SOCIOLOGY of WELL-BEING

Thank you for choosing a SAGE product!
If you have any comment, observation or feedback,
I would like to personally hear from you.
Please write to me at **contactceo@sagepub.in**

Vivek Mehra, Managing Director and CEO, SAGE India.

Bulk Sales

SAGE India offers special discounts
for purchase of books in bulk.
We also make available special imprints
and excerpts from our books on demand.

For orders and enquiries, write to us at

Marketing Department
SAGE Publications India Pvt Ltd
B1/I-1, Mohan Cooperative Industrial Area
Mathura Road, Post Bag 7
New Delhi 110044, India

E-mail us at **marketing@sagepub.in**

Get to know more about SAGE

Be invited to SAGE events, get on our mailing list.
Write today to **marketing@sagepub.in**

This book is also available as an e-book.

SOCIOLOGY of WELL-BEING

LESSONS FROM INDIA

STEVE DERNÉ

Los Angeles | London | New Delhi
Singapore | Washington DC | Melbourne

First published in 2017 by

 SAGE Publications India Pvt Ltd
B1/I-1 Mohan Cooperative Industrial Area
Mathura Road, New Delhi 110 044, India
www.sagepub.in

SAGE Publications Inc
2455 Teller Road
Thousand Oaks, California 91320, USA

SAGE Publications Ltd
1 Oliver's Yard, 55 City Road
London EC1Y 1SP, United Kingdom

SAGE Publications Asia-Pacific Pte Ltd
3 Church Street
#10-04 Samsung Hub
Singapore 049483

Published by Vivek Mehra for SAGE Publications India Pvt. Ltd, typeset in 10.5/12.5 pts Times New Roman by Diligent Typesetter India Pvt Ltd, Delhi and printed at Saurabh Printers Pvt Ltd, Greater Noida.

Library of Congress Cataloguing-in-Publication Data

Name: Derné, Steve, author.
Title: Sociology of well-being : lessons from India / Steve Derné.
Description: Thousand Oaks, California : SAGE, 2016. | Includes index.
Identifiers: LCCN 2016026479 | ISBN 9789385985720 (hardback : alk. paper) | ISBN 9789385985713 (epub) | ISBN 9789385985737 (ebook)
Subjects: LCSH: Well-being—India. | Quality of life—India. | Social indicators—India. | India—Social conditions. | India—Economic conditions.
Classification: LCC HN687 .D398 2016 | DDC 306.0954—dc23
LC record available at https://lccn.loc.gov/2016026479

ISBN: 978-93-859-8572-0 (HB)

SAGE Team: Shambhu Sahu, Alekha Chandra Jena, Shobana Paul and Ritu Chopra

Contents

Well, Michael, I'm against writin', seein' how many books there are in the world. It's the livin' of these things that counts. The livin' of them. Then after a long pause, But I do have some writin's, would ye like to see them? They're funny writin's.

—"Shiva Irons" (Murphy [1972] 1992, 103)

Preface: How I Came to Study Well-being in India

> *Fully conscious subjectivity ... holds the promise of being effective in a radically different way [than objectivity].... Write about it. Put your thoughts in a prologue.... It can be done.*

—Manulani Aluli Meyer (2008, 222)

> *Having had a cup of tea at my favorite tea stall, I'm sitting on a terrace as the sun rises, looking up at the Himalayan foothills, as horns honk in the background. I've just read the blog of my friend Brian McGuire. Later today, I'll have lunch with my longtime research assistant and friend Narendra Sethi. Tomorrow, I'll have lunch with the family of my closest friend in India, Harkirat Singh Jassal. The next day, I'll be on a train to Delhi to meet my wife, Lisa Jadwin. A lot of what I learned about well-being is apparent in this moment—bodily pleasures that break up the day (tea, the sun on my face), connections of love (my wife, my friends,) individual accomplishments (having completed 200 interviews).*

—Steve Derné, on preparing to leave Dehradun, December 14, 2011

This book aims to better understand well-being and how to live the good life by learning from what 203 Indians whom I interviewed told me about their well-being. Interviews are the main source of what I learned, although I also profit from the wisdom of Indian religions—a wisdom not unconnected to the distinctive sensibility of three of the founders of sociology in India: Benoy Kumar Sarkar (1887–1949), Radhakamal Mukerjee (1889–1968), and D.P. Mukerji (1894–1961). The book, then, tries to better understand well-being and how to live well by learning from Indian religious traditions, Indian sociologists, and, most of all, the 203 people who talked to me and my research collaborators.

In addition, I reflect on what this study taught me about doing better sociology. I especially suggest that more is learned by seeing similarities with the people interviewed than by objectifying them as different. I argue for the importance of including sociological introspection in any study. We should recount how our concerns shape what we study. We should ask how our findings might apply to ourselves and how we would answer the questions put to our respondents. The book intercalates such sociological introspection with the conclusions I reached based on what the people I interviewed said about well-being.

How did I come to study well-being as so much sociology emphasizes social problems? How did I come to see connections with the people I interviewed, rather than objectifying them?

Having completed my study of cultural globalization, I began to think about the next research project. I had well-being that summer of 2000, hanging out on the green grass of our home in Rochester, New York, with our cats Bert and Ernie, and enjoying being with my wife Lisa. My interactions with our kittens made me see eternity: How could a spirit such as our Ernie's ever die? In Lisa's garden, I watched the magic of dead organic matter turning into compost in the garden and regenerating life. In Rochester, big Bert licks my nose and kneads his sharp claws into my arm as I rub his stomach—it is kitten love, love for other beings. I began to imagine how heaven would be the blending of humans and kittens and horses into one. Nineteenth century Hawaiian texts show that Hawaiians didn't use categories such as human and nonhuman beings, gods, animals, geologic formations, and land (Holmes 2012). Buddhism and other religious traditions speak of the interconnectedness of all life. Sensing connections between me and other beings, I changed my practices: Loving nonhuman beings, I stopped eating meat.

That summer, I knew the limitations of academic discourse and wanted to learn something that would contribute to living a good life. I thought about how in India, in 1986 and 1987, I forced my questions on others. "What do you think about closeness between husband and wife?" I asked, "What are the advantages and disadvantages of arranged marriages? What do you think about joint-family living? Or nuclear family living?" Some of the people I talked to (my respondents) wanted to talk about the Ramayana, a sacred text they revered. Some wanted to talk about government corruption in

India and what it meant. Some wanted to talk about the USA and its attractions. But I brushed these aside. My questions sometimes mystified my respondents. In *Culture in Action* (1995), I told an academic story, but I didn't tell my respondents' story. My ability to understand others was limited because *my agenda* drove my consideration of others—and it diverted attention from considering the self.

More and more, the social scientific project seemed to involve me using people's talk to advance my career While I liked the people whom I interviewed, I also objectified them, turning their stories into my books and their lives into my academic career. What I did then makes my heart drop now. Both Dorothy Smith (1989, 1990) and Catherine MacKinnon (1989) argue that social science is implicated in the objectification of others and that the notion that some people can use other people to advance their own aims is how power works. By objectifying others in my writing, I was contributing to the way of thinking that uses others to benefit the self.

Years ago, at the beginning of my pursuit of the life of the mind, I realized (in the words of Norman O. Brown) that it was "closing time" for Western civilization:

> I sometimes think I see that civilizations originate in the disclosure of some mystery, some secret; and expand with the progressive publication of their secret; and end in exhaustion when there is no longer any secret, when the mystery has been divulged.... And so there comes a time—I believe we are in such a time—when civilization has to be renewed by the discovery of new mysteries. (Brown 1973, 30)

I began to see that Western civilization's secret was the chimera of material production and its attraction had faded. By the end of the twentieth century, it had become clear that the secret could not be sustained. The USA provides half of the world's grain exports. Losing a million acres of land each year to development and two million more to erosion, flooding, and soil destruction that are the outcome of intensive agriculture, the USA would not even be able to produce enough food for its domestic market in 50 years' time (McMichael 2000, 281). The USA's productivity has been bought by making withdrawals from nature's savings—withdrawals that will take millennia to replenish. For each calorie of food produced, 3 calories of fossil fuel energy are consumed on the farm—energy that did not come from this year's sunshine (McDaniel and Gowdy 2000, 63). And, so,

I began to search for principles other than material growth that could sustain our well-being.

In 2005, I learned of Gordon Mathews's most recent work on well-being. I'd long been impressed by Mathews's work on globalization (Mathews 2000) and on what makes life worth living in Japan and the USA (Mathews 1996). Thinking about the next project and interacting with Gordon, I somehow got invited to contribute a paper on well-being in India to a volume on well-being that he was co-editing. I began to learn something about well-being by re-reading the in-depth interviews about family life and about film that I had conducted in India in the 1980s and 1990s. Just re-reading those interviews while thinking of well-being made me see that Indians found well-being as much in being nurtured by groups as in taking individual initiative and that—consistent with Indian religious traditions—it's hard to experience well-being if one's actions harm other people; indeed, it's hard to experience well-being when others outside the self are unable to experience well-being, too (Derné 2009). In 2006, I chose to talk about well-being in India at a conference honoring the work of my mentor Arlie Hochschild, who was retiring from the University of California, Berkeley. I figured that this was an appropriate tribute as it was opening up a new field of sociology, much as her work had opened the field of emotions. The current book argues that an interactionist perspective on well-being can transform the study of well-being, just as Hochschild's work showed how an interactionist perspective on emotions could transform the study of emotions.

In 2007, I went to India to conduct interviews about well-being and I returned to conduct more in 2011. I knew immediately that these interviews were the most enchanting and insightful I'd ever conducted. In comparison to talking about family life or film, people loved talking about well-being. In my studies of family life and film, I started hearing the same things over and over after about 15 interviews. Even if people took different approaches to living in families or watching films, they were usually in dialogue with dominant discourses. (So, even those who married for love had to dialogue with the common "discourses" about why "love marriages" tend to fail.) But when it came to talking about the good life, people were not so ruled by discourses. People came to their own understandings based on their experiences with life, drew on diverse sources to understand well-being, and, ultimately, described many conflicting ways they experienced the feeling of enduring life satisfaction. I had done 100 interviews before someone talked about a good sleep or a good guru as a source of well-being. It was only after 200 interviews that for the first time a person mentioned giving up chewing paan (a betel-leaf intoxicant) as a source of his well-being. Although these interviews were following my agenda—talking about a sense of enduring life satisfaction—they encouraged people to talk about something about which they were enthusiastically engaged. In talking about the good life, people were addressing matters of spiritual or ultimate concern.

After conducting the interviews, I returned to the academic conference circuit to talk about what I had learned. I found more well-being and optimism in the academic pursuit's future than I had before I turned to studying how to live a good life. At a qualitative analysis conference in St. John's, Newfoundland, I stumbled upon a songwriters' circle in the Rocket Room above the Rocket Bakery where I heard the music of Sean McCann, Carleton Stone, and others. Well-being was there for me. There were connections. There was music. There was fun banter between the musicians—mimicking the Final Jeopardy time-ticking as a musician ran back to get the lyrics of a newly written song, joking about playing China Grove (by the Doobies!) for 40 minutes (which they didn't do). I saw puffins and icebergs. Ooooh hoooh!

The academic conference was great, too—and work is also part of well-being. The conference theme encouraged participants to consider how "we tell the stories of our respondents. Whose story is this? How do place and space affect the construction and interpretation of data narratives?" I had long realized that all of my studies have reflected my subject position—although I mostly didn't know it until they were done! My book *Culture in Action* recognized how social pressures shape Indians' lives, *because I needed to know about social pressures* growing up with a liberal family in Southern California that didn't put any social pressures on me. In *Movies, Masculinity, and Modernity* (2000), I focused on the influence of media on individuals *because media so influenced my own life*. In *Globalization on the Ground* (2008), I tried to understand the effects of transnational movement because of my own nomadism from my California roots.

And *Sociology of Well-being: Lessons from India* seeks to learn how to live a good life *because I want to have well-being.*

For me, the conference served to reinforce how important it is to place ourselves in our studies and apply the lessons of our studies to ourselves. It also came to highlight the importance of seeing ourselves as like the people we study.

Professor Tony Christensen (2012) gave a talk titled "Friends Don't Let Friends Do Ethnography," in which he reflected "on ethnography's tolls on personal relationships." I attended the talk because of my concerns with how I would write this book without taking a toll on my friends in India. But Dr Christensen was concerned about how his research on pickup artists affected his relationship with his girlfriend. He "left the field" because he found himself learning from the pickup artists, which strained his relationship with his girlfriend. I sensed Dr Christensen (who seemed to be threatened by pickup artists' methods) saw himself as different from those he studied—almost a different species (even though he reported that his girlfriend found that he "talked like a frat boy" when he was thinking about his pickup-artist research). He didn't present concern with harming any "friends" he made among the pickup artists whom he picked up to study. I wondered if he took the same sort of objectifying stance toward the pickup artists that I had taken toward the Indian men I interviewed in my previous studies.

Dr Christensen opened his talk by asking when people decide to leave the field. I replied, "You never leave it." Today, I'm able to keep in touch with many of the people I "studied" via email—and even phone. I don't think that my response was that unusual. Lori-Anne Dolloff (2012), another presenter at the conference, has been doing narrative research with an indigenous community in the Arctic. Between 2009 and 2012, she visited the Arctic five times. When there, she is very much part of the community—working on songs in church groups, for instance. Hearing her stories, her friends urge her to "write it up," but Professor Dolloff is concerned about doing that without involving her friends in the field—since it is, after all, their knowledge. Professor Dolloff is cautious about colonizing indigenous people, but she is clearly mutually sharing with them. By continuing to interact with the people she studied, Professor Dolloff has a relationship with them that doesn't end. Professor Dolloff seems to see herself as fundamentally like the subjects of her study with whom she has a long-term relationship.

The Qualitatives conference confirmed for me the *value* of seeing ourselves as being fundamentally like those we research, of trying to understand how we, too, would respond to the questions we asked our subjects. Dr Christensen, the scholar who studied pickup artists, left the field when he found himself unconsciously acting as an adept pickup artist during lunch at a pub, a situation that threatened his relationship with his girlfriend. Perhaps he left the field when he was becoming like those he studied; perhaps his self was threatened when he found himself applying the knowledge of those he studied. I think Professor Dolloff is interested in *gaining,* not from knowledge of the other but from the insights of the people who are studied. While I tried to advance scholarly understanding—and my academic career—in my earlier books, I now try to gain from the knowledge of the people I interviewed, whom I see as fundamentally similar to myself.

At the conference, I suggested to Dr Christensen that if one studied the good, the tensions about leaving the field would be less because what one learns from people would actually be good! One's good heart is threatened by studying pickup artists who use other people to experience their self. This book argues that studying the good is good for us, good for sociology, and good for society.

This book attempts to understand from Indians how to live the good life. My understanding comes partly from trying to apply their insights into my own life. Rejecting the approach of learning through taking an objective distance from those we study, I think that we can learn to live better lives by benefitting from the knowledge of the people we study.

Having situated the book in my concerns, there's a shift now to the more straightforwardly academic. This is *Wissenkunst,* after all. In *The Time Falling Bodies Takes to Light,* Thompson (1981) argues that different genres are important in different eras. For the Greeks, it was epic poetry; for the Renaissance, plays; for the nineteenth century, novels. For our time, it's *Wissenkunst*—what I take to be the playful mixing of art with (social) science. Indian philosopher Daya Krishna (1924–2007) (1989, 124–25) says that the arts, unlike the sciences, conceive of truth as "not merely reveal[ing] reality but also transform[ing] it, and, in a deeper sense, transcend[ing] it." "The encounter with a work of art transforms one's consciousness and not only takes it away from the so-called actual surroundings, but changes it in subtle ways." In this book, I hope my "social science" can also, like art, help transform consciousness, surroundings, and truth. I hope the social science I do in this book helps readers live better lives, construct better societies, and do better social science.

References

Brown, Norman O. 1973. *Closing Time*. New York, NY: Vintage.

Christensen, Tony. 2012. "Friends Don't Let Friends Do Ethnography: Reflecting on Ethnography's Tolls on Personal Relationships." 29th Annual Qualitative Analysis Conference, St. John's, Newfoundland.

Derné, Steve. 2009. "Well-being: Lessons from India." In *Pursuits of Happiness: Well-being in Anthropological Perspective,* edited by Gordon Mathews and Carolina Izquierdo, 127–46. Oxford: Berghahn Books.

Dolloff, Lori-Anne. 2012. "Confronting Lady Bountiful: Narrative Research in an Indigenous Community." 29th Annual Qualitative Analysis Conference, St. John's, Newfoundland.

Holmes, Leilani. 2012. *Ancestry of Experience: A Journey into Hawaiian Ways of Knowing*. Honolulu, HI: University of Hawaii Press.

Krishna, Daya. 1989. *The Art of the Conceptual*. New Delhi: Indian Council of Philosophical Research.

MacKinnon, Catharine. A. 1989. *Toward a Feminist Theory of the State*. Cambridge, MA: Harvard University Press.

Mathews, Gordon. 1996. *What Makes Life Worth Living? How Japanese and Americans Make Sense of Their Worlds*. Berkeley, CA: University of California Press.

———. 2000. *Global Culture/Individual Identity: Searching for Home in the Cultural Supermarket*. London: Routledge.

McDaniel, Carl N., and John M. Gowdy. 2000. *Paradise for Sale: A Parable of Nature*. Berkeley, CA: University of California Press.

McMichael, Philip. 2000. *Development and Social Change: A Global Perspective*. Newbury Park, CA: SAGE Publications.

Meyer, Manulani Aluli. 2008. "Indigenous and Authentic: Hawaiian Epistemology and the Triangulation of Meaning." In *Handbook of Critical and Indigenous Methodologies,* edited by Norman Denzin, Yvonna S. Lincoln, and Linda Tuhiwai Smith, 217–32. Newbury Park, CA: SAGE Publications.

Murphy, Michael. (1972) 1992. *Golf in the Kingdom*. New York, NY: Penguin.

Smith, Dorothy. 1989. "Sociological Theory: Methods of Writing Patriarchy." In *Feminism and Sociological Theory*, edited by Ruth A. Wallace, 34–64. Newbury Park, CA: SAGE Publications.

———. 1990. *The Conceptual Practices of Power: A Feminist Sociology of Knowledge*. Boston, MA: Northeastern University Press.

Thompson, William Irwin. 1981. *The Time Falling Bodies Take To Light: Mythology, Sexuality & the Origins of Culture*. New York, NY: St. Martins.

1

INTRODUCTION

Despite the sustained levels of growth in real income in industrialized countries over the last five decades, people are no more satisfied with their lives now than they had been in the past (Hamilton 2003, 3). There is, at best, a weak correlation between a country's income and the levels of satisfaction—and that weak correlation may be due to other factors such as tolerance of difference and political freedom (Hamilton 2003, 24). In Asia, the richest countries (such as Japan and Taiwan) have a higher proportion of unhappy people than the poorest (such as the Philippines; Hamilton 2003, 24). Within countries, too, once personal incomes are above about $10,000, the most affluent don't have more well-being than the least affluent (Hamilton 2003, 26). Even though "depth of social connections," rather than increased wealth, is associated with life satisfaction in the USA (Putnam 2000, 385), many academic studies of well-being, themselves influenced by individualistic assumptions of consumer cultures, focus on an individual's control of situations as the universal basis of well-being (e.g., Jankowiak 2009; Sen 2002). Although people who recognize the interconnectedness of things may instead experience well-being only when the earth and society are well, such approaches have been neglected by most scholars on well-being.

While happiness refers to a current emotional state, well-being refers to a sense of enduring life satisfaction. While quality of life uses objective measures such as poverty, literacy, and life expectancy, well-being refers to a subjective sense of life satisfaction

(Mathews and Izquierdo 2009). Subjective well-being resides within the individual and involves global assessment of a person's life (Diener [1984] 2009). For decades, scholars have shown that emotions and self-conceptions vary from place to place (Derné 1995; Lutz 1988; Lynch 1990). Like emotions and self-conceptions, subjective well-being is based on an internal state of mind and, so, varies cross culturally (Diener and Suh 2000; Mathews and Izquierdo 2009). Yet most psychological models, generated by research conducted in individualistic societies, do not adequately consider well-being in Asian societies (Oishi 2000). This book explores how Indian approaches to well-being demonstrate its universal aspects, especially those that have been neglected by Western scholars. The book identifies distinctive aspects of well-being in India and explores its variations within Indian society. By improving our understanding of well-being, the book seeks to improve our understanding of how to live a good life.

Most analyses of survey data seek to explain *variation* in the levels of well-being. I use the interviews I conducted not to explain differing levels of well-being, but to identify people's interpretation of their experience of well-being. But my interviews nevertheless confirm universal sources of well-being identified by experimental and survey analyses focused on explaining variation: The people I interviewed recognize access to material necessities, good health, connections with others, and feelings of specialness attached to the self as supporting well-being.

By talking with Indians I also learned that the fundamental basis of well-being rests neither in circumstances nor in individual traits, but depends instead on individuals' abilities to find meanings and day-to-day pleasures in life. Meanings and pleasures allow people to overcome the inevitable disappointments and difficulties everyone faces. Rather than focusing on people's individual characteristics or situations to understand their well-being, I argue that people themselves create well-being by interacting with other people, mutually increasing well-being in a self-reinforcing spiral. Rather than focusing on particular life choices as leading to well-being, I suggest that pursuing contradictory, inconsistent paths provide well-being. I urge that well-being resides in interactions, rather than within the person, and suggest that for most people well-being is transient and feelings of well-being are mixed. The book suggests that the interactionist approach, which revolutionized our understanding of emotions by seeing emotions not as automatic bodily responses but associated with interactions and meanings, can similarly improve our understanding of well-being.

While seeking to improve our understanding of well-being and how to live the good life, the book also suggests ways that sociology's method and approach could be improved by focusing on goodness, insisting on a basic similarity between the researcher and the people they study, and foregrounding the researcher's experiences in interacting with those they study. This discussion of rethinking epistemological and methodological approaches in American sociology follows not only from the study itself but also from the insights of some the founders of Indian sociology—Benoy Kumar Sarkar (1887–1949), Radhakamal Mukerjee (1889–1968), and D.P. Mukerji (1894–1961). I also highlight how the sociological approach that I advocate is consistent with strains in Indian religions and with the thoughts of some largely forgotten American sociologists such as Andrew Greeley and Pitirim Sorokin.

In what ways do I pursue "lessons from India" about the nature of well-being and how to live well? The main lessons follow from the wisdom of the 203 people I interviewed in India. The Indians I interviewed are often themselves philosophers of well-being—not formal ones, trained in university, of course, but people engaging in what might be called ethnophilosophy. Indian philosopher Daya Krishna holds that "in principle every human being is capable of original thinking, more or less without the crutches of quotations from others' thoughts" (as summarized by Chakrabarti 2011, 9). While I have also *analyzed* what people told me—such analysis is the second way I've pursued lessons from India—it is people's (informal) philosophical understandings of the good life that were most helpful. The insights of the people whom I interviewed are, of course, influenced by Indian traditions of Hinduism, Sikhism, and Islam (and, indeed, as scholars have recently shown there is a common *South Asian* religious tradition with parallel elements in Muslim, Sikh, and Hindu traditions—elements such as *darshan*, pilgrimage, submission, devotion, meditation, offerings, relationships with a spiritual guide, recitation, the sensate's self's connection to nature, and connections of the spiritual to the bodily [Bellamy 2011; Kent and Kassam 2013; Oberoi 1994; Taneja 2013]). A third way this study offers lessons from India is by identifying Indian religions' distinctive insights about how to live well. Indian religious traditions have, of course, influenced the thought of university-trained thinkers in India in the contemporary era. A fourth way this study offers "lessons from India" is by highlighting the insights offered by Benoy Kumar Sarkar, Radhakamal Mukerjee, and D.P. Mukerji—insights neglected by mainstream North American (and European) sociology. Finally, and less formally, the study offers lessons I learned from what it is like living as a foreigner in India for months at a time, over the last 25 years.

The Study: Interviews

In 2007 and 2011, I interviewed 112 men and 91 women, Hindu, Muslim, and Sikh, from the age of 18 to over 70, of laboring and a variety of middle-class backgrounds living in the city of Dehradun, India. Dehradun, capital of the state of Uttarakhand, is a diverse city that has attracted migrants from all over North India. I wanted to learn about well-being from this diverse sample of Hindi-speaking Indians.

Using questions employed by the "Everyday Well-being" component of the MacArthur Foundation survey of midlife Americans (Markus et al. 2004), I asked respondents to tell me what well-being (*khushhali*) meant to them, to tell me about situations (*paristhithi*) in which they felt (*mahasus*) well-being, and to tell me about situations in which they felt a lack of well-being. Following Gordon Mathews's (1996) interviews in Japan and the USA, I also asked questions addressing ultimate concerns. I told respondents that many people think that a person's life should have some purpose (*uddeshya*), meaning (*arth*), or something of importance (*mahatva*) and asked them whether they agreed. If they did—and they all did—I asked them what their purpose, meaning, or importance in life was. (I also asked a question relating to hobbies [*shaukh*] and one relating to pilgrimages.)

All of the interviews were conducted in Hindi (although about 10 people answered in English). The interviews, most of which lasted about 20–35 minutes, were open-ended, and were recorded and translated into English.

I used the term khushhali—described in the dictionary as "prosperity; well-being"—to capture the English concept of well-being. Hindi speakers I knew in the USA struggled a bit when I asked how they'd translate well-being. When I told them khushhali, many said "perfect!" But the fact they didn't volunteer it should have disturbed me a bit. A few English-speakers whom I knew in India limited khushhali's meaning to "prosperity," but that restricted meaning was primary for only two of the 200 people I interviewed. The literal meaning might be state (*haal*) of happiness (*khushi*). The answers were the answers I expected to get—sufficient income, health, good connections to others, and feelings of specialness associated with the self. So, I think khushhali is a good translation. But I should have wondered a bit more about whether the idea of an "*enduring* sense of life satisfaction" really translated. I did have to ask pretty often—"was this lasting (*sthayi*)?" This book will ultimately argue that well-being as an enduring state is actually pretty fleeting and that rather than existing as a steady inner state, well-being arises more in interactions–including the interview situation.

I began this research in 2007 without the benefits of a grant. But I also had freedoms I wouldn't have had with a grant. I started on a *char dham yatra* (pilgrimage to four holy spots in the Himalayas) bus tour pilgrimage, which allowed me to improve my rusty Hindi and think about my questions in an open-ended way, asking people about well-being informally. (The bus tour, which cost about $200 for about two weeks lodging and transport, was organized by the Garhwal Mandal Vikas Nigam and I was with other pilgrims.)

When I arrived at Dehradun in October, 2007, I joined with my longtime coinvestigator, journalist Narendra Sethi. Narendra, a Sikh in his 40s, first worked with me in 1991 on a study of filmgoing. In 1991, he was a cub reporter for the Hindi daily *Dainik Jagaran* (I met him because there was a dusty *Dainik Jagaran* office above one of the theaters in Dehradun). In 2007, he was an on-air news reporter for the cable outlet TV 100. (In 2011, when he again worked with me, he was the chief editor of a Hindi daily, the *Shah Times*.) He helped me improve my interview schedule and we started doing interviews. We typically approached people and explained our interest in studying well-being and what we wanted to ask. After explaining that we would not use respondents' names, that we would hide their identity, and that they were free to end the interview at any time, we began the interview. We recorded each interview, but Narendra also took notes. We recruited 21 people at their place of business, 18 people at religious places, 19 people at other public places (parks, markets, foodstalls, transport centers), and 5 people at their homes. We interviewed 11 of Narendra's acquaintances and eight of my own acquaintances.

Narendra notes that we got the best interviews with people we met in public places, including workplaces and religious places. One reason is that there was some self-selection. If we approached three friends, the most articulate might be the one to put himself forward. Perhaps, too, people in public might be more outgoing or have more time to talk. With some of the more reluctant interviewees, we often returned to the main questions about what well-being meant to them after they had had a chance to talk about situations of well-being and lack of well-being.

Narendra and I had difficulty interviewing women. We had never interviewed women before and thought perhaps we were old enough to be unthreatening in our 40s. But half of the women we approached refused to be interviewed (while no man refused to be interviewed). There are a number of reasons for the difficulty. First, women have less free time since they often work more hours than men (if they're in the paid labor force, they have a second shift, and if they're not in the paid labor force, housework never ends). Second, women may not be comfortable interacting with men, especially if their schooling was sex-segregated. Third, talking to men may threaten the women's honor or reputation. In my studies in the 1980s, men would tell me that "if my wife talks to you and another person sees it, our honor would go down." One woman insisted we interview her *with other people present*, presumably so that they could attest that nothing happened between her and Narendra Sethi and myself. So, early on I suggested to Narendra we ought to interview mostly men—that we would have enough variability by using our previous focus on men. We also interviewed few Muslims and a limited number of laborers.

When I returned to do more interviews in August, 2011, I especially focused on addressing these limitations. While I continued to interviews with Narendra Sethi, I was lucky to recruit educator Meenu Sharma as another coinvestigator. Meenu, a Hindu in her 40s, taught at a BEd college in Dehradun and subsequently earned an education doctorate at HNB Garhwal University. Meenu completed 85 interviews, all but four of which she recorded without my presence.

Meenu and I quickly learned that it would be better for her to do interviews with women on her own. When I was present, men wanted to be part of the interview process to interpret my questions for their spouses, sisters, or daughters—and to interpret their responses for me! Meenu sought out a diversity of women that Narendra and I would have had difficulty interviewing, including Muslims and lower-middle-class women. Meenu recruited neighbors, colleagues, relatives of colleagues, and people whom she met in workplaces, religious places, or in their neighborhoods (especially Muslim neighborhoods and laborer colonies). She also recruited people through acquaintances of her neighbors, friends, and colleagues. I learned a lot from people's faces, so it's disappointing that I only had a voice recording of the interviews that Meenu conducted. But Meenu typically reported what occurred in the interview.

(In the two research stints, I conducted 19 interviews without the help of a coinvestigator. Narendra Sethi helped me translate these recorded interviews.)

The rate of refusals was extraordinarily low. In the two research stints combined, 20 people declined to be interviewed, while 203 agreed to be interviewed. Eleven of the refusals were women who declined to be interviewed by Narendra and myself.

In the two research stints, we interviewed 112 men: 18–25 years old (25), 26–39 years old (28), 40–59 years old (30) and over the age of 60 (29). We interviewed 13 Muslim men and 21 Sikh men, along with 78 Hindu men, spread evenly across the age groups. We interviewed 10 laboring men, 25 lower-middle-class men, and 63 middle-class men, spread evenly across the age groups.

We interviewed 91 women: 18–25 years old (19), 26–39 years old (26), 40–59 years old (23), and over the age of 60 (20). We interviewed 13 Muslim women, 12 Sikh women, and 65 Hindu women, spread evenly across the age groups. (We also interviewed one Christian.) We interviewed 11 laboring women, 20 lower-middle-class women, and 59 middle-class women, spread evenly amongst the age groups. (Although we didn't intend to interview rural people, we also interviewed four men and one woman in agricultural jobs who turned up at public places, such as places of worship.)

Certainly, 203 people in Dehradun do not represent how villagers, people in more provincial towns, or people living in different regions might experience well-being. But I suspect I captured the range of experiences of people living in the more cosmopolitan cities and towns in the Hindi-speaking region of the North. It's worth noting, too, that my number of interviews compare favorably to the two qualitative studies I replicated. Mathews (while getting to know his respondents better) interviewed 52 Americans and 52 Japanese people. The Everyday Well-being component of the MIDUS study (while a sample from a broad survey) was based on just 83 interviews.

People were often focused and animated and occasionally emotional during the interviews. I got the impression many times that it was powerful for people to tell their stories and to relate their aspirations and the ups and downs of their lives. I think this was especially the case for laborers, many women, and the lower-middle classes, who so often are sidelined in today's globalizing India, which focuses so much on the more affluent classes (Derné 2008).

I didn't realize this until my last day in Dehradun in 2011, but my personality was apparently welcoming to people whom we interviewed. Narendra has always said that people feel very comfortable and happy when I talk to them and ask them questions. On that last day in Dehradun, I went on my usual running route and gave a photo to a gentleman with whom I shared the greeting "beautiful morning! (*su prabhat*)" most mornings. He remembered that I was leaving that day and we had a nice chat. In my first few days in Delhi, the Fulbright-appointed liaison encouraged me to speak Hindi with government officials. (I have always spoken English with government officials since their English is better than my Hindi.) But the liaison said people felt good that I had taken the time to learn (even inadequately) the language that they spoke. Perhaps this is one reason that I got such a positive reaction from the people that I interviewed. I think my interaction with interviewees was part of a positive chain that increased well-being.

What Interviews Reveal and What They Obscure

While people experience well-being—a sense of enduring life satisfaction—that sense of well-being itself does not always—or even usually—endure. Well-being is a sense of enduring life satisfaction that itself comes and goes. That sense of well-being is produced by many things: physical activity, contemplating the vitality of nature, and, perhaps above all else, felicitous interactions with other people. Such felicitous interactions include the interview situation itself.

A scholar at the University of Delhi commented to me that people are unlikely to tell an interviewer that they get well-being from engaging in malicious gossip. American students in a senior-seminar that I taught on well-being said that people won't say they get well-being from looking beautiful—it would seem shallow. Because they get well-being from felicitous interactions, the interview situation is biased against people talking about malicious gossip or shallow pleasures and biased in favor of people talking about publicly acceptable pleasures, such as helping other people.

Yet what people say in interviews nonetheless reveals sources of well-being (even if it doesn't reveal all of the sources or their relative importance). And we heard not just about publicly acceptable reasons, but also (surely less often) about some of those secret pleasures. The well-being people got from being interviewed—from being made important, being made the center of focus, and being able to talk about one's good life—and which was reflected in interviews represents a real (if perhaps transient) sense of enduring life satisfaction. Despite the biases, we were able to learn a lot about the range of experiences that give people well-being and how experiences give well-being.

The different gender, religion, and persona of Meenu and Narendra (and the fact I was with Narendra but not Meenu for the interviews) produced intractable differences in responses that makes the comparison of different sources of well-being for different groups problematic (since Meenu and Narendra interviewed different sorts of people). In 2011, when Meenu started interviewing large numbers of women, I was struck by how many women identified helping others as a source of well-being. Many even described housework as their hobby. When I'd left the field in 2007, having interviewed just 11 women, but 76 men, I felt I was swimming in data without patterns. Men mentioned so many things that patterns were slow to emerge. Raj Pattial, a flashy 19-year-old male business student whom I interviewed with Narendra in 2007, said the taste for helping others was the best taste, but he also talked about religion as a source of well-being, as well as the cool air of the mountains, good food, and how escaping the day-to-day on a picnic provides well-being. The young women Meenu interviewed talked more forcefully and with more focus on helping others: Young women students similar in age to flashy 19-year-old Raj Pattial said they experienced well-being from helping a mother with housework, carrying a backpack for a sick friend, dreaming of earning money to set up schools for the poor, or distributing sweets to orphans to celebrate a birthday. And it would not be untrue to report that the women we interviewed were more than twice as likely as the men we interviewed to report helping others as a source of well-being (35 percent of men [39/112] and 74 percent [67/91] of women). But this would be deceptive because the difference is much less significant when controlling for interviewer. Ninety-three percent (38/41) of married women under the age of 58 whom Meenu interviewed mentioned helping others as a source of well-being, but only 31 percent (5/16) of similar women Narendra and I interviewed mentioned helping others as a source of well-being. Thirty percent (18 out of 61) of the men under the age of 60 whom Narendra interviewed mentioned helping others as a source of well-being; 73 percent (8 of 11) of the men under the age of 60 whom Meenu interviewed mentioned helping others as a source of well-being. So, it appears that being interviewed by Meenu, rather than Narendra, led more people to mention helping others as a source of well-being.

While these differences could be due to some extent to the different ways we recruited respondents—perhaps people found in public mention helping others less often—I think the different gender, religion and appearance of Meenu and Narendra itself made people interviewed by Meenu more likely to talk about well-being in terms of service to others than people interviewed by Narendra. While Indian religious traditions emphasize service, these traditions are more imperative for women, perhaps making those interviewed by a female interviewer more likely to talk about such service in order to make the interaction enjoyable. Narendra's Sikh background (obvious with his turban) and Meenu's Hindu background would tend to similarly push interviewees to differentially discuss helping others as a source of well-being. While Sikh religion certainly emphasizes service, Sikhs also have a reputation for success, hard work, and living life in full, perhaps making those interviewed by Narendra and myself more likely to talk about diverse sources of well-being. Narendra often wore Western clothes, such as jeans and was accompanied by a Westerner, while

Meenu was alone and tended to wear Indian *salwar kamiz*. The different appearance might have pushed those interviewed by Narendra and myself to talk of more cosmopolitan pleasures. Meenu, as an educator, may have appeared to have a social-worker persona that might bring out the helping side of individuals who enjoy being liked by the interviewer.

Finding well-being from felicitous interactions, the people we interviewed, perhaps, highlighted those aspects of what gave them well-being that they sensed the interviewer would be attracted to, hence, leading to felicitous interactions. Thus, the apparently greater emphasis women placed on helping others as a source of well-being partly reflects the fact that women tended to be interviewed by Meenu Sharma, a Hindu, a woman, and an educator who might have appeared to value *seva* (service), while men tended to be interviewed by Narendra Sethi, a cosmopolitan-looking Sikh male accompanied by a Western friend who might have appeared to value free-wielding sources of pleasure.

Despite the "bias" in the sorts of things people were more likely to highlight in interviews, people *nonetheless do get well-being from what they mentioned in the interviews*. Raj Pattial really does get well-being from helping others, eating good food, and the cool air of the hills (even if he might be more likely to have highlighted helping others had he been interviewed by Meenu, rather than Narendra). The young women Meenu interviewed really do get well-being from distributing sweets to orphans, helping a friend with a backpack or helping their mother with housework, even if they might have also highlighted other things had they been interviewed by Narendra.

But comparisons are difficult: The different persona and religion of Meenu vis-à-vis Narendra and the situation of being interviewed by a woman as opposed to two men shapes people's responses. Because of these different interview situations and because we don't have a full accounting of the sources of each person's well-being (due to the open-ended nature of the interviews), *it is difficult to compare how important different experiences are for different categories of people*. The difficulty is intractable because Narendra and I could *not* interview the sorts of people Meenu recruited. The fact Narendra and I had a 50 percent refusal rate from women, while Meenu had a refusal rate of less than 6 percent from women meant whatever "sample" of women Narendra and I obtained is skewed toward women willing to talk with men. And there were many categories of women—lower-middle-class women and Muslim women, especially—that Narendra and I found it difficult to recruit (or "pick up," to use the term showing the objectification inherent in the interview situation).

Although Narendra and I interviewed 17 women and Meenu interviewed 16 men, there are often not enough people in an age category, for instance, to rule out chance variation. I think women do tend to more easily recognize (and emphasize) helping others as a source of well-being because of discourses about what it means to be a man and what it means to be a woman in the communities in which they live. Considering differences between men and women interviewed by a particular researcher points in this direction, *but the numbers are too small to make firm conclusions.* For instance, two of the three young women in school whom Narendra interviewed mentioned helping others as the source of well-being, while seven of the 14 young men in school whom Narendra interviewed mentioned helping others as a source of well-being. But had Narendra interviewed a fourth young woman in school who happened not to mention helping others as a source of well-being, the percentage would be the same. Twenty percent (4/20) of married men under the age of 60 whom Narendra interviewed and who lacked college education mentioned helping others as a source of well-being, while similarly situated married women (no college education, under the age of 60) whom Narendra interviewed were twice as likely (40 percent, 2/5) to mention helping others as a source of well-being. But had one of these women interviewed by Narendra not mentioned helping others as a source of well-being, the percentage would be the same. Eighty-one percent (13/16) of similarly situated women interviewed by Meenu (married, under the age of 60, no college education) mentioned helping others as a source of well-being while only 47 percent (4/7) of similarly situated men interviewed by Meenu did so. But had an additional one of these men mentioned helping others as source of well-being, the percentage difference would be much less (81 percent of women, compared to 71 percent of men). Evidence "suggests" a somewhat greater tendency for women to mention helping others as a source of well-being, but the difference is not large. Interviewer effect and the possibility of chance variation make this evidence less than compelling.

Of greatest significance is that the greater likelihood that both men and women mention "helping others" in interviews conducted by Meenu, compared to Narendra, highlights one of the primary findings of this book—*the fundamental importance of positive interactions as a source of well-being*. Respondents get well-being from interview interactions that feel good because they present a self that each respondent thinks the interviewer might admire. So, people interviewed by Meenu may have been more likely to emphasize helping others as a source of well-being, while people interviewed by Narendra and myself might have been more likely to mention more diverse, sometimes cosmopolitan pleasures because the interaction felt more affirming. While this might "bias" responses in some ways, it also highlights the fundamental importance of felicitous interactions as a source of well-being.

My caution about making generalizations about what sorts of people get well-being from different experiences is compounded by the fact that answers were all *volunteered*. So, I didn't ask people whether helping others—or singing, or religious ritual, or friendships, or money—gave them well-being. I asked them what well-being meant to them and to tell me about situations they experienced well-being and a lack of well-being. So, if someone didn't volunteer that helping others or earning a living is a source of well-being, that doesn't necessarily mean they would reject that proposition.

So, I don't make strong claims about different sources of well-being for different types of people. Given the fleeting, context-based nature of well-being, such claims may not make much sense in any event. Rather, the book focuses more on the particular experiences of well-being that people choose to describe in their encounters with Meenu, Narendra and me to understand the sources of well-being.

Ethnography

When I presented some tentative hunches at a University Delhi talk in 2011, I faced an audience of ethnographic sociologists. Some in the audience commented how different findings often turned out from researchers' initial understandings of what might be going on. Some were skeptical of my use of interviews and urged me to do more ethnography.

Interviews have a bias toward the cognitive, meaningful, and acceptable and are not particularly good at accessing physical pleasures that give well-being. In addition, there is sometimes a disjuncture between what people say and what they actually do. One man emphasized in talking about well-being that the body was nothing, but I knew that he enjoyed eating good food and riding his motorcycle fast!

While this is primarily an interview study, ethnography is a supplement. I often talked informally with people outside interviews, learning the most from the dozen or so respondents who became close friends and whom I got to know well and observe in multiple contexts. More significant, I learned what appeared to give people well-being from observations in locations such as tea stalls, barber shops, cinema halls, street demonstrations, park outings, pilgrimages, and temple visits.

This ethnographic supplement to interviews is limited by its focus on men. Restrictions on interactions between unrelated men and women are such that I only got to know five women well—and I knew them less well than the men I knew. I learned a bit from women's faces, but I didn't have as much opportunity to see women at leisure. Because I rely so much on interactions outside the interview situation to understand pleasures, I learned much less about *women's* pleasures than men's pleasures.

Some Ethical Concerns

Having learned so much from the people whom I got to know well creates an ethical dilemma. How can I disguise these people's identities sufficiently so that they could not be harmed by readers "guessing" their identity? The problem is that the people whom I got to know best are most identifiable because people whom I knew in India know who my friends are! Learning so much from my friends, I wondered how other researchers have handled the dilemma. Margaret Trawick's (1990) *Notes on Love in a Tamil Family* is a marvelous book, but one family is foregrounded in a book full of photographs—affairs are hinted at. Did this book have any effect on the people she studied given our global world? In *The Second Shift*, Arlie Hochschild

(1989) discusses a couple who invented a myth that they were doing equal amounts of housework by seeing the husband's work in the downstairs—the garage—as the equivalent of the wife's work in the upstairs—the rest of the house. When I first heard of the story in a college seminar, we all laughed. Generations of students have been laughing at "the Holts" ever since. How can you truly disguise people with such a distinctive story? It was these sorts of concerns that led me to attend Professor Christensen's talk "Friends Don't Let Friends Do Ethnography" at the Qualitatives conference. I didn't want to hurt any of my friends whom I interviewed!

Following the suggestion of Arlie Hochschild, I have changed characteristics and situations of people, even though this sometimes feels like I'm doing violence to the people's stories. Like George Vaillant (2002, 37) another researcher who uses pseudonyms and changes identifying characteristics, I have confidence that "if the narrative detail" appears to fit "any one of the reader's acquaintance too closely, it will almost certainly turn out that he or she has identified the wrong person."

I have also tried to be sensitive to what might be upsetting to respondents and have avoided mentioning such items, but it is difficult to predict what respondents will find upsetting. In 2007, I told a government administrator about my research interests and she asked to be interviewed. I didn't have my recorder, so I took notes. I found what she had said admirable and sent her a transcript of my notes. But she was extremely upset (perhaps about being objectified). I only became aware of the problem in this lone case because I had no recorder with me and so I decided to check with the woman to see if I had represented her well by sending her an email transcript. I deleted the interview and have not used it in this book. (Indeed, I have now forgotten what she said!)

I considered following the lead of researchers like Judith Stacey (1990) and checking with key interviewees featured in this book about my descriptions of them. After I returned to the USA, a hypnotherapist had me sign a release indicating that he could write about me, while disguising any identifying information. I considered asking him to check with me about any of his publications that profiled me. I realized, though, that reading such work in advance was more likely to disturb me than would the unlikely event of coming upon such writings after they were published. Putting myself in the shoes of my respondents made me see that I would prefer that the hypnotherapist change identifying information and think through whether there was any possibility of me being harmed by his writing (which I would be unlikely to come across in any event). So, I have carefully changed identifying characteristics, avoided writing about those with whom I was so close that they might be recognizable to those who knew me in Dehradun, and carefully considered the importance of mentioning potentially embarrassing information.

Sociological Introspection

Sociological introspection (Ellis 1991) is when a researcher thinks sociologically about his or her own experiences—as I have done in thinking about how I might feel about being written about by my hypnotherapist. I've done sociological introspection to see whether what my respondents said about well-being made sense, given my own experience. What would I learn about my respondents' insights by trying to live their suggestions? This sociological introspection has several components.

First, I looked at my own well-being in India to see if I could better understand the aspects of well-being that I mostly learned about through fieldwork and ethnography—things such as watching a film, exercising, getting a haircut, or having a cup of tea. These were *pleasures* that didn't come up much in interviews, but are nonetheless essential to well-being. Ethnographer Robert Desjarlais (1992, 19) rightly argues that by "participating in the everyday life of a society distinct from one's own," the researcher slowly learns "patterns of behavior previously unfamiliar to his or her body."

Second, I considered whether respondents' insights about well-being could be applied to my life. That is, I thought about whether learning from what my respondents said about well-being could help me have more of it. Trying out for myself what my respondents told me about pleasures and meanings helped me understand their contributions to well-being. It's notable that other well-being researchers also include personal anecdotes in their books to suggest the helpfulness of their usually quantitative findings about well-being (e.g., Seligman 2011). The proof of what we learn is often in the pudding.

Third, I thought about how I would answer the questions I put to my respondents if I were in a similar situation. I did this to see what aspects of life I might want to suppress in talking to an outsider. At first, small reflections I include here seemed like the odd part of the book—it seemed tacked on, or maybe self-indulgent. I remembered the old cartoon in which the "native" says to the anthropologist, "Enough about you, let's talk about me!" (in response to the 1980s focus on foregrounding the ethnographer's subject position [Clifford and Marcus 1986]). But I've come to see putting the questions you ask your respondents to yourself as the most essential element of sociological introspection. It keeps the researcher honest. If I wouldn't talk about well-being from sex why should my interviewees? As my wife said to me one day about one of my respondents, "I'm sure he doesn't tell you everything that he likes about his wife." Personal anecdotes that appear in this book serve to confirm my "findings" and to foreground my subject position to help the reader evaluate those findings.

The use of sociological introspection is uneven in this book—I don't systematically use it in all chapters (as Jeffrey Kripal [2001] does in *Roads of Excess, Palaces of Wisdom: Eroticism & Reflexivity in the Study of Mysticism*). In *When God Talks Back*, Tanya Luhrmann (2012) rarely describes her own experiences, but I found these descriptions helpful. For instance, her description of her own non-ordinary experiences—such as seeing druids—helped to highlight that the evangelicals considered in her book were not crazy. Even occasional introspection is, I think, helpful.

Well-being: An Interactionist Perspective

The social-scientific understanding of emotions was revolutionized by an interactionist perspective that saw emotions not as rooted within the organism, but arising through interactions and meanings (e.g., Hochschild 1983; Lynch 1990). The biggest social-scientific contribution of this book is to suggest that well-being, too, is not an inner state but arises through interactions and meanings.

My interviews revealed that well-being is often mixed, transient, and fleeting. Well-being may be produced by the interview situation in which people get well-being by being the focus of attention of the interviewer. People often received well-being in one arena (for instance, creativity), but not another (for instance, family), and their well-being shifted as interactions (even self-interactions) shifted their attention from one to the other arena of life. People surprisingly often got well-being and a lack of well-being from the same incident. One young man got well-being when he survived a bus crash, but a lack of well-being *at the same time* as he saw everyone dying around him. A woman got well-being when she entered college, but *at the same time* got a lack of well-being as she needed to leave her child in the village. On December 14, 2011, it was *vidaai* (farewell) time in Dehradun. I was sometimes moved to tears to leave my friends, but was experiencing well-being at seeing my wife soon. I knew I'd miss my morning *alu parantha*, but also knew that I'd soon enjoy a blueberry pancake again. Well-being—or lack of it—shifts as the interactions do. Talking to my wife gives me well-being about leaving; talking to my friends gives me sadness.

This book argues, moreover, that well-being is created through felicitous chains of well-being in which people interact in a supportive way with other people, mutually increasing their well-being in a self-reinforcing spiral. Cultivating pleasant, mutually supportive interactions with people may be the most important thing one can do to find well-being. After I returned to the USA, I often ran in the hills near my urban home. In these hills, I discovered many secrets, such as a beautiful maze. One day, I came upon two people walking in the hills and I showed them the maze. As I was running on, one of them said "I am so happy to have met you today." I replied how happy I was that they had enjoyed the maze that I showed them.

Researchers may be on the wrong track in looking at objective conditions or particular traits as causes of well-being. This book shows that *contradictory* conditions are often the source of well-being. Being on safari is great, and no matter what the Beach Boys sang you wouldn't want to be on safari to stay. Well-being involves feelings of specialness *and* connections to others, doing nothing *and* contributing to others through one's actions, horseback riding, *and* writing books such as this. One man I interviewed when thinking of his son's death said that "the body is nothing." But he nonetheless enjoyed sex, good food, and riding his motorcycle fast.

More important, it's not conditions that are important to well-being, but how people think about conditions. Meanings people attribute to conditions are more important than the conditions themselves. I interviewed two men about 80 years old, both in ill health, and both neglected by their families. But one was grumpy, focusing on his conditions. The other had an approach to life that kept him in wonder. He still saw every day as a new elegance. Rather than focusing on his physical limitations, he focused on how he could still walk to the park, even if slowly. Rather than focusing on how his family neglected him, he cultivated positive interactions. The two men's objective circumstances were similar, but one man kept well-being due to his approach and how he saw his circumstances.

Rather than focusing on particular activities that provide well-being, researchers might be better to focus on people's *ability* to find pleasures that provide relief from troubles. Some research identifies singing and camping as particularly good sources of well-being. But perhaps surfing, horseback riding, or running can contribute to well-being as well. It may not be *particular* pleasures that provide well-being, but individuals' commitment to seeking out pleasures, in general.

As many people I interviewed recognize, circumstances change. But the ability to cultivate felicitous interactions, to find an approach to troubles and a meaning to life, and to find pleasures can persist, and ultimately provide well-being.

This book shows, then, that well-being lies not in objective circumstances or particular activities but in felicitous interactions, the meanings people use to understand their situation, the ability to find approaches to handle troubles, and the ability to find pleasures in life. This study suggests the usefulness of focusing on how well-being arises through interactions and meanings, rather than some external objective circumstances. And the study suggests that because contradictory things lead to well-being, the source of well-being is multiple and can't be pinned down to any particular thing.

Outline

The first section of this book—"Universals"—examines what I learned about well-being from the men and women I interviewed. People identified sufficient income and health (Chapter 2), a feeling that the self is special (Chapter 3), and connections to others (Chapter 3) as the primary sources of well-being. But I ultimately argue that none of these conditions can ever completely endure. Everyone faces difficulties and troubles. Thus, the key to well-being—the only thing that can endure—is developing a *mental approach* to facing these troubles (Chapter 4) *and* a commitment to pursuing *pleasures* (especially of the body) that can provide escape from day-to-day necessities and troubles (Chapter 5). Thus, well-being is both inner—developing an approach—and outer—having bodily pleasures.

The second section of this book—"Variations"—examines variations in well-being. In Chapter 6, I consider how the understandings and experiences of well-being appear to vary by age, gender, and class in India. In Chapter 7, I consider what is distinctive about Indian approaches to well-being. Indian traditions, I think, make it easier for Indians to see the *contradictory* bases of well-being—that well-being comes from both self and other, both body and mind, both purpose and purposelessness, both work and non-work. These Indian traditions make it easier, I think, for Indians to recognize aspects of well-being, which I argue are important for people everywhere.

In the third section of the book—"Lessons"—I consider what we can learn from this study. I first suggest what we can learn about the nature of well-being (Chapter 8). This chapter focuses especially on how the interactionist perspective illuminates well-being. I then consider what this study suggests for doing better sociology (Chapter 9), and argue that sociologists should return to trying to understand the good life, combine ethnography with interviews, engage in sociological introspection as part of any interview study, and take a nonobjectifying approach that recognize continuities between the researcher and the people interviewed. In Chapter 10, I identify what we have learned about how to live better lives and how we might better construct societies to provide well-being.

In my concluding acknowledgments, I discuss my debts to sweet friends, assistants, teachers, and students in conducting this study. This gives me well-being as it connects me to others and allows me to see how my work is part of a chain of well-being with the mentors who came before me and the students who will continue to do sociological research. William Irwin Thomas suggested that *Wissenkunst*—knowledge/art—is the distinctive genre for our era. I've tried in this book to create a playful social science. Daya Krishna is right, I think, that "playfulness and not remaining boringly serious or teeth-gnashingly committed all the time, are the right mental milieu" for learning something new (paraphrased by Chakrabarti 2011, 10).

References

Bellamy, Carla. 2011. *The Powerful Ephemeral: Everyday Healing in an Ambiguously Islamic Place*. Berkeley, CA: University of California Press.

Chakrabarti, Arindam. 2011. "Introduction." In *Contrary Thinking: Selected Essays of Daya Krishna*, edited by Nalini Bhushan, Jay L. Garfield, and Daniel Raveh, 3–24. Oxford: Oxford University Press.

Clifford, James, and George E. Marcus. 1986. *Writing Culture: The Poetics and Politics of Ethnography*. Berkeley, CA: University of California Press.

Derné, Steve. 1995. *Culture in Action: Family Life, Emotion, and Male Dominance in Banaras, India*. Albany, NY: SUNY Press.

———. 2008. *Globalization on the Ground: Media and the Transformation of Culture, Class, and Gender in India*. New Delhi: SAGE Publications.

Desjarlais, Robert R. 1992. *Body and Emotion: The Aesthetics of Illness and Healing in the Nepal Himalaya*. Philadelphia, PA: University of Pennsylvania Press.

Diener, Ed, ed. (1984) 2009. "Subjective Well-Being." In *The Science of Well-Being: The Collected Works of Ed Diener*, 11–58. New York, NY: Springer.

Diener, Ed, and Eunkook M. Suh, eds. 2000. *Culture and Subjective Well-Being*. Cambridge, MA: MIT Press.

Ellis, Carolyn. 1991. "Sociological Introspection and Emotional Experience." *Symbolic Interaction*, 14(1): 23–50.

Hamilton, Clive. 2003. *Growth Fetish*. London: Pluto.

Hochschild, Arlie. 1983. *The Managed Heart: Commercialization of Human Feeling*. Berkeley, CA: University of California Press.

Jankowiak, William. 2009. "Well-Being: Cultural Pathology, and Personal Rejuvenation in a Chinese City, 1981–2005." In *Pursuits of Happiness: Well-Being in Anthropological Perspective,* edited by Gordon Mathews and Carolina Izquierdo, 147–66. New York, NY: Berghahn.

Kent, Eliza F. and Tazim R. Kassam, ed. 2013. *Lines in Water: Religious Boundaries in South Asia*. Syracuse, NY: Syracuse University Press.

Kripal, Jeffrey J. 2001. *Roads of Excess, Palaces of Wisdom: Eroticism & Reflexivity in the Study of Mysticism*. Chicago, IL: University of Chicago Press.

Luhrmann, T.M. 2012. *When God Talks Back: Understanding the American Evangelical Relationship with God*. New York, NY: Vintage.

Lutz, Catherine A. 1988. *Unnatural Emotions: Everyday Sentiment on a Micronesian Atoll & Their Challenges to Western Theory*. Chicago, IL: University of Chicago Press.

Lynch, Owen. 1990. "The Social Construction of Emotion in India." In *Divine Passions: The Social Construction of Emotion in India*, edited by Owen Lynch, 3–36. Berkeley, CA/Delhi: University of California Press/Oxford University Press.

Markus, Hazel Rose, Carol D. Ryff, Katherine B. Curhan, and Karen A. Palmersheim. 2004. "In Their Own Words: Well-Being at Midlife among

High School-Educated and College-Educated Adults." In *How Health Are We? A National Study of Well-Being at Midlife,* edited by Orville Gilbert Brim, Carol D. Ryff, and Ronald C. Kessler, 273–319. Chicago, IL: University of Chicago Press.

Mathews, Gordon. 1996. *What Makes Life Worth Living? How Japanese and Americans Make Sense of Their Worlds.* Berkeley, CA: University of California Press.

Mathews, Gordon, and Carolina Izquierdo. 2009. "Anthropology, Happiness, and Well-Being." In *Pursuits of Happiness: Well-Being in Anthropological Perspective,* edited by Gordon Mathews and Carolina Izquierdo, 1–19. New York, NY: Berghahn.

Oberoi, Harjot. 1994. *The Construction of Religious Boundaries: Culture, Identity and Diversity in the Sikh Tradition.* Chicago, IL: University of Chicago Press.

Oishi, Shigehiro. 2000. "Goals as Cornerstones of Subjective Well-Being: Linking Individuals and Culture." In *Culture and Subjective Well-Being,* edited by Ed Diener and Eunkook M. Suh, 87–112. Cambridge, MA: MIT Press.

Putnam, Robert D. 2000. *Bowling Alone: The Collapse and Revival of American Community.* New York, NY: Simon and Schuster.

Seligman, Martin E.P. 2011. *Flourish.* New York, NY: Free Press.

Sen, Amartya. 2002. *Rationality and Freedom.* Cambridge, MA: Harvard University Press.

Stacey, Judith. 1990. *Brave New Families: Stories of Domestic Upheaval in late Twentieth Century America.* Berkeley, CA: University of California Press.

Taneja, Anand Vivek. 2013. "Nature, History, and the Sacred in the Medieval Ruins of Delhi." PhD Dissertation: Columbia University, New York.

Trawick, Margaret. 1990. *Notes on Love in a Tamil Family.* Berkeley, CA: University of California Press.

Vaillant, George E. 2002. *Aging Well: Surprising Guideposts to a Happier Life from the Landmark Harvard Study of Adult Development.* Boston, MA: Little Brown.

PART I

Universals

2

HEALTH AND WEALTH

The meaning of khushhali *[well-being] is health [E¹] and wealth [E].
A disease-free* [nirogi] *body is the biggest* sukh *[comfort, happiness, pleasure] in life. The second thing is sufficient property [E]. Absence of disease* [nirogi] *and sufficient riches is what a family* [ghar] *needs for well-being.*

——Jivraj Sharma, 49-year-old male police sub-inspector

Khushhali *means to have a sound sleep every night, to have abundant food in the house, good education for the children and proper medical attention to the parents.*

——Harish Mishra, 40-year-old male shopkeeper

In fall 2007, I came down to Dehradun after a bus tour of the Himalayan pilgrimage sites Gangotri (the Ganga's source), Yamunotri (the Yamuna's source), Kedarnath (Shiva's mountain abode), and Badrinath (Vishnu's abode). Arriving in Dehradun, that world of glacial-river *sangam*s (confluences) and high temples seemed like a dream. I soon found a good place to stay with a garden and a kitchen and contacted my friend Narendra Sethi, the extraordinary journalist who had assisted me in 1991 and 2001. On the culminating day of 2007's Durga Puja festival, having completed just two interviews, Narendra and I wandered over to Gandhi Park, where we met and interviewed Prakash Tyagi, a 79-year-old who described

---

¹ Words marked [E] are words that were in English in the original.

himself as: "A common man, a little man," although he was actually a prosperous retiree from the Oil and Natural Gas Corporation (ONGC)]. When he talked about well-being, Prakash showed enthusiasm for life, saying, "You're human, don't let despair, dejection or disappointment into your heart." He shared maxims, which he said allowed him to "walk comfortably." One maxim was, "if circumstances do not smile on you, smile yourself on circumstances." The ability to see well-being as inner, rather than in external situations was a typical approach to maintain well-being in the face of adversity. Prakash referenced a Robert Browning poem to highlight his own optimism. According to Prakash, "[Browning had] optimism in pessimism. His conditions brought him pessimism, but he took pleasure in optimism." Prakash quotes Browning's "Last Ride":

Fail I alone, in words and deeds?
Why, all men strive and who succeeds?

Prakash interprets this to mean that, at the end, Browning thought, "Throughout life I have been discarded but now it is my last wish that you should travel with me on a horse for a long time, for a long way." Prakash says that he himself is alone, but still feels that: "In words and deeds while all men strive and succeed, all karma passes. My life is quite successful. All is well that ends well."

Prakash's health was declining rapidly and his family neglected him, but he says, "The world is wonderful." Reading, he says, is the "greatest bliss [*anand*]." Because he finds pleasure in *ghumna-phirna* (moving around), Prakash walks to Gandhi Park whenever he can: "Distance traveled in walking is more important than the destination." When we talked one day about a Bollywood film I had seen, Prakash dismissed "family films" as not worth seeing; it is the "sexy" films that move. Prakash's health is poor, his family neglects him, but filmgoing, walking, and reading are pleasures that give spark to his life. In some ways, Prakash is right to highlight himself as a "common man," since it is not his prosperity but his approach to living and easily-taken pleasures that are more important to well-being.

One day, Prakash excitedly visited me to share his conclusions about well-being in the form of a pyramid with the easiest available things at the bottom and proceeding to the heights. "First," he says, are three things that are "easily available"—"food, clothing and lodging." He is quick to recognize that good lodging should include a "comfortable home, good books, and a small garden." Higher up the pyramid one needs a "sound body provided by healthy surroundings." At the top of the pyramid are "good company and sweet relations with family and friends." Above all else are sweet relationships, which Prakash says are even a source of a sound body. The next chapter focuses on connections with others as a source of well-being, and subsequent chapters focus on the importance of pleasures (like walking, filmgoing, and reading) and approaches to life (like focusing on maintaining optimism whatever the circumstance). In this chapter I describe how people mention health and food, clothing, and lodging as foundations of well-being. But I also argue that quite limited health and wealth is not inconsistent with well-being; rather, the sorts of internal approaches, pleasures, and connections that Prakash focuses on are what are truly essential.

In 2007, Prakash had difficulty getting around and had a persistent cough, which he attributed to years of smoking. But these ailments didn't keep him from loving life—so, I think his focus on "a sound body provided by healthy surroundings" is belied by his own well-being! One day he told me that some people say he should want to die, but he insisted that he remained "satisfied with life. I want to live as long as I can." As is probably apparent, I was charmed by Prakash and his enthusiasms. And he seemed to enjoy our interactions, too, telling me that I revived the memories of his school life. He told me that I had met him too late. "I'm a fading rose, a fading man," he said. On the last day we met, December 15, 2007, he said, "life is too short, I wish I had more time." I sent him our annual holiday letter, but never heard from him again. When I returned in August 2011, the separate entrance to his home was overgrown. A neighbor confirmed that he had passed away and I left a volume of Browning poems that I had brought for him there in the growth from the current monsoon.

Health

Jayant Aorora, another Hindu man in his 70s, also mentioned diverse sources of well-being, which included good health. Narendra and I interviewed Jayant in the confectionary store, now run by his son.

Jayant, who migrated from what became Pakistan at Partition, points to the well-being he gets from the sweet relationships with a childhood friend who runs a retail shop near his own. But Jayant also says khushhali is "all spiritual [*adhyatmik*]. If a person is directly attached [*lagan*] to the almighty, a person is happy." While Jayant describes well-being as "all" spiritual and appears to get well-being from his relation with God, he *also* highlights a strong body as necessary for well-being; so, sources of well-being are contradictory, indeed. When I asked Jayant to describe a situation in which he felt well-being, he described recovery from ill health:

> When I was 40, I had a heart attack due to excessive smoking, and the doctor advised me to [quit] smoking and stop eating food prepared outside. After doing this, within 8 months, I became alright. Now I am 77, so for these years, I haven't had any ailment [*taklif*]. I have abandoned cigarettes and have never felt any desire for them. Just after the heart attack, my face became pale yellow but with proper treatment and good nutrition my face became rosy and gleaming again, blushed with good cheer and I retained my good health. The greatest happiness was when I was very happy to see my own face in the mirror.

When I comment that he looks like he still has such well-being, he says that when he came to know that we are interviewing people on well-being, it has given him even more happiness, showing how often interactions produce well-being. But certainly for Jayant, maintaining a healthy body—and his efforts to do so—help him feel well, too.

Armaan Singh, a 65-year-old unobservant Sikh, doesn't believe in God at all. "If there is a God," he asks, "why did my son die?" Like Prakash and Jayant, Armaan gets well-being from diverse sources. He enjoys watching cricket with the boys who crowd around his small shop and lights up at a "great cricket match." He, too, enjoyed sexy movies—in 2007 he urged me to see *Jab We Met*—and he pretends to flirt with schoolgirls in his shop. He said he had *budha mast*— the sexual intoxication of an old man. Despite his many enjoyments, like Prakash, Armaan described well-being as inner. "Khushhali means inner feelings," was Armaan's first statement on well-being. But he immediately pointed to health and wealth—two things that hardly seem inner: "The inner feeling of khushhali comes from three things—a physically fit body, wealth [*dhan*], and popularity"—the last was an English word, which he used to refer to the respect of others (which I will discuss in the next chapter).

An approach to life that sees well-being as inner, alongside connections to others and pleasurable activities such as cricket, flirting, and filmgoing, provide Armaan well-being; but a healthy body is also the key to his well-being: "The biggest part of khushhali—the biggest *sukh* [happiness, pleasure, comfort]—is the sukh of the perfect, healthy [*swasth*] body." Armaan compared the healthy person with the *hijras* (eunuchs) who are neither male nor female: "Both males and females can enjoy sex, but the middle ones—the hijras—they cannot enjoy sex." Perhaps because a *kothi* of hijras is in the neighborhood, they may be more familiar to Armaan than most people. While he is focusing on a healthy body in this discussion, Armaan also references limited social relations to explain why hijras—he thinks—can't possibly be happy: Hijras "can't marry; they can't have children; they're not accepted by society. This is the *dukh* (unhappiness) of their lives. Their lives are nothing but dukh because they are separated from society despite their humanness." For Armaan, the healthy body that hijras lack is necessary for well-being: "A man without an arm or without a leg or without eyes or a sick person has the greatest unhappiness [dukh], while a physically fit man can easily confront the woes and troubles which come in everyday life." Armaan, like Prakash, shows how mixed-up discussions of well-being often are. Like Jayant, Prakash says well-being is inner *and* is also in externals such as a healthy body, pleasures, and connections to others. While he emphasizes a healthy body as a key to well-being, when he thinks about his son's death, he sees the body as nothing (as will be described in Chapter 4).

A diversity of people identify health as necessary for well-being. Ahmad Siddiqui, a 63-year-old retired Muslim lawyer, said "good health [*swaasth*] is the first step towards khushhali. If you have money and you don't have health, you'll be unable to enjoy it. The first step to khushhali is good health." Tavleen Kaur, a 75-year-old Sikh widow living with her son, said health allows her to move about:

> By the grace of God, this body should remain healthy so that I can go for *darshan* [come before God in the *gurudwara*]. Now my knee joints are in a lot of pain. This is the trouble [*pareshani*] with my body. My aim is to have God shower blessings so that I am a little better, can go to

gurudwara, have a glimpse of the *sangat* [community], and do darshan of God. Then, my mind will have a little peace [*shanti*].

Maitreyi Chatterjee, a 65-year-old Hindu, prays to God to keep her healthy so that she can continue to "spend time with [her] friends and relatives." For Maitreyi and Tavleen, health allows interactions in community, the source of well-being I address in the next chapter. Shanti Kumar, a 36-year-old female Hindu domestic servant, said "khushhali is here when there is *sukh-shanti* [comfort, joy and peace] in the home and everyone in the family is healthy [swasth]." Madhvi Gupta, 48, says that she feels a lack of happiness anytime there is illness in the house, and that her own experience (*mahasus*) of illness is the source of the "greatest unhappiness. Being healthy [swasth] is the biggest happiness and lacking health is the greatest sorrow [dukh]."

While people themselves see health as an important component of well-being, my research suggests that people can often overcome ill-health to find well-being by cultivating good interactions or focusing on the satisfactions they manage to find *in spite of* ill health. Prakash Tyagi's health is in grave decline, but he focuses on how he can still walk to the park, if slowly. Despite health problems, Prakash has an approach to living that focuses on finding in each day "a new elegance." Prakash's objective health is not good, but he nonetheless has well-being. By contrast, Ishwar Kumar, an 80-year-old, is grumpy, even though his objective health is better than Prakash's. Although more hale and hearty than Prakash, Ishwar complains bitterly about his health, saying a leg injury makes it impossible for him to move outside of Dehradun. I'll compare the situation of Prakash Tyagi and Ishwar Kumar more fully in Chapter 8, but let me note here that while people see health as necessary for well-being, how one *sees* one's health may, in fact, be more fundamental.

Although my analysis suggests that approaches, pleasures, and connections are central to well-being, my sociological introspection, too, sees my health as a key component of well-being. For years now, I've stayed healthy in India, which is a basis of my well-being here. But anytime something goes wrong with health—the sting of a *jimuri* (insect) that made my arm swell, a cold sore after a trek, runs to the toilet—my pleasure in life is interrupted. Even worries about a root canal gone bad kept me from enjoying a trip to Paris some years ago. In August of 2010, my doctor said I had high triglycerides and I took up running. After running through the winter, I gloried in feeling superhuman in everything from mowing the lawn to spreading mulch, to shoveling snow, to trekking in the Himalayas, to circumambulating Mount Tamalpais in the Bay area. When I reflected on this to my friend Bert, he replied, "It sounds like you more than understand the value of conditioning when it comes to living life to the fullest! Well-being clearly involves being able to do what you want physically. It's odd to me how many people don't give themselves that gift." Consistent with what people told me, my introspection suggests that health crises do limit well-being, while the energy and ability to interact with people that one gets from the activities that produce good health is a source of well-being in day-to-day life.

My focus on approaches, pleasures, and connections as being more consequential for well-being than objective health is consistent with psychologists' quantitative survey findings examining how health shapes well-being. Like the people I interviewed, American respondents rank health as an important factor in happiness (Diener [1984] 2009, 35). Yet objective health has only a weak correlation with well-being, and once you control for leisure activities, the effect of health on well-being disappears (Diener [1984] 2009, 35–36). This suggests that running, swimming, or walking (for instance) are associated with good health, but it's the *pleasure* of walking, swimming, or running that produces well-being, rather than good health itself. Some research suggests that the causal direction is reversed: People who experience well-being develop good health because they feel well (Diener and Seligman [2004] 2009, 227). While objective health has, at best, a weak relationship to Americans' well-being (Lucas and Diener [2008] 2009, 85), subjective health—that is, how respondents report health—is strongly correlated with well-being (Bok 2010, 21; Cacioppo et al. 2008, 209; Diener [1984] 2009, 36). This suggests that how one sees one's health is a predictor of well-being, while actual health is not: Prakash is quite limited by his health, but focuses on how he can still manage to walk to the park, whereas Ishwar, whose health seems objectively better than Prakash's, is upset that he has to walk with a cane. Substantial research indicates humans' ability to adapt to adverse conditions. Thus, after suffering severe and lasting injuries people's well-being falls at first, but later rebounds as people adapt to their circumstances (Diener, Lucas, and Scollon [2006] 2009, 104). While the people I interviewed see health as a source of well-being, the fact that people adapt shows that having an *approach* to getting through troubles is central to feeling well (a topic pursued in Chapter 4). The fact that subjective health produces well-being more than objective health shows that how one views circumstances is crucial to well-being (a topic pursued in Chapter 8). The fact that the relationship between health and well-being disappears once leisure activities are controlled suggests the role of day-to-day pleasures in fostering well-being (a topic pursued in Chapter 5).

Wealth

Although economically prosperous, Prakash said his "aptitude" didn't lie in business and he often downplayed money's importance. "Khushhali," he said, "depends on attitude and temperament—on what we *think*. A poor man may be very happy and his well-being will be good, while a *crorepati* [millionaire] may always be ill and think dark thoughts. What well-being does that crorepati have?" While saying that because the person is first a "social being" and, so, "social friends" are necessary, Prakash also says the person should have "residential bliss, food, and clothing." Prakash's pyramid rightly recognizes how a comfortable home, good books, and a small garden that income provides are a foundation of well-being. Thus, Prakash remembers that he was miserable when he was without work: "After I left college, I at first wasn't able to find a job. In those days, I had no khushhali. But I found a job and those feelings passed." Yet his pyramid is also right that relationships with others are more central— and one reason sufficient income contributes to well-being is that it contributes to those relationships. My sociological introspection recognizes that income contributes to well-being: One of my great pleasures is enjoying books in the beautiful garden in our comfortable house. I love lying on the grass with cats, looking at flowers and lounging on a mat. Like Prakash, there was a time when my employment was in question—a department did not recommend renewal. That was a time when I felt a great lack of khushhali, but it passed and relationships and pleasures became again most important.

While seeing sufficient income as part of well-being, Prakash knows that craving for income can detract from simple comforts:

> Since I left college, I am fortunate to have had a good life. I never thought of money. I was always happy with whatever salary I had. I never crazed for much.... All of my family is now satisfied. All my children are married.

By contrast, he says, "the more ambitious you are the more you worry." Gurkeerat Singh, a 49-year-old Sikh living in a family with his wife and children, works long hours, but insists:

> I don't believe in toiling hard in the sun [*daur dhup*] running after money [*hapar tapar*]. We should remain happy. More tensions [E] only create more problems. So, tensions [E] should be less. By controlling our wishes [*ichchhaon*] and needs, tensions diminish. When a person's needs [*zarurat*] are less and there are limitations, it reduces tensions [E].

I once inherited a little money and found that it meant more work to do—more tensions. When I got my first tenure track job, other faculty memebers were discussing about making more money by teaching summer school. I said what seemed self-evident to me—surely you'd rather have more time than more money. Like Gurkeerat, I've tried to control needs—still getting basic cars, putting more into supplemental retirement accounts to offset every raise—and have found that this limits worries. I suppose I have an approach to work demands that parallels the approach that Prakash and Gurkeerat have—always keep money in its place.

For Armaan Singh, wealth, along with the body and social respect, is fundamental to khushhali. Armaan sees his money as "fine," saying says he has a pension and earns ₹10,000 a month from his shop. But Armaan, too, sees money as a poor determinant of well-being. In comparison to his brothers, he says, "[I am] the lowest on the monetary scale, but I'm the happiest of my brothers. I cannot afford a car. What do I need a car for? OK, I'm happy." He says that one of his brothers "has many cars, being not just a millionaire, but a billionaire through his manufacturing enterprise in Delhi." Yet Armaan believes his brother only donates to temples and gurudwaras for fame, rather than to actually help the poor.

Ahmad Siddiqui, the retired lawyer, mentions health as central to well-being, but also says that to be happy "the basic requirements of life must be fulfilled." Ahmad's discussion of lacking khushhali recalled a time when he earned "very little salary" because he could only get work on an "ad hoc basis." For Ahmad, the *dependence and loss of control* was the biggest reason for lack of well-being—a theme I explore below. Ahmad says:

> Because my salary was low, I was unable to meet the needs of my family. My father used to help me in meeting those expenses and every time it haunted in my mind that I am dependent on my father. This gave me a lot of dukh [sadness] because I thought that I should serve my mother. Instead my father is serving me.

Many men find well-being in earning because it supports their families. Arvind Rana, a 30-year-old Hindu, works in a tailoring shop to support his wife and children. Arvind is delighted with his family, smiling broadly when he describes his three children. For Arvind,

> The meaning of khushhali is linked with money. When money is there, the family is happy. When I excel well at work, my master gets happy and my mind is happy [khush] and in the home the family eats according to their desire. The gharwalle [family members] feel happy because of me; so I am happy. My mother and wife and my family members [pariwar-walle] are happy when I bring articles [sammaan] for them. My mind is happy when my family remains in happiness.

Arvind describes the ill-feeling he had when he was forced to work in a distant place while his wife was pregnant. Yet Arvind is also proud at his fortitude to earn in a difficult period:

> The situation [of the least khushhali] was when I had to go outside for money during that happy time when my wife was pregnant. My wife was in a pre-delivery state but for the sake of the livelihood of my family, I had to go outside. It was a problematic [samasyaatmak] and tension [E]-filled time because of my debt and because it was my wife's time, yet I had to earn money to clear off my debts. It was very painful and sad to be away during her delivery time. It was hard, but for her security, for the money and for the sake of the family I opted to go. Even today I remember that time when I left my wife in such a condition and went to earn outside!

Arvind described getting the "greatest happiness" when his brother phoned him in Darjeeling about his wife's delivery and told him he had a son. It is often, indeed, that well-being associated with money comes from helping others we love.

Fathers in the years while their children are growing commonly describe their well-being in terms of providing for their families. Surendra Kumar, a lower-caste Balmiki, who like Arvind passed Class 8, similarly describes well-being as "living in a good way without any difficulty." This 39-year-old who works as a menial clerk focuses especially on controlling spending: "It is in a person's own control to remain happy [khush]. If we spend more than we earn, we can never be happy. If we manage to spend only what we earn, whatever income we have, then we will be happy." But Surendra was troubled for four or five years of joblessness: "A human [*insaan*] without work will always remain without happiness [khushi] because that person won't be able to look after his children or even to feed himself." Men who are caught up in raising families commonly focus on earning money at their job as a primary source of well-being. Arvind Rana's boss, a 49-year-old Sikh, who has completed his masters in commerce, focuses on earning money as a source of well-being: "Khushhali is when everything is completely right in the family because business is running smoothly—there's nothing else."

One of the main reasons money is associated with well-being is that it facilitates the ability to connect with people whom one supports, gaining respect in the process. Ravi Chuhra, a 30-year-old Balmiki, owns his own electrical shop—which he calls both his "biggest happiness" and his "biggest achievement." Although marriage discussions are going on, Ravi doesn't want to marry until "my economic situation is sound because I don't want my wife to see a blank face when she asks for dresses or wants to go to the picture— she will be coming to my house all the long way from her family to live a life. I want to give all the peace and happiness to her." If quantitative studies show money "is associated" with well-being, it may be largely because it strengthens social bonds that make people feel well.

Women's discussion of how money provides well-being, similarly, focuses on how it facilitates helping other people. Sonali Pandey, a

19-year-old Hindu student, says that the purpose of her life is to help (*madad*) poor people (*garib log*): "When I get a job, I would like to support those poor people who cannot send their children to school because of lack of money." Parvati Aggarwal, a 68-year-old Hindu who had passed Class 8, says that rather than donating money at the temple, she would like "to give that money to be used in the marriage of some poor girls." Amrit Kaur, a 24-year-old Sikh college student, has ambitions to publish books of poetry. "Whatever money I get from that," she says, "I want to spend on the education of the poor children." Poonam Kumar, a 51-year-old female domestic servant, says that the purpose of her life is that if God "gives me enough money that I would like to help [madad] the orphan children."

For women, like some of the men described above, financial difficulties often led to a lack of well-being due to an *absence of control* over their lives. Women's feeling of lack of control is exacerbated when they themselves are not earners. Pooja Thakur, a 46-year-old postgraduate working as a librarian, emphasized that "there will be khushhali in the family when there is enough money to fulfill the family's needs." She described feeling ill-being when her husband quit his job: "I was very unhappy because at that time, my children were small and in school and I was just a housewife, so I didn't know what I should do then. How should my family fulfill its needs?" When her daughter eventually got a job and, later, a promotion, she found this to be the greatest happiness. Shanti Kumar, the 36-year-old female domestic servant, described herself as

> very unhappy [*dukhi*] when my husband used to drink a lot of *sharaab* [alcohol]. Then I was sad [dukhi] because that made the atmosphere in the house unpeaceful [*ashant*]. All of the money was spent on *sharaab*. Due to lack of money, there was always mental disturbance [*maansik klesh*] in the family.

Gaura Khanna, a 70-year-old committed to teaching, described how she lacked well-being when she was unable to get a "permanent job." She was "upset during those days" because she was "really working hard to find a job." She describes another situation in which she lacked well-being when her husband died: "I was very sad [dukhi] because my children were not settled and we had to depend on my income alone."

Control

As many situations described previously show, money is a source of well-being because it often provides a feeling of control over one's life. Without money, one is dependent on others. With money, one can control situations. For Surendra Kumar, controlling spending puts one's life under control. Recall that, for Surendra, who works as a peon, happiness can be yours if you control your wants: "Happiness is under our own control. If we spend only what we earn, we can be happy."

Dependence and lack of control are a common source of ill-being. When her husband was an alcoholic who spent the house's money on alcohol, Shanti Kumar felt ill-being. Ahmad Siddiqui describes his greatest unhappiness as the dependence he felt on his father when he could only find an ad hoc job. Gaura Khanna felt unhappy when her husband died because she was unable to support her family well. Poonam Kumar, the 51-year-old domestic servant who describes the purpose of her life as getting enough money to help others, described the lament she felt when her husband had a heart attack:

Last year, my husband had a massive heart attack. I was distraught because I thought and thought about what I would do if I lost him. My daughters are still to be married. None of the four of us were employed. What could we do?

Purnima Kumar, a 70-year-old widow living alone, lamented that when her husband died, she "had to cope with half a pension while [she] had three young children who were still studying." Rashmi Mishra, a 34-year-old college graduate, says that because she is a housewife, her "whole attention is focused on the family." For Rashmi, the uncertainty she felt when her husband was ill was the worst time of her life because she had no idea how she would provide for her children:

Four years back, my husband met with a serious accident. He was shifted to a hospital in Delhi and there he was swinging between life and death. My husband's illness made me very sad [dukhi] because at that time my children were very small. Every day this thought kept moving around in my head: "if anything happens to him how will I bring up my children because I am not very educated and I am only a housewife."

"The happiest moment" of her life was when her husband's health returned.

Often the lack of control comes from crises that limit opportunities. Ghalib Khan, a 21-year-old, says his work as an office peon in a hotel management institute "means khushhali to me. I like doing whatever work is given to me by the management of the institute." Ghalib's greatest sadness was that a few years after his father's death he had to leave his studies after Class 8 "because our family's economic condition was not good." For Chaand Rana, a married 32-year-old who works in a beauty parlor, well-being means serving her parents and other elders. But Chaand "felt quite sad [dukhi] at the moment my father took me out of school." Laughing, she says she "wept a lot" at her father's decision:

> I wanted to go further but that wasn't possible because we were poor [garib]. There were two sisters and a brother and my father needed me at home. I was taken out of school and those days I cried a lot [royi bahut]. My heart [dil] was very sad because I wanted to study higher and to become something, but I couldn't do it. It was hard [katin].

Chaand's goal remains "to make money and make a good name" for herself. She laughed several times recounting that far-off time when she had to leave school.

Restrictions at work can limit a person's sense of control and well-being, even if one is prosperous. Lochan Mishra, 68-year-old retired engineer, said that

> I gave the best of my efforts, my time, my energy, and my mind, for the work that I was paid to do but the department let me down. I was not promoted. And because of that, I had to leave my job. I took my retirement in 1990 before I wanted to retire. I ended up feeling that I wasted my time in that work.

While Lochan feels khushhali, enjoying especially his hobbies that involve everything from gardening to cooking, when he couldn't control his work life, he felt ill-being. Abdul Khan, a 61-year-old retired male principal, says, "[K]hushhali means peace—if you have peace in your mind, then you are happy [khush]. You're always happy if you do your work efficiently." But Abdul felt ill-being when his colleagues "without any reason, didn't cooperate with me. It affected my overall performance and my promotion was restricted." Whatever one's status, restrictions on opportunities can harm well-being. Chaand Rana and Ghalib Khan faced limited educational opportunities that harmed their well-being. Lochan Mishra and Abdul Khan were more economically successful but still felt a lack of well-being when their opportunities for advancement were limited.

On the other hand, many talk of well-being in terms of economic opportunities that provide control. Ghalib Khan described his greatest well-being as when he met the Hindu who became his best friend: "I was extremely happy because he helped me a lot even though I belonged to another religion. He offered me the job that I am doing now and until now he always helped me whenever I need his help." Raveena Chawla, a 21-year-old Sikh student, describes khushhali as

being financially independent. To achieve this goal, I am doing this course. When I went to the institute for the first time, I felt khushhali because I had never thought that I would enter the college gate.

For Raveena, garment technology studies made her "extremely happy because now I have a line in which I will work." Raveena, whose father died when she was young and who describes her greatest unhappiness in having to live with her mother's family when her father's family abandoned them, describes the aim of her life as "to become independent by getting a good job so that I can support my mother, and if God gives me enough, I would like to help others, too."

My focus on how control bolsters well-being confirms the work of economists (Sen 2002), quantitative psychological researchers (Diener [1984] 2009, 32), and anthropologist William Jankowiak (2009), who linked improvements in Chinese well-being since economic liberalization to Chinese people's greater control over their lives. Quantitative survey research, Jankowiak's study showing changes in well-being, and my study examining people's understandings of the sources of their own well-being confirm that control of circumstances is one way people experience well-being.

While people mention sufficient income as a part of well-being, mention obtaining employment as a time of well-being, and describe situations when they lacked money as causing a lack of well-being, it's notable that when asked to describe a situation of well-being, only three people mentioned obtaining anything material, and one of these mentioned the well-being he received when his family was able to purchase a home, after having lost a family home during Partition—surely a symbolic achievement as much as a material possession. No one mentioned improving their home or purchasing a car, or a scooter, or a television. That obtaining a material good was so rarely mentioned to illustrate well-being shows that while sufficient income may be necessary for well-being, higher sources of well-being emphasized by thinkers from Prakash Tyagi to the psychologist Abraham Maslow are more important.

The relationship between money and well-being is complex. Sufficient money is necessary to provide life's necessities. Working for money, as I explore in the next chapter, often provides a sense that one is special and competent and supports social connections that are a source of well-being: By earning, one can do things for other people. Money, though, can be a detriment to well-being—it can lead to running around, chasing after it. Money is, after all, only a symbol—it can detract from focusing on real realities (Brown 1959, 234–304; Loy 2002, 77–84).

Laborers' Woes

The complex relationship between income and well-being can be better understood by looking at laborers. Yashoda Kumar, an uneducated 53-year-old laborer, reflects that sometimes the elephant grass was extremely high, but the overseer only offered ten rupees to cut the grass. "There was grass all over," she said, "and I didn't want to cut it, but because I needed money I had to do it anyway." Yashoda, who lives with her husband and five children, only one of whom is still studying—the others having found employment in menial occupations—feels bad because she knows she is being exploited: "I used to do labor for ten rupees even when I was sick and sometimes I feel that rich people exploit us." Yashoda also recognizes the problems of not being able to provide for life's necessities:

> When my children were young, I had to face many difficulties because my husband was the only earning member in the family. Now, my sons are working. My daughters had to leave their studies—even though they didn't want to do so—and now they are working as domestic servants.

But lack of control and feelings of being compelled and exploited have, perhaps, as much to do with the problem of limited income as what the income buys.

Komal Kumar, a 37-year-old construction laborer, works to support her family on her earnings alone because her husband "drinks a lot" and, so, "brings very little money into the house." For Komal, though, the absence of any free time combined with the disrespect she senses seem to be the main sources of her unhappiness:

> Until now, there is no happiness in my life. Everyday in the morning I get up, prepare food for the whole family, and come to the work-site. The whole day I work here picking up the burden (*bojh*) and again when I return in the evening, I cook food for the children, eat it and go to sleep. This is the daily routine of life.

When Meenu Sharma asks Komal about whether she has a purpose in her life, she at first says she has no purpose, but then adds that her only goal would be to "get some free time and take a rest." Komal reflects, too, on the unpleasant interactions she is forced to endure with her supervisors: "We poor people work for the whole day and sometimes if the boss sees us resting for a few minutes, he starts abusing us. That moment is the saddest one because this is the work we have to do." Komal's job gives her no free time for the small pleasures that this book argues are so important for well-being (Chapter 5). Her job forces her to endure unpleasant interactions, rather than providing the felicitous interactions, which this book argues (Chapters 3 and 8) are central to well-being. The burden of supporting four children between the ages of five and 12 falls solely on Komal, but her lack of well-being perhaps has as much to do with her lack of a good relationship with her husband, the sort of relationship that this book argues (Chapter 3) is central to well-being. It's not just that she doesn't have enough basic resources, but she doesn't have a partner with whom she can join to struggle together. Like Yashoda, Komal experiences lack of well-being because her limited income fails to comfortably provide life's material necessities. But the lack of well-being from limited income also has to do with unhappy relationships and little opportunity for small pleasures.

Twenty-five-year-old Deeta Kumar, a laborer struggling to support her family, says that for her there is no "meaning to khushhali" because up until now "I've had no well-being (khushhali), but have only seen sadness (dukh)." The issue of supporting her family looms large. When her husband died of TB, Deeta laments that her younger son "was only a year old and I was unable to understand how I would bring up my children." While lack of earnings is a part of her problem, she also describes how her in-laws take all that she earns, yet she is unable to call on the support of her parents because she had married against their wishes. For Deeta, her problems with earning enough are complicated by her poor relationship with her in-laws and her parents. While her lack of subjective well-being "correlates" with her poor earnings, the root cause (of both the lack of well-being and poor earnings) could perhaps be found in her unhappy family life.

Vashisht Kumar, a 68-year-old laborer, complains that, today, very few people are happy (*sukhi*). Every person, Vashisht says, has troubles (pareshani). Poor, uneducated people like him, Vashisht says, "spend their whole lives in earning for their livelihood and for completing the basic necessities of life. If my hands don't work, who will give me the roti [bread]?" Vashisht was in difficulty when we interviewed him because he had to take a loan from a money-lender when his wife (who had a kidney stone) and his son (who lost two fingers at work) needed medical help. But, like some of the other laborers I've referred to, it's partly the pressing nature of a job that must be attended to, while giving no time for pleasure, that is the source of ill-being, too:

The whole life is spent in fulfilling the responsibilities of the family. Until now I have not obtained khushhali in my life. Since I was 15–16 years old, I had learned this work and started doing it. First I had the responsibilities of my parents and my brothers and sisters. After that, I had the responsi-bilities of my children. And, still, I am earning for my livelihood.

When Meenu asks Vashisht if he has been on any pilgrimage he replies that he has no free time (*phursut*) because he has to earn every day. While Vashisht's lack of earnings "correlate" with his lack of well-being, he appears frustrated that his children do not care for him. Vashisht spent his whole life meeting responsibilities to parents, brothers, and, finally, children, but says:

When the time for pleasure [sukh] comes, the children take their families and go out to stay somewhere else! Now, it is the time for my children to take the responsibility on their shoulders, but they are not doing so. Parents can look after their ten children, but ten children do not look after one parent. I'm still working with my hands to get two meals a day.

The root cause of Vashisht's lack of well-being—and his limited earnings—might very well be his lack of good relationships with his children. Like Deeta Kumar (who is mistreated by in-laws but can't return to her parents) and Komal Kumar (whose husband is an alcoholic), Vashisht's well-being is impeded by unhappy family relationships (as it is for many who are better off as well)!

Laboring Indians' well-being seems to be negatively affected by their limited earnings. But lack of control and lack of free time for the small pleasures that seem so essential appear to be important, too, as does poor social relationships that may sometimes cause or follow from limited earnings. Because they need to work today if they want to eat tonight, laborers often lack control of their lives and must accept employment even if they are mistreated and exploited. Some laborers seem to lack well-being because of lack of respect they receive from their employers and lack of good connections with their family. The "correlation" between income and well-being may, in fact, partly reflect that income is harmed by bad social relationships, which themselves directly harm well-being.

It is important to note, too, that many, many laborers still find a great deal of well-being. Vashisht Kumar enjoys listening to a radio at work, taking advantage of the small pleasures that helps people get through difficulties. Yashoda Kumar complains about having to work in poor conditions and for poor remuneration because she needs the money. But because she sometimes labors in a dairy she says that this gives her well-being because "in Hindu religion we say that cow service [seva] is the biggest service." Komal's attitude is that she should be able to live on what she gets: "Whatever money we get, we remain happy with that. God [*Bhagwan*] allows us to spend life according to what we get." Yashoda still has a purpose in life—to do good toward others. She describes facing her difficulties by praying to God that "he should not show such days to anyone else." In Chapter 4, I focus on how finding an approach to difficulties is central to well-being; Yashoda seems to have found approaches that help her feel well.

Reflections on the Relationship between Earnings and Well-being

This book is primarily concerned with people's understanding of what gives them well-being and a lack of well-being. While the book explores variations in what people think gives them well-being, it's not much concerned with explaining variations in people's level of subjective well-being. But some reflections on the relationship between earnings and well-being might be in order at this point.

When I first started studying well-being prior to conducting this research, the consensus in the literature was that income had very little to do with well-being. This consensus was based on a number of facts. First, despite vast increases in living standards over 50 years in the USA and other countries, levels of well-being in these countries have not gone up. In Japan, from 1958 to 1991, real income increased sixfold, yet reported satisfaction was unchanged (Hamilton 2003, 29). Between 1946 and the 1990s, American incomes increased fourfold in real terms, yet the proportion of people reporting themselves to be very happy declined (Hamilton 2003, 30). Despite the quadrupling of real incomes, fewer Americans were satisfied with their incomes in the 1990s than were satisfied with their income in the 1950s (Hamilton 2003, 30). Noting that doubling or tripling of real income in wealthy nations has not been accompanied by increases in well-being, Diener and Seligman ([2004] 2009, 210) conclude that it is "very clear" that "rises in well-being have not been remotely commensurate with increasing wealth"—a finding that appears to remain sound (Layard, Mayraz, and Nickell 2010). Second, the correlation between a country's income and self-reported life satisfaction is weak (although positive; Hamilton 2003, 24). So, a 2014 Pew poll found that 54 percent of people in rich countries (such as the USA, Germany and France) described themselves as happy, a percentage not much higher than the 51 percent of respondents in "emerging markets" such as India, Mexico, Vietnam, Russia and China who described themselves as happy (*Economist* 2014). In the 2014 Pew poll as well, Mexican respondents reported themselves happier than American respondents, Vietnamese respondents reported greater happiness than German respondents, and Chinese respondents reported more happiness than French respondents (*Economist* 2014). Third, longitudinal studies show most people's satisfaction with life tends to change little with rise and fall of income as they progress through their careers (Bok 2010, 11; Diener and Biswas-Diener [2002] 2009, 127–28).[2] Fourth, materialism and pursuit of externals (like money) are not associated with well-being. So, individuals oriented to extrinsic goals (such as money) have less well-being than those emphasizing intrinsic goals (such as relationships and personal growth; Hamilton 2003, 37). Placing money high in the rank of goals is associated with less vitality and more depression among Americans (Lane 2000, 145). Following up on American college students who said they preferred "high income and occupational success" over "having very close friends and a close marriage" showed that as alumni they were twice as likely as their fellow alumni to describe themselves as "fairly" or "very" unhappy (Lane 2000, 145). As the psychoanalysts are right to note, money is not an infantile desire (Brown 1959)!

But in the time while I was away from the literature doing this research between 2007 and 2011, the consensus had changed. Lucas and Diener ([2008] 2009, 84) concluded in 2008 that "many studies have been conducted and a number of consistent findings have emerged," the "most important" of which is that "at an individual level, correlations [between income and happiness] tend to be positive but *very small*" (my emphasis). Rather than emphasizing the *limited* effect of earnings on subjective well-being, researchers have recently emphasized instead the consistent positive correlation between earnings and well-being within a country (Bok 2010, 10–11; Cacioppo et al. 2008, 201; Diener and Biswas Diener 2008, 93). *Small* correlation between income and reported well-being within a society is *not* inconsistent with the findings I report: Well-being still might not increase as prosperity increases in a society; materialism might still be associated with unhappiness. I even suggest below that the *small* difference that is found might be entirely a product of the interaction between interviewee and interviewer producing less well-being for poorer individuals because the class difference with their interviewer makes the interaction less felicitous!

---

[2] Indeed, it may be more likely that feelings of well-being are a source of higher earnings, and, so, explain the small positive relationship (see Diener and Seligman [2004] 2009, 214)! One Australian study showed, for instance, that college students two standard deviations higher in Subjective Well-being subsequently earned 8–12 percent higher incomes (Diener and Biswas-Diener [2002] 2009, 129).

Rather than emphasizing the anomaly that individuals in some rich nations report less subjective well-being than individuals in poorer nations and that there's not much correlation between income and well-being in prosperous countries, recent scholars more often emphasized the positive correlation between income and happiness at the national level. Most of the extremely poor nations rank down in subjective well-being and most of the extremely wealthy nations are high in subjective well-being (Diener and Biswas-Diener 2008, 94–95). Diener and Biswas-Diener (2008, 94–95) note that "there is no nation with an average income of less than $2,000 a year that has a life satisfaction as high as any nation with an income of more than $20,000 a year." (So, the 2014 Pew poll found that fewer than 30 percent of Bangladeshi, and Ghanaian respondents reported themselves as happy and fewer than 15 percent of Kenyan and Egyptian respondents reported themselves as happy, while levels of reported happiness in Mexico, the US, Germany, France, China, and Vietnam were above 50 percent [*Economist* 2014].) While this may seem dramatic, it is not inconsistent with the often emphasized finding that after a threshold of around US$10,000 annual per capita is passed there is no strong correlation between national wealth and life satisfaction (Kesebir and Diener [2008] 2009, 68).

Many scholars continue to emphasize that increased earnings are particularly associated with increased well-being for people who earn very little money because money is so important for basic needs. This is consistent not only with Abraham Maslow's (1962) self-actualization theory that focused on how meeting "deficiency needs" for food and shelter is a prerequisite for the fulfillment that comes from meeting being needs, but also with the pyramid derived by my respondent Prakash Tyagi! Many studies show income has the largest effect on subjective well-being for those at the lowest income levels and in poorer countries (Biswas-Diener [2001] 2009; Diener and Biswas-Diener 2002; Diener and Seligman ([2004] 2009).

Despite the new emphasis, I remain persuaded that income has little direct relationship to well-being above an income level that provides necessities. My discussion of laborers suggests that limited earnings limit the well-being of people with very low income. But for many, the source of ill-being is that the pressure to earn is so pressing that there is little time for anything else in life. The lack of respect afforded to laborers, especially by their bosses, seem to also be an important source of ill-being. For many laborers, sources of limited earnings, such as poor relations with in-laws or having an alcoholic husband, may *themselves* be the primary cause of lack of well-being. This book argues that well-being arises not from situations but from the meanings people attribute to situations and the interactions people have that either facilitate or limit well-being. Yashoda Kumar seems to have more well-being than the other laborers I discuss in the previous section because she focuses not so much on her limited earnings and work situation, but instead on her ability to fulfill religious service and on what her work provides—enough to eat—rather than what it does not provide. As I argue in subsequent chapters, I have met many elderly people who grumpily focus on what they don't have, while others who have just as limited resources focus instead on the good interactions they can pursue. Thus, well-being may come less from circumstances than from how one sees and interacts with circumstances.

It's important to note that the observed correlation between income and well-being is quite small. It seems to me that a *small* correlation may be explained by the interactions between poor respondent and elite researcher themselves producing less well-being (in the interaction) than an interaction between a better-off respondent and the same researcher. Biswas-Diener and Diener ([2001] 2009) recently coordinated a study of slum dwellers, pavement dwellers, and sex workers in Calcutta. The interviews were conducted by "translators" fluent in Hindi, English, and Bengali. Some of the respondents were so unsophisticated that they couldn't understand a seven-point scale to evaluate their satisfaction with life domains (such as material resources, friendship food, morality, romantic relationship, family, and others) and so had to use a three-point scale or be shown facial depictions ranging from extreme smile (7) to extreme frown (1). Could it be that laborers who are interviewed by trilingual people who are probably university-educated might experience less well-being from this interaction (and, so, show less well-being in "objective" scales) than people with higher income when interviewed by the same sort of people? If, as I argue in subsequent chapters, well-being results more from felicitous interactions than objective circumstances, might the interaction an uneducated and poorly paid laborer has with a trilingual, university-related person be less felicitous for the laborer than it would be for someone closer to the university-related person in class background? *Given that the correlation between income and well-being is very small*, might the correlation be purely a product of how an interaction with someone so much above one in education and income *produces* less well-being than does the interaction between a better-paid respondent and a university researcher?

One of the themes of this book is the importance of a researcher's self-reflexive examination of the research process. I felt less comfortable interviewing laborers and poor Indians than I did interviewing Indians who were better off. I often felt—as the interviews I quote above confirm—that laborers were pressed for time. Although they were poorly paid, laborers' time seemed more valuable to me than that of more affluent Indians because I knew that laborers needed to work to live. Part of my discomfort had to do as well with my means of recruiting subjects at public places, such as places of work. Narendra Sethi and I recruited a number of laborers at job sites and at places where casual day laborers wait to be hired. These places were not only quite public (sometimes, a crowd grew), but I was also aware of my imposing on the laborer's time. Thus, it's fair to say that my interviews with laborers were less easy and carefree than they were with other Indians. More important, laborers themselves often seemed more reluctant to be interviewed. As I describe elsewhere (Derné 2008, 96–97), globalization and the liberalization of the Indian economy have sidelined the poor in many Indians' imaginations. Hindi films, which from the 1960s through the 1980s often featured and celebrated the poor and the marginal, increasingly focus on a transnational elite. Laboring Indians know they're less central in the Indian imagination and may feel less empowered to speak. My experiences interviewing filmgoers in 1991 and, again, in 2001 was that poorer Indians were increasingly reluctant to be interviewed. In that sort of situation, is it a surprise if poorer Indians feel less comfortable talking to trilingual university researchers than does a control group of university students?

I don't mean to discredit the important, innovative research that Biswas-Diener and Diener organized in Calcutta. The most important finding of the study, for me, is the overall satisfaction of the Calcutta poor *despite* their score on a life satisfaction score. While Calcutta pavement dwellers, slum dwellers, and prostitutes reported life satisfaction slightly below neutral, when it came to specific domain only

16 percent of respondents scored in the negative direction (Biswas-Diener and Diener [2001] 2009, 271) and overall the respondents fell in the satisfied range on all nine specific life domains (Biswas-Diener and Diener [2001] 2009, 274). Poor respondents were positively satisfied with morality (2.58), family (2.5), friends (2.45), romance (2.48), and food (2.55; the scales are 1–3). Surprisingly, they even showed better-than neutral satisfaction with their income (2.12) and housing (2.15). Thus, Biswas-Diener and Diener ([2001] 2009, 275) conclude that: "[T]ogether the multiple measures approach ... produced a picture of Calcutta's poor as a group that, while living in sub-standard conditions are satisfied with many arenas of their life," particularly social relationships. They are, the researchers conclude, "good (moral) people" who are "religious" and "have rewarding families." Yet the overall satisfaction score (1.98) was below neutral! Could that have anything to do with the comparison with the trilingual university researcher conducting the interview? And might interactions with other slum-dwellers or pavement-dwellers about all of the domains in which satisfaction was high produce a higher overall satisfaction score? Pavement-dwellers whom Biswas-Diener and Diener ([2001] 2009, 275–76) interviewed sometimes talked about how they preferred living on the pavement because of increased safety and better social relations than if they rented living quarters. Sex workers talked of how family members didn't look down on them due to their profession. If the Calcutta poor cultivated interactions with others *in their own milieu* to talk about their well-being, might their sense of life satisfaction rise from the levels arising after an interaction with university researchers?

Conclusion

The Indians I interviewed say that health is a foundation of well-being. Indians tell stories of how their well-being plummeted when facing health crises—and that's an experience I, too, have shared. Yet it's important to note that even those with health issues often experience great amounts of well-being; Prakash Tyagi and the 75-year-old Sikh woman who hopes to be able to walk to the gurudwara are good examples. That objective health doesn't correlate with subjective well-being after one controls for leisure activities suggests that it is the *pleasures and interactions* that themselves contribute to health (and are made possible by health) that are the main reason health is linked with well-being. That subjective health correlates with well-being, but objective health has no correlation to subjective well-being suggests the importance of *meanings* people attribute to their actual health. Prakash Tyagi sees he can still get to the park, while his age-mate Ishwar Kumar complains that he needs to use a cane. That people's well-being tends to rebound from crippling health problems suggests the importance of *developing an approach* to facing troubles.

Many of the Indians I interviewed similarly recognize money as necessary to provide some basis of well-being. Prakash Tyagi and others see meeting physical needs as an important basis of well-being. Just as loss of health harms well-being, so loss of means to support oneself harms well-being, too. Consistent with quantitative studies of other populations, my interviews with laborers show that income is especially important in bolstering the well-being of the poor. Yet, it's important to note again that even those with limited income often experience great amounts of well-being. Yashoda Kumar's earnings cause her distress, but she gets well-being from her religious life and from living on what she earns. Small pleasures (such as religious rituals), meanings (such as Yashoda's attachment to Hinduism), and an approach to troubles (such as Yashoda's focus on living within her means) allow people to experience well-being, despite objective difficulties.

My interviews suggest that money itself is often not the main source of well-being but is associated with other, more crucial, aspects of well-being. Money is associated with control of situation. Higher paying jobs are jobs that often don't involve unhappy interactions with people. Lack of money can represent weak social connections with, for instance, alcoholic spouses or in-laws that don't share the wealth. Money provides free time that allows little pleasures. But this discussion of work and money hasn't yet fully addressed two of the most fundamental ways that work provides well-being. First, one's work often makes one feel special and *specialness* is itself a source of well-being. Second, one's work allows a person to *contribute to others*, another key element of well-being. I take up these two themes in the next chapter.

The words of 58-year-old Fareed Khan put the relative importance of money in its place:

Whatsoever the business and whatsoever the size of that business is, it hardly matters. The basic thing should be that everyone in the family—the wife, the daughter, the son and everyone—should bond with each other living happily with love [*pyaar, mohabbat*]. For those who live with love, there is khushhali even if all they have to eat is sauce, while chicken or mutton can't serve the purpose if people don't feel happiness [khushi] towards each other.

As Prakash Tyagi and Abraham Maslow recognized, money is necessary to provide life's necessities. It meets deficiency needs. Without enough to eat, one lacks well-being. But money is not what well-being is all about.

References

Biswas-Diener, Robert, and Ed Diener. (2001) 2009. "Making the Best of a Bad Situation: Satisfaction in the Slums of Calcutta." In *Culture and Well-Being: The Collected Works of Ed Diener,* edited by Ed Diener, 261–78. New York, NY: Springer.

Bok, Derek. 2010. *The Politics of Happiness: What Government Can Learn from the New Research on Well-Being.* Princeton, NJ: Princeton University Press.

Brown, Norman O. 1959. *Life against Death: The Psychoanalytic Meaning of History.* Middleton, CT: Wesleyan University Press.

Cacioppo, John T., Louise C. Hawkley, Ariel Kalil, M.E. Hughes, Linda Waite, and Ronald A. Thisted. 2008. "Happiness and the Invisible Threads of Social Connection: The Chicago Health, Aging, and Social Relations Study." In *The Science of Subjective Well-Being*, edited by Michael Eid and Randy J. Larsen, 191–219. New York. NY: Guilford.

Derné, Steve. 2008. *Globalization on the Ground: Media and the Transformation of Culture, Class, and Gender in India.* New Delhi: SAGE Publications.

Diener, Ed. (1984) 2009. "Subjective Well-Being." In *The Science of Well-Being: The Collected Works of Ed Diener,* edited by Ed Diener, 11–58. New York, NY: Springer.

Diener, Ed, and Robert Biswas-Diener. (2002) 2009. "Will Money Increase: Subjective Well-Being? A Literature Review and Guide to Needed Research." In *The Science of Well-Being: The Collected Works of Ed Diener,* edited by Ed Diener, 119–54. New York, NY: Springer.

Diener, Ed, and Martin E.P. Seligman. (2004) 2009. "Beyond Money: Toward an Economy of Well-Being." In *The Science of Well-Being: The Collected Works of Ed Diener*, edited by Ed Diener, 201–66. New York, NY: Springer.

Diener, Ed, Richard E. Lucas, and Christie Napa Scollon. (2006) 2009. "Beyond the Hedonic Treadmill: Revising the Adaptation Theory of Well-Being." In *The Science of Well-Being: The Collected Works of Ed Diener,* edited by Ed Diener, 103–18. New York, NY: Springer.

Economist. 2014. "Happiness and Income: Everything that Rises Must Converge." *The Economist,* November 1, 58.

Hamilton, Clive. 2003. *Growth Fetish.* London: Pluto.

Jankowiak, William. 2009. "Well-Being: Cultural Pathology, and Personal Rejuvenation in a Chinese City, 1981–2005." In *Pursuits of Happiness: Well-Being in Anthropological Perspective,* edited by Gordon Mathews and Carolina Izquierdo, 147–66. New York, NY: Berghahn.

Kesebir, Pelin, and Ed Diener. (2008) 2009. "In Pursuit of Happiness: Empirical Answers to Philosophical Questions." In *The Science of Well-Being: The Collected Works of Ed Diener,* edited by Ed Diener, 59–74. New York, NY: Springer.

Lane, Robert E. 2000. *The Loss of Happiness in Market Democracies.* New Haven, CT: Yale University Press.

Layard, R., G. Mayraz, and S. Nickell. 2010. "Does Relative Income Matter? Are the Critics Right?" In *International Differences in Well-Being,* edited by Ed Diener, John F. Helliwell, and Daniel Kahneman. Oxford: Oxford University Press.

Loy, David R. 2002. *A Buddhist History of the West: Studies of Lack.* Albany, NY: SUNY Press.

Lucas, Richard E., and Ed Diener. (2008) 2009. "Personality and Subjective Well-Being." In *The Science of Well-Being: The Collected Works of Ed Diener,* edited by Ed Diener, 75–102. New York, NY: Springer.

Maslow, Abraham. 1962. *Toward a Psychology of Being.* Princeton, NJ: D. Van Nostrand.

Sen, Amartya. 2002. *Rationality and Freedom.* Cambridge, MA: Harvard University Press.

3

CONNECTIONS TO OTHERS
(AND THE SPECIALNESS OF THE SELF)

To do the self's work and to earn good money is the source of khushhali.

Interviewer: "Tell me about a particular situation in which you've experienced khushhali."

At work, we are always talking and laughing [hansna, bolna] *with each other. This daily give-and-take is the source of happiness.*

—Raghu Kumar, 30-year-old Bihari laborer

Work is a source of well-being because it allows one to show individual skill *and* to contribute to others. Arvind Rana, the 30-year-old working in a tailoring workshop, says that when he excels at work, the master tailor is happy, his own mind his happy, and his family is happy because they can eat whatever they want. Ahmad Siddiqui, the 63-year-old Muslim lawyer who lacked well-being until he found permanent employment, says he feels happy when he works for others without expecting anything in return. Krishna Notiyal, a married 49-year-old, felt the greatest happiness when he found a job at ONGC that allowed him to provide for his family. "Work," he says, "gives me energy [E] because I'm helping other people." Work leads to felicitous pride—the positive feelings that comes from others' recognition of one's contributions—and provides a way of contributing to family and society at large.

I start with work, but this chapter's general argument is that feelings of specialness *and* bonds with others are *both* central to feeling well. The primary contribution of this chapter (and, indeed of the sociological approach to well-being) is to show that by cultivating connections to others through their own interactions, people create a felicitous, mutually-reinforcing chain of interactions that contributes to the well-being of both self and others.

"Writing poetry gives me khushhali," says Amrit Kaur, the 24-year-old Sikh college student. "When people appreciate my poems, I feel happy [khush]." Amrit's aim is to become a "great poet and publish a book of poetry"—an aim that shows her sense of herself as special. She goes on to say that she will use the money she earns from writing poetry to contribute to "education of poor children"—showing her sense that work should contribute to others. Ravi Chuhra, the 30-year-old Balmiki who runs an electrical shop, says that owning his own shop is "the biggest happiness [*sab se badi khushi*] because it's my highest achievement." Ravi hopes to be able to eventually employ more than the two "boys" who already work for him, saying that then his "name will become known." For both Ravi and Amrit, successful work gives well-being because of a feeling of achievement and the pride and respect that come from helping others through one's work.

Asha Sharma, a 72-year-old, describes "the meaning of khushhali" as helping others. Asha, who mentions helping family members as a source of well-being, emphasizes that as a teacher she always helped her students. Parents of her students "used to feel very happy and praise me. At that time, I was very happy." Asha's discussion of her retirement shows pleasure at how much she was recognized by her boss and coworkers as well: "When I retired, all my staff members were crying. Then my boss said—'why are you all crying? You should adopt all the good qualities in her.'" When Asha's coworkers and the parents of her students were happy at her efforts, she herself found happiness in a mutually-reinforcing chain of interaction that increased the well-being of herself and those connected to her. Like Asha, 51-year-old Poonam Kumar says that the meaning of well-being is serving others. Poonam says she does her work as a domestic servant without overcharging anyone. She highlights her *own* ability when she says that "doing my own work myself gives me happiness." She proudly says that her employers give her a lot of respect (*izzat*) and don't treat her as a servant. This teacher and this domestic servant find well-being in selflessly making special contributions that make others happy, a happiness that rebounds on Asha and Poonam, increasing their own well-being.

Rajendra Rana, a 21-year-old television reporter, describes *khushhali* as coming from the "satisfaction [*santusht*] of work." Rajendra links his well-being to his own successes, which he defines by the positive reactions he receives from others and the good he is able to do:

Being a reporter, when I gather some news, after getting [positive] reactions from the telecast, I feel good. When I see the news I've collected being telecast or I give any message regarding AIDS or polio, I know that my message is affecting the people, so I feel satisfaction [*santushti*] and happiness [khushi].

Rajendra described experiencing well-being when he was able to convince a family that their child's life had been saved by medical doctors rather than the ritual ceremonies they arranged for her:

When the girl's parents realized that it was purely the efforts of the doctor which helped their daughter recover, this was the happiest moment in my life—because it was my initiative [*pahal*]. If the work I'm doing gives happiness to others, that is the source of khushhali for me.

Rajendra says his only aim is to never do any work that would give

dukh [unhappiness] to anyone. Anyone nearby should at least say that my work causes good things. I am never concerned about my own happiness [khushi]. But whatever I am doing must deliver happiness [khushi] to the person standing by me. That's why I work. There's a line in the Gita in which Krishna says "Keep on doing the deeds. Don't worry about the fruits." The person I am working for will realize that I am selflessly [*niswaarth*] engaged in that work.

Rajendra's *special initiative* that aims to *help others* is a source of well-being, especially when that initiative causes others to be happy, a happiness that spreads back to him.

Rajendra, a journalist, Asha, a retired teacher, Poonam, a domestic servant, Krishna, an ONGC executive, Amrit, an aspiring poet, Arvind, a workshop tailor, Ahmad, a lawyer, and Ravi, an electric-shop owner, all insist that personal gains are secondary to social contributions. Rajendra's discussion of the Gita's focus on selfless work as a way to live a good life was mentioned by several people

I interviewed, but the approach is embraced by Muslims, such as Ahmad, and Sikhs, such as Amrit, too.

In selecting from many possible examples, these men and women of diverse ages in all sorts of employment, Hindus, a Muslim, and Sikhs, I aim to illustrate the breadth of the emphasis on work as providing both specialness and connections to others.

Being Special

On a train to Dehradun, I met Vikram Aurora, a 70-year-old Delhiite pensioner, who earned money "coaching" students for their examinations in mathematics. Vikram told me that he enjoyed writing poetry and played me recitations of his poems from his mobile phone. When he heard about my project, he said simply that well-being came when one found a technique at which one could excel. When one excelled at a technique, he said, one became able to serve other people and support oneself. Using an English term focusing on the individual, Vikram said that through one's work one engages in a "calling" suited to the self, to which one is passionately committed.

In academic circles, there used to be a debate about whether individualism and community were opposed. Individuals in Western cultures, especially the USA, seemed to focus more on self-striving, while individuals in Asian cultures, especially India, seemed to understand the self as rooted in webs of connections in family and community (e.g., Bellah et al. 1985; Derné 1995). Scholars questioned whether the American emphasis on the importance of individual self-development threatened connections and community. While some Americans focused so much on self-development that relationships were contingent and could be abandoned if they no longer made one feel good, most scholars concluded that for most Americans strong connections and community bolstered the individual's self-development (e.g., Bellah et al. 1985; Cancian 1987). With a community behind you, you can take risks to develop your specialness. Similarly, while some Indians focused so much on their obligations to others that they buried personal desires and wants, most scholars concluded that Indians were able to pursue self-development and advance individual desires in the context of strong community and family obligations (Derné 1995). In my earlier work (Derné 1995), I concluded that a sense of both individual desires and the nurturing of connections to others are universals of human experience and, so, all cultures recognize the egocentric and sociocentric nature of human experiences, even as cultures differ in the *extent* to which they validate each pole of human experiences. Because Indians live in a sociocentric culture, they easily recognize contributions from family and society to the good life, but may only fuzzily recognize the individual efforts that may be just as important to their well-being.

The Indians I interviewed get well-being from feeling special, but the pleasure of their feelings of specialness mixes with the pleasure of contributing to others and being recognized for one's contributions, sometimes obscuring the importance of feeling special. The face of Vikram Aurora, the pensioner whom I met on the train, clearly showed delight at his ability to write poetry and to coach students. Perhaps his face showed even more his delight at connections to others—he talked with animation with me, others on the train, and his daughters on his mobile phone. Even as Vikram talks about his own specialness he also references how this specialness allows him to contribute to others.

Twice in 2007, I interviewed people whom I had seen showing delight in their special skills. But both times, the formal interview instead revealed a focus on connecting to others, too. When I met Gyan Prakash, he told me of his success playing soccer and proudly told me he had been nationally ranked and played in international tournaments. At the time of this discussion, I asked Gyan, 28, if this gave him khushhali and he replied that it did. And I could see his face beaming. But when I interviewed him, his sporting exploits didn't come up at all. Khushhali, he said, is "the combination of tradition [*parampara*], customs [*ritiriwaaj*] and the beauty of mountains." Tradition and customs reference—if abstractly—the society in which Gyan lives and the beauty of the mountains relates to his ancestral village. When I asked Gyan why he didn't mention sports, he said that you couldn't compare the happiness of that with the happiness that comes from the birth of a child, who will go through all of the rites and carry on the family.

Sunil Sharma, 38, showed delight in his specialness, even sacrificing income for his passions, yet his interview nonetheless describes well-being in terms of his connections to others. When I met Sunil, he showed me his artwork and how he designed modular furniture for his small house that allowed a sitting area to be converted to a bed. He showed me photos of himself singing on a stage in Nainital. He was excited about losing weight through his gym membership, and asked me whether I liked his look. Yet despite his passions for music that drive him to pursue his own vision and his obvious satisfaction with how his workouts transformed his body, he instead emphasized how social connections give him well-being:

> The greatest happiness [khushi] is when my father gets [milna] much happiness [khushi]. My father is a very emotional fellow and when I am doing good work, he starts weeping. If he sees me on television, he'll be so happy that he cries. One time I did a show—because remember I'm a singer—and my *mamaji* [uncle] was there, too. My mamaji told me [my father] was literally crying.

Sunil's face and talk of his passions clearly shows he gets well-being from his special abilities. But his discussion of his well-being highlights *family recognition* of his specialness as central to his well-being. So many Indians' discussion of their specialness is so directly linked to being supported by others and helping others that specialness is almost inseparable from the social connections in providing well-being. But the importance of a feeling that one is special shows in people's faces, even if it is sometimes more dimly recognized in talk.

When discussing the meaning of well-being, Indians commonly refer to helping others, but when discussing particular situations of well-being, they commonly refer to individual achievements, such as school admission, a promotion, or success in an examination. Thus, Shanti Kumar, the 36-year-old domestic servant who says khushhali comes from helping others, describes her greatest well-being as: "[When] I built my own house for myself because I never had the dream that one day I would have my own house." She emphasizes that it was she herself (*apna*) who did this; that it was her own efforts that produced the house. Suman Kumar, a 35-year-old female student, says she feels khushi (happiness) and sukh (comfort, happiness, pleasure) when she helps anybody "financially, physically, mentally or morally." But when she describes her greatest happiness she focuses on securing admission in the college institute she is now attending. Ayesha Khan, 20, left school after passing Class 10 and now helps her mother with the housework. When first asked about well-being, she says that doing the house's work gives her well-being, but she describes the most well-being she ever felt was when she got an award for her painting in school. Heena Ali, 19, says that khushhali means to help the handicapped people and give to beggars, but she got her greatest khushhali when she scored 95 percent in her Class 10 board examination in biology. "At that time," she reflects, "I was extremely happy because now I can give my entrance examination for PMT [Preparing for Medical Test]. 'Now,' I thought, 'my ambition to be a doctor will be fulfilled.'" Darpana Mishra, a 40-year-old lower-middle-class housewife, gets well-being from cleaning the temple and giving beggars enough food to fill their stomach. But she is also proud that she walked barefoot from Haridwar to Dehradun twice, carrying Ganga water to put on the *lingam* in a local temple: "It is because of the blessing of Lord Shiva that I have completed my barefoot walking *yatra* for about 70 km." These accounts all show that *contradictory* experiences lead to well-being—the experience of helping others as well as the experience of achieving as an individual provide feelings of wellness.

Achievements are a source of pride—the positive feeling from positive assessment of self by others (Scheff 1990). As Scheff (1990) argues, pride and its opposite, shame, are the emotions that signal the state of our relations with others. Although it has negative connotations in English and Hindi, pride is the emotion that signals positive connection with other people (while shame signals that our actions are looked down upon by others, threatening connections to them). Many people whom I interviewed talked about their specialness as a source of well-being, yet often the feeling of pride signaling strong connections is what is fundamental to well-being.

Armaan Singh, a 65-year-old, identifies a healthy body and wealth as two key sources of well-being, adding that the third source is popularity—"a person should have *yash* [fame, renown, reputation] and people should give praise for the person's qualities." Thinking back to his school days 50 years ago, Armaan remembers when he had an athletic accomplishment on the sports field: "My name was called in an assembly. I won a prize and came before the public and that gave me a lot of happiness [khushi]." Armaan's accomplishments surely were a source of well-being, but what he most remembers is that he was publicly praised and that this made him happy. He doesn't even tell me what the athletic event was, only that he was brought "before the public" and praised. "So, my happiest moment was winning the prize and getting applause; I was happy [khush]." Aiyasha Khan, the 19-year-old whose greatest happiness came from an award in painting, said she also got great happiness when she "got a lot of appreciation" for a speech that she had given in Class 9. It's not just painting well and speaking well that lead to well-being, but being socially recognized for one's accomplishments. Heena Ali, the 19-year-old who got happiness from her high biology marks, says she got an "extreme feeling of khushhali" when her photograph was published in the school paper after she earned a scholarship for her exam scores. It's not just getting high marks that leads to well-being but having a photograph published that recognizes the achievement. Heena also related: "When my parents are proud of my work it gives me happiness [khushi]." Working well makes one feel special and allows a person to contribute to society. But the well-being also stems from making those whom we love proud of us; it stems from how achievements connect us to others.

Harjit Singh, a 74-year-old, retired after a career of teaching math, says he devotes himself these days to chanting Sikh sacred hymns. Harjit talks of his abilities to chant these hymns:

> You may not believe it, but when I went to Amritsar for a year I used to chant hymns for almost the whole 24 hours. Officially, the Golden temple closes for about 4 hours but only officially. Even during those four hours, people can also worship and listen to their hymns and instructions. It's a 24-hour job and I hardly slept for just 1–2 hours— you can't even call it sleep, it was just lying down to rest the body. Otherwise, I was chanting hymns—even now I sometimes chant hymns for 18–20 hours without stopping.

Harjit explains that it took long years of training to be able to understand the hymns he chants: "I have been doing this for the last 35 years, but it doesn't come in a day—the poems are not that easy to understand.... I have to do a lot of preparation before going to recite these hymns." Harjit's chanting of hymns is a special ability, but he emphasizes that his chanting pleases others: "I chant the hymns and the people like it." In recounting his educational background that included a masters of science degree, Harjit interjects that he was a "gold medalist, also. I received two gold medals." For Harjit, reciting hymns and doing math are special abilities. The pride he feels in these special abilities recognizes that other people value his enterprise. Feeling of specialness and the feeling of helping others contribute to Harjit's well-being.

The desire to be recognized—what Armaan calls "fame"—is particularly strong. Girish Aggarwal, 48, enjoys the "freedom" that comes from running his own small shop. "A self-competent [*saksham*] man is the happiest man." Girish said he tired of the "boundations" of working at an office for which he had to go to work each day, "even if it was cold or raining." "Comfortable and happy" in his new venture, Girish describes "making my name known" as his main uddeshya [purpose]: "If the business flourishes, I'll have a name." Harish Mishra, a 40-year-old business owner, who focuses on the importance of coming home and having those we love greet us, says that he has no specific uddeshya but he wants that

> when I depart this world there should be at least five people, apart from my family members, who are shouldering me [in my coffin] and who will say "he is a nice man." There is one uddeshya—that everyone should love me. There should be at least five people who without any interest [*swaarth*] should say that he is a good fellow [English phrase].

I heard almost identical descriptions of the support of selfless pallbearers who will praise a person after their death from two other men. Wanting to be remembered for helping others or building a business, these men focus on their social connections. But they also want to be remembered *when few are*, showing a feeling of specialness also gives them well-being

A corollary of the well-being that we get from specialness is that failures threaten well-being. Sunil Sharma says he's unhappy if he's unable to execute a musical project he has planned. Ayesha Khan said she was very unhappy when she failed her Class 10 examination the first time. (She eventually passed the Class 10 examination.) Abdul Khan, the 62-year-old retired school principal, felt the most unhappiness when uncooperative colleagues stood in the way of a promotion. Specialness bolsters well-being; threats to specialness jeopardize life satisfaction.

Helping Others

People's recognition of how their own specialness contributed to their well-being was sometimes hidden, but the connection between helping others and well-being was usually out in the open. India's major religions—Hinduism, Islam, and Sikhism—all emphasize seva or service, so helping others is an important shared *discourse* around which people assimilate their experiences.

Kiran Chawla, a 45-year-old Sikh housewife, focuses on service to her religious community:

> Khushhali is serving people. Every day I go to the gurudwara and serve people there. This gives me happiness [khushi] because I feel that God has made me the medium of help to others. I always want to live for others and do *karseva* [service work] in the gurudwara.

Madhu Malhotra, an 18-year-old Hindu student, says khushhali is when she and her sister are both happy and she helps other people. Madhu experiences khushhali when she helps her mother with housework and she studies hard so that she'll be able to help her parents financially. But her greatest well-being was helping a classmate who had fractured her hand:

> I used to take her bag in the class and bring it down after the school was over. I used to help her eat at lunch. The girl's mother praised [*prashansa*] me in front of the whole class. I felt very happy [khush] at that time.

Madhu says she helped the girl, although she had not previously been known to her. Afterwards, the girl became her best friend. By mentioning how her injured classmate was not a friend, Madhu emphasizes the selflessness of her service. Like the mother's praise, the close friendship that developed lets Madhu know such help is valued in her social circle, contributing to Madhu's satisfaction.

Women commonly describe satisfaction from service to family, friends, and acquaintances. Rashmi Mishra, the 34-year-old who got the most well-being when her husband recovered from an illness, says that "khushhali means to help the needy people." Rashmi focuses on helping those in her family:

> Because I am a housewife, I get happiness [khushi] when I am fully dedicated to my husband and children. When I help my husband, I feel happy

because I think I am sharing his burdens.... Human life is a place of work [*ek karma bhumi*]. The aim of my life is that I should do whatever is possible for the family and society.

Sonali Pandey, the 19-year-old student who wants to earn money so that she can help the poor, describes an incident in which she was able to help a friend:

> When one of my friends had an accident, she had to be operated on. At that time, I gave my full support to her. I even used to write class notes out for her. I got the most happiness [khushi] from helping her prepare for her exam.

Chaand Rana, the married 32-year-old beauty parlor worker who cried and cried when her father had to take her out of school, describes khushhali as "serving [seva] mother and the father." She said she got great happiness from caring for her mother when her mother was ill and her handicapped brother couldn't help: "All of the work I did for her gave me happiness."

But people also say they experience well-being when helping people outside their own circles. Lakshmi Kumar, a 43-year-old administrative officer, describes khushhali as "anything which gives you satisfaction whether doing something creative or doing good things for others." She felt well-being donating blood to save a life and helping an arthritic man to the hospital. He lived alone and Lakshmi went to the hospital daily and looked after him for about a week until his son could return to care for him. Shazia Qureshi, a 60-year-old housewife married to a retired police officer, says that,

> When any guests come to my house I make my full effort to satisfy them. I desire that no one should ever leave my house with an empty stomach. This gives me a lot of khushhali.

Shazia, who only has a bit of education in the *madrassa*, describes her greatest moment of well-being as occurring when she was able to help a complete stranger:

> When my husband was in the job, one day the peon in his office came to me and started crying. I asked him, "What is the matter?" Then, he told me that [the peon] had fixed the marriage of his daughter and now he didn't have money to spend on her marriage. I gave him the clothes for

the daughter's marriage and some money. Seeing satisfaction on his face gave me a lot of khushahli.

Kantha Chopra, a 58-year-old Hindu, describes herself as a simple housewife who enjoys the routine of getting up and going to the temple. After telling me that the uddeshya of her life is to help the poor, she recounts an instance of helping a stranger in need:

> Eight years ago, on the way back from Haridwar during winter, I saw a lady who was shivering with cold. I gave her my own shawl. My husband objected. But I managed to convince him that she was more needy than me. I came home without a shawl, but I didn't feel cold. Even when my husband asked whether I was feeling cold, I said no.

The warmth her generosity kindled kept Kantha warm on her journey home.

Many women, including those dreaming of help they hope to do in the future, say they get well-being from helping others through social programs. Suman Kumar, the 35-year-old-student, wants to become so "financially and spiritually strong that I will be able to help all those people who are in need." She wants to raise money for a spiritual center she is associated with "so that it can be used by everyone in society." Heena Ali, the 19-year-old female student, describes khushhali as helping handicapped people and says her uddeshya is to "open an orphanage because there are many children who are forced into begging after the death of their parents." Heena envisions combining this orphanage with housing for elderly with no place to live. "Then, our culture will be transmitted from the older generation to the younger generation," and the orphans will simultaneously be educated. Although Heena describes her greatest khushhali as scoring well on a test that would allow her to continue her pursuit in medicine, her purpose is not self-directed, nor even directed toward using medical skills to help others, but to try to help orphans and older people become more independent so they, too, can help others. Santosh Prasad, a 30-year-old Hindu, who describes khushhali as the inner satisfaction she gets from her teaching work, says that she gets "satisfaction from doing the work of others," noting her involvement with liberating people from alcoholism (*nasha mukti*). Sanjana Atwal, a 37-year-old Hindu teacher, describes khushhali's meaning as "mental peace within the home when everyone in the family is happy [khush] and satisfied [santusht]." But she says she experiences the greatest feeling of khushhali when she helps others, whether financially or physically. Sanjana has formed an organization to encourage women to do prenatal testing for a blood disease. "Any time I help others, I feel happy [khush]," she says. Most men, like the women I've described so far, also experience well-being from helping others. Narendra Sethi and I met Raj Pattial, the flashy student who was home to visit his family for the holidays, in a youth-oriented café serving cold drinks and snacks. He tossed his motorcycle keys to a friend and was interrupted a couple of times to talk on his mobile phone. In talking about khushhali, he mentioned exploring a lonely, hilly place past Mussoorie. He mentioned eating good food and how important it was to find a way to make things move properly, put aside all tensions, and avoid chasing after money. (I'll elaborate on these points Raj made at greater length in the next two chapters.) It was only when I asked him about whether he had any uddeshya that helping others came up:

There's a purpose. Live and let others to live is a saying. But my motto is to live for others and enjoy living for others. You know what? Everyone does their own work. *But the taste in doing another person's work is the best taste.* Even if my friends call me in the night—2 in the morning—that "I want this or that," I'm helping them for sure [he snaps his fingers]. Even if I'm working and someone has some problem, I stop even if I don't know them.

Listening to Raj talk about the taste of helping others, I recounted how a bug had flown into my eye in Rishikesh and several people had gathered around to help me. Raj replied: "[T]hose are the good kind of people—but they are few. The thing is when I have a problem, everyone else may be doing their own things." For Raj, the beautiful taste of helping others also signifies his distinctive specialness—he's proud that he helps his friends. The image of the taste of helping others being the best taste is vivid and compelling, but amidst the many other activities and approaches Raj takes that give him well-being, I hardly noticed it when I first heard him talk and translated the interview, showing, I think, the *diversity* of factors that lead to a sense of enduring life satisfaction.

Like Raj Patial, Armaan Singh, the 65-year-old who describes the three pillars of well-being as health, wealth, and reputation, only brings up helping others when I ask about his uddeshya. His initial response is that his "only" uddeshya is that his "family is fine, my daughters are fine, my wife is fine, and I am fine." Then, Armaan recounts that in India there is a "general belief—especially among those who do *pujapath*—that you must give 10% of your earnings to the poor"—an especially common beliefs among Sikhs. (Recall that Armaan is of Sikh background, but is not practicing and says he doesn't believe in God.) For Armaan, helping the poor is "difficult; it's not easy." Armaan describes giving to the poor as his uddeshya. But he says he's not a saint—if he were a saint, he would have already started distributing his wealth [*daan*]. Although Armaan sees reputation as a source of well-being, he is not impressed with the rich who give donations to merely improve their name. "The donations given by the less privileged to the poor are the greatest. To share a roti with someone when you only have two rotis to begin with is not easy work."

Sachin Aggarwal, a 40-year-old Hindu father employed in the public works department, describes well-being as coming first, from his job, and second, from his family. When I ask the meaning of khushhali he says it's the peace (shanti) he gets at the *mandir*. It is only when I ask about his uddeshya that he mentions helping others: "To help the poor and downtrodden leads to satisfaction [santushti]." But Sachin says he does not have the earning capacity to engage in such help:

I would find satisfaction and happiness if an organization were formed to help the backward and downtrodden. Due to my government job I haven't [*milna*] the time to get involved in such social service.

Narendra asks Sachin, "If you're not able to help the needy, what does give you satisfaction?" Sachin mentions a specific instance of helping others: "I got the most satisfaction [santushti] when I had time to take an elderly couple to the hospital. They had no children and I was able to help them." Sachin is caught up in caring for his family and, so, helping people outside the family is not currently in the center of his thinking about well-being, which focuses more on work, family, and religious devotion. Yet, helping others still gives him life satisfaction. Somendra Mishra, a 47-year-old, operates a shop that supports his wife and three children. Like many men his age, Somendra emphasizes that well-being means clear "arrangements for earning bread for the family." While advancing his income is his uddeshya, Somendra also says,

> It's important [*zaruri*] that a person should not be self-centered and should be generous [*paropakaarii*, lit. benevolence, charity, altruism]. It's important that the person should be human enough to do good work, give properly to society, and keep the values of humanity [*maanavata*]. A person will feel good by doing good work.

Salim Khan, a 26 year-old news reporter, sees the interconnectedness of things and, so, can't be well unless others are well: "The meaning of khushhali is that my family is happy, people in the near vicinity are happy, people in the village are happy, people in the city are happy, and people in the whole country are happy." Salim is active in NGO that has helped 72 students. The saddest (dukhi) time in Salim's life was when he had to leave Darul-um-Deoband, an Islamic university, because of the costs. By participating in the NGO Friends of Education, he is fulfilling his dream of preventing others from facing the troubles he faced.

Like many women, men, too often find helping friends and family is a key part of their well-being. Pradeep Kumar, a 50-year-old, passed Class 5 and works in a dry-cleaning shop to support his family that includes his elderly mother, a 20-year-old daughter, and a 29-year-old son. For Pradeep,

> Khushahli means that the future of my children should be good. And when I serve [*seva karna*] my mother it gives me incredible [*bahut zyaada*] sukh.... As long as my mother is alive, my whole life stays always revolving around her [*ird gird ghumte rahana*]. To serve her, to take care of her, to get her food, medicine, etc. is my first uddeshya of life.

The service Pradeep gives to his mother makes him feel special: "I have three other elder brothers, but my mother is staying with me because she feels that I am the only one who will serve her well." Deepak Sharma, a newly married 28-year-old, describes getting the most well-being when he helped a friend who suffered an accident "No one was helping him out. I had known him for five years and it felt good to do something." Deepak, like Pradeep, also feels special in his help since no one else had stepped up to care for his friend.

Sweet Relations

Prakash Tyagi, the 79-year-old retiree, described good health and sufficient resources for essentials such as a small garden and a small library of books as two fundamentals of well-being. More difficult to find, he says, but crucial to well-being is "good company and sweet relations with family and friends." He says that because a human is

> a social being first, the friends should be social ones. This is the meaning of khushhali. Millionaires are not poor and dirty, but if they lack good friends, where is the khushhali?

Prakash emphasizes that he never thought of money or crazed for many things, but "all of my family is now satisfied—all have been married. This is the greatest khushhali." He describes one of the conditions of khushhali as doing "something good for others every day. This is the happiest thing." One day he wrote in my journal "man minus ego = God; man plus ego = devil." This thought—which he said he had heard "somewhere"—shows the importance of thinking beyond the self. For Prakash, sweet relationships with others are crucial. He said in English to me one day: "I feel that I am a man and I love men. That is the thing." Prakash has enjoyed good social relations from childhood—it's possible that I was his last new friend. Prakash's wife died less than two years before I met him and he describes their relationship as particularly close. He connects Browning's "Last Ride" to his relationship with his wife.

> The last ride is with her. I never felt alone in my time with my wife. Because of her, my life has been very smooth and I have never been in distress. We have been in tune with each other. If you never lose your love, your heart and beautiful body and proud mind will never fail you.

Doing work that provides for a family, helping others, and receiving praise for one's actions all form strong ties, providing community and well-being. The sweet relationships that Prakash refers to are for most people the most central parts of living the good life.

Armaan Singh, the 65-year-old shopkeeper who found well-being in the recognition he gained for his athletic accomplishments, enjoys talking and interacting. He particularly enjoys turning on the television in his shop and watching cricket with his friends and acquaintances, young and old. "My motto," he says, "is to give enjoyment." Armaan recognizes how good feelings are contagious from one to another. "If you're good, everybody is good. If you're happy, everybody is happy." Armaan senses positive chains of well-being where the well-being of one supports the well-being of another, a positive interaction I'll discuss further.

In the previous chapter I describe how Jayant Aurora, a 77-year-old, associates well-being with spirituality and a strong body, among other things. For Jayant, sweet relationships with his life-long childhood friend are also a big part of his well-being:

This is my good friend. Now, he is a crorepati [millionaire]. But we are both happy [khush] in our respective businesses. We meet every morning and have a lot of fun, throwing abuses at each other [in a fun way]. Being in the same age group, we discuss our day-to- day activities. He is satisfied and content with his business and with me, too.

Jayant's friend, also a 77-year-old, similarly tells me:

Every day I enjoy spending time with friends in my age group whom I have known for sixty years. Maybe sometimes people don't come to visit me, but I visit everyone. I visit those who are unwell, chat [gapshap] with them and drink tea with them. But as our friendship has been going on for decades, we're more than friends, we're brothers. We eat together and enjoy tea together, it's a way of passing the time.

Watching Jayant and his friend interact, it is clear they enjoy their sweet relationship. Jayant is certainly prosperous—and, perhaps, as prosperous as his friend. In mentioning his friend's money, Jayant is insisting money is less important than good relationships.

Sweet connections with friends and family were important for people, of whatever age, gender, religion, and income. For Kantha Chopra, the 58-year-old who got the greatest sense of well-being from giving her shawl to a cold person she encountered on a pilgrimage, sweet relations with her children and friends are a big part of her well-being. Every evening she enjoys walking with her friends and three days a week she gets up early in the morning and goes to the temple with her friends, too: "We all come together and I like that. Walking and talking together makes me feel good." Sonali Pandey, a 19-year-old, says her life's purpose is to earn money to support poor people's education, but sweet relations in her family are fundamental, too. Sonali defines khushhali as having a good relationship with her parents so that "the atmosphere in the home is peaceful [*shant*]. Then, I am sukhi." The importance Sonali gives to sweet relationships is also apparent in the unhappiness [dukh] that she felt when her grandmother died. "We were good friends [*dost*] to each other. Being very close with her, I lost a lot [when she died]." Kalpana Mishra, a 24-year-old, lives with her husband and her army-officer brother-in-law and his wife. Kalpana says she doesn't blame anyone for her husband's recent economic setbacks, and is happy that her beautician work is helping the family economically. Kalpana is currently experiencing great well-being because she has learned she's soon to be a mother: "I can't describe the level of happiness I felt when I tested positive for my pregnancy. I am happy in my inner core." But when I ask her to describe a situation of well-being she refers to the sharing of "deep inner thoughts" with her close [*khas*, lit. special] friends: "Sharing thoughts forms great happiness for us." Shekhar Kumar, a 23-year-old laborer, says simply: "Khushhali means pyaar [love], mohabbat [love], and *dosti* [friendship]. The most khushhali comes from sharing thoughts, heart, and feelings [*apna dil dilaana*] with friends [dost]." Bhairavi Kumar, a 21-year-old laborer, at first says she's never experienced any time of happiness, but, on reflection, she realizes that she sometimes "jokes and talks" with her brothers and sisters and this provides well-being.

Those living away from their families often describe well-being in terms of family togetherness. Avneet Kumar, 35, works as a cook in Dehradun, sending money monthly to his wife, children, parents, and brothers in a distant village. Avneet says that there's khushhali, "when my mother and brothers sit together in the home. I'm happy when we're together [*eksaath*]." Sushant Mishra, an 18-year-old commerce student who works in a phone-calling kiosk, says he feels well-being when he is in Gorakhpur and, "the whole family is together [eksaath], when we're all sitting together. I like spending time joking, and talking to people—especially people who keep on talking to me." Girish Aggarwal, the 48-year-old former office worker who enjoys the recognition and self-competence of running his own business, describes khushhali by focusing on "being part of the *sukh-dukh* [joys and sorrows] of others. This gives me happiness." Girish focused on the support of his parents who "nurtured and cared for me from childhood." Girish can't remember any situations of a lack of khushhali except for those "few incidents when my parents scolded me for one of my own bad acts." Sudhir Kumar, an 18-year-old, lives in Dehradun to attend a coaching institute a day's drive from his parents' home in Barkot where his father is a revenue officer. Sudhir describes khushhali as "spending time with friends and fulfilling the dreams of your parents. If my parents are satisfied, I'm happy [khush]." Sudhir, a lower caste Hindu, de-emphasizes his own desires:

I might have some desires, but it's not necessary that all my wishes be filled. It would be easy to enjoy the money sent by parents, to be self-centered and to think about myself. But real happiness lies in fulfilling my parents' dreams.

Echoing middle-aged Girish who has his own children, Sudhir, an 18-year-old student, says "I feel very good [*bahut achcha lagna*] sharing sukh-dukh with my friends." When Sudhir's mother recently died, he lost himself

completely. For two months, I didn't study and remained alone. Then, my friends started to ask 'what are you up to?' and 'where are you?' I still get emotional remembering that time. Mixing [*ghulna*] with friends and talking to them supported me. Now I'm happy.

Sudhir looks forward to returning to Barkot for Diwali because "I feel the most happiness with my parents. I will feel good at Diwali to be with my whole family." Like Girish, Sudhir enjoys sharing ups and downs of life with his friends, while also finding well-being by interacting in his family and fulfilling his parents' wishes.

Girish and Sudhir both say sharing sukh-dukh with others is the source of well-being. As Sondra Hausner (2007, 102) argues, *dukh-sukh* refers "to a complete range of human emotions. *Dukh-Sukh* is a term that refers not only to the pain or pleasure arising from a particular experience, but more accurately to the nature of suffering *and* delight in the universe [my emphasis]." The sharing of the range of human emotions with others, perhaps mixing suffering and delight, is what Sudhir and Girish say makes them feel good, overcoming any distress. The sharing of joys and sorrows as being fundamental to well-being was emphasized by a range of people. Lakshmi Kumar, the 43-year-old administrative worker who finds khushhali in creativity and helping others and who remembers finding great well-being in helping an arthritic man to the hospital, also values close relationships with her friends. She recalls how unhappy she used to be when her father was transferred because she would have to leave her friends. "Friends," she says, "should not just be there for a time of need or to pass the time with. You should share both good and bad with your friends." Gauri Mishra, a 69-year-old widow, is sometimes lonely staying alone in her big house. She prays to God that her sons and daughters-in-law will have the wisdom (*subuddhi*) to respect (*izzat karna*) her. For Gauri, well-being is "sharing sukh and dukh with others. Whether it's friends or relatives, I want to sit and talk with them, sharing sukh and *dukh.*"

The few people I met who complained about their connections tended to express a lack of well-being. Ishwar Kumar, 80, never had children and his wife has "gone up above," he says, pointing to the sky. When I ask him about the meaning of khushhali he replies,

To me there's no khushhali. How can a man who is alone [*akela admi*] get khushhali? What can be the meaning of khushhali for a man who is alone [akela admi]? I am living with my brother's son.

I press ahead and ask what khushhali would mean if he could get it. He says the meaning of khushhali is to meet with other good people (*dusre achcha log*). "This gives happiness and is the way to pass the time." When I ask Ishwar about a situation of an absence of well-being, he refers to his current living situation with his brother's son—"There is no one to listen to," he says, "no one with whom one can share one's woes and sorrows." Moreover, Ishwar says, the atmosphere in the home is one of altercations and misery (*klesh*).

Rather than being treated with respect, Ishwar relates that he is very sad (dukh) in his brother's son's home because the food that is prepared for him is not as good as the food prepared for all the other family members.

Ishwar complains about money, cursing "modern Indian society" which "neglects the elderly unless they have a bank balance." But I don't think it is absence of money per se that limits Ishwar's well-being. Rather, he blames his poor relationship with his family largely on his lack of a bank balance. "A person with a bank balance is respected in the family, but he who doesn't have one faces an uncertain situation." Ishwar complains that he had ₹3 lakh but his nephew "got it away from me." Ishwar says when he himself controlled the money, "I was the one to give and I got respect, but now I have to beg and don't even eat the same food as everyone else." While he lacks money, what really upsets him is not being treated with respect and not having sweet relations in the family.

I've presented Ishwar as grumpy, partly because he was grumpy in his interactions with Narendra and myself. This book suggests, however, that experience of well-being is fleeting, dependent on interactions. When thinking about arenas of life that are upsetting, a person experiences well-being. But if interactions shift attentions to other arenas of life, well-being can return. So, if I come to think of how smokers outside my office are killing me, I feel an absence of well-being. But if I encounter someone who talks of the smell of flowers in the air, I may experience all as good in the world. Perhaps something happened to Ishwar that made him particularly grumpy about his family that day. When we ask Ishwar about pilgrimage, he brightens and takes pride in doing the Amarnath pilgrimage, which he describes as very difficult—"I've done yatra of Amarnath and it's known to pass tough terrain. Everyone does Vaishno Devi, but not everyone can do Amarnath." When we ask him to think about a situation in which he experienced well-being, Ishwar thinks of how he tries to have good interactions with people: "Even if I happen to meet a rough-tempered [gussa, lit. angry] person I manage to talk to him and I get khushhali." Asked about his purpose in life, Ishwar says: "[M]eeting good people gives pleasure and passes the time in a good way. If I meet a good person, I'm going to pass the time well." But soon his thoughts return to his desire to change his living situation and Ishwar is again sour. He waits "for a place or a person where I can pass the rest of my life," but he knows his situation is intractable. It's notable, though, that when asked to think about pilgrimages and about his experiences of well-being, the interaction pushes Ishwar to experience some well-being as he reflects on his accomplishments and positive interactions.

Mixing and Connecting

Mixing with diverse people is one of the great pleasures in Indian life (see Trawick 1990, 83, 115). Prakash Tyagi, Armaan Singh, and others perhaps enjoyed mixing with me because I was a foreigner. I interviewed Sikh Jaspal Sidhu whom I met at the Shiva Tapkeshwar shrine in Dehradun and Hindu Deepak Sharma at the Sikh shrine Paonta Sahab—the pleasure of mixing with people of different religions was one of the pleasures of these spots (see Bellamy 2011 on Hindus at Muslim *dargah*s). Indians often talked to me about friendship with people of different religions. For instance, recall that Ghalib Khan, a Muslim, found his greatest happiness when he became friends with a Hindu who helped him (although his caste was different). People of Muslim, Hindu, and Sikh faith are devotees of Sai Baba of Sirdi (1837–1918). Sai Baba preached helping others and loving all living beings without discrimination. Such mixing— in the widest possible way, as Margaret Trawick (1990) puts it—is desired by many Indians. (On the other hand, Indians *also* enjoy the opportunities to interact with one's own people—so Sudhir Kumar looks forward to interacting at Diwali with family and others from his village, showing again how contradictory situations are necessary for well-being!)

Many Indians talked of the pleasures of close contacts with others. Armaan Singh always wants to interact and, especially enjoys watching cricket with young people. Jayant Aurora enjoys meeting with his childhood friend, throwing friendly abuses at each other. Kantha Chopra enjoys morning and evening walks with her friends and pilgrimages with her family. Lakshmi Kumar, Girish Aggarwal, and Sudhir Kumar all enjoy sharing sukh and dukh with their friends. Often closeness is in the home. Harish Mishra a 40-year-old married Brahman, draws a connection with my experiences with our cats (the photos of which I had shared with him) and his experiences in the home:

> You said you don't have children but you have cats. You are attached to them and the moment you go home, they come, they greet you, they jump on you. They're like "yes we're expecting you. You're slightly late, you've come back home. We were expecting you." It is only a matter of trust.

Krishna Notiyal, the 49-year-old who got the greatest happiness when he got his job at ONGC, says that he likes "social get togethers, with so many people interacting with each other. Several times in a week, I'll visit with my friends and feel relaxed." For Ghalib Khan, "Talking with my friends is my only hobby." Rajan Kumar, an 18-year-old coaching student, says that the meaning of khushhali is "inner satisfaction." When I ask him how one gets inner satisfaction he says, "From talking with others and making them friends.... I only get khushhali from talking to friends. That is my enjoyment—to try to know each other and to try know the problems of others."

But the importance of mixing and connection is most apparent in people's faces. People enjoy meeting friends at a tea stall or on a morning walk. They enjoy the people with whom they exercise or do yoga. Connection is particularly important at festival times—throwing colored paint at each other on Holi, squealing and dancing on the rooftop, while setting off firecrackers on Diwali. In people's faces I see delight and engagement. I see a focus on the moment only. I see engrossment in the flow (Csikszentmihalyi 1990) of what is happening in the moment. In late October 2007, I went with a friend to the outskirts of Dehradun to meet his uncle. I asked if we would go on motorcycle, and he said we'd go in a seven-seat *Vikram*. But as we crammed aboard there were 15 people all in each other's laps in the Vikram. What was notable was the delight at the contact, smiles, and laughter, all the way out to the cantonment.

The physicality of connections is central. Indians will take each others' hands and hug. Pressing wet *prasad* into each other's hands is common. Going to cinema halls, male filmgoers press tightly together to enter the hall and hold hands and connect when inside the hall (Derné 2000). Some Indians I know who have moved to the USA mention missing walking shoulder-to-shoulder with their fellow humans in the teeming crowds in India's cities. During festivals, pilgrimages, and wedding processions physical contact is part of the pleasure. Going to any pilgrimage site, pilgrims pack closely together to get to inner shrines and sanctuaries. When I was on the char dham yatra to Yamunotri, Gangotri, Kedarnath, and Badrinath in 2007, I sometimes slept in dormitories filled with snoring peasants from all over India. On pilgrimages it's not uncommon for exigencies, such as landslides to put many people together to sleep in small spaces. Sarah Lamb's (2000) study of a pilgrimage of elderly Bengalis who were mostly women reveals the hardships of renunciation in pilgrimage, but also the camaraderie, connections, and mixings that are fundamental (see also Gold 1988). Mixing with me—a white foreigner speaking Hindi—on these pilgrimages perhaps enhanced the experience of some pilgrims, some of whom I'm still in touch with years later. Indians I've talked with often report that they are still in contact with the people whom they met on pilgrimage, who may hail from different states of India. When Kantha Chopra, a 58-year-old, got so much well-being from giving her shawl to a cold person whom she met on pilgrimage, part of the pleasure may come from the connections and mixing with others. Years ago, E. Valentine Daniel's (1984) described the feelings of connection from living and bathing together in cramped, tight conditions as central to successful pilgrimage in India.

The sadness and even despair that comes with limited access to physical contacts and mixing shows their centrality to well-being in India. Abdul Khan, the 61-year-old retired school principal, described his greatest unhappiness as when his colleagues ceased cooperating with him without any reason. Amrit Kaur, the 24-year-old married student who wanted her poems to be appreciated, felt very unhappy when she got married because she missed interacting with her father after she had to leave her parents' house. Purnima Kumar, a 70-year-old widow, lost well-being when she was forced out of her husband's house after his death. Mostly she misses the interactions with others. "The best times," she says, "are when people visit."

Chains of Well-being

In some Buddhist traditions, one cannot be well as long as anyone is not well (Hershock 2005). How can eating a delicious chicken tikka make us well if the workers in factory farms that "harvest" the chickens are not living the good life? And, of course, what about whether being made into chicken tikka is good for the chicken? This Buddhist recognition of the interconnectedness of things parallels other Indian religious traditions. Indians' worship of trees and plants reflects a cosmology that holds that person and nature are inseparable (Shiva 1989, 40). Indians participating in the Chipko movement could not experience well-being as long as there was a threat to life-giving trees. Muslim Salim Khan can only experience well-being if his parents, brothers, and sisters are happy, "people in the near vicinity are happy, people in the village are happy, people in the city are happy, and the people in the whole country are happy." Only "then" do "we get more happiness." When others are happy, it brings us happiness and our happiness spreads well-being to others, too. As Armaan Singh says, "if you're happy, everyone is happy."

Lakshman Negi, a retired 61-year-old Hindu who enjoys gardening, says the well-being he gets in the home spreads to the rest of his life:

First, a human [insaan] gets [milna] khushhali in the home [ghar]. The wife is the biggest part of life and after that is the children. If there is happiness [khushi] in the home, there is happiness in every direction in the whole world. If you are disheartened [E] or frustrated [E] [in the home], then you'll never get happiness in this world. If we go to a five star hotel to have a cup of coffee and our mind is running in circles thinking about what is going on in the home—thinking about the treatment of the wife, 'is anything wrong?, are the children studying?'—then there is no sukh in that coffee. If happiness is absent from the home, then a person finds disturbance everywhere else. If you are happy in the home, then in every other direction you'll find happiness.

Lakshman says that if interactions in the home give you a peaceful (shant) nature, then you can never fight outside the home. No one can throw any abuse at someone of a peaceful nature. "When a person of violent nature meets a peaceful person, he will always quiet down." "Whatever words you say shape who you are," Lakshman says, so "saying sweet words is the important thing. We shouldn't utter words that hurt someone because that spreads unhappiness." Lakshman, who has a part-time job "to pass the time," says his boss is always in a bad mood, demoralizing employees who are, then, always in a bad mood, too. "When you think like a thief, then everyone will be a thief. But if you're clean and happy, everyone will be clean and happy." What Lakshman understands is the chain of well-being—one should talk sweetly because that positive interaction spreads well-being everywhere. One should avoid negative interactions that spread unhappiness to everyone.

Niranjan Kamboj, a 48-year-old Hindu, works in the oil business, supporting his wife, two children, and his mother-in-law. Niranjan focuses on sweet, supportive interactions with everyone as the path to the good life: "If we are attached to all in a right way and everyone is our best friend [E] and we're good to all, from that alone khushhali automatically [apne aap] arises." Niranjan sees his own happiness contributing to the happiness of others:

> If I am happy [khush], everyone is happy. If I experience [mahasus] happiness, others will experience happiness, too. But if I'm unable to be happy myself, others won't experience happiness and I will see all the people sad [dukhi].

For Niranjan, "[This] has nothing to do with whether a person is rich or poor; it has to do with whether a person remains happy [khush] and *mast."* To be *mast* (rhymes with bust), is to be intoxicated with life, to have joie de vivre (Kumar 1986, 52; Lynch 1990). "Whether one eats a [simple] roti or [a more luxurious] *halwa puri,* whether one is a corepati [millionaire] or a laborer, everyone rises with the question 'am I khush or not?'"

Emile Durkheim ([1912] 1915) theorizes that humans worship God as a representation of their society. Durkheim conjectures people are right to believe that there is something larger than them that provides moral guidelines that urge them to think of others. People conceive of that broader force as God but, according to Durkheim, it is actually society that urges people to act morally and to consider interests beyond their own selves. Niranjan, who lives near a Kali temple and hears the bells of the temple ringing every day, says the reason he is able to remain khush is that he is always

> attached with the [A]lmighty father [parampita] around the clock. The energy [E] which we receive from [this attachment] keeps us fresh and well. This house, these articles, this clothing, this body, this food, this furniture—all is [the Almighty's]. None of this is mine.

Niranjan says his focus on God gives him satisfaction (santushti) without which there can be no khushhali. I mention Durkheim to suggest that Niranjan's connection to God is actually a connection to society. Niranjan recognizes that he alone didn't make his "house, these articles, this clothing, this body, this food," but rather society contributed to all of those things. Only by recognizing this—that one is not doing everything oneself—does one experience satisfaction and khushhali.

Niranjan easily shifts from talking about his connections with God to talking about how his connections with other people gave him peace and satisfaction. When Niranjan said the Almighty gave him peace and satisfaction, I didn't quite understand the Hindi and asked him where he got satisfaction. Although Niranjan had been talking about God, he shifted to referencing relations with real people as keeping him peaceful: "Satisfaction [santushti] comes from having full faith and confidence [vishwaas] that [Narendra] Sethi is like my brother." Later in the interview, when talking about how he forgets himself in the temple, Niranjan comments that while many people see the images as just stone, whenever he looks at a stone image he sees the portrait of his father-in-law. "We honored [izzat karna] him during his lifetime, just as we worship in the temple." He says that the worship of the great mother (pratima) is like the respect for his own mother.

For Niranjan, sharing sukh-dukh leads to well-being. "If I have any problem I will share it with my brother," Niranjan says, referring to Narendra, whom he has just met. "This gives satisfaction and happiness. And if there is any dukh [sorrow, grief], I will share that with him, too." Niranjan relies on interactions with family to increase joy and decrease stress and trouble:

> With my bhabhi [older brother's wife] and with my sister, we share sukh [pleasure, joy] and dukh. There are a lot of relatives and this gives mental relief [E]. There are a lot of visits—this sister comes, then that one. By the visits of relatives and interexchange of views with them, the day-to-day stress-level [E] is reduced [kam ho jaana]. If I am facing some tension or some problem and I am alone, the stress keeps on increasing due to not sharing with others, so I won't be able to remain khushi. My smiling face will look sullen [latkana, lit. hanging] and I will keep on thinking. By sharing [tensions and problems] and cracking jokes, the stress-level [E]

is automatically reduced [kam ho jaana] and we forget about our sadness [dukh] and pain. By [sharing sadness and troubles] we are interconnected with society [samaaj].

When Niranjan has tensions, and problems, interacting with others reduces his stress level. But if he finds himself alone and unable to interact, sullenness lingers. As Girish Aggarwal similarly says, khushhali comes from sharing others' sukh and dukh. As Sudhir Kumar says, "[S]haring sukh-dukh with my friends makes me feel very good [bahut achcha laga]."

Ravi Chuhra, the 30-year-old Balmiki who owns an electrical shop, says the meaning of khushhali is to "see a person happy [khush] in front of me. To see others laughing and smiling is my happiness." Ravi's approach is to "always be cheerful," to remain in a "fresh [E]" mood and avoid carrying any conflicts into his relationship with others. Ravi's will to happiness makes others happy, creating his own well-being. Living in a large joint-family, unmarried 26-year-old Ishaan Rajput has a commerce degree and works in a retail store. Ishaan, whom I met at a Shiva temple, similarly says that he feels happy (khush) whenever he sees other people happy: "When the person in front of us is khushi, we, too, are khush. When the person in front of us feels peace [shanti], we too feel peace." When asked to describe a situation of well-being, Ishaan points to family functions, such as Holi and Diwali, when family members get together. Police officer Jivraj Sharma, a 49-year-old, says he never hides his happiness, but rather shares it with everyone. "If my talk is happy [khushi se bat karna], everyone is happy." Satveer Kumar, a 21-year-old jaggery seller, says he gains happiness whenever people "talk in a good way. If everyone is happy [khush], I'm happy." The wife of a school teacher, 44-year-old Daya Pandey enjoys regular walks with her friends. "When everyone else is in a sad mood, I feel sad," Daya says, "I'm happy when everyone else is happy."

Sociologists, starting with Durkheim ([1912] 1915, 215), have understood emotions are contagious—that a "sentiment" expressed "re-echoes" in "all the minds" of interacting individuals. Randall Collins (2005) describes how positive interactions in which people express good feelings build confidence, enthusiasm, and positive energy, creating a positive chain of emotional energy. Thomas

Scheff (1990) described how negative feelings of shame could build in interactants. Well-being, too, operates in chains and connections. One's own lack of well-being can depress the well-being of another person. The happiness, joking and *mast* that someone feels might transform the sullenness of anyone they encounter. Vitality and well-being increase with positive interactions. As this book will argue in chapter 8, well-being, then, might not reside within the person, but *within the interaction.*

Thus, when I ask Niranjan about the experiences of greatest happiness he refers to participating in festivals in which the intensity of interactions is great:

> When we grow from childhood to youth, there are many moments from which we experience [mahasus] khushhali—with someone's birthday, also with a sister's marriage, or with any other marriage, or going in the *baraat* [wedding procession], or whenever there is some function in the home, we are happy. Going in a baraat there is happiness [khushi] in each step we take. We experience khushhali.

Even though Niranjan's brother was murdered after a kidnapping, when I ask him about whether he experienced a situation in which he didn't get happiness, he said that while "there are some such moments—some incidents happen—where all of a sudden [*achanak*] we get too much [*zyaada*] sadness [dukh]," he insists that the "social atmosphere [E] in which we are always interacting helps us overcome that [sadness]." By contrast, the absence of interactions for Ishwar Kumar keeps his discontent lingering. Ishwar himself recognizes that doesn't experience khushhali in his current living situation: "there is no one to listen to; no one with whom one can share one's woes and sorrows." Because Niranjan has a social situation in which he keeps on interacting, discontent dissipates.

Reciprocity

Collins (2005) shows that people lose emotional energy when they are ordered about and when they are forced to give more attention to others than they receive from others. Scheff (1990) shows that people who are always criticized develop an absence of pride and an overabundance of shame. Indeed, *reciprocity of interactions* is vital to well-being. Equal interactions lead to felicitous chains of well-being. But if one person controls the interaction, well-being does not increase. The people I interviewed regularly talked of the importance of reciprocal connections across generations. A 57-year-old Sikh who was searching for spiritual guidance said his mind was always happy [khush] because just as he "used to do service to my father, my son is doing the same service for me." Many talked of how children should serve parents just as parents served children when they were unable to take care of themselves. When interactions are not reciprocated, people lose feelings of well-being. Ishwar Kumar is upset because his nephews are not caring for him in his old age. Vashisht Kumar, the 68-year-old laborer, complains that he handled the family responsibilities his whole life but now that it "is the time for my children to take the responsibility on their shoulders, they are not doing so."

Eighteen-year-old Raj Pattial is proud that if any of his friends call him at night he will drop everything to help them. Raj wants reciprocal interactions, but says people who help others "are few. When I have a problem, everyone else may be doing their own thing." For some, nonreciprocal actions seem to harm well-being. Komal Kumar, the 37-year-old laborer, is hurt that while she works the whole day, her boss abuses her if he sees her resting for a few minutes. Fulmala Rajput, 31, felt sad (dukhi) when she "was compelled to polish my husband's shoes or to press the clothes of other family members." She complains that despite her work, people in her family "talk sharply [zor se] with me or scold [daantnaa] me."

Well-being is in interactions. Positive interactions create positive chains of well-being. Interactions that are not reciprocal limit well-being. Positive interactions create a self-reinforcing spiral that builds emotional energy, while negative interactions create a spiral that lessens well-being.

Tensions between Specialness of the Self and Connections to Others

Usually, pursuing self-development *supports* connections to others as one's work contributes to society, especially supporting one's families. Vikram Aurora, the pensioner whom I met on the train, describes well-being as stemming from finding a technique at which one is excellent, *because* it allows one to earn and help other people. Pursuing a technique at which one excels is a way of fulfilling obligations and contributing to others.

But sometimes the pursuit of the special vision and techniques that contribute to one's own well-being is in tension with the well-being one also gets from fulfilling obligations to others. Sunil, the 38-year-old Garhwali singer, tells me he only feels fulfilled pursuing his passion for Gahrwali song. He tells me that while he could easily get a high-paying job, it wouldn't fulfill him, so he makes what he can from his singing. But Sunil's hard-working wife is unhappy that he doesn't pursue a more remunerative career—as both Sunil and his wife tell me. Her nursing work and his income from ancestral property brought in the bulk of the family's earnings; Sunil's singing contributed little. Sunil loves his wife and family, often praising his wife's qualities from cooking to caring for the children. Sunil's face shows well-being not only when he is working on his Garhwali songs or playing them for me on cassette, but also when he is interacting in his home with his wife and children. Sunil describes himself as lazy with the children, but he seems more connected to his young children than the majority of Indian men I observe. Sunil says that marrying the wife that he did was like winning the lottery. (The marriage was an arranged marriage.) Knowing how unhappy his wife is, Sunil tells me he has given his wife full freedom to leave him, but this is an empty offer as Sunil also well knows. "In India, the wife cannot leave the husband," he tells me.

So, while Sunil's unremunerative musical focus gives him well-being, Sunil recognizes that his well-being is simultaneously threatened by his restricted earning capacity. When I ask Sunil about situations of a lack of well-being, he first tells me that he never misses out on an opportunity for happiness (khushi). He, then, reflects that if he is unable to execute a project that he has planned that this frustrates his well-being, a statement consistent with my observations that he shows greatest animation and engrossment while working on his music. But Sunil, then, reflects on how his limited earnings threaten his well-being:

> In some ways, I don't experience khushhali—I'm not repaid for the work that I do. To look after family, I need good money. [The money I earn] gives me unhappiness, because I'm not paid well. Along with my creative

work, I want to earn a lot and because I don't, I feel *dukhi*. I am having difficulty accessing *lakshmi* [prosperity, the Goddess of wealth] and this gives me sadness. If there is no lakshmi in my hand, then there is a lack of khushhali.

Although Sunil repeatedly said he is a happy, simple man, who doesn't care much for money, he is simultaneously unhappy that his approach to earning threatens his relations with those he loves. As I argue in Chapter 8, it is not unusual for people to experience a simultaneous mixture of well-being and absence of well-being.

The well-being Sunil gets from supporting those he loves is in tension with the well-being Sunil gets from pursuing his special creativity. Vikram Aurora, the pensioner whom I met on the train, suggested that finding work at which one excels supports not just the self, but the other people one helps through one's work and the family one can support with the fruits of one's work. Sunil has not found work he loves that also generates sufficient earnings, putting Sunil in a conundrum. Sunil gets well-being from his musical ability (the "specialness" that bolsters well-being, which I emphasize in this chapter), but Sunil also wants to connect to lakshmi (a source of well-being described in Chapter 2) and make his wife happy (highlighting the social connectedness that this chapter also focuses on as necessary for well-being). Sunil remains hopeful—even convinced—that his musical career will eventually be remunerative, which would be a way of solving the conflicting pulls he experiences. Sunil also remain hopeful that his wife will become satisfied with what he is able to earn: Sunil knows his wife is unhappy with his earnings, but he also insists that his wife "understands" him; that she knows he has to fulfill his passions. For now, though, Sunil's desire to pursue his individual specialness through music conflicts with his desire to properly support his family. For many people, there is a happy concordance between earnings and a loved job. But sometimes the two sources of well-being described in this chapter—individual achievement and connections to others—come into conflict, and this is one reason well-being, as I argue in Chapter 8, is so often mixed.

This chapter confirms the findings of survey researchers that both higher levels of work satisfaction (Diener and Seligman [2004] 2009, 234) and higher levels of social connectedness (Diener [1984] 2009; Diener and Seligman [2004] 2009, 237; Kesebir and Diener [2008]

2009, 68; Larsen and Prizmic 2008, 274; Putnam 2000) are associated with higher levels of well-being. This chapter shows that people themselves recognize achievements and connections as a source of well-being and perhaps suggests some of the reasons why achievements and connections are so satisfying.

References

Bellah, Robert N., Richard Madsen, William M. Sullivan, Ann Swidler, and Steven M. Tipton. 1985. *Habits of the Heart: Individualism and Commitment in American Life*. New York, NY: Harper and Row.

Bellamy, Carla. 2011. *The Powerful Ephemeral: Everyday Healing in an Ambiguously Islamic Place*. Berkeley, CA: University of California Press.

Collins, Randall. 2005. *Interaction Ritual Chains*. Princeton, NJ: Princeton University Press.

Csikszentimhalyi, Mihaly. 1990. *Flow: The Psychology of Optimal Experience*. New York, NY: Harper.

Daniel, E. Valentine. 1984. *Fluid Signs: Being a Person the Tamil Way*. Berkeley, CA: University of California Press.

Derné, Steve. 1995. *Culture in Action: Family Life, Emotion, and Male Dominance in Banaras, India*. Albany, NY: SUNY Press.

————. 2000. *Movies, Masculinity, and Modernity: An Ethnography of Men's Filmgoing in India*. Westport, CT: Greenwood Press.

Diener, Ed. (1984) 2009. "Subjective Well-Being." In *The Science of Well-Being: The Collected Works of Ed Diener*, edited by Ed. Diener, 11–58. New York, NY: Springer.

Diener, Ed, and Martin E.P. Seligman. (2004) 2009. "Beyond Money: Toward an Economy of Well-Being." In *The Science of Well-Being: The Collected Works of Ed Diener*, edited by Ed Diener, 201–66. New York, NY: Springer.

Durkheim, Emile. (1912) 1915. *The Elementary Forms of the Religious Life*. Translated by Joseph Ward Swain. New York, NY: Free Press.

Gold, Ann. 1988. *Fruitful Journeys: The Ways of Rajasthani Pilgrims*. Berkeley, CA: University of California Press.

Hausner, Sondra L. 2007. *Wandering with Sadhus: Ascetics in the Hindu Himalaya*. Bloomington, IN: Indiana University Press.

Hershock, Peter D. 2005. *Chan Buddhism*. Honolulu, HI: University of Hawaii Press

Kesebir, Pelin and Ed Diener. (2008) 2009. "In Pursuit of Happiness: Empirical Answers to Philosophical Questions." In *The Science of Well-Being: The Collected Works of Ed Diener*, edited by Ed Diener, 59–74. New York, NY: Springer.

Kumar, Nita. 1986. "Open Space and Free Time: Pleasure for the People of Banaras." *Contributions to Indian Sociology*, 20(1): 41–60.

Lamb, Sarah. 2000. *White Saris and Sweet Mangoes: Aging, Gender, and Body in North India.* Berkeley, CA: University of California Press.

Larsen, Randy J., and Zvjezdana Prizmic. 2008. "Regulation of Emotional Well-Being: Overcoming the Hedonic Treadmill." In *The Science of Subjective Well-Being*, edited by Michael Eid and Randy J. Larsen, 258–89. New York, NY: Guilford.

Lynch, Owen. 1990. "The Mastram: Emotion and Person among Mathura's Chaubes." In *Divine Passions: The Social Construction of Emotion in India*, edited by Owen Lynch, 91–115. Berkeley, CA: University of California Press; New Delhi: Oxford University Press.

Putnam, Robert D. 2000. *Bowling Alone: The Collapse and Revival of American Community.* New York, NY: Simon and Schuster.

Scheff, Thomas. 1990. *Microsociology.* Chicago, IL: University of Chicago Press.

Shiva, Vandana. 1989. *Staying Alive: Women, Ecology and Development.* London: Zed.

Trawick, Margaret. 1990. *Notes on Love in a Tamil Family.* Berkeley, CA: University of California Press.

4

MEANINGS AND APPROACHES

What [people] seek is "significant living," i.e., a life in which there occur,
to a great extent, experiences which are felt to be of utmost significance
and importance. That such experiences occur in the life of most persons
is a fact. It is equally a fact that they want an increasing rate of frequency
for such experiences.

—Indian philosopher Daya Krishna (1989, 187).

Eighteen-year-old Vijay Sharma whom we met at Lakshman Siddh—a temple celebrating a *siddha* (person of spiritual accomplishment)—sees the quest to find himself as the secret to well-being:

Khushhali isn't in money. It's not in worldly things. My idea is that the biggest happiness [khushi] is to know ourselves. To know ourselves is why we have come into this world. It can't just be that we're here to take birth, go to school, get married and then die. I need to know the reason behind it—these questions erupt in my mind—the curiosity to know myself. The biggest thing of khushhali is obtaining peace [shanti] within yourself.

Narendra and I press Vijay, a student of English, history, and defense, about money. He says, "I don't respect [*mannana*] money very much. I receive peace [shanti] inside the self. I will only get happiness if I get a face-to-face glimpse of Bhagwan. It hardly matters whether myself or my brothers get any employment or any money or any worldly things." Vijay, whose hobby is listening to sad songs, enjoys (*pasand*) the isolation (*ekant*) of going to temples where he can meditate (English: meditation). Perhaps he is a young man finding himself—his father is a police officer and he is studying defense, too. Perhaps the particular situation of Vijay—we interviewed him at a temple celebrating a siddha—led him to highlight knowing the self as fundamental to well-being. Perhaps his religious tradition pushes him to emphasize finding the self. For whatever reason, Vijay highlights the quest for meaning as the key to his well-being.

To say that to have well-being one needs to pursue one's creativity whether as a poet (as for Amrit Kaur) or as a Garhwali singer (as for Sunil Sharma) is to say that life has to have some *meaning* or purpose. To say that to have well-being one must help others whether by contributing to housework (as for Ayesha Khan) or participating in an NGO to educate children (as for Salim Khan) is to say that life means something. Few people emphasize the quest for meaning as exclusively as Vijay does; but with few exceptions, finding meaning in life is fundamental to the well-being of the people we interviewed; meanings especially help people get through troubles and discouragements. Finding an approach to living that helps in hard times seems central to experiencing well-being.

Prakash Tyagi, the ONGC retiree introduced in Chapter 2, has a zest for life despite a persistent cough he attributes to years of smoking and the unmentioned neglect by many in his immediate family. Prakash shared with me a few "maxims one can walk comfortably with," including "if circumstances do not smile on you, smile yourself on circumstances" and "try to give grace even to afflictions." Prakash's objective difficulties but clear sense of well-being shows the importance of developing an *approach* to life to guide actions and provide understanding of life's troubles and painful necessities. Despite his declining health, the loss of his much loved wife and the neglect of his family (the last of which he didn't comment on, but which both Narendra Sethi and I noticed), he remains happy. His approach of de-emphasizing tensions may contribute to his well-being. One of his maxims to walk comfortably with is that "for well-being, tension has no meaning. No room must be there for it." As Prakash himself recognizes, khushhali "depends on attitude and temperament—on what we think and believe." Prakash, thus, says that the millionaire who thinks only the "darkest" thoughts can have no khushhali despite their material wealth. Prakash seems to have recognized the perils of pressures to earn—"the more ambitious you are," he says, "the more you worry"—and developed an approach to limit his own desires. He says that after leaving college he "never crazed for much" and was always "happy" with "whatever salary" he earned. Perhaps especially since his wife died he sometimes focuses on how transience means one should temper attachments: "Enjoy the garden and company but don't be bewitched [*jaadu*, lit. magic, charm, spell]. All surroundings should be loved, but don't be enamored, enchanted or tempted." Prakash's *approach* of loving life, while limiting attachments and de-emphasizing tensions, is one of many meaningful approaches to handle difficulties and challenges.

Armaan Singh, a 65-year-old, only discusses his approach to life when he considered his misfortunes. In talking about well-being, Armaan focused on the external world—good health, sufficient earnings, and connections to others But when I asked him about his situation in which he experienced a lack of well-being he told me that his son had died seven years before due to witchcraft. "What greater sadness [E] can there be! If anyone's son dies, the death is not a hurt of 1–2 days which ceases, but is a lifelong process which gives sadness [dukh] as long as a person lives." As I empathize with him, Armaan showed the approach he has developed to handling misfortunes: "It's nothing [*kuch nahin*]. We can't do anything in this life. We should keep on doing the deed [*karm*] and not expect the fruit of it. All we can do is our work [karm]." Armaan was extremely disturbed for several years after losing his son. He planned a suicide that would be a peaceful (shant) way to leave the world—alcohol followed by sleeping pills and sleeping outside in the cold. But a passerby saw him and intervened. Although Armaan does not believe in God—"if there is God, he says, why would my son die?"—he relates how he luckily came into contact with a guru who helped him "realize that this body is nothing [kuch nahin]. We have to make ourselves feel that we are bodyless." Armaan's story illustrates how meanings often come to us when coping with misfortunes. When life is flowing easily and we are caught up in the flower of the moment, meanings are less important. Armaan is a *mauj* and *masti* individual [an individual with joie de vivre] who enjoys life to the fullest, seeing movies, watching cricket, and interacting with everyone. He learned to approach his son's death—which he described as a lifelong sadness—by focusing on how ultimately the self is without a body. Surely, finding a way to approach that sadness is central to his ability to enjoy life fully.

Social-science research demonstrates an association between meaning and greater levels of well-being (Kim-Prieto and Deiner 2009, 447; Steger, Oshi, and Kashdan 2009, 43; Vaillant 2002, 206). These findings especially show that meanings speed people's adaptations to negative events (Larsen and Prizmic 2008, 270–71) and that religious beliefs that offer meaning are correlated with subjective well-being (e.g., Bok 2010, 21–2; Diener [1984] 2009, 29; Myers 2008, 327). Such quantitative studies show an association: Greater meanings, especially religious meanings, are associated with greater subjective well-being in individuals. This qualitative study identifies the range of approaches Indians take and shows that people *themselves* recognize the importance of meanings to experiencing well-being.

Religion is a focus of this chapter because for many people religion highlights meanings that stretch beyond one's individual joys and sorrows; the true self and God endure whatever one's circumstances. The last chapter's reference to the Hindu discourse of seva, *langar* rituals which feed the community, and the Muslim obligation to guests suggested how religion urges thinking of others' needs. Prakash is not a highly religious person—he doesn't "believe in rites and rituals,"—but he says he "always remembers Him." One of his maxims to walk comfortably with is "we must be grateful to the almighty for every moment." Thinking like Durkheim (e.g., [1912] 1915, 236), Prakash connects worship of God with the worship of humanity: "We are human beings and if we worship humanity we worship God. People who do not worship humanity cannot recognize God." So, in being grateful for what the Almighty gives him, Prakash is grateful to humanity. Hence, one of his "maxims" is to practice "altruism, generosity, and tolerance" Religion helps Prakash think of others. The emphasis on helping others, celebrated within Indian religious traditions, surely attributes meaning to necessities—from housework to earning—that may not always seem fulfilling to the self.

Although religion is central to this chapter, I don't want to overemphasize it. Many people didn't mention religion at all—even though Indian religious principles often echoed in what people said. Armaan, a man of Sikh background who is clean shaven and says he doesn't believe in God, says that one should see well-being as inner—that one can't modify circumstances, but one can modify how they see these circumstances. In coping with his son's death, Armaan describes how he focuses on the "deeds" rather than the "fruits"—that one must keep doing one's work no matter what one gets from it. Both of these ideas are central to the Bhagavad Gita, but Armaan doesn't mention that connection. Consistent with Geertz ([1966] 1973), religion has perhaps affected Armaan's ethos—his approach to life, even if he didn't learn this ethos through religious preaching. Armaan uses the Gita's words and concepts without referencing them, but it is perhaps significant that in his time of crisis—when life seemed so meaningless he contemplated suicide—he turned to a religious guru and learned that the body is ultimately nothing. Religion provides a reservoir of resources people can use in crafting an approach to living with misfortune—but it is not all-encompassing and is not referenced by all of the Indians I interviewed.

Meanings and Pleasure in Combination

Enjoying connecting and mixing, whether in a shared autorickshaw, at a cinema-hall, or on a pilgrimage, shows that the *pleasure* and fun outside of our often individualistic daily lives is *also* a source of well-being. For Prakash, one regular pleasure was walking to Gandhi Park. Although he walks "slow and seldom," Prakash says *ghumna* (wandering) is a great pleasure. When he was younger Prakash enjoyed going to theaters to see films, but now he only sees them on TV. When I suggest family films are the best to see, Prakash says he enjoys "sexy" films, by which he means titillating (not pornographic) films. For Armaan, pleasures include watching cricket on his shop television with young friends and occasionally seeing films in theaters (he enjoyed the mainstream hit *Jab We Met*, which he called "sexy"). Armaan also enjoys tea, good food, a good sleep, and riding his motorcycle fast—all of which are among the many small pleasures that provide a break from the day-to-day (and which I'll discuss in the next chapter).

Religion's contribution to well-being goes beyond helping people craft a sense of purpose and find meaning; it also provides *pleasures*, especially through ritual *activities* that take one away from the ordinary, away from a focus on self. The physical movement in the leadup to pilgrimage or temple worship, the handling of prasad, and the ringing and sound of temple bells are among the bodily pleasures associated with religious rituals. In discussing meanings and approaches alongside pleasures (albeit in separate chapters) I try to highlight the importance of well-being of both the body and the mind. Discussing meanings and approaches alongside pleasures shows the need to pursue life with some purpose, while also having time for fun purposelessness. Pleasures are often of the external world and the body, while meanings and approaches are of the mind—how one sees things. One theme of this book is that well-being relies on diverse, even contradictory elements. Thus, Armaan says that the external world—health, wealth, and social connections—are key to well-being. His discussion of health emphasizes that hijras (eunuchs) can have no well-being as they can't have sex. Yet, in thinking about his son's death, Armaan says that he came to understand that "this body is nothing," that "we are bodyless." For Armaan, a healthy body is central to well-being, as is the understanding that ultimately the body is nothing. One theme of this book is that well-being comes from combining contradictory parts of life. There is no one key to well-being, but a diversity of keys to playing a well lived life. (Oooh, it's a mixed metaphor, but perhaps the mixedness of it makes the point!)

As I will discuss more fully in Chapter 7, the focus on contradictory imperatives is characteristic of Hinduism. Thus, Hinduism focuses on *both* the affairs of the world and transcending the affairs of the world, and makes it imperative for individuals to *both* renounce the world and fulfill our meaningful obligations to the material world (Kinsley 1982; Sharma 2005, 46). Hinduism stresses both the joys of desire and of transcending desire, of the carnal and the spiritual (Varma 2001, 69–70). Shiva enjoyed sexual play with Parvati for such an extended period that the gods worried, but at other times Shiva was immersed in sublime meditation oblivious to the world (O'Flaherty 1973; Varma 2001, 70). To experience the bliss of the infinite one must play on many contradictory paths.

I considered presenting a single chapter on the contradictory pulls of meanings and pleasures, just as the previous chapter discussed *both* connections to others and the specialness of the self. But Indians find a lot of pleasures and embrace lot of meanings, making such an approach unwieldy. So, this chapter sticks with a discussion of meanings, holding off pleasures for the next chapter. But the reader should know the other side of life is coming next.

Religion and a Meaningful Life

Durkheim ([1912] 1915, 355) identified how religion works to help persons think beyond egocentric concerns associated with individual aspirations or troubles. Rajendra Rana, the 21-year-old news reporter who wants to combat harms like superstitions, quotes the Gita to emphasize selfless activity: "Krishna urged us to just keep on doing deeds without worrying about the results we get." Niranjan Kamboj, the 48-year-old in the oil business, says that the reason he is able to remain khush is that he is connected with the Almighty father (parampita) around the clock. For Niranjan, focusing on God allows a person to forget selfishness and personal troubles and focus on a wider whole of which one is only a small part:

> As long as I remain in the temple, I forget about myself. There are a lot of festivals here, too. For the [festival] time, we forget about ourselves—what we are, what we do, whether we are facing any difficulty [pareshani]…. For whatever time we're in the temple, this state continues. The chime of the bell and the tantalizing sound of the bell takes us to the "zero zone" [English phrase]. Our mind [E] goes into zero with the vibrating sound of the bell. We forget everything. Then, there is only God in front of us.

Although he focuses here on the time in the temple, Niranjan says it's not necessary to go to the temple everyday because Bhagwan resides in our mind and is present everywhere in everything. He says he accomplishes his meditation and prayers during his 45-minute drive to the office! When Niranjan focuses on God, his own difficulties are not so important.

Suraj Singh, a prosperous 58-year-old real estate dealer, begins describing khushhali by focusing on externals—"proper food, housing, and clothing. Even a car, which used to be a luxury is a necessity for the middle class today." Suraj says he is "sound and happy [khush] in all areas—politically, socially, in business, and with my friends." Suraj only brings up religion when discussing challenging times. He says that Sikh holy book, the Guru Granth Sahab, teaches the importance of maintaining a positive attitude in the face of sorrow:

> The book says that the king of the whole world's king is dukh. But after reciting the almighty's name, he becomes sukh. Even the creator of the whole world is unhappy but by reciting and remembering the almighty, he too becomes happy.

Although not a devotee, Suraj's religious beliefs help him see that even the most wealthy have troubles that can be put aside by focusing on the broader reality that is God: "If you keep *Prabhu*'s name in your remembrance and chant *kirtan*s you'll remain happy and peaceful whatever your troubles." Jayant Aurora, the 77-year-old who maintains a sweet relationship with a childhood friend, similarly says that as long as a person is attached (lagan) to God, "that person is happy. Nothing can make me unhappy. If I have a financial setback, I would be happy as long as that attachment [to God] is there." Sukhraj Singh is a 33-year-old newspaper hawker who overcame the poverty that resulted from his father's early death and is embarrassed to have not passed Class 10. Sukhraj is consistently cheerful and very much in love with his wife, which he says is the key to his happiness: "I love [pyaar] my wife. If I didn't have any regards for her, then how could happiness be there?" But Sukhraj, of course, also has troubles, like everyone, and this is where his shauk of "keeping praying to God irrespective of whether I am getting anything or not" helps. When he thinks about God at the gurudwara, he says,

> I feel like I have no relations, no family, and just am in the service of God, chanting "Wahe guru, wahe guru" all the way. There are no worries or tensions about business profit or losses.

Sukhraj gets well-being from the very family relationships he forgets while at the gurudwara. Religion gives him something even bigger to contemplate which puts any particular "worries or tensions" in a broad context in which they can be minimized.

Focusing on God especially helps people turn from their own material troubles when facing a serious crisis. Priya Kumar, a 52-year-old widow, says she feels khushhali when she "helps others": "It gives me internal [*aatmik*] sukh to cook food for anyone who comes to my house." Priya, who now lives alone, recounts that when her husband died, religion helped her turn from the material world that was so full of troubles: "After the death of my husband, my mind hated [*virakti*] the material world and I became associated with spirituality [*adhyatmikta*], which is the ultimate truth of life [*jivan ke antim sachai*]." Kavita Kumar, a woman in her 80s, similarly says that khushhali means doing for others (*paropkar*, lit. charity, altruism, benevolence). She illustrates her experience of khushhali by referring to when her relatives come to stay at her house: "I feel happy because I cook different dishes for them. When they eat the food, I feel very satisfied." Yet, like Priya, Kavita finds that devoting herself to God takes her away from the material world. Kavita wants to focus on God because "ultimately in this stage I don't know when he'll come to take me with him." Like Priya, Kavita finds well-being in helping others in the material world, but because of her age and its hardships, she also wants to think of God so that she can forget this material world and focus on the spiritual world.

Devotee Sukhpreet Singh, a 74-year-old, similarly says that chanting Sikh kirtans pacifies "whatever disturbance there is in the mind. I really get satisfaction by reading that—that is the beauty of the whole book." Sukhpreet told me how the scripture helped him cope with his son's death. One day when Sukhpreet's son was resting on a cot, Sukhpreet went to the tap to get him water. "When I went to wake him up to give him water, he was dead, like a stone," he says, face in his hands crying. Crying, he asks whether we "can imagine what a person will feel at the time. It's the most [not understandable through the tears] thing to happen to me." "For a couple of seconds or minutes, I was simply mad," he says, crying and crying. When his son died, Sukhpreet was frantic and "did not know what to do. But suddenly, I realized our tenth guru had lost his four sons on the battlefield. I only grieved for my one son." After regaining his composure Sukhpreet says that "perhaps if I had not been reading the hymns it would have been impossible for me to accept that situation." Leaving behind his trauma, he opines that all scripture has this "purpose" to offer help, but says he still thinks "our scripture is the best in that way." His religion helped him see that others had suffered even more than him, allowing him to leave his anguish behind.

Gopal Chopra, a 73-year-old Hindu who administers a government program, similarly finds religion provides meanings to get through the hard times. When I ask Gopal about a time he experienced a lack of well-being, he speaks of how focusing on God helped him overcome the death of his son-in-law:

Even in bad times, I feel happy because I believe in God. God is good for that. I didn't feel khushhali when my son-in-law met with an accident and died—but I overcame that situation by remembering God. In the

Gita, Arjuna asks Lord Krishna some different questions and Krishna replies that 'We're all under Bhagwan. We should surrender to God' [English phrase].

A characteristic of people's talk about well-being is reference to a diversity of sources. Gopal, a Hindu who came from Pakistan during Partition, continues by referencing a poem by Bulleh Shah (1680–1757), the Sufi whom Gopal calls a famous Punjabi poet. "According to Bulleh Shah's preachings," Gopal recounts:

> We should not think of ourselves. We should "think of God" [English phrase]. From this we will get khushhali. When one stops thinking of self and starts thinking of God [English phrase], [the person] gets a vibration in the brain that provides khushhali. We should keep our brain busy with God—not with the worldly things. This is anahad naad bani [a mysterious sound within and only audible to the yogi.] We should physically remain in society—we should do seva to society, but in our minds, we should be with God. This is another source of khushhali. I try to not simply pass the time step-by-step but to be engrossed in God. Without Bhagwan, it's nothing; we're wasting our time.

What is significant is that belief in God helps Gopal sideline his particular, individual problems, and focus instead on surrendering to a larger reality that God represents.

Many people think of God's role in their successes to see their own accomplishments not as the result of egoistic striving, but fulfilling a larger purpose. Niranjan Kamboj says that

> when we bestow everything on the Almighty, whatever we have attained— this house, these articles, this clothing, this body, this food, this furniture— all is Your's [the Almighty's]. None of this is mine. You are owner [maalik] of all this—whether I am a farmer or I am having a job. All is because of You. It's Your's [the Almighty's].

Niranjan's activities have meaning because they're not just for himself, but for others. Krishna Notiyal, the 49-year-old man who enjoys social get-togethers and got his greatest happiness when he found a job at ONGC, had just completed an improvement on his house. I said it was a great house now and could be in a Hindi film. "I would be exultant," I told Krishna. But Krishna sat calmly on his balcony, no smile on his lips. "It's just roti [bread], clothing [kapra] and housing [*makaan*]. It's the basic needs of the family. I'm doing nothing. All of this comes from God." When I visit the home of 45-year-old Hemant Kapoor, I couldn't help but be dazzled by the garden and the house. Again, I said I would feel like a king if I had built such a house, but Hemant, like Krishna, said it was all because of God. Religion helps Hemant and Krishna see what they accomplish as not a selfish pursuit but participating in God's accomplishments for the broader society. By focusing on God, they see their accomplishments as moving forward God's work.

Thinking of God helps many faithfully pursue their duties at work or home. Gajendra Rajput, a never-married 69-year-old retired forestry officer, said that by "doing yoga and remembering God" he was able to "do good service [seva] to others" and to love people (*pyaar mohabbat apas me*). Gajendra complains that people think about money so much that they "forget honesty [*imaandaari*] and even adopt the wrong ways of earning money." Gajendra says that only the person with a clean mind (*saaf man*) who knows right (*sahi*) and wrong (*galat*) is able to walk on the path of inspiration (*prerna*) from God (Prabhu). Gajendra says one should focus on "wealth of satisfaction [*santosh dhan*]" rather than the elephant's wealth, eagle's wealth, or precious stones. Gajendra did "service in the government sector," rather than speculating for monetary gains. "I am satisfied that I'm at least trying to be with God [Prabhu]." Thinking of God helps Gajendra see his work as service to others—work he should accomplish to the best of his abilities. Gurkeerat Singh, the 49-year-old Sikh who doesn't want to run after money and enjoys sweet relations and interacting with people during festivals, says

> Khushhali means do your work everyday with virtuous [*nek*] intentions. Then, the Almighty automatically gives khushhali. I don't drink. I'm a vegetarian. I do pujapath every morning and evening. I have taken *amrit* [a sign of devotion to God]. All of this is the secret [*raaz*] of my khushhali.

Gurkeerat sees earning as part of his religious devotion. Hindu Surendra Kumar, a 39-year-old menial lower-caste clerk, similarly focuses on the effects of "faith" on working dutifully: "Faith helps us see that the duty of a person is to work hard [karm], to make efforts and toil [*mehanat karna*]." Thinking about God helps both

Gurkeerat and Surendra see their hard work as devoting themselves to broader purposes rather than narrow individualistic ones. While I've emphasized how faith in God helps people attribute meaning to their activities at work and in the home, faith also *strengthens* the individual's resolve. Meanings help people pursue duties with energy. Durkheim ([1912] 1915, 242) argues that a person has more "confidence, courage and boldness of action" when that person "feels the regard of his [or her] God turned graciously towards him" or her. Thus, Richa Mishra a newly married 27-year-old teacher, says a person achieves results by combining

three things—your actions, your love, and the grace of God. It's a Thanksgiving when the three elements combine. When you visit a shrine like Vaishno Devi, you get confidence in yourself; you get that grace of God in yourself that, yes, you have committed your faith and you have done your part and now His part is there, too.

Sukhpreet Singh, the 74-year-old Sikh devotee, says that "there is a miracle in reciting the name of God. If you do that, you will not have anything missing in you. You feel that God will provide whatever you demand or whatever your requirements are." So, the devout often feel that God not only gives meaning to their actions, but He empowers them as well.

Religious meanings are ready-made. Individuals don't need to invent them. Several of the people whom I interviewed enjoy spiritual or religious readings, but it's also notable that several, like Armaan Singh, found gurus at the time of losses. Santosh Prasad is a 30-year-old anti-alcohol crusader who gets inner satisfaction from her teaching work and helping others. She said that the situation that caused her greatest unhappiness was too painful to recount. Santosh has found a guru who gives her inspiration (prerna) to do her social service work. She finds visiting her guru's ashram a great pleasure (anand) and from him she realized that God will provide for her well-being.

Because of the ready-made nature of religious approaches to life, religious discourses had a powerful effect on people's approaches and meanings. But for many—and probably most people—the effect of religious discourses on finding an approach that helps one cope with difficulties and guide life is more indirect. Maitreyi Chatterjee, a 65-year-old, finds khushhali in giving a meal to the beggar who comes to her house every day and finds happiness in her chats (*baatcheet*)] and kitty parties [E] with her friends and relatives. When Meenu Sharma asks her if she's done any pilgrimages she says that while she has done them,

> I don't believe too much in doing pujapath and going to mandir [temple]. I'm not much devoted [*bhakt*] to God. I think that if you're loving [*prem karna*] the human being, you'll find God [*ishwar*] within that person. There is no need to go to temple or pray to God or read religious books. If you're doing good for others, this is equal to worshiping God and this—helping others—gives my mind [*dimaag*] and inner self [*aatma*] peace [shanti].

Surely Maitreyi knows the religious discourse of love and service, but she doesn't foreground religion in describing her focus on helping others and interacting with friends, an approach that helps her find meaning in life. While it might be possible to trace religious doctrine's influence on people like Maitreyi, people often talked about how to approach life without talking about religion at all. What is most significant for this book is that finding meanings in one's actions and, especially, finding an approach for facing the inevitable troubles of life contributes to feelings of well-being.

Gaining Knowledge

For many, knowledge—and the quest for it—provides meaning and purpose. Jaspal Sidhu, a 22-year-old coaching student who became clean shaven after Class 12 signifying he is not a strict adherent to Sikh religion, describes Paonta Sahab—a Sikh pilgrimage close to Dehradun—as a place that gave him "peak satisfaction [santushti]. I got pleasure [E], adventure [E], and knowledge [E] at that place." Jaspal values the good historical knowledge of the 10th guru who did *tapasya* (austerities) at that place. For Jaspal, such knowledge "gives peace and satisfaction no matter what sadness [dukhi] a person faces." Salim Khan, a 26-year-old journalist, faced his greatest unhappiness when he had to leave an Islamic university for financial reasons. He gets well-being from participating in educational NGOs to help educate those with limited funds. When I ask Salim about what he gained from his travels through India, he pauses for so long that I asked him whether he had gained anything. Salim, then, focused on getting knowledge from these travels:

> No, I've gotten a lot. It's truly said that travel [*safar*] gives a lot of education in learning. Today, whatsoever I have become, I have become because of these journeys. After leaving my studies, I had become an Islamic teacher. But I was a blank in worldly knowledge, whereas these yatras gave me a lot of learning. These journeys gave me a lot of inner strength whereas I used to live in a very limited circle consisting of my religion and my religious books and religious activities. These journeys gave me boundless knowledge [*apaar gyaan*] and the opportunity to meet great knowledgeable people from different walks of life whose thoughts and teachings, inspired me to study again. And this inspiration ignited me to do something big in life. I got this [milna] from these yatras.

Salim describes his interest in setting up an educational center as following from what he learned visiting Bijapur district in Karnataka. According to Salim, the district was totally destroyed in the 1857 revolt and the area remained "illusioned" for 90 years (until India achieved independence). Salim says what he learned in Bijapur

> taught me the importance of educational centers for development. In Bijapur, there were many educational centers, but in the 1857, everything got destroyed. When the educational centers were revamped, things improved. Everything in the world can be destroyed, but if a lamp of knowledge is lit, its flame is inextinguishable. Knowledge is the one thing which can never be destroyed. Books pass on the information to a second and a third. The torch of knowledge is ever-glowing and it keeps on passing from one generation to the next. From these yatras I learned that the more you spread and share your education, our level of education will automatically increase. It widens our knowledge, passes on the good knowledge.

For Salim, pursuing knowledge gives meaning to his life.

Santosh Prasad describes two situations in which she experienced khushhali, the second being when she got knowledge (*brahma gyaan*) of God through her guru. But the first thing that comes to her mind when she thinks of an experience of well-being is when she "topped" in her BEd (bachelors of education) examination. The latter, of course, also reflects the feeling of pride at her special accomplishment, but together both reflect that for her knowledge leads to well-being. Somendra Mishra, a 47-year-old, focuses on raising a family, saying that clear arrangements for earning a living are the source of well-being. When I ask him to describe a time in which he experienced well-being he referred to being a student:

> The student life was the greatest [sab se badi] happiness [khushi]. That life was the best [*sab se achcha*]. Then, there were no responsibilities [*zimedaari*] and the sole objective [uddeshya] was just learning. That was the limit.

While Somendra surely found well-being, too, in the absence of responsibilities, he mentions the ability to devote himself to learning as "the limit." While Santosh and Maitreyi have found knowledge through religious gurus, others seek out people who can help them understand. Thus, Raveena Chawla, the 21-year-old Sikh student, says that she is always looking to "meet those people who are independent in their field because I want them to share their life experiences with me so that I can learn good things from them." Finding a guru who can help one understand is one path to knowledge, but, however one does it, pursuing and gaining knowledge is one way to give purpose and meaning to life.

My discussion of how learning and knowledge gives purpose highlights a key characteristic of well-being that I'll return to later—well-being involves participation in numerous different spheres of life. For Santosh, Maitreyi, and Raveena, knowledge was associated with a special connection to a guru, one of the things that keep us from feeling alone. For Santosh, knowledge was associated with her special achievements. For Santosh, Maitreyi, Jaspal, and Salim, knowledge was associated with religious community. For Somendra, pursuit of knowledge was associated with freedom from responsibilities (but also with being able to earn a living). For Jaspal, the experience of knowledge was also associated with the pleasure, adventure, satisfaction, and peace of escaping day-to-day life on pilgrimage. For Salim, gaining knowledge in his lengthy travels was associated with the pleasure of traveling beyond his limited circle. And, as the Gita suggests, the path to knowledge is one of several paths one might pursue to become close to God. And, finally, my friend Prakash Tyagi, who obviously enjoys knowing, says ironically that "sometimes wisdom becomes too heavy [*bhari*] and is a hindrance." Knowledge, indeed, can detract from the pleasures of the body, emotions, and other aspects of the good life, which I'll discuss in the next chapter. As I'll argue in Chapter 8, the nature of well-being is to be contradictory. To experience well-being, we need to participate in many arenas of life; we need to feel well in many of life's arenas.

Pursuing a Purpose

Having a purpose and working towards it is central to life having meaning. Pursuit of knowledge is one such purpose—Raveena Chawla wants to learn from those who have achieved things in their field; Salim Khan pursued knowledge by traveling through India. Shazia Qureshi, the 60-year-old housewife who finds well-being in serving her guests and got the most well-being when she gave money to an office peon to help with his daughter's marriage, got great joy of fulfilling her longtime goal of completing her Haj pilgrimage:

> When I went for Haj I landed at the airport and straight away went to Medina and as I reached there tears of happiness [khushi] rolled down my eyes because it was my aspiration and longing [*tamanna*] from childhood to visit this place and now God has given me the chance to go there after completing all my family responsibilities.

Although she has fulfilled this "aspiration," Shazia still has other aims:

> The aim of my life is that whatever time is left for me, I want to spend it for pujapath. Moreover, I always want to help the poor and all those who are in need of help.

It seems even when one's greatest aspiration is fulfilled, one still needs other senses of purpose to give life meaning.

Pursuing a career is often in the forefront of people's minds. Thus, Richa Mishra, the newly married 27-year-old who has just begun teaching and does pilgrimages to aid in accomplishing her purposes, says

> I want to rise up in life. I want to at least do my best. I'm a teacher, so naturally I will want to rise to the status of principal—maybe that will be the highest point of my career.

One reason Raveena Chawla wants to meet people from whom she can learn is that her goal is to "do something in my life," which can only happen when she is "financially independent." Thus, she was very happy when she was accepted into a garment technology course "because now I got into a line in which I have to work for my future."

Being able to throw oneself into a meaningful purpose helps when times are hard. Purnima Kumar, the 70-year-old widow who lost well-being when she was forced out of her husband's family, is distressed because

> The purpose [uddeshya] of my life has finished. Even now, I don't have tears to cry over it. I pray to God "do take me as soon as it is possible."

When the thing that gave Purnima purpose is lost, she feels despair. But Purnima was beginning to find another purpose in life, perhaps giving her more well-being. Immediately after describing her purpose as finished, she goes on to describe "a temple near my house. Every day in the morning I go there and do all the cleaning [safai] work and I feel satisfied in doing that work." So, even as she presents despair, finding a bit of purpose in life keeps her going. We need a purpose, even if it changes over time.

Well-being as a State of Mind

One common way that Indians address unpleasant, upsetting or disappointing circumstances is to approach life by seeing khushhali as being inner. Although this resonates with the Gita, people usually don't highlight religion in talking about seeing well-being as in the mind. Armaan Singh is not a religious man, although he found a guru when he coped with his son's death. Armaan's first words on the subject of khushhali are that it consists of "inner feelings." As we chatted after the interview, Armaan put it this way: "In any circumstance, you should remain happy because you cannot change the circumstances; you have to mold your mind according to the circumstances." Armaan says that although his brothers all have more wealth than he does, he is happier than them because of how he sees his life. Armaan's approach of seeing well-being as inner, as a state of mind that one achieves through viewing the world through positive eyes is not uncommon. But Armaan also finds pleasure in the body, in food, in joking, in exercise, and in watching sports. After referencing inner feelings as the source of well-being, Armaan quickly goes on to refer to how these good inner feelings are brought about by externals—health, wealth, and *shoharat*, an Urdu word Armaan translates as "popularity," but might be rendered as respect. Armaan's *contradictory discussion* highlights a fundamental characteristic of well-being: well-being follows from contradictory arenas of experience—in this case, both external circumstances and internal thoughts. But what's most important in this context is that Armaan has developed an approach to facing life's difficulties: By seeing happiness as inner, he is able to move beyond despair at events like the death of his son and to use his positive attitude to generate happiness in others, creating a felicitous chain that increases his own happiness. In doing so, well-being is not just inner, but is actualized in his relationships, too.

For Yash Singh, a 58-year-old, meditation helps him focus on well-being as an inner state. Yash, a master pakora maker, lives with his mother and wife, his adult son having moved to another state. For Yash, khushhali means satisfaction from "all sides"—both money and family. Daily meditation, he says, gives him peace of mind (*man ke shanti*), preventing bad thoughts (*galat uchhaal* [lit. wrong waves]) and any ill will for others. Without meditation, he says, the mind never "rests in a proper way." You don't need to "become a priest or perform *havan* [a fire sacrifice]," he says, "if you just meditate a half hour daily. Offering prayers to Bhagwan without demanding anything, your mind will be free." Without daily meditation, he says, the mind "flickers here and there". Because of his meditation, he never "experiences unhappiness" and is not bothered by external circumstances:

> For instance, whether my servant works or not, I don't get pain from that and I hardly get too irritated over the actions of my servant. I have peace of mind. Whether my work is being done or not, I won't complain about that. Instead, I will simply focus on my work and my mind and do pujapath.

Yash demonstrates an approach that I'll discuss further later—that one should be balanced and not focus exclusively on one sphere. Like Armaan, he finds well-being in multiple life spheres—work, family relations, earning money, and daily meditation. What I'm emphasizing here is that by focusing on the inner nature of well-being, Yash is able to be unbothered by small irritations, such as a servant who doesn't work diligently. Whatever the external circumstances, he maintains a felicitous internal approach—he can't change circumstances, but he can affect how he thinks about them. A large number of people approach life by seeing happiness as springing from the inner self, rather than external circumstances. Sukhpreet Singh, the 74-year-old Sikh devotee, uses almost the same words as Armaan: "You cannot mold your circumstances but you can definitely mold your state of mind to be happy with those circumstances." Sukhpreet begins his discussion of khushhali by saying it is "actually a state of mind." He says we must see whatever our circumstances are as a gift from God:

> Even if your circumstances are not good and you feel disgusted or unhappy, you should be grateful to God for those circumstances because there is some happiness in that, too. You don't know why God has willed those circumstances and they may be the most happy moment of your life.

When I ask Sukhpreet how he came to understood this, he refers to the good scripture of "Guru Govind Shahab." One of the maxims that retiree Prakash Tyagi says a person can walk comfortably with is that "if circumstances do not smile on you, smile on your circumstances." "Give grace even to your afflictions" is another of his maxims. He says that humans should never let despair, dejection, or disappointment in their hearts. Abdul Khan, the 61-year-old retired school principal, says that keeping the mind peaceful provides happiness. "If your mind is peaceful, you will be happy." A retired 51-year-old military man working as a private security guard says that "khushhali is in the inner core of a person." Surendra Kumar, the 39-year-old menial clerk who focuses on controlling his spending, discovered the inner nature of well-being after the anguish of lacking a stable job. "Khushhali," he concludes, "is combining being sukh in comforts and remaining happy in bad times, too." Surendra recognizes even comforts can overwhelm well-being and that learning to be happy in hard times is fundamental to well-being, as well.

Gaura Khanna, 70, is so passionate about teaching that she took a job in a private college after retirement. Gaura, a widow who lives with her son, daughter-in-law, and grandchildren, gets well-being from diverse aspects of life—reading spiritual books, singing in her own way, and meeting former students who have succeeded. Ultimately, she describes how maintaining her mind's positive outlook is key to maintaining well-being:

> Why feel tired? It's the brain that says you're tired. If you don't put those words in your mouth you won't feel tired. Tiredness is in the brain, it's not in the body. If you don't think about your being tired you won't feel tired. I have never been angry about anything. Why be angry? You should just divert your mind to other things.

Suman Kumar, a 35-year-old student, says she tries to find happiness (khushi) in everything she does. Yakin Kaur, a 43-year-old, takes in some tailoring work while her husband works in a jewelry shop to provide a modest living (they now own both a fridge and a scooter). Yakin, too, gets well-being from diverse sources, saying that khushhali means "everything is moving well in the family, everything is sukh shanti in the family, everyone's health [swasth] is good, and everything is good financially, physically and mentally." When Meenu Sharma asks her about a situation of a lack of khushhali she emphasizes that "sukh and dukh are two sides of the same coin. Dukh doesn't affect [prabhav] me much in life because I use my mind to overcome it." Tulsi Kumar is a 33-year-old domestic servant with little formal education. When asked about a situation in which she experienced great well-being, Tulsi replies that she has "never experienced any great happiness even from childhood because my mother expired when I was only ten years old. Then I learned cooking and looked after my other brothers and sisters." She describes the happiness of her children as the meaning of khushhali, saying that she spends the money she earns on her children. The aim of her life is that her children will study so that they don't have to be a laborer or a domestic servant. When asked about a situation of a lack of khushhali, Tulsi replies that "without money, life itself causes unhappiness [dukh] and troubles [pareshani]," so she works the "whole day to fulfill my family's needs." While this sounds like a difficult life, Tulsi's first response when asked about well-being is to emphasize that she finds happiness in whatever she does:

> Whatever work I do, I feel happiness [khushi] in that. For example, like washing utensils, cleaning floor, etc., I try to feel happy in all the situations I face whether it is in my favor [paksh] or not in my favor.

Gaura, a prosperous English-speaking teacher who is the widow of an executive; Suman, a student; Yakin, a mother of modest means who takes in tailoring work; and the domestic servant Tulsi, all focus on how their mental approach to situations helps them maintain their well-being.

All these people realize that well-being cannot be based in circumstances because circumstances are always changing. Only focusing on the unchanging—whether the self or God—will provide well-being because those do not change. Thus, Gajendra Rajput, the 69-year-old retired forestry officer, says, while it might appear well-being comes from both the soul (aatma) and the "show world," this is actually a "misconception. The general public's opinion is that money is the way of khushhali. But actually when our soul [aatma] is satisfied [*santusht*] that is what leads people to obtain khushhali." Gajendra says only the person with a clean (*saaf*) conscience (*man*, literally mind) who finds inspiration (prerna) in the self can achieve well-being. After referencing the self, Gajendra immediately references God, saying you get inspiration by walking on the path of Bhagwan (God). In many strands of Hinduism, there is a strong recognition of the ultimate identity of soul and God. Focusing on either (or both) is to focus on the unchanging that can be an eternal source of pleasure. So, a 75-year-old pujari (Hindu priest) whom we interviewed said Bhagwan Ram was his love and he only sang the name of Ram. He described himself as pleased, happy and cheerful (*prasann*) because he could remain aloof (*alag*) from the world which is changeable by focusing on praising Ram who is always present. "Baghwan Ram remains here and this gives me a lot of happiness [khushi]." A 41-year-old pujari whom we interviewed said "bodily problems are natural, but our soul [aatma] is very powerful. Our body is changeable, but our soul is not changeable—it remains forever." For this pujari focusing on the unchangeable soul is the source of well-being (khushhali).

The contrast between the grumpiness of Ishwar Kumar, an 80-year-old, and the zest of Prakash Tyagi, a 79-year-old, shows the importance an approach to life takes. Both are in ill health and both might choose to focus on the neglect of their family. But Ishwar focuses on these things and is, thus, "fed up" with his family and "curses" modern India. He focuses on his health problems as contributing to his sufferings. Prakash has medical problems, but focuses on still being able to walk to the park, if slowly. He is neglected by his family, but focuses on forming new relationships. He's crushed by the loss of his wife, but remembers her fondly. In short, Prakash has a felicitous approach to facing his situations, while Ishwar grumpily realizes he can't easily change his situation by moving out of his brother's son's house. Prakash's mental approach to his circumstances (rather than the circumstances themselves) is what provides well-being.

The conclusion of well-being researchers William Tov and Ed Diener ([2008] 2009, 157) is probably correct: People experience "pleasant or unpleasant emotions in part because they pay more attention to pleasant or unpleasant stimuli." But perhaps the Indian philosopher Daya Krishna (1989, 195) better explains humans' ability to focus on the pleasant. "Art, religion, and contemplative enjoyment of the Nature world ... give to [a person's] life a 'significance' which he [or she] can always achieve if he [or she] *so desires and wills.*" Krishna is arguing that focusing on what is beautiful gives significance. "Interpersonal communication," he argues "can crown this experience of 'significance' by an intense give-and-take where each feeds on the other and increases a thousandfold." That is, seeking people out to interact with about what is significant increases that significance. "In short," he concludes, "heaven and hell are not far from [a person] and it depends to a very great extent on [that person] whether he [or she] would make of his [or her] life and that of others a heaven or hell." By attending to the beautiful and sharing it with others, one's own life is good and that of others is good as well. Or in American sociology, it's presented as a theorem (the so-called Thomas theorem): If people see situations as real, they are real in their consequences. Or as William James (1902, 90) puts it: "[S]ince you make [things] evil or good by your own thoughts about them, it is the ruling of your thoughts which proves to be your principal concern. The deliberate adoption of an optimistic turn of mind, thus, makes its entrance into philosophy." The pre-Socratic Greek philosopher Democritus held that "a happy life does not depend on good fortune or indeed on any external contingencies.... The important thing is not what a [person] has but how he [or she] reacts to what he [or she] has" (Tatarkiewicz 1976, 29, cited by Diener [1984] 2009). The ordinary people whom I interviewed—that is, the nonacademic, but actually extraordinary, ordinary people—think like philosophers and social scientists.

As I was beginning to write this chapter, my friend Bert Sandell sent me an email link to a YouTube video by professor and inspirational speaker (that's quite a combination!) Shawn Achor with the subject heading "happiness rocks!" Bert, who brings a sense of awe and positive thinking to his projects from cultivating berries, to backpacking, to designing storage facilities, was surprised that so many American undergraduates are unhappy despite all the great things in life. Achor's (2010) book, *The Happiness Advantage: The Seven Principles of Positive Psychology That Fuel Success and Performance at Work*, highlights how "happiness rocks!" to use Bert's summary of one of Achor's inspirational talks. Achor uses social science to show the role of positive thinking and a positive approach to people's happiness and success. Bringing in Achor's book shows important differences between the USA and India. Achor's focus is not well-being, but using well-being for success at work! The channels through which approaches are disseminated in the USA include social science and self-help literature. But Achor's book suggests that maintaining well-being by focusing on positive thinking is a *universal* way of approaching life's difficulties; it's a way to find well-being whatever it is one is facing.

I mostly succeed in taking this approach—although sometimes I find it challenging to think beyond the crush of circumstances (from health issues to coping with cigarettes being smoked outside my office). Some days, it's easier than others to "feel groovy" and focus on the beauty of the morning:

Slow down, you move to fast
You got to make the morning last
Just kicking down the cobble stones
Looking for Fun and Feeling Groovy

—Paul Simon, 59th Street Bridge Song, Columbia Records 1967

I think that approaching life by seeing every morning as a new elegance (to quote Prakash Tyagi) and seeing well-being as stemming from within helps cope with circumstances that are usually not too terrible after all. And this is, after all, the lesson of Indian religious traditions associated with Tantra—pay full attention to whatever is before one in every moment without preconceptions (Becker 2004, 57), while seeing everything as nondifferent from Shiva.

Now that I'm enjoying writing this book in November 2011, it's hard to remember that a few weeks ago (or was it 10 days ago?), the India lifestyle felt like a bit of a grind. Sometimes, I miss a sit-down toilet, a good shower and a banana pancake. I know those things are available in India, but I like my hotel near my friends with a nice garden (although not a good table for writing!). (And, with the US dollar soaring—or the rupee plummeting—it's now just 10 US dollars a night!) Like Shiva (and consistent with the theme of this book), I like to mix in a bit of renunciation with my pleasures. A Thai monk told travel writer Joe Cummings: "[Y]ou know why you like to travel? Everywhere you go nothing belongs to you. When you're home surrounded by your possessions, you're weighed down." "I think he was right," Cummings reflected, "it is liberating being stripped down to one suitcase" (McRae 1993, 250). (But, of course, Joe also liked the pleasures of Southeast Asia.) Still, a couple of weeks ago I was focusing more on the horns and noise and separation from my wife and cats. And that focus was probably a choice. I could instead choose to remember the magic of India—someone balancing 14 bricks on their head or another person fixing my mobile phone combining flame from a lighter for soldering and liquid poured from a rootbeer bottle (that's called *jugaar*—making it work somehow). Or simply eating delicious alu paranthas every morning. That shift to focusing on the enchantment of India was/is so complete that it's hard to remember the bummed-out feeling I experienced. This odd little paragraph should highlight that well-being is fleeting—it comes and goes. It involves many things coming together—pleasures and renunciations, work (on this book), and aimlessness (watching someone balancing bricks on their head). And it also involves an approach—seeing the mind as more important than the circumstances—to cope with life's difficulties.

Controlling the Mind, Controlling Ambition

Some maintain equanimity through ups and downs by controlling their expectations or not getting too attached to fleeting things. Prakash Tyagi says that he is "fortunate to have had a good life." He "never crazed for much" and was "satisfied" with "whatever salary he got." Because he sees "no room" for tension in a life of well-being he focused on supporting his family, but not running after money. Prakash loves life and the world, but says the world should be enjoyed in a "natural way":

> We should not, be enamored with joys and sorrows. We should enjoy the garden and the company of friends, but we shouldn't be spellbound [*jaadu*] by these things. We should love all our surroundings, but shouldn't be enamored, enchanted or tempted.

As a 48-year-old Hindu wife of a property dealer told me, "we get happy from normal life."

Krishna Notiyal, the 49-year-old who sees the wonderful home he has had built as only a reflection of God, emphasizes controlling ambitions:

> You should keep your mind under control. One shouldn't be proud [*ghamand*]. One should be ambitious but not overambitious Needs should be in a balanced form. They should be neither higher nor lower.

Lochan Mishra, the prosperous 68-year-old retired engineer, focuses on limiting expectations in all fields, including family:

> Khushhali means that you don't expect much from the family and do whatever you can do for them. You will always be satisfied and you will never [have] regret. But if you expect something, you'll be disappointed and, then, you can't have khushhali. Expect little. Give more.

Raj Pattial, the flashy 19-year-old Punjabi student who enjoys eating good food and exploring hilly places, but who sees the greatest taste as helping others, is studying to earn a bachelor in business. For Raj,

> Money does count but only to a certain level. That is, I am not poor and I am also not too rich. I am above the necessities, but not to the point that you want fancy cell phones, gold everywhere. It's not like that. I want a plain. I want simplicity. You want to be a well-being person you need simplicity. If you are running behind things, it's taking your attention and if you're not running behind things, persons would give you attention.

Raj says many people in the world think of what they don't have and strive for this or that. Perhaps they see a car and all of a sudden they want a "car, personal camera, aeroplane space shuttle. What will you get in a space shuttle that you won't get in a car?" Raj says that when someone asks him what he wants to earn he won't say one lakh or two lakh, but rather that he would like to "contribute to fulfilling the wishes of my mom and to help my father." Happiness stems from many things, for Raj, including controlling his wants. The important thing here is that Raj sees running after too much money as detracting from a simple life. It's especially important that he holds that if a person runs after money, others won't give that person any "attention." That is, running after money *detracts* from sweet interactions that produce positive chains of well-being.

People of modest means often focus on limiting desires as an essential component of the good life. A 40-year-old laborer recounted this guiding philosophy that limits expectations: "Keep eating *daal* and roti; keep praising God." Surendra Kumar, the 39-year-old menial clerk, says that "it is in a person's own control to remain happy [khush]": simply live within one's means and don't desire more than what one can afford. Yashoda Kumar, a 53-year-old laborer, recalls the hardship of her husband being the only earner in the family when her children were young. But now she is working alongside her husband, both sons are laboring, and her daughters have left their studies and are domestic servants. Yashoda says that khushhali is being "happy" with "whatever money we get from our work." When Meenu asks her about a situation in which she experienced great happiness, she replies that there has been no such situation, but that Bhagwan has allowed her and her family "to spend life according to what we've been able to get."

One important reason people limit desires and ambitious is the tensions that expectations often produce. Although Gurkeerat Singh, the 49-year-old Sikh, works long hours, he says he doesn't believe in "running after money [hapar tapar]" because this only creates "more tensions [English] which creates problems." For Gurkeerat "controlling our wishes [ichcha] and needs" diminishes tensions. "When a person's needs [zarurat] are less, tensions are less, too." Recognizing that in India "tensions emerge from many directions," Raj Pattial counsels that "to not be in tension, you must not give attention to tensions." Raj describes for me the Indian concept of *jugaad*—making something work with whatever means possible (see Jeffrey 2010, 204). For Raj, focusing on jugaad and *chalta* (to move things along) allows people to "not take tensions as tensions whatever the tensions may be." Raj goes on to describe how the happiest people see their "shortcomings as strengths." As an example he describes the director who makes many movies all of which are flops. Rather than worrying about making more successful films, Raj says that person should just say "OK, I'm a flop maker." "Or if you're alone," Raj says, "accept that and have no tension. Be peaceful. Take this weakness as strengths." Raj sings me a line from a Hindi film song—*mai zindagi ka vakt ko chala gaya/har fakr ko dui me*—to highlight that as life goes on, our worries go up in smoke. When I suggest to Raj that he has a lot of well-being, he says he would "never say that" because "when you're in a good mood, one day a bad mood will come back" just as "when you are in a bad mood, a good mood will come back." He, then, translates a line from the Gita into English, which he said, illustrated this principle: "Whatever you do, whatever you get, just do the deeds in your life." Raj's approach to well-being relies on his own experiences, Hindi film songs, and respected religious texts. Well-being arises for Raj, not just from his joys of doing for others, eating good food, and exploring mountainous areas, but from taking an approach of not paying attention to tensions. Raj is able to maintain well-being in the face of difficulties by seeing even shortcomings as strengths and by recognizing that a good mood is sure to follow a bad mood.

Staying Level, Staying Balanced

Many people recognize that well-being comes from balance between different life spheres—that over-emphasizing one aspect of life often brings trouble. Yakin Kaur, a 43-year-old woman who takes in tailoring work, says in life there should be balance (*samman*, lit. equality) financially, physically, and mentally. Yash Singh relies on meditation to help him have peace of mind, but emphasizes that you only need to do meditation for a half hour a day—"you don't need to become a priest or perform a fire sacrifice." Raj Pattial similarly values religion, but counsels against an overemphasis on religion:

Being religious is a good thing. Being devoted to God can only give you good things. You must have noted that there is enjoyment in church, is it not? You're listening to your guru, you get a feeling inside that's different from your normal feeling. Even if you have 5 lakhs of rupees behind in credit, for that period, you will think "no problem, it's fine." So, being religious is not a problem, but being over-religious is: like wearing yellow clothes and babas and all that—you must have seen that in all India. That is a problem.

Yakin, Yash, and Raj all emphasize that one should stay balanced, rather than investing too much in one sphere of life.

Others emphasize avoiding becoming either too excited or too down about life. Bhagat Kumar, a 70-year-old laborer who said that he's never had great happiness (khushi), focused on recognizing the inevitable ups and downs of life: "In life, there are downs and ups.... When there is too much [zyaada] khushi, we shouldn't start jumping up and down and when things are down [niche] we shouldn't cry, either." Bhagat emphasizes remaining content with what he has: "My only motive is to remain content [santusht rahana]. I don't want to get turned up with my neighbors having this or having that. Lust for anything has no priority for me."

Fareed Khan, a 58-year-old fruit seller, lamented the pains of being too invested in his children. Fareed, who described love between family members as bringing khushhali even when all one has to eat is sauce, told me that when his son was born he was "extremely happy, extremely [bahut zyaada khushi, bahut zyaada]." But he quickly adds that he should not have been so happy and he started crying:

> I should not have been that happy because the Almighty is witness to it that whenever there is extreme happiness in someone's life, a sudden sorrow [gam] arrives the next moment, spoiling your happiness [khushi]. Too much happiness is not good. It's right [sahi] to remain level. The stationary level of happiness is much better. Stationary. Moderate.

Fareed lamented that the disobedience of children has become rampant and hurts the head (mukhya) of the family. He says that the woe (gam) has now become great (zyaada) as his son has gone to his wife's parents' house, abandoning him on Id, the festival day when Muslims normally remain very happy. Fareed is crying so much that I work with Narendra Sethi to be sure that he knows he doesn't need to continue the interview. Fareed says that his heart has been lightened from talking and he is grateful. He says he is thankful for the moral support of his daughters. In the midst of his pain, Fareed sees that he wants to try to be "level," "moderate" or "stationary" in his attachment to his sweet relationships, because his son may leave to go to his wife's house during a festival season. Narendra Sethi and I may have been witnessing Fareed's development of an approach to handle sorrows that have just arisen after his son's wedding.

Positive Attitude

As I show in the last chapter, the approach of many Indians is to maintain a positive outlook to cultivate good relationships. Thirty-year-old Ravi Chuhra aims to "always be cheerful," to maintain a "fresh mood" and to avoid carrying any conflicts into his relationship with others. As Armaan Singh says, "if you're happy, everyone is happy." Sixty-one-year-old Lakshman Negi focuses on maintaining a peaceful nature and "saying sweet words." "Hurtful words," he says, "spreads unhappiness," but "if you're clean and happy, everyone will be clean and happy." Forty-eight-year-old Niranjan Kamboj similarly says that if he lets himself experience unhappiness, he will see all the people sad, but if he is happy, everyone is happy. As 70-year-old medical doctor Om Sharma puts it, "khushhali comes from behaving good with others, helping others, thinking good of others, never thinking bad of others, not keeping jealousy [English] with others, never having ill [*buri*] feelings [English] with others."

Prakash Tyagi emphasizes that each day is a new elegance. He approaches the beauties of the world with a sense of wonder. I, too, find that you can will a focus on the beauty of the natural world. Indian philosopher Daya Krishna (1989, 194–95) says that one can "become increasingly aware of" the "transcendent pole of life" and "love it or be overawed by it." There exists, he says, "the world of colours and sounds and tastes and smells. And there remains the world of imagination where these are transmuted into a realm where beauty reigns supreme." Krishna (1989, 195) says that communicating with others about this beauty can intensify the significance of such beauties. As Krishna (1989, 195) says, a person can make his or her own life—and that of others—a heaven or a hell. That is why Prakash Tyagi chooses to focus on the beauty of the day.

Meanings and Significance … and Pleasures

Finding an approach to life is a key to well-being. There are many approaches we could take: Some find meaning at striving to their potential; some find meaning by seeing well-being as coming from a state of mind. Even if people's meanings and approaches change, the ability to find meaning in life often lasts. People who continue to find meanings despite changed and changing circumstances experience well-being.

But an approach is not all we need for well-being. We also need pleasures, especially of the body and especially that escape the day-to-day. There are many pleasures that provide such an escape: For some, pleasure comes from singing, for others, it's running; for some, it's following the Giants, for others, it's dancing. But no pleasures really stand out much above others—what is needed is pleasures that are bodily, that separate us from day-to-day trials, and that usually connect us to others.

I find it fruitful to discuss both meanings and pleasures together to highlight the importance of the joys of the mind (which are so often associated with meanings) and of the body (which are so often associated with pleasures). An important theme of this book is the contradictory nature of well-being. A person needs meaning, but bodily pleasures provide well-being, too. Even though I want to discuss pleasures *alongside meanings* to highlight some aspects of the contradictory nature of well-being, I'm going to do it in a separate chapter—the next one—to give the reader a chance to relax (maybe take a break, have some pleasure). Reader, refresh the mind. Do some hula. Have a cup of tea. Take a nap. Have some bodily pleasures before continuing. Come back refreshed.

References

Achor, Shawn. 2010. *The Happiness Advantage: The Seven Principles of Positive Psychology that Fuel Success and Performance at Work.* New York, NY: Crown.

Becker, Judith. 2004. *Deep Listeners: Music, Emotion, and Trancing.* Bloomington, IN: Indiana University Press.

Bok, Derek. 2010. *The Politics of Happiness: What Government Can Learn from the New Research on Well-being.* Princeton, NJ: Princeton University Press.

Diener, Ed. 1984 [2009]. "Subjective Well-Being." In *The Science of Well-Being: The Collected Works of Ed Diener*, 11–58. New York, NY: Springer.

Durkheim, Emile. 1912 [1915]. *The Elementary Forms of the Religious Life*. (Tr. Joseph Ward Swain.) New York, NY: Free Press.

Geertz, Clifford. 1966 [1973]. "Religion as a Cultural System." In *The Interpretation of Cultures*, 87–125. New York, NY: Basic Books.

James, William. 1902. *The Varieties of Religious Experience: A Study in Human Nature*. New York, NY: Penguin, 1982.

Jeffrey, Craig. 2010. "Demoralizing Developments: Ethics, Class, and Student Power in Modern North India." In *Ethical Life in South Asia*, edited by Anand Pandian and Daud Ali, 192–208. Bloomington: NY Indiana University Press.

Kim-Prieto, Chu and Ed Diener. 2009. Religion as a Source of Variation in the Experience of Positive and Negative Emotions. *Journal of Positive Psychology* 4(6): 447–60.

Kinsley, David R. 1982. *Hinduism: A Cultural Perspective*. Englewood Cliffs, NJ: Prentice Hall.

Krishna, Daya. 1989. *The Art of the Conceptual*. New Delhi: Indian Council of Philosophical Research.

McRae, Michael. 1993. *"Farang* Correspondent." In *Travelers' Tales Thailand*, edited by James O'Reilly and Larry Habegger, 245–55. San Francisco, CA: Travelers Tales.

Myers, David G. 2008. "Religion and Human Flourishing." In *The Science of Subjective Well-Being*, edited by Michael Eid and Randy J. Larsen, 323–41. New York, NY: Guilford.

O'Flaherty, Wendy Doniger. 1973. *Siva: The Erotic Ascetic*. Oxford: Oxford University Press

Sharma, Arvind. 2005. *Modern Hindu Thought: An Introduction*. Delhi: Oxford University Press.

Steger, Michael F., Shigehiro Oishi, and Todd B Kashdan. 2009. "Meaning in Life Across the Life Span: Levels and Correlates of Meaning in Life from Emerging Adulthood to Older Adulthood." *Journal of Positive Psychology* 4(1): 43–52.

Tatarkiewicz, W. 1976. *Analysis of Happiness*. The Hague: Martinus Nijhoff.

Tov, William and Ed Diener. (2008) 2009. "The Well-Being of Nations: Linking Together Trust, Cooperation and Democracy." In *The Science of Well-Being: The Collected Works of Ed Diener*, edited by Ed Diener, 153–173. New York, NY: Springer.

Vaillant, George E. 2002. *Aging Well: Surprising Guideposts to a Happier Life from the Landmark Harvard Study of Adult Development*. Boston, MA: Little Brown.

Varma, Pavan K. 2001. *The Book of Krishna*. New Delhi: Penguin.

5

PLEASURE

I'm at spring training, getting away from work. I sleep well. I don't know where I am in a strange bed—but not the kind of strange bed where you wake up with someone else! Coffee tastes better waking up in some strange place. Does it seem like Rome or Florence even though guys are walking around in bowling shoes going to their Camaros? The previous week, my students had talked about [a dance called] the Harlem shake. They had been buzzing, intensely interacting with each other, laughing before class. I let it go on. Afterwards we talked about why they found it rewarding. They mentioned the Harlem Shake is interactive, bodily. A student opened his computer to instruct me in the Harlem Shake. "It's just crazy; it's wild; it's done for no purpose," he said. On the ride to the airport, our longtime cabby—from Romania—was playing classical music. My wife asked him whether he sang, too. He played us some folk Romani music and sang for us in a beautiful voice. But he said he needed to mark out time separate from work to do the singing. He talked of how his best singing was when he was young, living in Ceausescu's Romania.

—The author's personal journal, February 27, 2013, Phoenix, Arizona

Om Sharma, a 70-year-old, gets well-being from the satisfaction of practicing medicine. Slow to respond when asked about a particular situation that gave him well-being, Om finally says "there are many times a patient is cured and that brings happiness." But Om seems to emphasize even more that it is sweet relations with others that lead to well-being: "Khushhali comes from behaving well with others, helping others, thinking good of others, never thinking bad of others, not keeping jealousy [E] with others, never having ill

[*buri*] feelings [E] with others." Such sweet relations create a positive chain of well-being. Om has an approach to life, too, that helps
him stay well. He eschews focus on money, saying "finance always
gives trouble." There have been many times, he says, "when I was
sad [dukhi]. I have diabetes and I feel weak and this gives mental
depression [English phrase]." But Om's focus on God helps him
get through these troubles: "Being spiritual [E] helps. Everything
depends on Ishwar [God]. Nothing is in our own hands. Whether it is
good [*achcha*] or bad [*bura*], all is fine [*thik*]." Om, thus, recognizes
the sources of well-being I've discussed thus far—health, meaningful work, sweet ties to other people, and a felicitous approach to life.

But there is something else that anchors Om's well-being—regular
pleasure. For Om, singing and listening to music is a delight: "I love
vocal music, both listening and singing." Every day, he listens to *bhajans* on the radio and he delights in the opportunity to sing. Everyday
pleasures are a direct source of well-being and also help get through
life's inevitable troubles. A variety of pleasures provide well-being.
"Whatever gives the mind [*man*] peace [*shanti*]," Om recognizes, "is
actually the source of khushhali."

Pleasures which also include bathing, food, sex, sleep, wandering, gardening, exercise, experiencing nature, and watching film or
sports—often provide well-being because they *separate us from day-
to-day lives*, especially work and troubles—at least briefly. Often (but
not always) *pleasures are bodily*—very different from the pleasures
of the mind discussed in the last chapter. Pleasures often (but not
always) *empty the mind* rather than use the mind to understand what
it all means. Sometimes pleasure *pleases the self*; sometimes pleasure
ushers in a *different mode of consciousness*, one that *connects us to
everything*. Whether pleasures are of the mind or the body, whether
pleasures put us in touch with self or with a mode of consciousness
that recognizes the unity of all things, may have something to do
with our day-to-day life. Since a key aspect of pleasure is separation
from the day to day, those with few social connections in their daily
life may find more connections in pleasures, while those who are
engulfed in tight networks of people may find pleasure of the self in
their escapes. Those who live in the world of the mind may touch the
body in their pleasures, while those whose day to day involves bodily
work may touch the mind.

Sometimes pleasures (alcohol, tobacco, even playing cricket) interfere with our connections with others by taking us away from our social obligations. The meaningless and self-focus of pleasures is in tension with obligations to other people. Pleasures are an important part of the good life, but as with work and connections, there needs to be *balance*. You can have too much of a good thing (just as you can have too much of a bad thing!). Work is good, but too much work doesn't provide well-being. Connections are good, but we also need time alone. Any of the pleasures described in this chapter can swamp life, showing the importance of balance between different spheres of activity that make up well-being. Gurkeerat Singh works hard, which is why he has to warn himself that there is no well-being in toiling hard and running in the sun. He needs to make time for the pleasures of food and prayer and festivals. Yash Singh, the 58-year-old pakora maker who finds that meditation allows his "mind" to rest, also "likes" to drink a little sharaab (alcohol) after work—it's another way that he rests the mind. But he emphasizes that he never drinks "on the job," but only at the end of the day. Focusing on pleasures shows the tension between pleasures of the self and obligations to others, pleasures of the mind and pleasures of the body, contributing meaningfully and engaging in meaningless fun.

Because an interview is an activity of the mind, pleasures come up rarely and usually in the interstices of the interview, such as when I asked about shaukh (hobbies) or pilgrimage. In talking about their shaukh, people were not strictly talking about well-being, although I prefaced the question by asking about hobbies that lead to well-being. Talking about shaukh seemed to provide a little break from the "heavier" discussion of well-being itself. On a few occasions, I interviewed people precisely because I had seen them enjoying bathing, exercising, or creating artwork, a poem or a piece of furniture. On these occasions, I was usually disappointed: In an interview, people did not discuss these things, which I had observed giving well-being. In one instance, I had not taken my voice recorder with me because I was going to a dinner at a friend's house. At my friend's insistence, I interviewed one of his friends without a voice recorder. He talked about the pleasure of bathing every day in the river near his home soon after awakening. But when I returned the next day with voice recorder in hand, none of this came up in the interview. At first I thought I was unlucky that I didn't take my voice recorder with me to the party. But later I realized it was lucky I hadn't: If I'd pulled out the recorder he never would have told me the story about bathing—and I never would have visited that fantastic bathing place. I almost always kept my small voice recorder in my pocket. The fact that I hadn't brought it with me shows one important part about pleasures—they're outside work. I knew I was going to a *friend's* house, so I wasn't "at work" at the time.

Sometimes, paying attention to people's *faces* is more important than *what people say in interviews*—a theme I take up in Chapter 9. Because of the limitations of interviews in accessing pleasures, this chapter also references day-to-day interactions with people, secondary literature that resonates with what I learned in Dehradun, and my own self reflection—I'm aware of the pleasures of sex, bathing, good food, a good sleep, travel, exercise, and following the 2010 World Series champion San Francisco Giants—to understand how pleasure provides well-being. Because I got to know more men well than I did women, and also because I'm a man, my discussion of pleasures may have only a limited understanding of women's experiences.

It was only because I knew Armaan Singh outside of interviews that I knew about how his pleasures contribute to his well-being. In responding to interview questions, Armaan focused on health, wealth, and esteem as the source of well-being and said the body is nothing. But each day he enjoyed roaring away from his shop on his motorcycle to have a delicious alu parantha at his favorite *dhaaba*. Armaan smiled large with exaggerated animation as he interacted with young customers or watched cricket with youngsters and neighbors. Armaan delighted to tell me about Hindi filmgoing experience he enjoyed. Pretending to flirt with the teenage girls who come to his shop and call him uncle, he dances, smiles, and rolls his finger, whispering to me about the masti (joie de vivre) of the old man. In talking about the importance of health, he mentions how hijras can't have sex, perhaps the only time a bodily pleasure came up in the interviews I did with him—and, then, only indirectly. Recognizing that Armaan is a mauj and masti individual (that is, an individual with joie-de-vivre who enjoys life) highlights how you can often learn more from faces than you can from formal interviews—at least when it comes to pleasures. I should also highlight, of course, that the sources of well-being that Armaan talks about in the formal interviews—health, wealth, social connections, and meanings—are *also* part of his well-being. But the pleasures discussed in this chapter are an important part of his well-being, too.

After I conducted the 2007 interviews, I directed three senior seminars in which my undergraduate students conducted similar interviews about well-being with respondents in the USA. One student, Patrick Maney (2010), argued that physical sensations were a source of well-being that were neglected in interviews. His insight was based on his own subjective understanding of well-being. He subsequently did further interviews for a senior thesis that showed how physical sensations were important to people's well-being, even though they rarely came up in interviews using the questions I used in India and my students used in the USA. I describe Maney's work to highlight three things. First, his work shows that when you ask about physical sensations, people *do* recognize they cause well-being. Second, one of the concluding themes of this book is how this work on well-being connects me to both my teachers and my students. Maney developed a research question from absences in our interview schedule. Thus, Maney was engaged in the "Great Cycle of Explanation" (Wallace 1971) which I first learned about from Claude Fischer, one of my first mentors, who taught me sociological methodology. Thus, there is a connection that links my mentor's teaching, my work and teaching, and my student's work. This serves to highlight the links of well-being between teachers and students. In this book, I'm getting well-being recognizing my mentors and also in recognizing my students' accomplishments. Finally, Maney's findings show that open-ended interviews often have a bias toward the mind and the meaningful, the sources of well-being addressed in the last chapter, but may neglect pleasures.

Another student, Brooke Adams (2010) found that undergraduate students who were not on school athletic teams were more likely to volunteer physical exercise as a source of well-being in open-ended interviews than were students who were on school athletic teams. Her paper "Team Work?: The Effects of Structured Leisure Time on Well-being" suggested that when something becomes like work, such as taking on the obligations of being on an athletic team, the associated pleasures contribute less to well-being. The pleasures discussed in this chapter often provide well-being by taking one away from one's work. When exercise becomes work, it loses some of its fun. Adams's paper again shows how one can theorize from the data generated, part of the cycle of explanation I learned from Claude Fischer. Adams's findings show the importance of pleasures outside of work as a fundamental part of the good life.

Purposeless, Emptying the Mind, Moving Away from Day-to-Day Concerns

A key part of many of the pleasures discussed in this chapter is emptying the mind. Niranjan Kamboj, a 48-year-old, describes how the pleasures of festivals or temple-going include forgetting himself. When he hears the tantalizing sound of the bell, he enters a "zero zone" in which the "mind goes to zero." He forgets everything except God. When talking about going on pilgrimage or to temple, the widow Tavleen Kaur, like many others, describes how her "mind" gets "peace." Because meditation calms his mind, Yash Singh, the 58-year-old pakora maker, isn't bothered by troubles, such as his employees' misdeeds. When asked about *khushhali*, Gaura Khanna, the 70-year-old with a passion for teaching, emphasized ceasing to think: "When I think nothing, I feel happy. What I feel when my brain is vacant I cannot express in words." She enjoys singing in her "own way," and reading spiritual books, both of which put her mind at peace. Another 32-year-old teacher says that while things like listening to music can make her happy, "doing nothing makes my mind happy [khush] as well." One day Gurkeerat Singh was looking happy and I asked him why. He replied that he was just happy and didn't know the reason.

In my college years, we used to call movements without a purpose "actionless activity." These days, I go on a morning run, with temple bells ringing in my pocket, bells I tie atop a local hill, to ring in honor of Lord Shiva. The bells help me enter that zero zone where the mind calms. Actionless activity is important because we so often have a purpose. Indians often repeat the Gita's sentiment that one should do one's actions without regard for the fruits, showing how nice it is to get away from the purposeful. "Hey, I got nothing to do today but smile, da-n-da-n-da–da and here I am.... Half of the time we're gone and we don't know where and we don't know where." (On researching this lyric, I found someone gave this comment on YouTube: "Ain't it the truth. Or maybe it's a half truth. Maybe we're *always* gone and we don't know where." There's the mystic talking in that one—if your self and purposes are gone all the time, you're not in this world; you're a mystic.) In college, a scrawled crayon sign above my door said "don't think" and even today I enjoy the emptiness of those long plane rides and the blue of airports. Moving without a purpose, without pursuing a goal, doing nothing, and finding a way to empty the self are ways of getting into the moment. Many of the pleasures discussed in this chapter—eating, sleeping, walking, reading, listening to music, playing sports, exercising, watching television, joking, drinking, and engaging in religious ritual—have the pleasurable effect of calming the mind. "Hello, lamppost, what cha knowin', I've come to watch your flowers growin', ain't cha got no rhymes for me, doot-in' doo doo, feelin' groovy."

One gets away from work responsibilities, but also from the self one has to present at work. Work is a source of well-being; pleasures provide well-being because they move us away from work, away from the purposeful. Philosophers, economists, and social scientists, all realize work can detract from the good life. The young Marx (1844, 74) in Paris wrote that because labor is "external to the worker," the worker denies, rather than affirms the self, "does not feel content, but unhappy, does not develop freely … physical and mental energy but mortifies" body and mind. Keynes (1932, 370) knew how difficult it is to embrace the moment, making each day a work of art, but still critiqued purposive people who find well-being in tomorrow, rather than today. For the purposive person, Keynes says, "jam is not jam unless it is a case of jam tomorrow and never jam today." Or Janis Joplin: "If you got it today you don't want it tomorrow, man, 'cause you don't need it,' cause as a matter of fact, as we discovered in the train, tomorrow never happens, man. It's all the same fucking day."

Philosophers, thinkers, and singers understand the importance of getting away form work; so do hard-working Indians. When Meenu asked 37-year–old laborer Komal Kumar about her purpose in life she says simply: "It would be enough if I could find some work in which I could get some free time to take a rest." When Meenu asks 68-year-old laborer Vashisht Kumar whether he's done any pilgrimages, he replies that he's done nothing like that since he never gets "free time [phursut] from my work. Unless I'm sick, I don't take any vacation [*chuti*] because I have to earn each and every day." Harish Misrha, the 40-year-old businessman who looks forward to being greeted by his family whenever he returns home, emphasizes that he lives "happily all the time" because he lives for today: "The key to well-being [khushhali] is to think that I may die tomorrow. That is why I'm living to day." Harish takes the approach urged by Keynes and Prakash Tyagi—savor each day.

Victor Turner (1969) argued that rituals often reverse day-to-day realities, providing people with a "liminal" period outside of the usual structures of life. Rituals refresh people for a return to day-to-day realities of economic and family structures. Many of the pleasures discussed in this chapter work this way. Instead of focusing on obligations to others or on worklife, people can enjoy the pleasures of a meal, a bath, sex, reading a book, or listening to music. Instead of being encompassed in tight relationships, one gets a chance to have solitude. Instead of living with purpose, one enjoys purposelessness. Pleasures refresh for a return to the day-to-day and provide well-being.

A theme of this book—consistent with Turner—is that one needs *both* work and pleasure. It's *too much* work that harms well-being. And well-being is sapped by *too much* pleasure, too. One needs back and forth between work and play. Recognizing people need *both* work and pleasure makes well-being a real possibility. Keynes (1932, 366–67) said humans could only look forward "to the age of leisure and abundance" with dread because so few of us would know what to do with our leisure. Singers will find leisure "tolerable—and how few of us can sing." But we don't need to sing *well*—and we won't get pleasure singing all the time (that would make it work!). Rather, we need both work *and* pleasure.

Using psychoanalytic thinking, Norman O. Brown (1959, 53) suggested humankind "will not cease from discontent and sickness until the antimony of economics and love, work and play is overcome" (see also Marcuse 1955). For Brown (1959, 38), "our indestructible unconscious desire" is to return to childhood, to return to the pleasure principle that is ruled by delight in all surfaces of the human body. But, for Brown (1959, 38), "childhood cannot be recovered and paradise cannot be regained. For the infantile experience of freedom and absorption in pleasure has a fatal flaw. It has not come to terms with the reality principle" which insists on work and repression. But here Brown is wrong. We don't need to exile work. We only need to make room for pleasure.

Marx (1845–46, 160), too, envisioned a communist society of pleasurable work—hunting in the morning, fishing in the afternoon, and philosophizing after dinner (without thinking too much, as Catharine MacKinnon [1989] rightly points out, about who cooks dinner). Norman Brown (1959, 33) questions Fourier's similar "utopian dream" of "pleasurable work." And, indeed, some necessary work can not be made pleasurable. Is hunting, fishing, and philosophizing all society needs? But if the goal is not to *eliminate* economic activities designed for self-preservation, but to *balance* these activities with purposeless pleasure, provision of well-being (which is, after all, what utopian thinking aims to do) is, I think, a real possibility.

Religious Ritual

Turner's analysis focused on rituals, and indeed Indian rituals and festivals *themselves* provide many of the diverse pleasures, described in this chapter. For many Indians, daily religious ritual, as well as regular (if occasional) festivals, are an important source of pleasure—and well-being. Ritual is particularly multivalent, touching on sources of well-being from previous chapters: People can show they are special with special ritual skills, such as the ability to recite or sing hymns, the strength to do arduous pilgrimages, the resources to sponsor rituals, or the connections to bring people together. People are able to contribute to others—people can give to beggars outside temples and Sikhs are especially proud that everyone can contribute something to langar (ritual serving of food to all visitors at a gurudwara). Rituals are especially important in connecting people to those around them, to their wider families, and to others in the community Rituals also highlight religious meanings that can help get through hard times.

But religious ritual is also a pleasure. Unlike many of the other pleasures mentioned in this chapter, it is a *sanctioned* relief—one that there need be no excuse for. Daily worship and special festivals of Hindus and Sikhs drip with sensuality: bathing, eating, physical contact, and singing. Hindus and Sikhs bathe before daily and festival worship. Sikh gurudwaras always have a place to wash and at Sikh pilgrimage spots one walks through water after removing shoes. Of course at both Hindu temples and Sikh gurudwaras, people remove shoes and experience the pleasures of the often cold (or hot!) marble or brick striking the feet. At Sikh gurudwaras, langar is pressed into hands; at Hindu temples it is prasad (ritual food, first offered to a deity, then consumed by the worshiper) that's pushed into the hands. Eating is a bodily pleasure, as is feeling the food in one's hands. There is jostling with the others at the ritual or ceremony and songs are sung, voices loud, pleasure in voice, and ringing in the ears. Bells vibrate; harmoniums play. Flowers and incense give pleasure to the sense of smell. (I have less personal experience with Islamic rituals—although I witness the throngs moving together at times like Id, and hear the sounds from the mosques. Bellamy [2011] describes the physical experience of smoke and smell at some dargahs.) So, ritual experience includes a mixture of bodily pleasures—food, bathing, sounds, the feel of cold stone on the feet, of food in the hands.

As I hint earlier, I have personal experiences enjoying the pleasure of ritual. My Sikh and Hindu friends invite me for daily and special rituals. Interviewing at gurudwaras, Narendra Sethi and I participate in langar. Interviewing at Hindu temples, we participate of giving and taking of prasad. I have 'fieldwork notes' of many such experiences. Perhaps I'll just tell you my experience of Guru Nanak Jayanti—a festival celebrating the birth of a Sikh Guru. A friend, who knew about my research, invited me to participate, saying I should write a chapter about it. In the leadup, there are firecrackers and a procession to the gurudwara—sounds of explosions, the pleasures of packing tightly together and, always, escape from the day-to-day world. The friend who invited me feels the pressure of business, but says "there's money in his pocket" but he needs "this"—the festival—"to move my heart." The festival morning, my friend enjoys his recitations and has some tea before setting off at a fast pace. Saying he didn't get exercise that morning, we rush to the event. We're a bit late and there's a stampede for *puri bhaji* and tea. We enjoy pressing tightly together and enjoy the food too. Celebrants participate in the giving of langar: donating money, bringing food, cooking food, or serving it. I ask someone at langar if beggars can come to langar, as many are there, and someone tells me, "Yes, that is one of the first things that Guru Nanak said." Leaving the big hall, skipping some speeches, my friend lights up seeing friends he's known since his childhood, 30 years ago. There's talk of Guru Nanak (although perhaps for me!), but more laughing and jokes. When the female school groups start singing in the main hall, we rush back in for a song. Rushing back to the shop at 1:30 PM, my friend works urgently so he can get back for the lights and crowds of the evening festivities. There were meanings in the speeches and in talk among friends. The feeling of community is clearly important as is the feeling of helping others. But the pleasures are important, too: Exercising the body walking quickly to get there; washing at home and, then, before and after *langar*; feeling and eating that sensuous food; the bodily feeling of being close together; and hearing and singing songs.

By providing a liminal time and space away from daily life, rituals provide a vitality that re-energizes everyday life. I could march through Victor Turner's (1969) inspiring work and the work of those he inspired, but given this book's emphasis on celebrating Indian sociology, it's worth noting similar arguments of Calcutta sociologist Benoy Kumar Sarkar (1941, 347–49). Each Hindu ritual, he argues, "serves in the first place to break the monotony of life." Each ritual, he says, "provides the family with a holiday atmosphere. Relaxation from the daily round of conventional duties as well as the leisure to enjoy life in a new setting are two important items associated with each festivity. All festivities are recreational of course." Each ritual, he says, allows people to enjoy art. "A conscious cooperative creativity is in the air." Rituals, he says, help people live "a somewhat enlarged life." Festivals, Sarkar says, provide "seasonal and regular chances for camaraderie" with family and caste mates. There are pleasures and escape from day-to-day to a life enlarged to touch a larger whole.

The first interview Narendra Sethi and I conducted for this project was in October 2007 with Sachin Aggarwal, a 40-year-old man working in a government department and living in a joint-family with his wife, parents, and his two young children. Our first question was "What is the meaning of khushhali?" "It's going to the mandir," Sachin replied. "I get [milna] the most peace [shanti] and khushhali there." I ask Sachin if such peace is lasting and he says: "[W]henever you go to the temple, you will gain peace. [Going to temple] gets rid of any tension [*tanav*], allowing a return to well-being." It turned out to be relatively rare for people to mention visiting temple, gurudwara, or mosque in responding to an initial question about the meaning of well-being, but it was not uncommon for people to mention in the course of the interview the importance of regular visits to a temple or gurudwara.

Many emphasize the peace they get that contrasts with day-to-day pressures. Sukhraj Singh, the 33-year-old newspaper hawker who describes his love for his wife as his main source of khushhali, forgets even that at the gurudwara: "When I get to the gurudwara, I feel like I have no relations, no family and just am in the service of God, chanting guru wahe guru all the way. There are no worries or tensions about the business profits and losses." A 35-year-old Hindu meat-seller, with a master's degree in organic chemistry and living with his parents and wife and two children, mostly focused on earning in discussing well-being and lack of well-being. But, then, he recounted that "in the normal course, pujapath [worship/meditation] keeps on going. I go to the temple in the morning and, after breakfast, come to the shop. This feels good and gives peace [shanti] of mind. I realize God is there." Yash Singh, the 58-year-old Sikh pakora maker, says *pujapath* gives him peace (shanti) of mind (man). Because of pujapath, he never gets any "bad waves of thoughts" in his mind. "By doing *pujapath*, ill-will never arises. If you don't do pujapath, then your mind won't rest in a proper way." Sudhir Kumar, the 18-year-old lower-caste coaching student, tells us he has photographs of gods in his room to remind him of God. He says he gets pleasure on pilgrimages from being with his "own people" and looks forward to Diwali as a festival time when he will see his family again. Sudhir mentions the pressures of his studies, but says that he still finds time for daily *puja*. "I devote five minutes each day to doing puja with God. Through the concentration of puja I get [milna] the utmost happiness [zyaada khushi]." A 60-year-old Hindu housewife living in a family that includes her married son and daughter-in-law says "doing housework means well-being [khushhali] for me." Perhaps it's not insignificant that she continues in the next sentence to mention the peace and happiness of temple-going: "Also, whenever I go to mandir and do pujapath, I feel happy." Kantha Chopra, the 58-year-old who described getting well-being when she gave a shawl to a cold person on a pilgrimage, says for at least a month after a pilgrimage she keeps "discussing it with our friends." Describing herself as a "simple housewife," Kantha, like many women, says she gets happiness from "normal life" activities like the morning walk to the temple: "We get up early in the morning. We say Ram's name, do some pujapath, go to the temple." And in the evening, as I'll describe later in this chapter, Kantha enjoys a walk with her friends.

Some mention *sounds* as important in pulling one away from daily life. Praveen Joshi, a 60-year-old medical doctor, gets khushhali "when we're reciting the guru's name." Praveen especially praises the "magnetic and magical voice" of a guru's bhajan (ritual song). "A person will forget everything and get engrossed in it. Our mind [man] gets completely peaceful [shant]." For Niranjan Kamboj the sounds of the bell on entering the temple helps him forget himself and think only of God:

> As long as we remain in the temple, we forget about ourselves. There are a lot of festivals here. For that time, we forget about ourselves—what we are, what we do, whether we are facing any problem, whether we have to take dinner at home or not. For whatever time we remain in that temple this state continues. *The chime of the bell and the tantalizing sound of the bell takes us to the zero zone* [English phrase]. Our mind goes into zero with the vibrating sound of the bell. We forget everything. Then, there is only God in front of us.

"The energy which we receive by doing this," Niranjan continues, "keeps us fresh and happy." In the last chapter I emphasized how 75-year-old Sukhpreet Singh's reading of Sikh texts helped him cope with his son's death. But the ritual of chanting and the breathing associated with chanting is also a pleasure that leads to satisfaction:

> Any disturbance in the mind is pacified by chanting hymns. I really get satisfaction in that. I chant for the sake of pleasure—for pleasure and satisfaction. Chanting hymns gives complete contentment. My aim is only to do this—to recite God's name. Even with each breath—in and out— you should recite the name of God.

For Sukhpreet, ritual provides both meaning and pleasures. But for many, the absence of thought and the emptying of the mind is most important. Praveen Joshi is so engrossed in a guru's bhajan he forgets everything. Niranjan Kamboj's mind goes to zero and he forgets everything in the vibration of the bell. Gaura Sharma, an alert 70-year-old still working as a lecturer and living with her son and daughter in-law, maintains equanimity. She's never tired, she says, because she doesn't give voice to any tiredness. She's never angry because she just diverts her mind to other things. Gaura says that whenever she goes to the temple she is "empty minded. My mind becomes dumb at that time." On reaching home she sometimes thinks she should have "asked God for such-and-such things. But when I go there, I am totally blank." Meanings are important, but escaping thought is important as well.

Like the anthropologist Turner and the sociologist Sarkar, the Indians I interviewed know that ritual is a pleasure of life. Rituals are especially important to break from day to day. But many activities— exercise, filmgoing, bathing, or dancing—provide similar relief outside the religious context.

Bahri Alang: Pleasure as Multiple, Bodily, and a Separate Way of Feeling and Thinking

Nita Kumar's (1986) classic article, "Urban Space and Free Time: Pleasures for the People of Banaras" is a touchstone study of well-being in India. I was in India and subscribing to *Contributions to Indian Sociology* when it came out, so I was perhaps one of the first people to read it! Kumar's analysis resonated with my experiences in Banaras, the city in which I was then living. Kumar focuses on male artisans in Banaras to describe the pleasures of *bahri alang*—going outside. The daily bahri alang ritual starts by moving to a lonely place outside the crowded city lanes. The place should be open, quiet, well-watered, and with the appropriate stones—some used to beat clothes against, some used to grind *bhang* (a hashish mixture), some used to squat on to "do latrine." Once outside, the first task is to wash clothes vigorously with lots of soap, making them very clean. Next the reveler grinds and strains bhang very fine and makes a drink out of it with milk or fruit juice (or drinks it dry as a ball). The bhang acts as a laxative and "nature calls." After doing latrine, the reveler massages himself with oil and exercises (for instance doing push ups and situps). Then comes the bath, usually involving "repeated immersion." By this time, the clothes washed at the beginning have dried. The reveler winds homeward, perhaps stopping to have paan [a betel leaf mixture], comb hair, or put on *tika* and *kajal* (Kumar 1986, 40, 50–51). Bahri alang, a secular ritual, is worth discussing because it highlights characteristics of the range of pleasures described in this chapter.

As with other pleasures, bahri alang's pleasures are *multiple*. Kumar (1986, 41) reports that if you ask people[1] about their *manoranjan* [entertainment] "you hear about a *constellation* of activities." "Foremost among these are: the preparation of bhang, defecation and bathing (*nipatanaa-nahaanaa*), and washing clothes (*saafai lagaanaa*). These are presented under the general rubric of *bahri alang jana* (going to the outside)." Like many pleasures "the rituals of bahri alang are centered on the *body*. It is the body that is given a treat, that is allowed to indulge in sensation, first that of *divya nipatan* (divine defecation), then of cooling and cleansing, and lastly of intoxication" (Kumar 1986, 53). Massage, bath, exercise, and defecation[2] are all bodily pleasures. As Norman Brown (1959, 32) puts it "pleasure is in the active life of the human body." The pleasures are to the individual body; Kumar (1986, 53) describes how "self-indulgence and self-satisfaction" result from bahri alang. Yet she's also right to recognize that the healthy body is also "equivalent to a good person," symbolizing "the highest civilisation and wisdom. Bhang is," she says, "Shiva's prasad" (Kumar 1986, 53).

Bahri alang introduces a *different consciousness or feeling* separate from the day-to-day. Kumar (1986, 52) describes mauj-masti as the distinctive feeling associated with bahri alang:

> Mauj-masti is the sense of freedom and contentment that comes from the *malish* (massage) and the *snan* (bath), the exercise, the *saaf pani* [clean water], the bhang, the outdoors. It means to feel on top of the world and also to feel intoxicated. The swaying walk of an elephant is masti. To have your pan dissolve in your mouth and be able to squirt out a mouthful of juice is masti. To have it drip out of your mouth and onto your clothes is even better! To wear a bright flower garland around your neck, a large tika on your forehead, kajal in your eyes, and perhaps *itra* (perfume) liberally on yourself, is masti. To *forget time* when at bahri alang, when with friends, listening to music is what being mast is all about. (Kumar 1986, 52; my emphasis)

---

[1] Kumar (1986, 31) addresses "Pleasure for the people of Banaras" (the article's subtitle), but also recognizes bahri alang is the "monopoly of males."

[2] In a recent survey (Coffey et al. 2014, 49), 47 percent of respondents say they defecate in the open because it is "pleasurable, comfortable or convenient." Respondents said open defecation provided opportunity for a "morning walk, see[ing] their fields, and tak[ing] in fresh air" (Coffey et al. 2014, 53).

The person is *outdoors—separate from daily life*. "The requisites for a venue are simple, access to water, or river, tank, pond or well; and openness to the sky and fresh air" (Kumar 1986, 42). Nature— as opposed to social life—is a part of bahri alang: Inside is the "complex, crowded city, with its packed lanes and localities and its busy life of men, the venue of *chitas* and *chintas* (cremation pyres and worries)"; outside it is "open, fresh free" (Kumar 1986, 45). And it is a different consciousness outside of daily life: the reveler forgets time and "feels intoxicated."

Sometimes bahri alang is done in *solitude*, but at other times it is done *with friends, in connection to others*. Kumar (1986, 42) describes how bahri alang places should be "places of soli- tude (ekant). Thus, the distinction is not only between outside and inside, but between crowded and quiet." Although bahri alang trips "are essentially individualistic activities, performed in solitude, with the premium on peace," sometimes a person becomes "fed up with being alone" and "goes to bahri alang with friends" (Kumar 1986, 51). At such times, people enjoy "clothes washing *sammelan* [conferences]. Daily bahri alang is often done individually, while seasonal and distant bahri alang tips to nearby places are more often done with others" (Kumar 1986, 51).

Ultimately, bahri alang is just plain fun. Kumar (1986, 53) empha- sizes that *bahri alang* like "most leisure activities" "stresses discipline, and *simultaneously* exemplifies what is considered the profound- est philosophy of life: *the experience of pure play*" (emphases are mine.) Play must be taken in moderation—it must be combined with discipline. But the fundamental element of leisure activity is nonetheless "experience of pure play." The poets recognize play- ful bodily pleasures as the source of delight, as in Blake: "Energy is the only life, and is from the Body.... Energy is Eternal Delight" (quoted in Brown 1959, 31).

Bathing and Grooming

I wanted to interview Hemant Kapoor, the 45-year-old who says his wonderful garden is God's blessing, because of what he told me about bathing. One day in October 2011, a friend—I'll call him Gurmaan— invited me to dinner at his uncle's house in a Dehradun suburb.

We piled into a crowded shared Vikram; people were sitting in each other's laps. The smiles were broad as we enjoyed close contact. Hemant's shop was near the uncle's house and when we arrived, Hemant and Gurmaan's uncle wanted to enjoy sharaab [liquor] (while Gurmaan and myself did our best to ward off the invitation). Hemant wanted to be interviewed when Gurmaan told him about my research. Although I didn't have my recorder, I conducted a sort of an interview. In thinking about well-being, the first thing Hemant mentioned was bathing in the river with his friends each day before breakfast. Then, Gurmaan's uncle said, "Wait until you see his garden, then you'll know about well-being." Before returning to Dehradun, Gurmaan and I were taken to Hemant's amazing garden and house. Gurmaan's uncle introduced me to Hemant's wife and said that she is the *Lakshmi* (goddess of prosperity) of the house and that Hemant gets well-being from this, too. Hemant agrees, but I think that in the interview, he only mentioned bathing.

Excited by Hemant's interview, I traveled out to see him in a private rickshaw the next day. But with the voice recorder rolling, Hemant does not mention bathing when asked about *khushhIali*, but instead mentions India's development!

> First our country should be in a happy state [*khushhal*]. If our country is happy, our state of Uttarakhand will also be happy. By this our state will also progress and in this way we'll be marching ahead. Our country, our state, our culture all are well. Then, this situation provides us happiness.

At the end of the interview, I ask about his pleasure from bathing and he provides a full account in a sentence, connecting bathing with meditation, meeting friends and cracking jokes:

> We go in the morning to that place, we do bathing-meditation [*snan-dhyan*], meet friends, crack jokes and the atmosphere of happiness forms.

Hemant invited me to dinner that night. Before I returned to Dehradun, his son took me on his motorcycle to that bathing place—a temple is nearby for morning worship, a hot spring bubbles up to make the stream warm. It is wonderful. I enjoy roaring on the motorcycle to the bathing spot, back to Dehradun, and later back to Hemant's house in the evening. Again, alcohol is flowing for the men and there is pressure to drink it ("it's our way of welcoming you"). The evening goes long and I eat early—10 PM. The women of the household are happy—and anxious—to see me enjoying the food. Hemant's daughters and wife beam and ask me back—but can I really know from their faces that this is a pleasure for them? The party is going on, but Hemant and Gurmaan's uncle interrupt to walk me through the streets to their car to drive me (yes, drunkenly, through empty streets) back to the city.

Bathing is not a big part of the discourse of well-being, so it doesn't tend to come up in a formal interview. Why Hemant mentioned bathing—and only bathing—when I first asked him about well-being without a voice-recorder on, I don't know. Bathing is a pleasure of the body. It's a ritual pleasure that is done at the same regular time. It's a pleasure outside of the usual purposes and meanings of life. It's a pleasure outside of day-to-day work. It can be combined with other pleasures, such as singing, worshiping, meditating, meeting friends, cracking jokes, and laughing. It's part of many other aspects of Hemant's well-being—a wonderful house, feelings of specialness about building his house, gardening, eating good food, having a happy family, welcoming guests, drinking alcohol, roaring around on a motorcycle, wandering drunk through the streets, and driving a wobbly car back to Steve Derné's "Hotel Heritage" (where because the US dollar rocks! rent is less than US$10/night—I thought those days were over for me!).

Bathing is one of my great pleasures, too (see Derné 1998). A day starts with a great shower (except in India where it starts with pouring water from buckets over my head! That is, it's still great but not a shower.) In India I enjoy bathing after a run and after breakfast. I enjoy washing my running clothes and wringing them out to dry. It's a sensuous, bodily ritual experience.

Life in India is full of such small pleasures of the body. One day in October, I took a holiday after writing work. I talked with my wife on skype. I had a good run. I had a great breakfast. I watched a baseball game on mlb.tv. I visited with two friends who had had me over for Diwali meals (yes, Diwali was early that year). I went shopping with Meenu Sharma for a birthday present for my wife and was able to get Meenu a shawl as well. But the thing that really made it a holiday was a haircut. You sit in the chair—you're the special one.

All attention is paid to you. And at the end, the barber massages your head—an extreme pleasure of the body. After that pleasure, I couldn't help smiling the rest of the day. And I couldn't help smiling every time I walked by the hair salon. While the pleasure is in the body, the *interactional nature of well-being* is apparent in how my barber and I smiled at each other every day. Some men in India are shaved most mornings—and I even see modest outdoor hair salons operating early enough for my morning run. The hair salon where I go to have my haircut is full of smiling faces (along with a small black-and-white TV with old Hindi films playing). I considered interviewing the barber—who always waves as I go by—to better understand the pleasures people get from being groomed. But I figured there was really no need. I could see it in the faces.

A pleasure, like getting a haircut, puts a person in the moment, not thinking of past or future. It's a good on its own with no connection to meaning or purpose. This had such a big effect on me, I was sure I'd remember it—I just put "great haircut–pleasures of the body" in my personal journal. But when it came time to write about it, I had trouble conjuring up all that happened—I remember now barber's massage created a ring with his hands that circled around my head. I found an email to my friends called "Stevie D's vacation," but it just said that there was a great massage after the haircut. I assumed I'd remember it all, but I didn't. This highlights a characteristic of pleasures—one is often in the moment, in the flow, not thinking about past or future (Csikszentimhalyi 1975, 1990; Walker 2010), not putting pleasure into words, but just experiencing pleasure.

I've discussed my own experiences to highlight the importance of small pleasures of the body (eyes closed, feeling yourself being shaved, feeling the various creams on the face, feeling the head massage and the back massage)—pleasures not mentioned in interviews (no one mentioned a good shave or a good haircut, although they are surely a source of well-being). My discussion also highlights how pleasures take a person away from the day-to-day work. Having a haircut and watching a ball game and talking to my wife on skype was a holiday from writing this book! This discussion also highlights how often pleasures are combined with other pleasures. My smiling interactions with my barber, my feeling of being special at the barber's, and watching Hindi films while waiting my turn are all part of the pleasure—and this pleasure is *combined* with other pleasures: watching baseball, calling my wife, eating good food, meeting with my friends, and shopping for gifts for my friends and coworkers.

Being well groomed also provides well-being by connecting someone to others. People will praise my "look" after a haircut and I'll praise others, too. When people learn I have a camera, they often want to strike a pose and clamor for a print (easily done now that it's all digital). In earlier eras, going to theaters was a special time and men would be sure they were looking good, often admiring themselves in the shiny cinema-hall mirrors (Derné 2000). Among the people I interviewed for the well-being study, a 22-year-old beautician mentioned "wearing good clothes" as her hobby, while a 40-year-old lawyer described his hobby as "wearing brand clothes." Marx (1844, 74) mocks workers who are only "freely active" in animal functions— eating, drinking, procreating, or at most in [their] dwelling and in dressing up." For Marx, creativity is necessary for freedom. But animal pleasures—eating, drinking, bathing, or procreating—as well as the pleasure of dressing up are pleasures, too and provide well-being. And, indeed, dressing up, eating, drinking, and procreating can all be creative, too. Marx needed a bit more imagination!

Kumar's article and my discussion here focus on men's experiences of bathing and grooming. I don't have as many windows onto the world of experiences for women. It's long been said—and I don't know if it's true—that in the days when women were confined to the home, women enjoyed interacting each other each day as they awoke before dawn to go outside and defecate and urinate.[3] There appear to be nearly as many beauty parlors in India as there are men's hair dressers. Although I haven't seen any cheap outdoor parlors catering to women, some beauticians who lack the English skills needed to work in salons go to the houses of clients to apply beauty treatment, suggesting there may be lower-cost alternatives for women that parallel the outdoor-shaving "establishments" men can frequent. Narendra Sethi and I interviewed two women in the beauty salon in which they worked (beauty salons have signs that say "ladies only," but a female shopkeeper whom we were interviewing suggested we interview her friends in the salon and we went right over). The women seemed to

---

[3] In one recent survey, Nepali respondents (whose gender is not given) "lauded open defecation as wholesome, healthy, and social" (my emphasis) (*Economist* 2014).

have personalities like my barber—refreshing and engaging. So, it's possible that the beauty parlor and bathing rituals are pleasures for women, as well. Because my discussion of men's pleasures is so often based not on interviews but fieldwork and observation that I didn't have opportunities to do with women because of ongoing, if diminishing, gender segregation in India, a full exploration of women's pleasures awaits a woman scholar who might explore these issues. (This shows, again, the value of the "cycle of explanation" I learned from Claude Fischer.)

Wandering, Walking, Exercising

Going outside is a key pleasure of bahri alang. In Banaras, revelers sometimes hire a boat to go to the far side of the river. Because it floods during the monsoon, the far side is a sandy stretch, devoid of habitation, 100 meters wide in the dry season. When I lived there in the 1980s, people crossed the river to bathe and wash clothes and to escape the city; I was among those revelers. More commonly, people go for a lonely stroll in one's locality. *Going outside*, perhaps the fundamental experience of bahri alang, is captured with the words ghumna-phirna—strolling or wandering. "In their free time," Kumar (1986, 44) reports, people "like to indulge in ghumna-phirna: to stroll in the *gali*s (narrow lanes), wander in the bazaars, hang around the ghats, visit the temples, take in the ambience of evening lights, bustle and activity."

The *Gummukar Shastra* (*The Shastra of Wandering*, Sankrityayan [1948] 2004), the alternative shastra by Indian wanderer, philosopher, Marxist, polymath, and novelist Rahul Sankrityayan (1893–1963) emphasizes the pleasures of travel and wandering. Ann Gold's (1988) and Sarah Lamb's (2000) ethnographies show villagers of even modest means going on extensive pilgrimages. Sanjay Srivastava's (2005) discussion of the Leave Travel Concessions show how often government servants enjoy travelling. While my interviews indicate many laborers find extensive yatras beyond their means, many nonetheless enjoy going to local temples, gurudwaras, and mosques. I feel cooped up if I don't have a chance to wander. I keep making pilgrimages to India, to warm waters—Hawaii, Samoa, Fiji, Burma, and Baja—to open spaces, like the Sahara and Patagonia, where

I ride horses fast. On my wanders through India, I often meet Indians who enjoy travels, too.

The people whom I interviewed in Dehradun talk about the pleasures of wandering. Rajan Kumar, the 18-year-old coaching student who gets happiness from talking with friends, says that he's been to the hill stations Shimla and Mussoorie and he just "keeps on traveling. By ghumna, I get enjoyment." Raj Pattial, the flashy 18-year-old who enjoys eating food but says the best taste is to help others, describes his experience of most khushhali as when he

> went to Dhanaulti—a place beyond Mussoorie—on a picnic. I like being in a place in mountains. I discovered the place on my own. No one took me to that place. We went to a picnic spot, but I kept climbing. There were construction barriers, but I jumped all that stuff and found an apple orchard. The fragrance of apples was everywhere. That was a special thing—a downsizing. All three sides were mountains, but on the fourth side you could see to Rishikesh and Ganga. It's like AC-air coming on your face. Your face is cool. It's coming and touching you and I'm telling you, yaar, this is the best part you could ever live. You could have chips. You could have coke. You could have whatever you like. Food is the best part, isn't it, la? I like to eat. It's the best thing of living.

Raj's switch to discussing food—which I'll come back to as an important pleasure—is characteristic of the discussion of pleasures—they're multiple. Sachdev Kaur, a 27-year-old, engaged to be married and looking for a job having completed college training in computer applications, says she gets khushhali from meeting and talking with friends and new people. But she also feels very happy when she goes for ghumna-phirna to new places. She says her hobbies are traveling (English), shopping, wearing good dresses, and enjoying life.

Like Raj Pattial's trip to Dhanaulti, ghumna-phirna often involves trips to nature. For me, it's getting to the Sierras, to the Southwest of the USA, to the California coast and desert, to the Pacific Islands, to those Himalayan landscapes. And it all changed in 2014 on a kayak trip to Baja—hearing the dolphins breathing offshore and seeing the phosphorescence in the water at night, pelicans dive-bombing into the ocean, the pink mountains at sunrise dropping into that turquoise blue water. In Dehradun, there's Deer Park with wildlife and landscapes that throngs with people. Natural beauty takes a person out of the day to-day gritty realities. Immersion in natural beauty is a pleasure.

The pleasures of wandering compliment other sources of well-being—good food, good relations, helping others, and earning a living. Govind Kumar, a 71-year-old private-school principal, says khush-hali is primarily a state of mind, which requires means (Chapter 2), but more centrally close relationships (Chapter 3): "Peace [shanti] of the heart [dil] is khushhali. Though money is important [zaruri], more important are friendship [dosti; E] and family relations." Like so many Indians, helping others gives Govind happiness:

> If I move out of my house and I see a man lying outside my house, whether it's because he's a drunkard or because of disease, or whatever reason, I feel sad [dukhi] that my fellow countryman, my brother, my friend is in such a condition. How we can improve this situation is my concern. Happiness [E] can only be obtained when all around is the atmosphere of happiness [E].

But after talking about the well-being that follows from a world that is well, Govind talks about the pleasures he gets from traveling in nature

> I also get happiness [E] from natural [E] surroundings. If we are destroying [dabna] or spoiling [E] nature, happiness [E], will diminish. If we go to Mussoorie our heart feels so soothing that we think of remaining there forever, but we are in the worldly affairs [duniya ka kam], so we have to come back

Govind says that for a "long time" he has wanted to "complete a tour of my own India" because of the "pleasure" of "seeing new places and nature." Govind likes pilgrimages because "through yatra, you get ghumna and you get nature [E]." Govind's well-being can't be pinned down—it comes from money, connections to others, and contributing to others. The pleasures of travel and nature, though, are surely part of Govind's well-being, too.

For many, ghumna-phirna is a refreshing, bodily daily activity, a good in itself. The day after I interviewed him, Armaan Singh spotted me while he walked and shouted that a "morning walk" was key to his well-being. Prakash Tyagi, who was happy that he could still walk to Gandhi Park, highlighted the pleasures of ghumna in just a sentence: "Distance in walking is more charming than the destination," suggesting walking *itself* is the source of well-being. It's being in the moment. It's not thinking about the past or the future. The *destination*—where one is going—has no importance to the pleasures of walking. Pleasures are not about what one is *aiming for*, but rather are goods in themselves. Somendra Mishra, a 47-year-old, like many men his age, focuses on earning money for his family as the main source of his well-being. But when I ask about his shaukh he explains: "The morning walk [E] makes me feel fresh. I concentrate at work well. When I skip ghumna, I feel lethargy." The *bodily* activity of the walk refreshes Somendra to meet the requirements of each day.

For some, walking connects to other people. Tavleen Kaur, the 75-year-old widow, describes her only shaukh as God keeping her fit enough to "keep on walking. I'm very fond of walking." Tavleen's movements are very limited—she spends much time in bed watching television. She says walking refreshes her and takes her to the gurudwara where she glimpses community. Kantha Chopra, the 58-year-old who says for at least a month after a pilgrimage she keeps "discussing it with friends," describes regular pleasure of walking:

> The evening walk gives us happiness. We all come together. Normally, we are four in the group, but today we're only two. I always feel good [achcha lagna] [from our walks].

For Kantha, as for Tavleen, connections with friends are a part of the pleasure of strolling; pleasures often connect with other sources of well-being.

When I reached India August 1, 2011, I'd been running "most days" for more than 11 months. I'd started running the previous August, when my doctor suggested I address high triglycerides. I started for health, but kept running because I loved it. I got new energy. I got out of the house daily. Mostly I ran in Mendon Ponds, a nearby county park, over hilly trails, but, especially in the following summer, I started running in my neighborhood, seeing all the people out on their front porches. I ran all through winter 2010–11 with the yak trax cleats on my running shoes. I ran over the Continental Divide (in New Mexico) and to the Pacific Ocean (from Point Reyes), and on the pavements of Phoenix for spring training. I didn't think I'd continue in India, but I did—smelling incense, hearing temple music, through the crowded streets. My journal describes a run in Dehradun in November: "great morning run, cool mountains out, waving at people, hearing the temple bells and the music, followed by a good cup of tea." Jane Brody (2012) reports when people ask her why she walks, bikes, and swims, she says "weight control" and a "desire to live long and well." Indians don't make excuses for religious ritual and Americans don't need to make excuses for exercise as it's positively sanctioned in the USA. But, Brody admits, weight control and health are not the real reasons she gets

> out of bed before dawn to join friends on a morning walk and then bike to the Y for my swim. It's how theses activities make me feel: more energized, less stressed, more productive, more engaged and, yes, happier—better able to smell the roses and cope with the inevitable frustrations of daily life.

So, it's a ritual of physical pleasure that is a source of well-being

Running through Gandhi Park, I see many Indians enjoying a morning run, squats, yoga, or breathing exercise, sometimes alone, sometimes in a large group under a "shelter." In my hotel, the hotel workers run on the grass or do a snakelike movement to music. Very often on my morning run, I see elderly men and women out for a walk, sometimes together, enjoying the sun and bantering with each other. When I do qi gong exercises on my rooftop each morning, I see a lone woman who does pacing patterns on her own rooftop and a man doing exercises with his arms. One man who used to do morning exercises on his rooftop said he disliked being observed there and, so, began exercising instead in city lanes, suggesting the importance of getting away from *it all*. My systematic counts at Gandhi Park revealed about two men for every woman, showing that women, too, enjoy daily exercise.

Only a few people mentioned exercise in response to interview questions about well-being. One who did was Gajendra Rajput, the 69-year-old retired forestry officer, who reported that "Doing yoga, remembering God, doing good service [seva] to others and sharing love [pyaar mohabbat aapas me] gives [*milna*] satisfaction [santushti] and peace [shanti]." Gajendra mixes yoga with helping others and loving others as one of many things that contributes to calming the mind.

But ethnographic encounters showed the importance of daily exercise in calming the mind, providing energy, and separating from day-to-day responsibilities. Sunil Sharma, a 38-year-old, told me how his gym membership transformed his body and provided new energy. It was still monsoon when I accompanied him to Cantonment one morning for a workout on the wet grass. Just as Sunil was pleased with his newly thin (*patla*) body, I was pleased when he praised me for having such stamina at my advanced age of 51. Gurkeerat Singh, a 49-year-old, usually does morning exercises to prepare for a day of work. But one day he was collecting money for a Sikh charity and missed his exercise, and told me, "I missed my exercise, so my mind is tired."

At a tea stall that I often frequent, people who had exercised together met for morning tea and continued companionship. They were regulars and had special teas prepared for them (such as tea without sugar or milk) or special sandwiches (such as bread with cucumber, tomato, and onions). Having a third place—the tea stall, as well as the tennis courts—was an important escape from their day-to-day lives of work and home. Every Saturday morning, they'd arrive on their scooters or motorcycles, store their tennis rackets in special places, await tea made for them specially, and enjoy bantering with friends with whom they'd just played tennis. The pleasure of exercise is combined with the pleasures of food and drink and good company. As I've become a runner, I've similarly enjoyed sharing the running lifestyle with my friends and coworkers like the person administering the grant under which I did this research and the (former) chair of my department.

The exercise-wallah at the tea stall show important aspects of pleasures of this chapter: They're often combined with community, they're often part of a regular ritual that helps one through the day, and they're often an escape from day-to-day realities. I considered interviewing exercise wallah at my tea stall or at a gym, but I ultimately decided I knew all I needed to know from the smiling, laughing faces of friends meeting each other after a workout. And, besides, interviews with people who had smiled exercising at Gandhi Park and interviews with Sunil Sharma and Gurkeerat Singh (whom I also observed smiling while in their daily exercise) did not produce any discussion of physical activity as a source of well-being. I think the faces tell the tale, showing the limitations of interviews, which tend to bring out the serious, cognitive, and heavy.

Teatime, Food, Sleep, Sex

When I arrived in India in 2007, I didn't have a grant, and was on my way to the high(er) Himalaya on a char dham yatra. A gentleman whom I met on the train to Haridwar told me he still was in contact with people whom he met on his char dham yatras, showing the pleasure of sweet relations. He told me I would learn more from the "hilly people" than I would from *purohits* (priests) I'd see at temples. We shared a cup of tea—one of the great pleasures of India. Teatime, I thought, is central to well-being—a break that takes me away from day-to-day life. I learned that Philip Lutgendorf was writing a book about tea in India and I thought, "What a good idea." At the end of 2007, my wife and a friend Lynne joined me and we did a little horseback riding on a tea estate in Assam—showing a bit, perhaps, of my pleasures in ghumna. Lynne said she'd almost enticed a boyfriend to come to Assam just to learn about tea culture he loved. My wife, a coffee drinker, enjoyed the pleasures of bed tea so much she considered shifting from coffee. In 2011, a hotel I stayed in did not prepare tea. A male friend of mine, about 30 yeas old, asked me in mystification, "What will you do?" "Exactly," I replied. (But I found a good tea stall! It's all good!)

My hotel had no tea facilities, so each morning I went to the tea stall at which I observed the exercisers. I later learned the tea stall is reasonably renowned for offering a large cup of tea, exactly how you like it. And a cup of tea costs ₹8, more than the more usual ₹7 at nearby tea stalls. (Of course, the renown may have only come to my attention when people knew I enjoyed that tea stall—the pleasant interaction about the tea stall was a source of well-being!) A cup of tea, especially with generous milk, sugar, and spices, is a bodily pleasure and a pick-me-up. At this tea stall the exercise wallah get a sense of specialness from having tea prepared just as they like it, for instance without milk and sugar or in a glass rather than a cup. The pleasure of teatime is as much social as bodily. Bantering between people is a big part of the pleasure of the break away at teatime. I saw young coworkers on breaks sitting outside sharing tea and listening to music on a mobile phone, all smiles. Many small-business proprietors look forward to the two tea breaks in the long workday. Many are even more happy for a break when someone (as they usually do) stops by right about teatime to share tea with them. Joking is a big part of teatime, perhaps especially at tea stalls where the tea stall proprietors are often a source of fun. (Like barbers, tea-stall proprietors often have an outgoing personality that contributes to pleasure.) Being able to offer small hospitality with tea is also enjoyed—I have been offered hospitality by the homeless who can afford to buy the foreigner a cup of tea. Again, perhaps, it would have been appropriate to interview people at a tea stall or a tea stall proprietor. But I think the faces say it all.

When I asked people in the midst of a tea break whether it provides well-being, there were smiles and affirmation. But no one mentioned tea or a tea break in a formal interview about well-being. Pleasures in faces are not revealed in interview discourses, making it unclear how widespread these pleasures are. Is a cup of tea a pleasure for women who are often the ones who have to make the tea? In the 1980s, men imagined that women who worked outside the home would make the husband do everything by his own hand—"He even has to make his own tea!" they would say. In the many homes I've visited where women work outside the home (as is more common today), women still make the tea, so men's concerns were ill founded. Certainly in some homes women often appear to enjoy a tea break as much as men. But in other homes, women would bring tea to me and their husband and then depart. I've rarely seen women in tea stalls in Dehradun. So, drinking tea at stalls is at best an uncommon pleasure for women. Since it was through "fieldwork"—I love that I've finally done "fieldwork" in the pleasurable tea stall!—and not through interviews that I learned the pleasure of tea, other researchers would have to examine whether women share this pleasure (or perhaps substitute it with another one).

Food is one of life's pleasures, mentioned in interviews, but not as often as it deserves. Armaan Singh says he gets well-being from health, wealth, and esteem, but eating well is a big part of Armaan's well-being, too, as he travels by motorcycle to his favorite dhaaba (cheap eatery) for breakfast each morning. Like the tea stall, the dhaaba we both go to prepares special food for all of us regulars. Some people like yogurt rather than chole with their paranthas. Some like sugar in their yogurt, too. Some people take onions in their paranthas, while others don't. While there's not as much banter at the dhaaba, operators and patrons enjoy talking with each other. I first ate at the household of my friend Harkirat Singh on what by chance was Thanksgiving Day, 2007. We had *makki roti* and *sarson ka sag*, after which I felt a calm strength and peace. Harkirat says the food is best in the home as the corn for the makki roti comes from his in-laws' farm and the women of the household churn fresh butter. But, certainly, it's also the community—Harkirat, his wife, his two brother's wives, and about six children—all enjoying food after Harkirat chants Prabhu's name. It was Thanksgiving after all.

People mention food in interviews, but often in the context of a shaukh. Raj Pattial, the flashy 18-year-old motorcyle rider, talked of escaping to a special place he found beyond Mussoorie, but then seamlessly moved on to discuss food. He said the natural place he found was wonderful, but then added: "You could have chips. You could have Coke. You could have whatever you like. Food is the best part, isn't it, la? Food is the best part of living. I like to eat. It's the best thing for every person." A 21 year-old-male Muslim menial office worker described his hobbies as: "[D]oing my work, talking to my friends, and eating Chinese food." A 49-year-old Muslim housewife described her shaukh as "eating good food and eating *chaat* [fried crispies]." A 68-year-old Muslim widow described her shaukh as "eating sweets and eating paan [a betel concoction]." A 40-year-old Muslim lawyer described his hobbies as "eating chaat, eating good food, and wearing brand-name clothes." For a 74-year-old Hindu widow laborer, smoking is her hobby; "eating spicy food" is the hobby of another elderly Hindu laboring woman. It is perhaps significant that everyone discussed in this paragraph talk about the pleasures of eating food *outside the home*. Is part of the pleasure escaping day-to-day life? Is it especially a pleasure for women to have food made by someone else? (I often saw women enjoying food at street stands that sell momos and chowmein.) Is outside food especially a pleasure for laborers and laboring women?

I've always found well-being in food. There's the routine of food, including, for instance, my alu parantha at my favorite dhaaba or juice at Ravi's stand. There's the community of food—eating at Harkirat's but also taking food at my dhaaba. There's the specialness of food: In the 1980s, one used to look forward to having a sweet at Nirula's in Delhi after months in provincial India. In 2011, I was trekking to Harkidun and a returning group of Indian business interns handed me a most delicious chocolate chip cookie as I was making my way up a leg of the 16-km trek. There's sharing food with others, making cornbread raspberry pancakes for my friends or Huevos Rancheros for a vegetarian on a backpack trip. And enjoying the food of others—Bert Sandell's home-made berry blasts or fish caught from a lake on a backpack trip (and cooked with sorel collected by another friend, Mark Berry). There's the community food of a backpack trip, spiced with Marie Sharp's jabinero sauce. There's the creativity and exploring of finding berries. Food is a physical pleasure and a time out of the normal day to day realities.

I had interviewed more than 100 people when I first noticed someone had said a good sleep was essential to well-being. This confirmed how there's no discourse controlling what people said about well-being—I was still hearing new things after the 100th interview. As soon as I started telling people about this interview, many agreed that a good sleep was essential to well-being. Priyanka Sharma, a 26-year-old teacher, describes her uddeshya as to have her family run well with the cooperation (*sahayog*) of husband and in-laws. Priyanka enjoys the hobbies of cooking, listening to music and dancing. Situations in which she felt khushhali included scoring better than her sister on an examination and getting her first job—each of which surely made her feel special. But at the outset, Priyanka mentioned a good sleep alongside helping others as the source of well-being:

> When I make others happy and keep them happy, then, I, have khushhali.
> When I have a good sleep (*achchi nind*), I experience happiness.

After rereading the interviews, I later realized that the ninth person I interviewed, Harish Mishra, a 40-year-old, had also mentioned sound sleep. Harish's uddeshya is that when he dies there will be at least five people who, without any interest, shoulder his coffin and say he was a good man. He gets well-being when his family greets him when he returns home. But when I first ask about well-being, Harish replied that in his opinion, "khushhali only means to have a sound sleep every night, to have abundant food in the house, good education for the children and proper medical attention to the parents." Harish here is mentioning the themes of sufficient health and wealth and connections to others mentioned in earlier chapters. He wants to help others, but he also wants to have a sound sleep.

You awake from a good sleep refreshed. If you're lucky you can remember sweet dreams. India, for me, involves pleasures of asceticism. So, while bathing with buckets and washing clothes is a sensuous pleasure, abandoning a shower and sex and banana pancakes is ascetic. Sometimes I awake in India remembering vivid dreams of sensuous breasts. Freud—the visionary Freud interpreted by Norman Brown (1959)—is wrongly out of style. "Hasn't Freud been debunked?" the students ask me. But Freud was right to recognize the unconscious in dreams. Like many of the pleasures discussed in this chapter, sleeping and dreaming is an escape from the mind. These pleasures are an escape from the day-to-day life. When I was in India dreaming of my wife and being home in Rochester with her and Ernie our cat, I knew as I was waking that it must be a dream. "If it wasn't a dream, and I walked in the front door, I'd be jetlagged," I thought to myself. That was the return of logic and thought, highlighting that dreaming takes us away from the day-to-day world. And how we wake up refreshed.

Indian religious traditions of Shaivism—worship of Shiva; Vaishnavism—worship of Vishnu, especially Krishna; and Tantra all celebrate physical passion and love-making as a window to the divine. Wendy Doniger O'Flaherty (1973) describes Shiva, one of the most popular gods in Dehradun, as the "erotic ascetic." Shiva is the best at tapasya—asceticism. But when he comes out of his asceticism to make love with Parvati, the world shakes. Nita Kumar's classic article on bahri along describes Shiva's appeal to men—he is unconstrained, with wild matted hair, but he is also the best lover. If anything, Krishna devotion celebrates sex even more. Krishna is famous for his connections with the gopis. As Pavan Varma (2001, 40–41) puts it in a devotional and academic book,

> Without physical union with Krishna, [the gopis] were in genuine suffering.... Making love with him gave them sukha (bliss), joy, and it is at this point that ... the carnal and the spiritual make a surprising fusion.... The gopis became *jivatmas* (individual souls) seeking merger with the *paramatma* (the absolute). Physical passion became an aspect of *bhakti* (devotion). The erotic was sanctified; the spiritual was sexualized.

A friend of Indian origin gave Lisa and me a Krishna statue as a wedding present. I questioned the giver whether that was appropriate for a wedding considering Krishna was with all the gopis. She replied, "But Stevie D, he is the most desirable of all men." I don't apologize for using popular sources (e.g., Varma 2001) as well as academic sources (e.g., O'Flaherty 1973). I'm an academic *and* a devotee of Shiva, Krishna, and the Goddess. And I learned about Indian religious traditions more as a devotee and a lover of Indian society than as a scholar of religions!

In my interviews, sexual physical pleasure barely came up even in the interstices. Armaan Singh mentioned that hijras—eunuchs—can't have well-being because they can't have sex. When I asked 42-year-old Rajendra Prasad about situations of happiness, his assistant interrupted and said "after the wedding, after the wedding." Rajendra ignored him, but did talk about the happiness of having children. A couple of men were excited that talks about marriage were going on. One man whom I knew was always looking for sex outside marriage when his wife was away. He told me that when he goes to the drug store to buy condoms, he just would say "give me those [*woh, doh!*]." Another friend told me he was looking forward to time alone with his wife when other members of his joint family were going to be away in Delhi for a few days. His smile in this discussion indicated the pleasures of physical intimacy. In my 1987 interviews in Banaras, one man told me his wife's best quality was only sex that she never refuses. Physical pleasure of touching bodies is a great pleasure that should connect to others and that should go beyond the mind and the day-to-day. But it's not talked about much. My student Patrick Maney wanted to research pleasures of the body *because* it is absent from interviews. Money never appears in dreams because, as Norman Brown points out, it's not an infantile desire. Sex appears in dreams, but not in interviews. In the liberating Freud of Norman Brown, the polymorphous perversity of sexual play is pure pleasure. The pleasure is in people's faces—even if an observer doesn't know the cause. In our 20s, my friends and I called it the "well-laid look."

Psychoanalysts would suggest that because unconscious infantile desires that drive sexuality existed before language they aren't easily accessed by the conscious mind. There might be some truth to that, but I think it's a cop-out. In my twenties, I discussed these pleasures with my friends and I've always discussed them with my wife and, previously, my girlfriends. The fact that sensual, bodily, and sexual pleasures did not come up in the interview situation highlights again how interviews tend to focus on the conscious, purposive, and meaningful, neglecting important pleasures. My reliance on Indian religious traditions and a few comments is certainly inadequate. How widespread and important are sexual pleasures? Do women, who often have less control of their sexuality, get as much pleasure from these traditions as men do? Marx (1844, 74) denigrates animal pleasures—"eating, drinking, procreating." But aren't we animals, too? Aren't physical pleasures important?

Prem Saran (2008, 165), anthropologist, government servant, and initiated Tantric practitioner argues the "ludic and purposeless worldview of *lila* [play]" remains central in Indic civilization. "Even today," he says "customary breaks are pervasively available to interrupt the flow of linear time." Teatime, food, sleep, sex—all are pleasures that breakup the purposeful and mindful parts of life.

Flirtation

There was just a glimmer of flirtation in my fieldwork.[4] A sober Khalsa Sikh in his 20s focused on virtues (nek)—avoiding smoke, drink, and relationships outside of marriage. He always had a smile on his face. He was impressed that I saved my wife's phone number with the words "sweet queen." One day he showed me that he had saved a female friend's phone number with the word *chamakdar*—shining. He told me he enjoyed talking to her on phone—but that it was only talk. But it was talk outside of his work, outside of his day-to-day responsibilities, outside of his relationships based on obligation, maybe even outside of his usual nek (virtuous) world. Another Hindu man, about thirty, received a call from a "friend" he enjoys talking with. He pointedly told me not to worry about his relationship with his wife—I should understand it's just talk. David Haberman (1994, 105) shows that for Krishna devotee, the greatest love is between a man and a woman married to someone else. Such love is never tempered by social responsibilities, but exists only between two individuals. Such love only exists hidden, in the forest, at night; it's Radha and Krishna on the Yamuna at moonlight. Flirtation is a

---

[4] Singh (2015, ch. 6) describes how the intensities of life that go with flirtation contribute to the quality of life in an impoverished area of rural villages in Rajasthan.

connection of others based not on what one does for them or one's obligations to them but just based on a one-on-one relationship. Could it be this sober Sikh gentleman, whose life is so taken up with family, work, and devotion to God, gets a bit of pleasure and escape from small talks with the one who is shining? And doesn't it give pleasure because it is outside of his day-to-day relationships? And does it give pleasure to the one whom he finds to be shining?

Solitude; Song; Reading; Gardening

Indians often live lives of tight relationships in jobs and homes. While many middle-class people whom I knew had spacious houses, many others lived with six or more adults and five or more children in a couple of rooms with big beds. Indian streets and shops and public places are often tightly packed. Social expectations of proper behavior are often strong.

While Indians find well-being in connections to others, sometimes escaping into solitude—as in daily bahri alang trips—is a source of well-being, a pleasure that takes one out of one's day-to-day life. Vijay Sharma, 18, enjoys going to Lakshman Siddh, a mandir celebrating an accomplished religious person, because he likes (pasand) "isolation [ekant]—I like being alone." Nitin Kumar, a 36-year-old, described the "different [alag] experience [*mahsus*] of finding mental peace [*maansik shanti*] at places like Lakshman Sidhh or any temple." For both of these men, being alone and escaping from the day-to-day life is part of the pleasure of their temple visits—visits which for Vijay are spontaneous, while for Nitin they are a regular fortnightly program. Gaura Khanna, the 70-year-old with a passion for teaching who emphasized the pleasures of thinking "nothing," says she experiences khushhali when she sings in her "own way" and lives in her "own way." She describes happiness as a purely innate feeling she sometimes gets. The pleasure is singing and living as one wishes, without being guided by the social expectations and pressures Indians so often face. Earlier in this chapter, I described how Raj Pattial enjoyed finding an apple orchard in a place beyond the hill station of Mussoorie. A key aspect of his pleasure was that he found it on his own and that he broke away from the group he was with. "There were a lot of construction barriers and all that," he says.

"I jumped all that stuff and went to that place." He says the fragrance of the apples was pleasant and the air was cool—bodily pleasures, too, certainly. He calls his experience a "downsizing." Could it have also been an escape from the tight connections with which most Indians live and, which, usually is a source of well-being for them?

In discussing shaukhs, people discuss reading and music, both of which can be enjoyed alone. Gaura Khanna mentioned reading in her discussion of khushhali itself: "When I read good and spiritual books, it gives me khushhali." Richa Mishra, the newly married 27-year-old who gets confidence to accomplish her goals from her pilgrimages, describes her shaukhs as music, gardening, and reading. She seems to enjoy music in solitude, since she says she listens to sad songs if she's gloomy and hip hop if she's happy. "If I'm in a dancing mood," she says, "I'll shift to dance music." Bhajans are Om Sharma's favorite kind of music and he listens each morning on the television. A 68-year-old laborer with very little time for pleasures said that as soon as he got to his workplace he turns on his radio and only switches it off when he leaves work. A 19-year-old male college student who enjoys soccer as an "energetic game, which keeps the body clean and fit" says that listening to music brings "peace to my soul [aatma]." Madhvi Gupta, 48, says listening to music makes her feel good (achcha lagna). "A bad [kara] mood turns into a good one after listening to music." Ethnomusicologist Judith Becker (2004, 38) argues that one reason Americans resist car pooling is their attraction to the "absent-minded, dreamy state one gets into when driving a car alone and listening to music on the radio.... We sometimes enjoy the feeling of nothing but our own bodies in a space that holds no other human being."

But music is, of course, something that is often enjoyed together, too. Devotional songs at festivals are often enjoyed together. I often observed people listening to music on a mobile phone together. Singing together is of course a great pleasure through which people connect to others. A 37-year-old lower middle-class housewife described her shaukh as "singing bhajans [devotional songs]," a sentiment echoed by another 40-year-old lower-middle class housewife who said that as soon as her children were settled her only uddeshya would be to "serve God and perform bhajans and pujapath."

British musical artist Brian Eno (2008) describes why singing is a source of the good life. It's a bodily activity—you use your lungs. You need long vowels, he says, because it's a chance to express yourself. The thrill of rhythm and harmonies produced together is a great pleasure. Eno reports, based on his experiences with an acapella group of 15–20, that "singing aloud leaves you with a sense of levity and contentedness." For Eno, singing with a group is a loss of self-consciousness and mind:

> When you sing with a group of people, you learn how to subsume yourself into a group consciousness because a capella singing is all about the immersion of the self into the community. That's one of the great feelings— to stop being me for a little while and to become us.

Eno gives singing meaning as, well, saying it produces "empathy, the great social virtue."

Eno (2008) reports that a "recent long-term study conducted in Scandinavia sought to discover which activities related to a healthy and happy life. Three stood out: camping, dancing, and singing." We're all afficionados of our favorite pleasures be it surfing, camping, singing, dancing, or horseriding (and I love all of those). Without taking anything away from Brian Eno or the Scandinavian study— camping, singing, and dancing all connect with others and use the body and get one out of daily life—one theme of this book is that the key thing is to embrace pleasures *whatever they may be.* We all need work and health and connections. We all also need approaches to living life and pleasures that divert from its troubles. But I think this chapter shows there are *many pleasures* that can fill this function. It's a chimera to search for the best pleasures. Rather, for well-being each person needs to find those pleasures that work for him or her at particular times—that engage the body, that empty the mind, that provide relief from daily life.

The diversity is so great that I can't describe all the pleasures mentioned by those I interviewed. Reading, crafting, and gardening were among the many things that gave particular individuals pleasure.

Sports, Cinema

Sports—both playing and watching—is another pleasure that separates a person from the day-to-day world. Krishna Notiyal, the 49-year-old who enjoys social get-togethers and sees the great house he has built as all God's work, is also, as he says, a "sportsman." He enjoys watching cricket these days, but in college he "represented the university" in cricket and hockey. The pleasure here is pride of excellence and connections—representing a university. But it's also the pleasure of the game. "From playing cricket, I got the most happiness [khushi]." A police constable visibly brightened when we asked about his hobbies. "Even though I'm 48, I still play volleyball, which gives me happiness and relief." We can see in this the pleasure of specialness—still playing sports beyond his youth—but also the "relief" from the day-to-day world. Besides being an active bodily pleasure separate from the day-to-day life, playing sports also provides the pleasure of connections to others. Mamraj Kumar, a 22-year-old-laborer, says: "[Khushhali] is when I have an enormous [*bhayanak*] celebration [*jashan*] of happiness [khushi]. Like when I play [cricket] and it's a good play, that gives happiness [khushi] and there is a celebration."

While many people mentioned cricket in discussing their hobbies, sports is another arena that I know provides pleasure primarily from people's faces. Young people playing cricket on makeshift pitches or school corridors have a concentration on their faces, which I rarely see. There's a joy at movement to bowl the ball, a mad concentration at batting. Sports is a bodily enjoyment and a connection to others. I remember a rainy day Thanksgiving football game in upstate New York—the Thomases versus the not-Thomases in a family with a lot of people named Thomas, me carrying the youngest over the goal line.

Sports-watching, too, offers pleasures of celebration and separation from the day-to-day life. Yesterday, as I write this morning on November 27, 2011, India and the West Indies played to a tied draw in test cricket, only the second ever—that is India made up a big chase, but not all the way and ran out of balls in an exciting game. A couple days before, Sachin Tendulkar failed to get his 100 test ton by just six runs. On my street people sat riveted, watching, and shouting. (I remember in 2007 as I started my char dham yatra, sitting in a hotel in Rishikesh and hearing what appeared to be a terrorist attack outside; it turned out that India had defeated Pakistan in cricket.)

Mentioning the *watching* of cricket points to the joys of *virtual* realities that so many enjoy today. Now that my wife is a Giants fan we, amazingly, could watch games together on mlb.tv, her in the USA, and me in India, while we talked on skype! (I've also had a couple of great experiences watching the Giants at their beautiful park in San Francisco.) There is excitement in the virtual realities—and one reason is that they're different from day-to-day realities. So, thinking about the Giants, we don't have to think about work or family or politics or anything with a real effect. Virtual reality of sports allows the mind's application (baseball and cricket fans are both interested in statistics—how we wait for Tendulkar's 100th test 100—will it ever, come?) to something of no consequence in reality, something outside our day to day worlds. As Grant Brisbee (2011), of the McCovey Chronicles (a San Francisco Giants fan blog) says,

> the whole reason I've written over a million words about baseball over the last eight years or so is because it doesn't mean anything. That's what makes it one of my favorite things in the world.... [T]he individual results of a baseball season are frivolous nonsense, and they're what help me deal with the stuff that isn't frivolous nonsense. Or, to dumb it down, I'm looking at an unopened medical bill right now. Don't want to open it because I don't think I'll like what's inside. But then I lean back and think of Matt Kemp in a room with a "CONGRATULATIONS MVP" banner, slumped in a folding chair, and tooting a party favor ironically with every exhale. [Kemp did not win the MVP—Most Valuable Player]. Now I feel better! That's what baseball does for me.

And there is a lot of joking in sports, too, as Grant's column suggests: Let Timmy smoke. Following baseball, like following Tendulkar's quest for 100th test ton, provides escape from the day-to-day world that so often is full of troubles. But one gets to do serious play engaging in following baseball.

My earlier studies of filmgoing (Derné 2000, 2008) showed how often people get well-being from escaping tight family and work situations through moviegoing. Eating food, pressing tightly together with other filmgoers, and enjoying the cool of the cinema-hall provide bodily pleasures. Some people whom I interviewed for this study mentioned filmgoing as a shaukh. Thus, Jaspal Sidhu, the 22-year-old coaching student who enjoys pilgrimages, also says that he likes Bollywood films very much; his favorite film—*Hum Dil De Chuke Sanaam*—gave him great happiness. Mamraj, the 22-year-old laborer who described well-being as enormous celebration at sporting events, also describes seeing good films as a hobby: "A good role of a hero impresses me." Armaan Singh and Prakash Tyagi were among the many who continue their enjoyment of filmgoing into their 60s. The world of film, like the world of sports watching, is a virtual world—a world of events that are made-up and separate from day-to-day realities. Shared attraction to these worlds connects people.

Intoxicants

Mild intoxicants—paan, tea, sweets—are a regular part of Indian pleasures. Bahri alang revelers are among the many who enjoy bhang, which Prem Saran [2008, 166] well describes as a "psychedelic relaxant" commonly used "in festivals like Holi and Shivaratri."

Nonordinary consciousness is a large part of the pleasure of activities like bahri alang. Serge King (1988, 44–50) was taught by a Hawaiian elder to see several levels of consciousness beyond the ordinary world. What is a meadow in ordinary consciousness, in psychic consciousness is seen as connected to animals, air, and soil. In dream consciousness, a person might see the meadow as representing openness to life and love. In being consciousness, you see yourself not as standing in the meadow; instead you see yourself as the meadow *itself*. The shift to these different modes of consciousness away from ordinary consciousness is one thing that makes pleasures pleasurable.

Drugs—like bhang—often induce nonordinary consciousness, but such psychedelic drugs aren't necessary. Drumming and music are ways to enter nonordinary consciousness (Becker 2004; Harner 1988, 12–13). The movement of exercise, the sound of bells, the wandering through town, vigorous bathing, or washing clothes are pleasures described in this chapter that induce the nonordinary consciousness that separates people from daily life.

Alcohol is another technique people use to create emptiness of the mind and forget day-to-day realities. Yash Singh, the 58-year-old pakora maker, finds that drinking a little sharaab (alcohol) after work rests his mind. Ashok Kumar, a 25-year-old who works at a tea stall, hopes to someday start his own business. "Money, wife, ghar [home]—that's khushhali," he says. His greatest well-being was having a girlfriend "because everyone else had one," and his least well-being was when he lost the girlfriend. Ashok describes his hobby as drinking alcohol:

> I like to drink sharaab. I like drinking in the evening, not during the regular business hours I sit together with my four friends and we all feel good (achcha lagna) while drinking.

Lakshman Negi, a 61-year-old, often talked of the pleasures of drinking, saying when we would go to the Himalaya together, we would do fine with a bottle in our pocket. A man I knew who was constructing a building said that we'd get real pleasure when we partied afterwards in Mussoorie with lots of alcohol. When I went to his house for dinner he lit up at the thought of alcohol. At parties I attended, men often enjoyed drinking and dancing to music. While people will respect your wishes to not eat meat in India, I had a hard time having them respect my wishes not to drink—although I noticed that they would respect the wishes of my khalsa Sikh friends—perhaps if the reason you don't drink is religious it's taken more seriously! On these occasions, people usually said they just wanted me to drink as a welcome to me, but they very much enjoyed their drink, lighting up while bringing out the bottles. Alcohol came up rarely in interviews, but, again, I saw it on people's faces—men's faces. Every time I've seen alcohol being consumed in India, it's been an all-male affair. Indeed, as the next section describes, women often pay the costs of men's drinking.

Pleasures That Overwhelm Life Harm Well-being

Pleasures provide an escape from day-to-day responsibilities. While connections to others are often an enjoyed part of pleasures, pleasures might threaten one's responsibilities to others and one's connections to others, in turn, threatening one's well-being.

Too much attachment to any pleasures might harm social relationships. Surfing, or mountain climbing, or camping may be great escapes, but if they become a person's whole life, family and bonds are neglected. Too much attachment to sexual pleasures can threaten social bonds. I knew a businessman who caused tension with his wife, two children, and friends and even harmed his business because of his pursuit of extramarital affairs. In the 1980s, when contact between unmarried men and women was more limited, men talked of the danger of running behind the back of girls and losing themselves in the intoxication for sex (Derné 1995). Sunil Sharma realizes that his attachment to his music limits his earning ability, threatening his wife's love and respect for him. One day he asked me to have some street food with him and mentioned that his pleasure at eating chowmein outside the home may upset the wife who is busy cooking for him after a long day of nursing work. Watching or playing cricket all the time can prevent a person from fulfilling their responsibilities to others. Thus, Mehar Khan, a 26-year-old middle-class Muslim housewife, described her lack of well-being as stemming from her husband's focus on cricket:

> My husband does not pay much attention to his business. I wish that he should pay more time in his shop so he can fulfill his family responsibilities well. My husband is very fond of playing cricket, so most of the time he is in the cricket field with the boys all around him. [I tell him] "Instead of playing with those boys, you should pay more attention to your business."

One person's pleasure may be another person's pain, disrupting the felicitous chain of mutual well-being. Listening to music too loud may harm others. Enjoying smoking may disturb others. I miss the pleasurable monkeys that have been chased from Delhi, but the monkeys were a pain to people living in the city—they stole people's washing and worse! In short, the pleasures of the self can cause a conflict with the desire to get along with others.

The problem of pleasures overwhelming responsibilities and connections is most obvious with alcohol. A little alcohol might empty the mind and provide escape from the day to day, but a person who empties the mind altogether through alcohol becomes a burden to others and can't maintain relationships. One 54-year-old man told me that he was "unable to follow through with anything except alcohol and tobacco." Although he said that they were ruining his life and work, he said he couldn't give them up. Many women hate alcohol because of what it does to their families.

Many of the women we interviewed describe problems associated with men's drinking. Komal Kumar, a 37-year-old construction laborer, says one reason she lacks well-being is that her "husband drinks a lot. He doesn't bring money into the house most of the time. He fights with me and beats the children." A 25-year-old college-educated Hindu housewife describes how she experiences a lack of well-being

> when my father-in-law and brother-in-law drink a lot of alcohol and they shout and create scene in the family. They fight with each other. Then, everybody is upset in the family and some of the time I think that I should run from here and settle down somewhere else with my husband and child.

A 39-year-old Hindu says that khushhali is sukh-shanti (contentment and peace) in the home (ghar) and that she feels (mahasus) khushi when she serves others. She suffers a lack of well-being when her husband drinks a lot, comes home, and fights with everyone in the house: "We have to sleep hungry without any food. At those times, I got a lot of unhappiness [dukh]." A laborer in her 60s says that she wishes "the atmosphere of my home would be peaceful and happy," but that unfortunately her husband "has been a drunk from the beginning of marriage—he always fights and shouts and often sells the household things for his drink." In discussing her purpose in life, this woman first says that she hopes her son gets a good job, but then adds: "I hate sharaab [alcohol] and I want that the government should close all those shops that are selling sharaab because it is spoiling many families."

These complaints about alcohol all come from women. Women may be less likely to take the approach that well-being is inner, precisely because external circumstances *are* the cause of so many of their troubles. Because family looms so large in so many women's lives, family situations were often key factors in determining women's well-being.

On Moderation: Pleasure as *Part* of Well-being

Pleasure is only *part* of well-being. One can't experience well-being having sex *all the time*, surfing *all the time*, chanting God's name *all the time*, drinking *all the time*, or travelling *all the time*. Contra the Beach Boys, you can't be on safari to stay. Because the sources of well-being are diverse *and contradictory,* no single principle helps us understand well-being. We need pleasure, but we also need individual striving, meaning, and social connections. Pleasures are often purposeless and meaningless. But purposefulness *is* important to individual striving that is *also* necessary for well-being. Pleasures are often bodily and involve emptying the mind, but the mind needs to be engaged to provide meaning that helps us come to terms with our troubles.

A fundamental aspect of pleasures as a source of well-being is that there needs to be a back and forth between pleasures and responsibilities. Too much life in structure is arid. Too much life in pleasure keeps one from contributing to others.

If pleasures dominate life, they don't lead to well-being. If you're always gone and you don't know where, you don't have a purpose in life and you don't have connections to concrete other people. Any pleasure taken to extremes threatens social connections. Those who pursue extreme pleasures, such as mountain climbing expeditions above 8,000 meters, usually have frayed relationships at home (Coffey 1989). If you want to meditate all the time and become a *sadhu*, your family connections are finished.

I'm writing this book now (in 2014) on sabbatical. Without administration, teaching, and grading, I miss the vitality that came from freedom that is *occasional.* Perhaps I'll head into the office! Shamans who work in nonordinary realities are usually grounded in ordinary realities as well—because you can't live in nononordinary realities all the time (Harner 1988, 12). Indeed, you can't enjoy the nonordinary realities without experience of ordinary ones!

As Bharat Gupt (2004, 17) points out, traditional Indian society recognized the pleasures of flirtation: "*Shringara* or the romantic emotion was to be indulged only in the *grihastha* or the householder state of life and it was not only to be encouraged but was obligatory." But Gupt is right to point out that "the judicious person" must "seek sexual fulfillment and yet not transgress on his [or her] other obligations." Citing the *Kamasutra*, Gupt points out "one should conduct oneself in such a way in the world that all the three aspirations"—dharma (duty), *artha* (profit) and *kama* (emotional gratification)—"are achieved without any one obstructing the other two." Anthropologists such as Victor Turner and shamans such as Michael Harner understand pleasures must be balanced with daily life. The fact that the idea is so strong in Indian culture may be one reason the people I interviewed recognize this as well—and one reason their well-being is strong.

For well-being, a person needs to have sufficient income and health, individual pursuits, connections to others, approaches to handling life's difficulties, and pleasures to escape the day-to-day. But too much of any one of these things harms a person's well-being. If you have so much connection to others that the self dies, you lack well-being. If your work for others means there's no time for pleasures, you lack well-being. If you only have individual pursuits, life has no meaning. If you pursue pleasures all the time, connections to others and meaningful pursuits of goals can be ruined. One day I was in a qi gong meditation class, tears streaming down, as I meditated on love of those I disliked (smokers). I felt at one with the world. I asked Lisa O'Shea, my qi gong instructor, what would happen if I felt this way all the time. She said that, then, I would be a mystic. Pleasures help us empty the mind and feel purposeless. But for most people pleasures only satisfy because they are only a *part* of living the good life. One gets joy from purpose and meaning, *too*. If we're gone all the time and don't know where, we're a mystic, feeling oneness, union, and communion, but missing purpose and individual pursuit. So, pleasures, *alongside* sufficient income and health, self pursuits, connections to others, and approaches that give life meaning are the main source of well-being. But no *one* of these elements can dominate over the others if one is to live well.

Any Pleasure

For well-being, people need pleasures that separate from day-to-day, often engaging the body and emptying the mind. Pleasures are often purposeless, while the day-to-day is full of purpose, and they often are ritualized, providing breaks in daily activity.

On the other hand, it is, I think, a *chimera* to search for particular pleasures, the best pleasures. Brian Eno (2008) quotes a Scandinavian study that suggests camping, singing and dancing provide a happy life. And they do. You get outside your day-to-day life, you connect with others, and you use your body. But for other people, surfing, chanting God's name, or bahri alang might work as well. The key thing *is to have pleasures whatever they may be*. As 70-year-old doctor, Om Sharma, says, "*Whatever* gives the mind [man] peace [shanti] is actually the source of khushhali." Ultimately, the ability to find pleasures is the thing that lasts. A person might lose the ability to surf or climb peaks or jump trees on a horse. But that person will have well-being if they are able to find other pleasures that move them.

At the 2012 American Sociological Association conference, I was delighted to run into Claude Fischer, one of my graduate school mentors. Claude was looking good and he asked me if I was still horseback riding and traveling to Fiji (as I probably had been the last time we'd seen each other). I realized that I'd since taken up running and returned to studying India. I've continued to find pleasures throughout my life—running, horseback riding, surfing, hula dancing, singing, backpacking, and kayaking—but they've changed over time. What pleasures one chooses is probably not as as significant as finding *some* pleasures. And the *ability* to find pleasures, to find meanings, and to find connections to others is what truly persists. Every circumstance that 'correlates' to well-being is transient—you can lose your job, your health, someone you love, or your ability to pursue certain pleasures (physically, financially, or because of circumstance). But if you have the ability to find pleasure, meaning, and connections, you will keep an enduring sense of life satisfaction.

References

Adams, Brooke. 2010. "Team ... Work? The Effects of Structured Leisure Time on Well-Being." Geneseo Undergraduate Research Conference. Geneseo, New York, USA.

Becker, Judith. 2004. *Deep Listeners: Music, Emotion, and Trancing*. Bloomington, IN: Indiana University Press.

Brisbee, Grant. 2011. "Angel Villalona and the 40-man Roster," November 23, 2011. Available at: http://www.mccoveychronicles.com/2011/11/23/2582207/angel-villalona-and-the-40-man-roster#storyjump (Accessed on November 28, 2011).

Brody, Jane E. 2012. "Changing America's Anthem on Exercise." *New York Times*, August 28, D7.

Brown, Norman O. 1959. *Life against Death: The Psychoanalytic Meaning of History*. Middleton, CT: Wesleyan University Press.

Coffey, Diane, Aashish Gupta, Payal Hathi, Nidhi Khurana, Nikhil Srivastav, Sangita Vyas, and Dean Spears. 2014. "Open Defecation: Evidence from a New Survey in Rural North India." *Economic and Political Weekly*, XLIX(38, September 20): 43–55.

Coffey, Maria. 1989. *Fragile Edge: Loss on Everest*. Madeira Park, BC, Canada: Harbour.

Csikszentimhalyi, Mihaly. 1975. *Beyond Boredom and Anxiety*. San Francisco, CA: Jossey-Bass.

———. 1990. Flow: *The Psychology of Optimal Experience*. New York, NY: Harper.

Derné, Steve. 1995. *Culture in Action: Family Life, Emotion, and Male Dominance in Banaras, India*. Albany, NY: SUNY Press.

———. 1998. "Feeling Water: Notes on the Sensory Construction of Time and Space in Banaras." *Man in India*, 78(1–2): 1–7.

———. 2000. *Movies, Masculinity, and Modernity: An Ethnography of Men's Filmgoing in India*. Westport CT: Greenwood Press.

———. 2008. *Globalization on the Ground: Media and the Transformation of Culture, Class, and Gender in India*. New Delhi: SAGE Publications.

Economist. 2014. "Sanitation in India: The Final Frontier." *The Economist*, July 19, 35–36.

Eno, Brian. 2008. "Singing: the Key to a Long Life," This I Believe Feature, National Public Radio, November 23, 2008. Available at: http://www.npr.org/templates/story/story.php?storyId=97320958, (Accessed on November 25, 2011).

Gold, Ann. 1988. *Fruitful Journeys: The Ways of Rajasthani Pilgrims*. Berkeley, CA: University of California Press.

Gupt, Bharat. 2004. "The Genesis of the *Nayika* in the *Natyashastra*." In *A Celebration of Love: The Romantic Heroine in the Indian Arts*, edited by Harsha V. Dehejia, 17–22. New Delhi: Roli.

Haberman, David L. 1994. *Journey through the Twelve Forests: An Encounter with Krishna*. Oxford: Oxford University Press.

Harner, Michael. 1988. "What Is a Shaman?" In *Shaman's Path: Healing, Personal Growth and Empowerment*, edited by Gary Doore, 7–16. Boston, MA: Shambala.

Keynes, John Maynard. 1932. *Essays in Persuasion*. New York, NY: Harcourt Brace Jovanovich.

King, Serge. 1988. "Seeing Is Believing: The Four Worlds of the Shaman." In *Shaman's Path: Healing, Personal Growth and Empowerment*, edited by Gary Doore, 43–52. Boston, MA: Shambala.

Kumar, Nita. 1986. "Open Space and Free Time: Pleasure for the People of Banaras." *Contributions to Indian Sociology*, 20(1): 41–60.

Lamb, Sarah. 2000. *White Saris and Sweet Mangoes: Aging, Gender, and Body in North India*. Berkeley, CA: University of California Press.

Maney, Patrick. 2010. "Well-Being and the Sensory Construction of Happiness." Geneseo Undergraduate Research Conference. Geneseo, New York, USA.

Marcuse, Herbert. 1955. *Eros and Civilization: A Philosophical Inquiry into Freud*. New York, MA: Random House.

Marx, Karl. (1844) 1978. "Economic and Philosophic Manuscripts of 1844." In *The Marx-Engels Reader*, 2nd ed., edited by Robert Tucker, 66–125. New York, NY: Norton.

———. (1845–46) 1978. *The German Ideology.* In *The Marx-Engels Reader,* 2nd ed., edited by Robert Tucker, 146–200. New York, NY: Norton.

MacKinnon, Catharine. A. 1989. *Toward a Feminist Theory of the State.* Cambridge, MA: Harvard University Press.

O'Flaherty, Wendy Doniger. 1973. *Siva: The Erotic Ascetic.* Oxford: Oxford University Press.

Varma, Pavan K. 2001. *The Book of Krishna.* New Delhi: Penguin.

Sankrityayan, Rahul. (1948) 2004. *Gummukar Shastra.* Allahabad: Kitab Mahal.

Saran, Prem. 2008. *Yoga, Bhoga and Ardhanariswara: Individuality, Wellbeing and Gender in Tantra.* New Delhi: Routledge.

Sarkar, Benoy Kumar. 1941. *Villages and Towns and Social Patterns.* Calcutta: Chuckerverty Chatterjee.

Singh, Bhrigupati. 2015. *Poverty and the Quest for Life: Spiritual and Material Striving in Rural India.* Chicago, IL: University of Chicago Press.

Srivastava, Sanjay. 2005. *"Ghummakkads, A Woman's Place, and the LTC-walas: Towards a Critical History of 'Home,' 'Belonging,' and 'Attachment.'" Contributions to Indian Sociology,* 39(3): 375–406.

Turner, Victor W. 1969. *The Ritual Process: Structure and Anti-Structure.* New York, NY: Aldine.

Wallace, Walter L. 1971. *The Logic of Science in Sociology.* New Brunswick, NJ: Aldine.

Walker, Charles J. 2010. "Experiencing Flow: Is doing It Together Better than Doing It Alone." *Journal of Positive Psychology,* 5(1): 3–11.

PART II

Variations

6

AGE, GENDER, CLASS, AND INDIVIDUAL LIVES AND CHOICES

For khushhali, there should be no mental tension. Life should be easy and work should be done smoothly. I got the most khushhali when I got my first job and when I became the mother of my son.

Interviewer: "Tell me about those situations when you experienced a lack of well-being."

I felt dukhi [sad] when I was compelled to polish my husband's shoes or to press the clothes of other family members. If anybody talks sharply [zor se] to me or scolds me [daantana], I'm unhappy.

—Fulmala Rajput, 31-year-old with a government job like her husband

Married to a property dealer, Madhvi Gupta, a 48-year-old mother of two, sees well-being as each person's own choice:

Khushhali is each person's *alag alag* [own individual] thinking. It's personal. Some feel khushhali in the home. Some people feel happiness [khushi] from their children's happiness. Some people receive happiness by doing religious work [*dharm karne se*]. Some receive happiness by attending to their family. Some receive happiness by a little gardening. It's their alag alag choice.

While we might translate "alag alag thinking" as a person's "own individual thinking," alag alag literally means "separate separate." While people need connections, individual accomplishments, pleasures, and meanings, Madhvi is right that they have a variety of ways of feeling well-being in those areas: Some find connections with friends, others with family; some find pleasure in singing, others in gardening; some find individual accomplishments in journalism, others in writing poetry.

Yet situations rooted in religion, gender, class, and age limit opportunities and options, limiting choices. In the epigraph that opens this section, Fulmala Rajput describes experiencing well-being when she got her job and when she gave birth to her son. Later in the interview, when asked about her hobbies, she describes reading as an important pleasure in her life. Yet when Meenu turns the conversation to experiences of ill-being, she points to being scolded in the family as limiting her well-being. Fulmala, a government servant married to another government servant, still finds her well-being limited by her gender. I found that even people in the most limited circumstances seem to find at least a glimmer of well-being and sometimes find felicitous arenas of life to focus on. Yet their choices are not fully "separate" but also shaped by obdurate cultural and structural limitations, which channel and shape well-being.

Sociologists specialize in finding patterns. The regularity (or patterning) of a *dominant discourse* shapes not what people think, but what is thinkable (Barrett 1991; Swidler and Arditi 1994). If dominant discourses identify money as central to life, people will tend to think that money is central to well-being. If religious traditions identify service to others as important, people will find well-being in contributing to others.

Social theorists also focus on how *structural constraints* limit the way people think about their well-being. Social theorists use the term *social structure* to focus on the patterning of positions within society (Derné 2008, 59–70). While "discourse" highlights the patterning of ideas that are available, "structure" highlights the patterning of opportunities. Opportunities are more limited for women than they are for men; for less educated, poorer people than they are for more educated, more prosperous people. People with limited opportunities may find their well-being more affected by the actions of others compared with people with more autonomy in their lives. Family positions shaped by age and gender channel people's focus into particular arenas of life, affecting the arenas from which they derive well-being.

Diversity of Resources and the Multiple Paths to Well-being

The next chapter suggests how distinctive aspects of Indian life (social structure) and thought (discourse) shape Indians' approaches to well-being—and how non-Indians can learn from these approaches. But one of the main findings of this book is the tremendous *diversity* of paths to well-being and of discourses people draw on to understand their well-being.

When I returned from the field in 2007, having interviewed 11 women and 76 men, I was stunned by the diversity of things I heard about well-being: People got well-being from a good sleep, a good guru, giving up chewing paan, surviving a bus crash, becoming a mother, helping a neighbor to the hospital, or bathing in a river. I was equally struck by the diversity of sources people referenced— the Bhavagad Gita, Sikh scripture, Shobha De, Robert Browning, Khushwant Singh, Urdu poetry, Hindi-film songs, and the slogans outside an educational institution. In 2007, I was surprised that 87 interviews were not enough to exhaust what Indians had to say about well-being. Indeed, it turned out I was still hearing new things *even after 200 interviews*!

This diversity was stunning because in my study of family life (Derné 1995) and my studies of filmgoing (Derné 2000, 2008), 15 interviews or so was enough to exhaust the range of ideas male respondents had about family life and about films. Of course, interviewing larger numbers was important to understand variations in ideas and to understand the prevalence of different ideas, but I didn't hear many new stories after about 15 interviews.

People's familiarity with religious discourses about the importance of service certainly led people to talk about their well-being in terms of helping others. But I think that the *absence of a dominant discourse* about well-being is vitally important in contributing to the diversity of ideas people have about what gives them well-being, ideas that follow more from their experience than from any discourses. In considering their well-being, Indians have diverse, legitimate discourses that they can draw on. As a result, Indians understand a variety of paths to well-being. Some may take a religious path; some may reject religion. Some may focus on material pleasures, others on serving others. More fundamentally, people include contradictory elements in their understanding of well-being. Raj Pattial helps others, but he also enjoys good food, feeling cool air, escaping from day-to-day pressures, which engage him as he hopes to earn good income, partly to help his parents. So, Madhvi Gupta is right in one way—well-being is partly an individual's own individual choice.

Limits of Quantitative Analysis to Understand Individual Variation in This Study

While a sociologist will look for patterns to try to understand whether the sources of well-being are different for people of different religions, classes, genders, or life stages, individual biographies and choices shape people's approaches to well-being. Comparisons are difficult in a study like this that was primarily open-ended (I asked what well-being meant to each person, rather than asking them to address, for instance, whether they got well-being from religion, work, family, tea-drinking, or a good sleep). The problem is compounded by the "interviewer effect"—the effects of different interviewers on respondents' responses that I reference in the introduction.

In 2011, when I started hearing interviews with large numbers of women conducted by Meenu Sharma, I was struck by how many women talked of helping others as a source of well-being. Many even described housework as their hobby. When I'd left the field in 2007, having interviewed just 11 women, but 76 men, I felt I was swimming in data without patterns. The people we had interviewed in 2007 mentioned so many things that patterns were slow to emerge. I initially hypothesized that women focused on helping others as a source of well-being—or at least said they were—because of the strength of discourses about women as nurturing and because of the structural constraints they faced. But it turned out this focus was perhaps *more* the result of being interviewed by Meenu Sharma, who perhaps gave off a sense of concern for others, rather than by myself and Narendra Sethi, both of whom perhaps gave off a sense of enjoyment of a more free-wielding, cosmopolitan life. Seeking well-being from felicitous interactions with the interviewer, people were more likely to mention helping others as a source of well-being if they were interviewed by Meenu than if they were interviewed by Narendra and myself. Ninety-three percent (38/41) of married women under 58 years old whom Meenu interviewed at least indirectly mentioned helping others as a source of well-being, but only 31 percent (5/16) of similar women Narendra and I interviewed mentioned helping others as a source of well-being. Thirty percent (18/61) of the men under the age of 60 whom Narendra and I interviewed mentioned helping others as a source of well-being, but 73 percent (8/11) of the men under the age of 60 whom Meenu interviewed mentioned helping others as a source of well-being. Given the strength of an apparent interviewer effect and the fact that Narendra and I interviewed the bulk of the men, while Meenu interviewed the bulk of the women, a quantitative analysis of gender differences in how people talked about what gave them well-being did not reveal many differences.

Indeed, a substantial minority of women—34 of the 91 women interviewed—did not explicitly focus on helping others as a source of well-being. Very few women—I identified only three—focused *exclusively* on helping others as a source of well-being. Women emphasize contradictory things alongside helping others as a source of well-being. The sources of well-being for women are as diverse as they are for men. Sonali Pandey, the 19-year-old college student described in Chapters 2 and 3, seems to focus a lot on helping others as a source of well-being: Her purpose is to earn money so that she can contribute to the education of the poor and her greatest experience of khushhali is when she gave her "full support" to a hospitalized fellow student by writing out notes for her and helping with exams. But good relationships with her parents define khushhali for her, she finds sukh in the home's peaceful atmosphere, and her greatest lack of khushhali was the death of a grandmother who had been like a friend to her. Sonali's discussion of her hobbies calls to mind pleasures, such as dancing, painting, and listening to music, and thinking about pilgrimages reminds her of the peaceful atmosphere (*shant vatavaran*) that relaxed (*aaraam*) her mind. Although "waiting in line to get darshan" tired her, she was rewarded with the experience of total relaxation (aaraam). Heena Ali, another 19-year-old college student referenced in Chapter 3, seems very focused on helping others. Heena initially says: "Khushhali means to help the handicapped people because they need somebody's support and I would also like to help the beggars." Later in the interview, when asked her purpose in life, Heena dreams of opening an orphanage so that children are not "forced into begging after the death of their parents." Yet when asked to describe a situation of khushhali, Heena references scoring 95 percent on biology in her Class 12 examinations and having her photograph published in the paper when she earned a Class 6 scholarship. Her parents' praise also gives Heena khushhali: "It gives me happiness [khushi] when my parents feel proud [E] of my work." When asked about her hobbies, Heena described individual pleasures—painting, drawing, dancing, and composing poems. Heena gets well-being from helping others, but also from her pleasurable hobbies and her own accomplishments, especially as they are recognized by others. Asha Sharma, the just-retired 72-year-old teacher, focused almost exclusively on service in responding to the questions on well-being, but she clearly also enjoys her "hobbies" that include gardening and cooking. When asked about pilgrimage, she describes a "peaceful atmosphere" that was so strong she "didn't feel like moving from that place. The different vibration (*anubhuti*) that I got when I visited that place was something I never experienced before." All of these women talk about helping others as a source of well-being, but all of them also mention facets of well-being beyond helping others, including the pride of individual success and the relaxation of hobbies or religious activities.

My initial impression, then, that women talked more about helping others as a source of well-being was not fully supported by closer quantitative analysis or closer consideration of women's and men's responses.

Despite the problems associated with open-ended questions and with interviewer effects, this research still revealed important ways that age, gender, class, and religion limited people's pursuits of well-being and pushed them to find well-being in ways that were not only their own individual choice. But even while discourses and structures limit and influence people's approach to well-being, even people like Fulmala Rajput who are limited by their roles nonetheless find well-being in important areas of their life. Madhvi Gupta is also right to recognize that each person's own "separate" thinking also plays a role: Despite the patterns I note below, there is great individual variation within any category associated with gender, religion, class, or age.

Lifecycle

Because men and women in their 30s and 40s are in the cycle of earning and rearing children, many find meaning and well-being in work and family—the areas in which they are most involved. Most, of course, have pleasures, too—a daily walk, or *puja* in the morning are some examples. Many find pleasure in the particulars of their job or family—cooking special dishes or developing expertise at work (for instance, fixing phones, tailoring clothes, or being a good journalist).

By contrast, younger people—especially, perhaps, men—often focus on diverse life arenas as their main source of well-being. So, an 18-year-old working at a telephone-calling booth enjoyed joking with friends as his main source of well-being. Or Ashok Kumar, a 25-year-old operating a tea stall, seemed to get the most well-being from drinking alcohol in the evening with his friends. Mamraj Kumar, a 22-year-old laborer, loves cricket and film. Rajejndra Rana, the 21-year-old college student, finds satisfaction (santushti) and happiness (khushi) when he gets positive reactions from a telecast he does on AIDS or polio. Several of the young men whom I interviewed made a love-affair they were pursuing the center of their well-being. Shekhar Kumar, a 23-year-old laborer, says: "[K]hushhali means pyaar [love], mohabbat [love], dosti [friendship]. I get khushhali by expressing my thoughts, heart and feelings." For Shekhar, the greatest time of well-being was when he met a young woman whom he loved (*pyaar karna*): "I was together [*saath*] with her in friendship [dosti] for a whole year. When [she] was with me, I was khush [happy], etc. [*vaghera*]." Shekhar says that ever since the young woman married, he has always been in sadness (dukhi). Shekhraj Sharma, a 19-year-old, studying in a prestigious institute in Dehradun, hails from a successful family of government servants. Shekhraj says well-being means "to love [pyaar karna] Arthi because at this stage of life Arthi means everything to me." Indeed, both Arthi, an 18-year-old, and Shekhraj came to study at the same institute from their homes as a "joint venture." When I ask Shekhraj about the situation that gave the most well-being he gives the date when he first met Arthi. "It was the happiest moment of my life."

Young women mentioned a diversity of areas less often than young men. Many of the young women interviewed by Meenu seemed institutionally-channeled. They focused on pleasing their parents by doing well in school or by contributing to family support. It is difficult to know if this difference is influenced by the fact that so many were interviewed by Meenu. It's also possible that men, more than women, have more time in their 20s to explore before marriage and career are settled. During this time, men can focus on things such as drinking, cricket, a love, or being a good journalist, rather than family and earning as a source of well-being.

Women *themselves* see marriage as a defining break that may alter what gives them well-being. Sushma Sharma, 34, lives with her husband and two children. Sushma contributes more to the family's income with her nursing work than her husband does with his musical career. When I ask Sushma what khushhali means to her, she replies with her own question: "Before or after marriage? Before marriage, getting my job was what gave me happiness. After marriage, my children were my happiness." Sushma wanted to complete her BA, but said she could not after getting married. She had ambitions as an artist but, again, marriage kept her from pursuing them. Anthropologists report that Indian women's change of households at marriage is a significant change that men don't undergo (e.g., Lamb 1997). Women not uncommonly describe the difficulties of this transition. Amrit Kaur is a student living separately from her husband to pursue her studies. When Meenu asked Amrit about a situation of a lack of well-being, she replied that when she married, "I felt unhappy because I had to leave my father's house because my father was a source of inspiration for me. So, I was very sad [dukhi] at that time."

Geetika Bapna's (2012, 109) ethnography of a Delhi neighborhood confirms that many women distinguish between "time before marriage and time after marriage" and that women found difficulties in the transition. One newly-married woman complained that "marriage ties you up." A middle-aged woman described "unmarried life" as "without cares" while "married life has many worries." A young wife said "a girl's real life is before marriage only. After marriage you are tied up in responsibilities" (Bapna 2012, 111).

In their 30s and 40s, most men are caught up in earning a living and most women are caught up in raising a family (and increasingly with earning a living, as well). Certainly, there are many men and women in their 30s and 40s who continue to focus outside of work and family to find their well-being, even if this is a source of tension. Sunil Sharma feels the tension between his love of Garhwali music and the demands of supporting his family, but for Sunil, being a musician is central to his well-being—even if it doesn't adequately support his family. But for many, being immersed in the circle of family and work means that this is the primary source of well-being.

In Chapter 2, I describe how Arvind Rana, a 30-year-old, gets well-being in earning money for his family. He smiles broadly when asked about his children and is delighted to say that he has three. When we ask Arvind about his shaukh, he reminisces about how he used to love cricket:

> I had a shaukh, but now it's become a distant thing, a dream, but I used to have a shaukh of cricket from childhood. I was so mad for it I used to skip my tuitions and not study during the studying times and remained batting and throwing the ball.

But "now," he says, "all is happiness [khushi]. Now life is going very well. I have children. I earn daily and feed the family and enjoy life. I am most happy because I am the reason for my family's happiness. For a common man [aam aadmi] there is nothing greater than his family's happiness. Though we are not well off [itne height (E)] whatever we are, whatever small work we have we make the best of it and provide for the family." Arvind's radiant well-being shines through and his well-being from playing cricket is a "distant thing." Arvind's boss, Hardayal Singh, a 45-year-old Sikh, gets well-being from earning for his family. He says the meaning of khushhali is "when everything is completely right [thik] in the family. Secondly, when the business is running smoothly. That's all [bas]." Hardayal says he has no shaukh and while he has been to the Sikh pilgrimage spot of Hemkund, he says the happiness passed after a few days. Hardayal seemed to me to have enduring life satisfaction, which, like his employee Arvind, centers on earning for a family, which is his main involvement in life.

As I recount in Chapters 2 and 3, a focus on earning a good living is common in the well-being talk of men of a range of classes, especially in the 30s and 40s. Gunjan Kumar, the 35-year-old son of a forestry official, supports his wife, children, and parents with the earnings from his meat shop. For Gunjan,

> Khushhali means there should be no scarcity of anything at home. The children, the wife and myself should live comfortably [aaraam se] in the

home and our needs should be easily arranged. The needs of the children and wife being fulfilled is happiness. My daily business should generate such that all is able to be made right for the parents and everyone.

When I ask Gunjan about specific situations of well-being and a lack of well-being, he describes particular ventures that were successful and others that were not. Gunjan has no shaukh: "I am simply a shopkeeper who starts his business in the morning until night." His purpose is simply to get his two daughters "the best education" and he hopes that by "getting into engineering or the medical field" they will earn and marry well. There is some room for pleasure in Gunjan's life. When I ask him about his pilgrimages he describes the peace [shanti] and good feelings [achcha lagna] he got from visiting Vaishno Devi. "It was temporary, but my heart prompts me to visit that place again and again."

Laborers often seem particularly focused on gaining well-being by supporting their families. A 30-year-old Muslim from Bihar says: "To me khushhali means doing labor to eat. Doing labor, having food, sleeping comfortably [aaraam se] is khushhali. What else?" Raghu Kumar, a 30-year-old Hindu laborer from Bihar, earns a little to help his wife who earns from grazing cattle in Bihar. Still, he says, "doing one's own work and earning money" is the source of khushhali. Pradeep Kumar, a 50-year-old laborer, defines khushhali as the certainty that "the future of my children will be good." Pradeep takes special pleasure in supporting his mother: "When I serve [*seva karna*] my mother it gives [milna] me a lot of happiness [sukh]." Surendra Kumar, the 39-year-old peon working to support his wife and two children, describes his biggest shaukh as "to get work, to do the work, to look after the family. Only he who can nurture the family realizes the biggest happiness [sukh] of the family." Like Gunjan, Surendra also finds pleasure in travel to holy places, like Haridwar. "My soul [aatma] got satisfaction [santushti] and peace [shanti] from those yatras. Whenever we see something beautiful we definitely get [milna] mental peace [*maansik shanti*]." And some of the pleasure is in the memory: "The effect is there for life, because the memories remain for life."

Women in their years rearing children similarly describe the enduring satisfaction they receive from the family life around which their lives often revolve. Yakin Kaur, a 43-year-old, takes in some tailoring work to help support her husband and two children. For Yakin well-being means that "everything is moving well in the family, everything is *sukh-shanti* [happiness-peace] in the family, everyone's health [swasth] is good, and everything is good financially, physically and mentally." Pyara Kaur, a 36-year-old mother with a teaching job, says:

> When my son gets good marks, I'm happy. When people appreciate the food I've cooked, it gives me khushhali. When there is sukh-shanti and prosperity [*samriddhi*] in the family, I experience khushhali.

Gamini Rajput, 34, earned a masters degree in education before devoting herself to keeping house for her husband and two children. "The meaning of khushhali," Gamini says, "is when the family is happy. If the family is happy and the husband is happy, that is the best happiness." A 49-year-old housewife with little education says: "[K]hushhali means doing my household work and doing *namaaz* [prayer]. If my children are happy, I am, too, because my happiness lies in the happiness of my children." A 27-year-old Hindu housewife who passed Class 12, works in the home with the support of her husband who has a menial job. "Khushhali," she says, "means to look after the house and my children and to do the household work." Tulsi Kumar, a 33-year-old, works as a domestic servant and along with her laborer husband raises a family of three daughters and a son. "The happiness of my children means khushhali for me," Tulsi says. "Whatever money I earn through my work I spend on my children so that they can get at least two meals a day."

Life cycle, of course, is not merely based on age. It's not *age* that makes people find well-being from supporting a family, but *lives that immerse them in these tasks*. So, for those who are immersed in these tasks even though outside the 30s and 40s, well-being often comes from the work of supporting families. Amar Thakur is only 20, but has had to work to support his family since his father died. Amar realizes that he had the most happiness "when my father was alive and I had a chance to study." He finds that today all of the weight of the family is on his shoulders. Now, Amar says, "my objective is to work and earn and to look after my family. These are my inner feelings." Amar is young to have responsibility to care for his family—and he enjoyed studying before this. Immersed in earning, it is his source of well-being. Giribala Kumar, a 23-year-old, is unmarried but still faces the pressures of doing housework for her parents and brothers and sisters, who struggle to get by. Giribala, who passed Class 8, says that "doing household works brings happiness [khushi]. This only means khushhali for me." Chandan Kumar, an uneducated gardener in his 60s, has four children in their 30s—and he still hopes to find wives for two of his sons. Chandan still hopes to find a permanent *pakka* [built-up] room to live in and was pained when his eldest son and daughter-in-law left to live separately. "By khushhali," he says, "I mean that I should carry on with my work and earn daily bread. I don't want to be dependent on my children and I want to finish up my responsibilities by [arranging the marriage of] both of my sons."

Indian religious traditions urge older adults to eventually move beyond the stage of being the central care-givers of their families. Indeed, many people in their 60s and beyond find well-being in being supported by their families (see also Lamb 2000; Vatuk 1990) and in spiritual quests, which were often less central in their 30s, 40s, and 50s. Alka Kumar, a 74-year-old Hindu widow in the laboring class, is unable to "move much because of too much back ache." But her daughter-in-law "looks after" her. "Now in this age," she says, "I am getting cooked food [to eat] and washed clothes to wear. This is khushhali for me." Geeti Kumar, a 70-year-old, says that for her khushhali is that all members of her family look after her and respect (izzat karna) her. A 56-year-old Muslim housewife similarly says she gets well-being because all of her children "respect [aadar] me a lot." A 69-year-old Sikh widow says that the "khushhali of old age" is that her son and daughter-in-law take care of her [khayaal rakhna] and respect [izzat karna] her. Sarla Gupta, a 65-year-old, described how her sons made arrangements for her to continue meditation while she traveled. "I feel very happy [bahut khush lagna]," Sarla said, "because both my son and my daughter-in-law respect and love me a lot." Others, of course, complain about not being supported by their families, limiting their well-being. Ishwar Kumar is bitter about lack of family support in his old age, as is the 68-year-old laborer Vashisht Kumar. Vashisht complains that his children should take responsibility on their own shoulders. "Because they aren't doing so, I'm still working with my hands in this age to get two meals a day."

Certainly, many Indians focus on religion at all stages of the life course—and some older Indians don't focus on religion. But many Indians talk about how they turned to religion as their material responsibilities waned. Kavita Kumar, a woman in her 80s, describes well-being as cooking for others and doing for others. She was especially happy when her granddaughter married into a rich (crorepati) family since her own background is "simple middle class." But Kavita, a Hindu, says that today she wants to devote herself fulltime to doing pujapath. "All the day through I remember Bhagwan because ultimately in this stage I don't know when he'll come to take me." Purnima Kumar, 70, was once very concerned with her family's economic conditions. Her greatest sense of well-being came when her daughter got a government job to help bear the expenses that were difficult to meet on her husband's pension. As I detail below, Purnima, who lives alone, has been bothered by unhappy relationship with her son and daughter-in-law who eventually threw her out of the house, causing a grief so great that she doesn't "even have tears to cry over it." Today, she says "religious works and pujapath mean khushhali to me." There is a temple near where she lives and she is "satisfied" going there every day, cleaning the temple and doing pujapath. Abad Khan, a 77-year-old Muslim, says he is from a rich family that lost their wealth during Partition. While still doing some laboring work, Abad is increasingly turning to religion. When asked about a situation in which he got the greatest khushhali, he replies that he has now

> become a religious person [dharmik vyakti]. God [maalik] has saved me from doing many sins [bahut paap]. I used to drink liquor, but when I got the [religious] knowledge I started hating [ghrna] it by the grace of God. I got the greatest happiness [khushi] that my God [maalik] called me to his doorstep [apne dwaar par].

A 61-year-old Muslim widow has become focused on helping her children know about their religion—"they should follow all the rituals and should follow all the good things in the Muslim religion." Tavleen Kaur, a 75-year-old widow, describes her greatest well-being as when her "husband was alive. When the husband doesn't have any vices, it is the greatest happiness for the wife." But today, her greatest happiness is being with Bhagwan. "Khushhali is directly interacting with the almighty and listening to the preachings and religious hymns to learn God's lessons." Pagat Singh, a 57-year-old Sikh, finds that "doing reverential service at the feet of the almighty [*parmatma*] gives khushhali." Pagat describes how he used to do service to his father and son, bringing happiness (khushi) to his mind (man). But now he is searching for a good saint (*sant*) who can help him come

> at the feet of God with reverential service. My ultimate goal is to leave all these worldly things and go in acquaintance with some saint [sant]. The meaning of khushhali in life has changed. Materialistic things do not give khushhali to me now. My khushhali will only be when I find a saint to lead me to the desired path. Whether there is profit or loss in the business no longer matters at all. Fifty-seven years have already passed and now I am on the verge of being a follower of a saint. I have myself bestowed my life in reverential service to the almighty.

Disadvantages of Class and Gender and the Pursuit of Well-being

Some laborers, women, and elderly people complain about their lives. Elderly people are sometimes neglected by their families. Women can be limited by households that oppress them. Laborers often have to work longer for less compensation than other Indians and are not treated well by supervisors. Although structural circumstances limit their well-being, they often (like Fulmala Rajput) still find some well-being in parts of their lives. Many have pleasures. Those oppressed by family circumstances find well-being in work. Laborers with unhappy work may sometimes find well-being in family. As Chapter 8 argues, interactions that push people to think about areas of life that are going well lead even oppressed people to experience some well-being.

Vashisht Kumar, a 68-year-old laborer, recognizes that needing to work today in order to eat tonight limits his pursuit of happiness:

> Until now I have not obtained khushhali in my life. Since I was 15–16 years old, I had learned this work and started doing it. First I had the responsibilities of my parents and my brothers and sisters. After that, I had the responsibilities my children. And, still, I am earning for my livelihood.

Asked about any pilgrimages, he says he's never done any because he doesn't get any "free time [phursut] from my work." Vashisht gets a little pleasure from listening to the radio at work—this is the glimmer of well-being in the interview. Yashoda Kumar, a 53-year-old laboring woman, says her work serves cows and she anticipates well-being in the future when her children succeed. She seems to have more meanings and hope around her life than Vashisht. But, like him, she finds that laboring limits her well-being: "Until now there's been no situation in which I was very happy. That's it [bas]. Bhagwan allows us to spend the life according to what we get."

Even Vashisht enjoys radio and Yashoda has hopes and gets pleasure from helping others and serving cows. Komal Kumar, a 37-year-old, and Deeta Kumar, a 25-year old, are laborers who seemed to be so distressed about their lot that they got little, if any, sense of well-being in current days. Deeta, a 25-year-old widow, despairs that, "There is no meaning of khushhali because until now I have not got it. I have always seen sadness [dukh] in my life." Deeta's troubles partly stem from her husband's untimely death. She married against her parents' wishes and, so, gets no support from either in-laws or parents now. As I described in Chapter 2, Komal Kumar despairs,

> Until now, there is no happiness word in my life. Every day in the morning I get up, prepare food for the whole family, and come to the site. The whole day I work here picking up the burden (bojh) and again when I return in the evening, I cook food for the children, eat it and go to sleep. This is the daily routine of life.

Her husband "drinks a lot. He does not bring money into the house most of the time. He fights with me and beats the children." When asked about her purpose in life Komal says that her only aim is to "get some free time and take a rest." External situations—an alcoholic husband and unremunerative, unrelenting work—limit her well-being. Yet, Deeta married for love and was perhaps happy once. Chapter 8's discussion that well-being is mixed and fleeting suggest that times may change and provide Deeta and Komal well-being as they continue living life.

Some women have ongoing, enduring distressing family circumstances, which make it difficult to find an enduring sense of life satisfaction. Komal Kumar would have a difficult time seeing well-being as inner: Her husband is a drinking wife-beater, who sells household items to get more drink. Shanti Kumar, a 36-year-old domestic servant, similarly was always in sadness because her husband "used to drink a lot. Then I was sad [dukhi] because that made the atmosphere in the house unpeaceful [ashant]. All of the money was spent on sharaab." Pooja Thakur, a postgraduate with a government job, finds khushhali if the home has a peaceful atmosphere and there is enough money to meet the family's needs. Yet she was helpless to assure this when her husband quit his job in a pique.

> When my husband left his job, I was very unhappy because at that time, my children were small and in school and I was just a housewife, so I didn't know what I should do then. What should we do? How should my family fulfill its needs?

Janki Kumar, a 25-year-old, earned a BA and says her husband is a good husband and father. Although disappointed her parents made her quit her studies to marry, she says passing the day in housework gives well-being. Yet she is in a large joint family and her in-laws cause her distress:

> When my father-in-law and brother-in-law drink a lot of alcohol, they shout, create scenes in the family, and fight with each other. Then, everybody is upset in the family and some of the time I think that I should run from here and settle down somewhere with my husband and child.

Purnima Kumar, a 70-year-old widow, recounts multiple situations in which her lack of control of family matters harmed her well-being. When her husband died, she had to live on a half pension while her three young children were in school. Later, her son and daughter-in-law were both very sharp (*tej*) in speaking with her and forced her out of the house. When Meenu Sharma asks her about a purpose in her life, she says that when her son threw her out of his house, all aim of her life had finished. "Even now, I don't have tears to cry over it. I pray to God to take me as soon as possible." One woman described having to leave her father's family after his death and move to her mother's family where she was not treated well. Circumstances sometimes grip so strongly that it's not possible to gain well-being by changing how one thinks of those circumstances.

Because women often live in tight family circles, family relationships sometimes seem to have a stronger effect on their well-being. Husbands or in-laws who drink harm well-being. Tavleen

Kaur, the 75-year-old Sikh widow who is happy to be able to go to gurudwara, emphasizes how much a husband affects the wife's happiness:

> I had khushhali when my husband was alive—he was a very good person. He had no vices, no drinks, no gambling, no chewing tobacco, no eating of paan. He hailed from a very good family. Life goes on. In life, if a husband and wife get along well and understand each other well, then that's happiness. What else? *If husband doesn't have any vice, this is the greatest happiness for the wife.*

Although Tavleen describes a situation of well-being as when her husband was alive, she says that today the biggest source of well-being is that her own beloved (*premi*) children love (pyaar karna) and respect (mannana) her. Sushma Sharma complains by contrast that her husband

> doesn't take work seriously. He takes everything for granted and takes everything jokingly. I'm a mute spectator to the things going on. He's not serious with his work. I am the only one who is nurturing the children and he isn't looking after them. I have to look after everything.

A 56-year-old Muslim housewife reflects that her children are very good and respect her a lot. I think she is right when she concludes that "when relationships in the family are good, there is khushhali." For women, especially, family often dominates life so much that relationships in the family are crucial to well-being.

Some women recognize how their well-being changes when family circumstances change. Alka Kumar, a 74-year-old widow, gains well-being because her daughter-in-law cooks her food and cleans her clothes. Thinking about times of sadness, Alka described how in earlier years her mother-in-law "used to harass" her a lot. Alka says she served her day and night but was nonetheless "abused" all the time. "Then I felt unhappy because all the time I am busy doing the household work and then looking after [my mother-in-law], but she did not pay any good response to me." Geeti Kumar, a 70-year-old widow, has well-being because her son and daughter-in-law and grandchildren "look after my health and my medicines. When I am in pain, they take me to the doctor." Geeti describes her daughter-in-law as like a "Lakshmi" to her and says her grandchildren, too "look after me and love me a lot." Yet in her 30 years of marriage, she constantly experienced deep troubles [pareshani] because her husband used to beat her: "After my son married, everything is alright. My unhappiness [dukh] is much less." For some women being a mother is a great happiness—sometimes because it improves their relationships in their in-laws' house. One 49-year-old describes, for instance, how she will never forget how her eldest son was the first son of his generation in her joint family. "My mother-in-law and father-in-law distributed sweets in the neighborhood and I will never forget when my father-in-law blessed me and my son with great affection." A 51-year-old Sikh gains happiness when people come to her house and eat food. She reflects that the first seven years of marriage were unhappy because her in-laws used to say bad words until her son was born. "Since my son's birth, I have had nothing but happiness."

With limited opportunities, women and the poor seem to focus more on getting well-being from day-to-day things. Vashisht Kumar is a poor laborer whose pleasure is the radio. Raghu Kumar, the 30-year-old laborer, finds happiness in the daily routine of "talking and laughing [hansna bolna]" at the worksite. As I describe in the last chapter, Kantha Chopra, a 58-year-old, like other women, finds well-being in her round of walks and puja:

> We have a routine life. We're simple housewives. We get up early in the morning. We say Ram's name, do some pujapath, go to the temple. The evening walk, too, gives us happiness.

Like many women, Madhvi Gupta, a 48-year-old, describes getting "happiness from normal life. We do pujapath in the morning. It feels good (achcha lagna) to do Bhagwan's darshan." "We do a satsang (gathering) to temple every Thursday, too," she says, but "we keep on discussing it for 2–3-days afterwards and soon enough it is time for the next week's satsang." The hobbies women talk about are often small activities, such as gardening, reading, and listening to music. A 23-year-old unmarried Hindu woman with a bachelors degree in science summarized the focus on small things well:

> Well-being is like this—the small [choti moti] happiness [khushi] of daily life is the main khushhali. We shouldn't wait to say "wah" at a bigger

happiness [khushi]. We should take happiness from everything that can be [*jitna ho sake*]. We should accept things as they are. It's not necessary that happiness should be some special [*khaas*] thing.

The married 34-year-old Gamini Rajput came to a similar conclusion: "One doesn't get happiness from bigger things. It comes from smaller things. Some days pass with less happiness than others"

More advantaged people also get happiness from such small things. Many men mentioned morning or evening walks as important. But given their opportunities, these small things were often not their main focus. Abhilash Aggarwal, an affluent 75-year-old retiree, describes how he gets well-being and "inner satisfaction" from giving service to anyone in any way that he is capable. After the interview, his wife brings us tea and he remarks that the best thing about India is the devotion of Indian wives. He tells how his wife cared for him when he had cancer. "Is that a source of khushhali, too?" I ask. He laughs and says, "It is, but we take it for granted. I can't cook. I can't even make a cup of tea. When I turn on the gas, she runs and says 'let me do it.'" Men, then, get well-being from small things, too, but they may not recognize them as much.

People from disadvantaged groups—especially women and Muslims—seem more focused on how well-being includes not just their own well-being but the well-being of society. Since so many women and Muslims were interviewed by Meenu Sharma, it is possible that there is an interviewer affect here. But it does seem that lacking opportunities in some ways may make one see that for the world to be well, others beyond the self must be well.

A 35-year-old mother says that "the meaning of khushhali in society" is interacting with "mutual respect." "If all the people of society and the country are prosperous," she continues, "it would feel most right." Upjeet Kaur, a 51-year-old, has passed Class 10. Her husband's spare parts store provides the comfort of a scooter, TV, and fridge, but they are not prosperous. Upjeet describes experiencing khushhali when she prepares food for relatives who come to her house. She describes great feeling of khushhali as occurring when she gave medicine to a poor man whom she met on her way back from a pilgrimage to Hemkund. In addition to the satisfaction of helping particular people, Upjeet describes herself as "very happy" whenever she "see[s] somebody progressing in life.

I am very happy because I want that everyone should lead a good and prosperous [*unnati*, lit. advanced] life." Ghadda Khan, 30, is a married postgraduate, but her husband's shop doesn't even afford them a scooter. When Meenu asks her what well-being means to her she replies, "By khushhali, I mean that everyone should be educated. Only then will my *Bharat* [India] be well. I pray to God to give everyone good health." Women, it seems, are more likely than most men to recognize that well-being includes not just their own well-being, but the well-being of society.

Muslims—less educated and prosperous than other Indians, less represented in government jobs, and sometimes the targets of Hindu violence—similarly, seem to better recognize that well-being must extend beyond the individual. Ghadda Khan, the 30-year-old who would find well-being if everyone in India is educated and healthy, notes further that to attain sukh-shanti (happiness and peace) there must be no differences between Hindus and Muslims. Aarif Khan, a 35-year-old plumber, wants to do service (seva) to all members of society, no matter what caste (jati) in order to bring unity (*ektaa*) among people in society. Salim Khan, the ambitious 26-year-old journalist, defines well-being in a way that includes not just himself, but all of society:

> *Khushhali* means your family is prosperous [*sampann*]. In the family is khushhali. The parents are happy [khush], the brother and sisters are happy. Everyone is happy. After that, people in the near vicinity are happy, people in the village are happy, people in the city are happy and people in the whole country are happy. Then we get more happiness.

In his mind, Salim sees the necessity of a felicitous chain of well-being. Wahid Khan, a 21-year-old engineering student, defines well-being as "universal peace. First and foremost, if I am happy or satisfied, I want every other person to be happy." Wahid doesn't think he could truly have well-being unless the state is equipped "with all of the amenities and infrastructure be it environmental, social and economic." Wahid does not feel he could have well-being unless the roads are good! Razia Khan, a 33-year-old, has experienced discrimination. It was tough enough to find an apartment to rent as a Muslim, but when people learned her husband was a lawyer, potential landlords shied away because of a fear a lawyer might somehow capture the house. Perhaps it is this situation that shapes Razia's definition of well-being.

> To me, khushhali means to help others. Whenever anyone comes into my house, whether known or unknown, I prepare food for them and ask them to eat it. I would like that all the people should live together peacefully. *Khushhali* means to help others without any selfish emotion [*niswaarth bhavna*].

Conclusion

There are many ways to find meanings and many pleasures to enjoy. There are many satisfying individual pursuits and many sorts of connections that can be valued. So there is tremendous diversity in how people find well-being.

But life circumstances of age, gender, class, and religion push people into certain circles of life, shaping people's choices. Because people in the middle of life are pushed into the circle of work and family, they find well-being in these areas in which they are most involved. Circumstances also affect opportunities, sometimes causing hardships, which limit the sources of well-being people can pursue. Being disadvantaged due to social circumstances seems to help people empathize with others, leading them to emphasize how well-being truly only comes when happiness is widespread through society.

References

Bapna, Geetika. 2012. "Marriage, Language and Time: Toward an Ethnography of *Nibhaana*." *Economic and Political Weekly*, XLVII(43, October 27): 109–117.

Barrett, Michele. 1991. *The Politics of Truth: From Marx to Foucault*. Stanford, CA: Stanford University Press.

Derné, Steve. 1995. *Culture in Action: Family Life, Emotion, and Male Dominance in Banaras, India*. Albany, NY: SUNY Press.

———. 2000. *Movies, Masculinity, and Modernity: An Ethnography of Men's Filmgoing in India*. Westport, CT: Greenwood Press.

———. 2008. *Globalization on the Ground: Media and the Transformation of Culture, Class, and Gender in India*. New Delhi: SAGE Publications.

Lamb, Sarah. 2000. *White Saris and Sweet Mangoes: Aging, Gender, and Body in North India*. Berkeley, CA: University of California Press.

———. 1997. "The Making and Unmaking of Persons: Notes on Aging and Gender in North India." *Ethos*, 25(3): 279–302.

Swidler, Ann and Jorge Arditi. 1994. "The New Sociology of Knowledge." *Annual Review of Sociology*, 20: 305–29.

Vatuk, Sylvia. 1990. " 'To Be a Burden on Others': Dependency Anxiety Among the Elderly in India." In *Divine Passions: The Social Construction of Emotion in India*, edited by Owen Lynch, 61–90. New Delhi: Oxford University Press; Berkeley, CA: University of California Press.

7

INDIAN WAYS OF LIVING THE GOOD LIFE

One should meditate upon the Supreme—the limitless, unchanging, all-knowing cause of the happiness of the world, *dwelling in the sea of one's own heart as the goal of all striving.* (my emphasis)

—*Maha Narayan Upanisad* (Muller-Ortega 1989, 72)

Those who make the passage to India can expect no simple answers, no answers at all; rather perhaps to become more aware of the mystery. Those who want answers had better go elsewhere; or stay elsewhere. In India Blake's 'dread forms of certainty' melt away. Certainties are lost, rather than found.

—Kathleen Raine (1990, 5)

Poet Kathleen Raine came to India, like me, as an outsider. Like me, Raine learned from India. Although I am a 'South Asianist' and I studied Hindi in school, I didn't come to India as a seeker looking for spirituality. When I was 21 and living in Cloyne Court, a student cooperative in Berkeley, Laurie Troyer would rhythmically dance in the basement, bells on her ankles, the hard thump of her feet punctuating the ring of the bell. Intoxicated, enchanted, I'd ask, "Where did you learn to do that?" At the time, I knew next to nothing about Nepal: I was surprised it was in the northern hemisphere. When I asked at a discount travel agency from which I got my air ticket whether there was a "Let's Go! Nepal," I was surprised to learn that there was such a thing as *Lonely Planet Travel Survival Guide,* which came in at 157 pages—scant compared to today's versions! Laurie had written me about being content in Nepal and intoxicated in India, and preferring intoxication. After Nepal, I, too, turned to India.

When I got to Nepal at the age of 22, I was profoundly skeptical of religion. I walked the grounds of Pashupatinath, the temple celebrating Shiva as lord of the beasts, but I politely obeyed the "no non-Hindu sign" and didn't enter, seeing myself as nonreligious. As an academic sociologist, I thought India was a good foil to compare with the USA—diverse (Hindu, Muslim, Sikh, so many languages), democratic with large cities, although most of people lived in villages, too. And my studies were concerned with sociological questions about culture, globalization, family, and gender. I saw myself as secular, anti-religious. At the age of 26, when I lived in Banaras, I was going into Kashi Vishwanath—which also barred non-Hindus—but as a scholar. Back then, I didn't know yet I was a Hindu. I got to India for academic reasons and for intoxication and adventure, not for spiritual growth. I learned the spiritual attraction slowly, learning mythology reading *Amar Chitra Katha* comic book stories of the gods and goddesses to improve my Hindi and learning about Indian religions from my interviews and from my interviewees who took me to holy places. By the time I got to Kedarnath, the *jyotirlinga* that is an abode of Shiva in the Indian Himalaya in 2007, I was beginning to sense I was a Hindu and to sense my special connection to Shiva and to Mahadevi too. Chanting *om namaha shivay*, bubbles came up from a spring high up at Kedar. By 2012, I was making the trek to my fourth jyotirlinga, Jageshwar. Like villagers in India's flat plains who see the sacred spots in the Himalaya in their own smaller hills, I began to see how my neighborhood runs in Rochester, New York, USA took me to Yamunotri (Graduate Theological Seminary), Gangotri (Highland Park Reservoir), Kedarnath (Pinnacle Hill), and Badrinath (Summit Drive; Derné 2013). My wife was Ganga; the ice at the end of my driveway that melted into water was Gaumukh. I assumed if I ever got back to Pashupatinath, it would be obvious I am a Shaivite and I'll come on in.

It took a while for me to even begin to make sense of Hinduism. I was looking for core beliefs, but ultimately Hinduism recognizes that it is all good. Shiva is the greatest ascetic, but also the greatest erotic. The Gita counsels that one should be vegetarian. Unless one can't; in which case, be a warrior! I was confused because I thought I was looking for *a* doctrine, but actually it is all good. As Chaudhuri

(1979, 148) puts it, "A Hindu is under no compulsion to subscribe to any dogma or profess faith in a particular thing." The Hindu "might even extend" faith to a "number of dogmas which are utterly inconsistent with one another."

As the first epigraph of this chapter suggests, Hinduism focuses on well-being. This chapter argues that *distinctive* aspects of Indian traditions—and especially its religious traditions—provide insight into living the good life. Indian religious traditions embrace contradiction and physical pleasure, both of which are fundamental to well-being. The immersion in spirituality and ultimate matters urged by Indian religions contributes to well-being as well.

While I make some references to Sikhism and Islam, it is Hinduism I know best—all of my earlier studies were with Hindus—and, so, I mostly reference the Hindu tradition. As I mention earlier, recent scholarship is right, I think, to focus on common *South Asian* religious tradition with parallel elements in Muslim, Sikh, and Hindu traditions—elements such as darshan, pilgrimage, submission, devotion, meditation, offerings, relationships with a spiritual guide, recitation, the sensate's self's connection to nature, and connections of the spiritual to the bodily (Bellamy 2011; Kent and Kassam 2013; Oberoi 1994; Taneja 2013). This scholarship is consistent with my experiences of knowing Hindus who regularly visit Islamic dargahs, meeting Hindus at Muslim and Sikh religious spots, and meeting Sikhs at Hindu religious spots. The scholarship, moreover, is not just recent. Calcutta sociologist Benoy Kumar Sarkar (1884–1949; 1941, 351) argued that while Islamic "religious dogmas" don't have affinity with Hindu dogmas, the *"mores* of Indian Muslims and Hindus are common" and "many of the customs and folkways of the Muslims of India are identical with the *samskaras* of the Hindus" reflecting common roots in "pre-Hindu or non-Hindu and pre-Muslim aboriginals" of India.

Anthropologists and psychologists recognize that well-being varies from place to place. Summarizing anthropological evidence, Mathews and Izquierdo (2009, 1) argue that happiness is not the "same everywhere; the experience of happiness is culturally specific." Psychologist Ed Diener and his colleagues identified different correlates of happiness in different cultures (Diener and Suh 2000; Diener et al. 1995). Indians may experience well-being in different ways than Americans. Because of their traditions, Indians may more easily accept the contradictory experiences necessary for well-being.

They may more easily recognize connections and pleasures as central to well-being. Americans, who lack these traditions, may not as easily recognize these sources of well-being. But I suggest that the sources of well-being highlighted by Indian traditions are a source of well-being for Americans as well.

The chapter is eclectic—it draws on academic work on Indian religions, but popular sources, too. It draws on what I've learned about religion from the people I've interviewed all of these years. I draw on the texts that have appealed to me and come into my hands as I've been living with and in India (off and on) over 30 years. I'm not a religious studies scholar, so I haven't tried to systematically review the scholarship on Indian religious traditions. The gentle complaint T.N. Madan (1997, 189) applies to D.P. Mukerji's references to Indian religion probably applies to my analysis, too: "One has the uncomfortable feeling that [Mukerji] himself operated more in terms of intuition and general knowledge than a deep study of the texts." It took me some years to identify the features of Hinduism I focus on in this chapter—and I did so more by living with and in India than studying these traditions. But, I nonetheless think that most people familiar with Hinduism will recognize as commonplace or self-evident these features of Hinduism that I focus on here. What I try to do that *is* distinctive is to highlight some fundamental features of Indian religious traditions and thought by identifying how Indian sociology (and to a lesser extent Indian philosophy and Indian psychoanalysis) have been influenced by Indian religious traditions and thought. It's an odd way of highlighting Indian religious traditions and thought that shape Indians' understandings of well-being, but it lays the groundwork for a later chapter that identifies important insights of Indian sociology that have been neglected by mainstream sociology in recent years. And it perhaps allows me to add some sociological insight to understanding Indian religions.

Sociocentrism: Recognizing Well-being from Social Connections

When I first lived in India in 1986, I was struck by how the upper-caste Hindu men whom I interviewed saw themselves as part of family groups. Often living in tightly-packed joint families, they valued guidance from family. A cohort of brothers often developed a strong sense of interconnectedness. People easily saw their achievements as supported by families even more than by their individual effort (Derné 1995). I had stumbled upon sociocentrism of Indian thinking, which had been recognized by anthropologists and psychoanalysts long before me (e.g., Kakar 1981; Roland 1988; Shweder 1991).

Early Indian sociologists, too, recognized that the individualistic assumptions of Western sociology were of questionable relevance in India. D.P. Mukerji (1884–1961) found that the sociology texts he read missed the "elementary fact" that India's history, economics and philosophy "had always centered in social groups, and at best, in socialized persons" ([1955] 2013, 213). Mukerji (1955 [2013], 213) judged these scholars "competent" in their own fields, but thought that they missed "India's social system of action," and, so, their work appeared "narrow, circumscribed, fragmented and partial." Mukerji (1955 [2013], 217) found Parsons's action system did not apply for the simple reason that action for the Indian is "not individualistic" but is inherently structured on normative, teleological bases. Indian sociologist Radhakamal Mukerjee goes further and argues that methodological individualism is not only a poor theory of motives in India, but in the West as well.[1]

Like the East Asian cultures of Japan and Taiwan (Larsen and Eid 2008; Suh and Koo 2008), Indians seem to require a greater social component for happiness than people in individualistic cultures. They don't find well-being as much in self-esteem and positive emotions as people in individualistic cultures do. Indians, like the pseudononymous Niranjan Kamboj, seem to more easily recognize chains of felicitous interactions as necessary for happiness. Perhaps people in individualistic cultures have more sensitivity to violation of the self—I'm driven mad by dogs barking and horns honking in India and I'm not that keen on crowding into tight buses or dealing with crowds in the streets (and, of course, in the USA I'm bothered by smoking, bad driving, and so on)—while people in sociocentric cultures have more sensitivity to disruption of relationships.

---

[1] Radhakumal Mukerjee (1960, 79) criticizes social science for giving a "distorted picture of" an "isolated and self-contained individual self" that focuses on the individual's "elemental predispositions and strivings." For Mukerjee (1960, 77) this "false metaphysical individualism" is the basis of the social sciences' "inadequate" and "false theories and concepts."

So, Girish Aggarwal describes well-being as being "part of the sukh-dukh [joys and sorrows] of others." When he told me about a situation in which he experienced well-being he said that "the biggest happiness came from the way my parents brought me up. Right from childhood, they nurtured and cared for me." When I asked about a situation of a lack of well-being he said, "Except for a few instances when my parents scolded me for my bad acts, I don't remember any circumstances which made a lack of well-being in my life."

I argue, *not* that Indians are more likely to get well-being from these chains of interactions, but that the cultural sociocentrism allows them to more easily *recognize* they get well-being from such felicitous interactions. In short, I think that because of their sociocentrism, Indians *recognize* sources of well-being that people in individualistic cultures often miss.

Seva

India's major religions—Hinduism, Islam, and Sikhism—all emphasize seva or service. Islam emphasizes service to guests and to society. Sikhs focus especially on service to the poor and the elderly. The institution of langar in which Sikh gurudwaras provide community meals (which has parallels among some Hindu Vaishnavas) is perhaps the clearest Sikh celebration of service to the poor—a celebration Sikhs themselves often comment on. Everyone can contribute something: farmers can give grain, pulses and potatoes, some can give money to support langar, and others can cook or serve the food. Sikhs often comment that everyone is welcome at langar. I always experience a feeling of community sitting side by side with my fellows, receiving food from metal buckets. The poet Raine (1990, 234–35) describes the experience (as an outsider) well:

> Rich and poor, a high ranking officer covered with medals side by side with gardeners and the women who swept the pavement ... were all served. One Sikh gentleman who served us was a High Court judge ... another a well-known Punjabi writer. Our shoes removed, we sat in lines facing one another in the welcome shade of a wall. Again and again the chapatties, the dahl, the curried vegetables, the cool water, were brought round—excellent food of this rich land, the best dahl I have ever tasted.

So it should be—no money was involved, nothing bought or sold, all was fruit of the earth and the work of human hands.

How can one not see the well-being of helping others?

Seva is, of course, a dominant Hindu principle. Referencing Krishna devotion, ethnographer Peter Bennett (1990, 189–90) describes *seva* as "an expression of selfless love for Krishna and the delightful experience of loving Krishna." Bennett quotes a Pushti Marg perceptor who says that in "seva, love [*sneha*] and Bhagwan's happiness come first." A devotee recounts that a real Vaishnava has such feelings of love (*premabhava*) for God, that if something is needed in the temple, the real Vaishnava "gives quietly and expects nothing in return." Untouchable leader Ambedkar criticized the implied subordination in Gandhi's service to untouchables. For women, seva was often service to husbands. Well known among Hindu women, Annapurna, the Hindu goddess of nourishment, celebrates the provision of food. Yet Manuela Ciotti (2012, 153–54) has recently shown how both women and untouchables say they are empowered by seva. Untouchable women in political movements shift their role from 'receivers' of social service to 'providers' of such service. Women appropriate the legitimacy of social service (samaaj seva) and social work (*samaaj karya*) to justify political work outside the home.

While embracing *seva* can be ambiguous for oppressed groups, early Indian sociologists recognized the importance of a focus on *seva* in shaping Hindu communities. Calcutta sociologist Benoy Kumar Sarkar (1941, 363) argued that Vedic sacrifices "comprise a set of social services" which "serve to render the individual community-minded in a comprehensive manner." Sarkar quotes the Bengali writings of another Indian sociologist Ramendra Sundar Trivedi (1864–1922), who argued the Vedic sacrifices regard the "entire world" as a "divinity. Whatever exists on earth is a God." The human being has "debts to everything." Therefore, the individual has to "sacrifice something in favour of everybody and everything to repay those debts" (Trivedi 1921, 172 as quoted and translated by Sarkar 1941, 364). Sarkar (1941, 355) reports that Bengali sociologist Trivedi interprets sacrifice as a "cult of active social service. The sacrificial rites or rituals thus come to imply nothing but the self sacrifice of the individual in the interest of the collectivity." Indian sociologist Radhakamal Mukerjee (1951, v) quotes the *Mahabharata*'s counsel that "doing others good is the highest virtue." Or in a popular contemporary Hindu text: "When we freely give time to work that benefits others, we make offerings to the lord" (Easwaran 2006, 166). "It is good to remember that old age will come to all of us. Spiritual awareness teaches us to serve someone in this condition cheerfully and lovingly" (Easwaran 2006, 69).

The most common sentiment offered by the people I interviewed was that helping others is part of well-being. Perhaps Indians easily see this because of the religious highlighting of service as a value. But I don't mean to argue that those in more individualistic cultures don't also get well-being from connections to others. Moreover, if those in individualistic cultures more easily recognize the well-being that comes from self-fulfillment, that doesn't mean that Indians don't find well-being in such fulfillment as well, only that they may not recognize it as easily. That is why I tried to put these two aspects of life together in Chapter 3—people get well-being from both individual pursuits and connections to others.

Pleasure and Play

Grounded in the "ancient texts" he cites, Indian sociologist Radhakamal Mukerjee (1889–1968; 1951, iii) emphasizes that "the drive or energy emerging from *desire* is *Divine* as it sheds the passion for enjoyment, indulgence or anger" (my emphasis). Mukerjee (1951, 3–4) argues that in Indian traditions the person's "enjoyment of pleasures" in a "brief span of life" is what "conquer[s]" "finiteness and mortality." Citing the Gita, Mukerjee (1951, iii) describes how such "desires" also drive the proper "pursuits" of "marriage, family, wealth and happiness." Hindu ethics, he recounts, are not based on any sense of guilt. Rather, Hindu ethics focus on "constructive strivings toward regeneration and fulfillment" (Mukerjee 1950 [2005], 445). Mukerjee (1950 [2005] 445) argues that Hindus, thus, put less emphasis "on inhibition and repression and more on self-development and self-transcendence." D.P. Mukerji's ([1942] 1948, 125) analysis of Indian culture similarly finds no "trace of priggishness in matters of sex.... Everywhere the man-woman relation is healthy. Gods and goddesses, princes and courtesans, princesses and their lovers obey the dictates of nature without fear of offending against a superior moral law." Indeed, ancient Hindu poets indicate how yoga practice helps a lover delay his or her own orgasm so as not to stand in the way of the "pleasure from simultaneous orgasm for both" (Chaudhuri 1979, 234; see also Mukerjee 1957, 297). The *Krishna Jamna Khanda* describes in detail the coitus of Krishna and Radha (Chaudhuri 1979, 275) and Hindu festivals make provision for "sensual enjoyment" (Chaudhuri 1979, 299). D.P. Mukerji ([1942] 1948, 127) describes the Upanishads as celebrating "joy of living in tune with the Infinite." Tantric initiate Prem Saran works in the Indian administrative services, but also writes as a scholar who earned his PhD in cultural anthropology from the University of California, Santa Barbara. Saran's scholarship offers an insider account of Hinduism's focus on pleasures. Hinduism, he says, has a "purposeless and playful cosmogony and worldview" (Saran 2008, 22). Saran describes his own approach to the deity as "playful," and he wanted to teach this playful mentality to his children.

Sensuality and dance is fundamental to Indian religion. To play with Radha and Krishna on the Yamuna at moonlight is to be playfully religious. Most Hindus are familiar with Shiva's *Nataraja* dance and the dancing of Krishna and the gopis. Indian literature, art, and music clearly highlight the passions, bodies, and carnal pleasures of Krishna and of the gopis (e.g., Spink 2004).

The pleasure and sensuality of food is central in Hindu rituals. *Panchamarita*—five nectars of honey, milk, ghee, and yogurt—are often distributed just before prasad. Pushpesh Pant (2006, 210) describes the sensuality of taking prasad: "One receives the spoonful respectfully in cupped hands, raises the cup to the lips and wipes the hand clean by passing the palm over the hair." As Pant (2006, 209) notes, "Ancient Indians made no distinction between the supreme cosmic reality Brahman and *anna* or food that nourishes and sustains us. Food for us is synonymous with life, its very sap, essence of existence or *rasa*" (see also Lynch 1990, 103–04). As sociologist Radhakamal Mukerjee (1957, 305) puts it, food seeking is "physical and personal, psychic and social, spiritual and cosmic."

Terms such as "flashing, glittering, gleaming, glistening, twinkling or sparkling" (Muller-Ortega 1989, 119) suggest the pleasures of the "enlightenment experiences" (Muller-Ortega 1989, 14) sought by Tantric practitioners. In Tantra, the practitioner combines *bhukti* (sexual enjoyment) with *mukti* (spiritual freedom), and *yoga* (spiritual practice) with *bhoga* (sexual enjoyment; Muller-Ortega 1989, 55; Saran 2008, 142). The goal is to obtain *jivan mukti* or liberation while still alive (Muller-Ortega 1989, 37). As Saran (2008, 142) puts it, one approaches all things in the world with *sukha-bhavana* or a joyful attitude. Indian art historian Harsha Dehejia (2008, 14) describes the supreme delight and condition of perfect joy one seeks as arising "from a multiplicity of sources such as the pleasure of eating and drinking, seeing a relative or a friend after a long time, the bliss of music and the delight of sexual union." Radhakamal Mukerjee (1957, 174) describes Hinduism's "primordial pair" as symbolizing the "identity between enjoyment (bhukti) and salvation (mukti), between bondage and freedom. Here then is an uplifting of normal marital sexuality as contrasted with the oppressive sense of sin with which it was invested by Christianity in medieval Europe."

Hinduism (whether inside or outside Tantra) celebrates the eroticism of Shiva and Parvati and of Radha and Krishna. As Pavan Varma (2001, 72) puts it, "unconstrained joy" is the "essence of divinity." While not the whole of that joy, sex is an "aspect of divine joy." Thus, "Krishna's presence in Vrindavan" gave "sanctity to the joys of the flesh." As Chaudhuri (1979, 271) notes "love for Krishna as God must correspond to sexual love between men and women." Indian philosopher Daya Krishna (1924–2007) (1989, 135) rightly describes a distinguishing feature of Indian art and Sanskrit literature as "dripping sensuality." *Kama* [passion] is one of the four classical aims of life valorized in Hindu religion. Thus, Gupt (2004, 17) summarizes that "traditional Indian society was very clear that *shringara* or the romantic emotion was ... not only to be encouraged but was obligatory. The judicious person was one who knew how to seek sexual fulfillment and yet not transgress other obligations." Thus, the *Kamasutra* urges that "right conduct (*dharma*), profit (artha) and emotional gratification (kama) are achieved without any one obstructing the other two." As Radhakamal Mukerjee (1957, 299) puts it, Indian religion not only "enjoins the fulfillment of sexual impulse" but has evolved ways of "blending the goals of sex and mysticism" "for the consecration of senses and desires."

William James (1902, 171) describes how in Christianity the self often appears divided. Augustine felt he had two wills, "one carnal, the other spiritual," which contended with each other and "disturbed" his soul. In the Hinduism of Shiva and Parvati and of Radha and Krishna, there is no conflict. As Pavan Varma (1993, 64) points out when Krishna makes love with Radha, "the carnal and the spiritual make a surprising fusion." "The Hindu view of life," he says, "was always informed by two parallel themes: one emphasizing the legitimacy of desire, the other stressed the joys of transcending desire" (Varma 1993, 119). Saran (2008, 10) summarizes the truism that in Indic thought there is no "rigid distinction between the body and the mind" or between the "sacred and the profane." So, one "visualizes oneself as God or Goddess" (Saran 2008, 10) and experiences the sacred in eroticism and sexuality (e.g., Muller-Ortega 1989, 53–55). As the devotee becomes Shiva or Parvati (or both!) incarnate, the body and senses are radically transformed.

So, in Tantra, yoga processes lead to *both* inner enlightenment *and* physiological transformation of the body (Muller-Ortega 1989, 28). Because the body is perceived as composed of all deities, Tantra worships the body as a vessel of the supreme and sees the body as a central tool for enlightenment. As the body becomes God-like, the cosmos becomes like one's body (Muller-Ortega 1989, 53–60). As Indian religious traditions recognize the pleasures of sexuality and the body as promoting rather than hindering spiritual development, is it any surprise that so many Indians recognize the importance of pleasures in a life of well-being? This book argues that all people need pleasure and play for well-being. While I've emphasized James's argument that Christianity often divides the self, T.M. Luhrmann has recently showed how Christian evangelicals today include playful elements. They play that God is walking alongside them or they pour God a cup of coffee or set a dinner plate for Him, encouraging a "light, fanciful, not-real-but-more-real-than-real quality to the experience of God" (Luhrmann 2012, 83). Yet this focus on playful pleasure still seems more consistently celebrated in India. Because Indians live in a culture that celebrates sexuality, food, and dance and associates these with divinity, Indians perhaps more easily recognize pleasures and dripping sensuality of life more easily than most.

Well-being in Living the Contradictions

The distinctive feature of Hinduism and one with great implications for living well is its embrace of contradictions. While Hinduism embraces pleasures of the body, it *also* embraces renunciation of the body in fasting and mortification. David Kinsley (1982, 176) puts it well: "The distinctive nature of Hinduism resides in its *simultaneous affirmation* that people have an obligation to uphold the world, on the one hand, and to transcend the world on the other." The essence of Hinduism, he says, lies not in compromise, but in

> the clear demand that *both obligations are absolute*. Over the centuries, Hinduism has been characterized more by a desire to push each obligation to its limit than by the desire to reconcile the two and risk compromising either of them. It is the tension between dharma [duty] and *moksha* [liberation] that characterizes Hinduism and lends it its special appeal. (1982)

As Lannoy puts it,

> The Indian style of living favours alternations between sensory deprivation and sensory bombardment. On the one hand, fasting, yoga, meditation, reduction in the hours of sleep, concentration on silent and solitary rites. On the other, lights, music, perfumes, flowers, sudden noise, rhythmical movement, surging crowds. At one moment, everything conspires to turn the individual inward only to be thrust at the next into a maelstrom of noise, movement, colour. (2002, 129)

What distinguishes Hindus, Chaudhuri (1979, 234) argues, is "their capacity to face all realities, and wherever possible derive pleasure from them." "Hindu spirituality," he says, "can quite naturally be brought within the worldly framework of their religion" (Chaudhuri 1979, 311)—that is, spiritual and worldly values are not in conflict. Radhakamal Mukerjee (1951, ii) argues that Indians achieve "freedom" only "through a proper scaling of the four-fold values of life, wealth (artha), enjoyment (kama), righteousness (dharma) and self-realisation (moksha)." Quoting an "ancient text," Mukerjee says that these goals are "to be equally striven after; and one who pursues a single goal deserves censure." McDaniel (1989, 154) describes tantrics as ultimately reaching a stage in which they have "experienced all possibilities and extremes, and gone beyond traditional moralities to one in which all objects and actions are equally valuable." Radhakamal Mukerjee (1957, 303) argues that the "mother-deity (Sakti) unites in her appearance ... love and hate, goodness and evil, beauty and ugliness, exhibiting the *mutually contradictory modes of the cosmic energy* that endure untouched by the scale of human valuation." By identifying with Shiva, he says, the "devotee contemplates all the symbolic pairs of opposites and reaches beyond these to the unrelated, ineffible totality of the cosmos."

The current study suggests that well-being involves the pursuit of multiple goals. For well-being one needs togetherness and solitude, bodily pleasures and mindful meanings, and connections to others and individual striving. Hinduism deeply and fundamentally refuses to privilege one side of experience over another or even to draw compromises between them, but rather urges pushing each side of life to extremes. Thus, the government administrator-Tantric-academic scholar Prem Saran (2008, 121–22) summarizes: "The Indic running together of the sacred and the secular, the divine and the human, is part of a *non-modern* and pervasive civilisational ability to be quite comfortable with supposedly dichotomous categories that would cause serious cognitive noise in the Aristotelian cultural universe." Saran (2008, 122) cites T.N. Madan (1989), another Western-trained Indian sociologist, as noting how often Western ethnographers are uneasy with Indians' ability to combine "mortality and fertility, solemnity and fun, seriousness and frivolousness, metaphysical speculation and folk belief."

Mircea Eliade lived in Calcutta in his 20s. He fell in love, he studied Sanskrit, he experienced the supernatural, he practiced yoga, and he lived in an ashram in the Himalaya. In his autobiography of those years he described India as a "mixture of asceticism, metaphysical exultation and sexuality" (Eliade 1981, 134). His book on yoga, which made his career, recognized that the word yoga "means many things" "because yoga is many things" (Eliade [1958] 1969, 150). For us Westerners who lived in India as young people, India is a moveable feast. (Eliade's autobiography goes cold, but unlike me he didn't keep returning to India; he didn't adopt an Indian lifestyle in Europe or the USA.)

The same mixture of opposites is apparent in Raja Rao's ([1960] 1986, 99) insider account: The Gita is "an affirmation not of the good but of Truth. *Truth can take no sides—it is involved in both sides.*" As is well known, the Gita proposes several paths to salvation—knowledge, devotion, and action—and the paths themselves are contradictory (Varma 2001, 130; Eliade 1958 [1969], 120). The Gita says the self is an illusion, but also the self extends to the whole universe. Krishna says to Arjuna that the self is "deluded by individuality" when the self thinks, 'I am the actor'" (Varma 2001, 129). Yet Varma (2001, 130) notes that the Gita also "exalts the ego, by claiming that it too is part of the infinite Atman, the supreme spirit."

Trawick (1990, 41, 37) points out that the pervasiveness of ambiguity in Indian culture means "South Asian deities" "are not consistent. Each has a dual nature; each is split." Varma (2001) notes that Krishna in Vrindavan gives "sanctity to the joys of the flesh," but that his absence from Vrindavan conveys the "limitations of the joys of the flesh." Shiva is the best ascetic, but also the best erotic (O'Flaherty 1973). Shiva can be completely engrossed in meditation in the Himalayas, but when Parvati brings him down for sex, the earth shakes. Trawick's (1990, 38) summary is a good one:

> Siva, whose sign is the phallus, is said to be half female. In his form as Ardhanariswaran, his body is split down the middle, woman on the left, man on the right. He is the king of ascetics—men who give up all physical pleasures and keep their sexual power within themselves. He is also king of philanderers; he makes love to his yogini wife as well as to many others not out of any sense of duty ... but for the sake of pleasure only.

The tenth century Kashmiri Shaivite Abhinavagupta said that the goddess should not be conceived as different from Shiva: "The reality of Siva, therefore, has neither beginning nor end and it is luminous with its own light. Within itself [the reality of Shiva] embraces all principles, which are in effect identical with it" (Muller-Ortega 1989, 86–87). Or in the *Shvetashvatara Upanishad*: "You are woman, you are man/ You are the youth and the maiden, too./ You as an old man, faltering along with the staff;/ you are the dark blue bird/ You are the green (parrot) with red eyes.... Having no beginning, you are everywhere" (Bokhare 2006, 35). Shiva is wild God, but also "the most romantic, faithful and docile of husbands" (Lannoy 2002, 138).

The sensibility of recognizing the contradictory paths in life is apparent in theories of personality developed by early Indian sociologists. Drawing on classical Sanskrit texts, Benoy Kumar Sarkar (1941, 79–80) identifies humans as having four "fundamental instincts"—kama (sex), *kamchana* (wealth), *kirit* (reputation) and karma (work, action, or creation). It's notable that these relate well to the "universal" aspects of well-being I identify in part I of this book: Kamchana has parallels to wealth, karma to individual striving, kirit to connections to others, and kama to pleasure. Sarkar (1941, 25, 79–80) criticizes (Western) sociological interpretations for tending to advance "monistic" interpretations emphasizing sex or economy or politics, for instance. Instead, Sarkar (1941, 25) urges that sociologists should "stress" "the pluralistic make-up of the mind or personality." Radhakamal Mukerjee ([1950] 2005, 430) argues that people whose self is harmonized by yoga can "see the self abiding in all creatures and all creatures in the self." Because a person sees "equality in life with all sentient creatures" the person experiences "profound joy and absolute compassion from which well forth infinite sharing and service to the world."

Western traditions of noncontradiction and emphasis on specialization may militate against recognizing the felicity of pursuing contradictory paths associated with well-being. Such paths are more easily seen in India where contradiction is celebrated. Jivraj Sharma, the 49-year-old police officer and husband, describes himself as an ardent devotee of "Bhagwan Shiva, Bhagwan Bholenath. He is complete God and on the other hand he is totally incomplete. So am I too. I am not perfect in any field but have the knowledge of every field." Following the Hindu path of identifying with the deity, Jivraj identifies with Shiva's contradictory traits. With Hindu traditions that identify seeing the lord in everyone whatever their path, perhaps Indians more easily see the well-being that comes from connecting to diverse other people. To be well, it helps to recognize that it's all good—and Hinduism helps people recognize that.

Religion's Pervasiveness

At least until recently, religion was pervasive in India. Vishwanath Naravane (1978, 95) remarks that religion is the national life music and is used to understand even economics and politics. Naravane (1978, 17–18) retells Vivekananda's tale that if you ask the average Westerner a deep question about religion, the reply will be simply that he or she attends church.

> But if you ask [the Westerner] about the elections to the Congress or the state of the economy, he [or she] will talk to you with enthusiasm. On the contrary, if you ask an average Indian about political issues he [or she]

will say: 'I don't know. Some one comes every year to collect revenue on my land.' But if you ask [the Indian] about the nature of God, or the creation of the world, or human suffering, [the person] will warm up and talk to you about *maaya, samsara* and mukti.

In pointing to ultimate realities, religion pushes away from a narrow materialist focus, allowing people to experience more well-being. Indian philosopher Daya Krishna (1989, 98) rightly recognizes "there are moments in everybody's life when one has a vague feeling of the Transcendence Beyond towards which one feels an intimate relation with overtones of peace and joy and calm suffusing one's whole experience." By encouraging "a *seeking* for something beyond this world" (Krishna 1989, 114), religion encourages the "opening of one's self" to experiences of transcendence (Krishna 1989, 98). "The concern is not with the world at all, but rather with something that is to be realized by taking our minds away from it" (Krishna 1989, 114). Sociologist D.P. Mukerji ([1942] 1948, 2) argues that Indian culture emphasizes this religious, "mystical" "world-view" which promotes "indifference to the transient and the sensate," "dissolv[ing] the "little self" in "the Supreme Reality." Radhakamal Mukerjee (1957, 287) says that in "Indian thought" love has been viewed as an "*inner experience.*" Thus, he says, there is a "stress on the subjective feelings rather than on the objects and situations of love."

Pervasiveness of religion suggests the presence of the divine in the world, contributing to finding meaning in life. Makarand Paranjape (2006, 215) easily recognizes the divine in everything:

As an Indian, a Hindu, and a *sanatani*, the idea that gods can be confined to temples is rather strange. The temple is a place of concentration, no doubt, which reminds us of the deity, but the divinity that the gods represent is everywhere. As the Isha Upanishad says, all these worlds and whatever is contained in them is imbued with the divine In other words, gods can be found where you look for them.

Consecrating life, seeing all actions as service to God or as divine play, and seeing each person as reflecting divinity, all support well-being by providing approaches and ways of seeing that make actions meaningful. As Daya Krishna (1989, 187) concludes, people seek "significant living"—"a life in which there occur, to a great extent, experience which are felt to be of utmost significance and importance." Seeing the world as divine and one's actions as enacting actions of the Gods provides that sense of significance.

As Lata Mani (2009, 57) argues, the principle animating the cultural matrix in India has been a nonmaterialistic one so that Indians can pursue "creative life force" and a "subjective sense of worth" without being hemmed in by materialism's "narrow understanding of value and worth" (Mani 2009, 177). Those who feel separate and fail to develop the ability to recognize the "oneness of all" or the divine essence of everything can be "caught in an interminable cycle of desires, large and small," and, so, "shuttle between the sense of 'too much' and 'too little', self-aggrandisement and self-deprecation" (Mani 2009, 145). Religion's pervasiveness facilitates nonmaterial pursuits that facilitate well-being, helping to divert attention from pursuits battered by the ups and downs of life's external circumstances.

As this suggests, Indian religions provide approaches and meanings to get through times when circumstances are troubling. I repeatedly heard both Hindu and non-Hindu interviewees talk about how well-being rests not in external circumstances, but in the mind. External circumstances aren't a stable source of well-being because individuals can't control them. What individuals can control is how they think about these circumstances. The people I interviewed cited this as a truism. A source was rarely cited, but their statements—and phrasing—echo statements in the Gita and other religious texts. In the Gita Krishna counsels Arjuna that the person of action should "renounce the fruits" of his or her action, acting impersonally, without desire. Seeing that situations influence different people differently, the Gita counsels that value is not inherent in an attribute of the situation itself; rather its origin is in the value imbued by the person (Varma 2001, 127). Varma (1993, 182) rightly emphasizes that the Gita describes harmony, serenity and composure as resulting from being impartial to

> gain or loss, victory or defeat, failure or success. [That person] neither exults nor hates,... is unmoved in fortune or misfortune, honor or disgrace ... is calm, controlled and poised and possessed of a quietness of mind. Forever content, [that person] is autonomous in [the] source of delight which is [the] inner self.

As Anandamayi Ma put it, "Happiness that depends on anything outside of you, be it your wife, children, money, fame, friends or anything else, cannot last. But to find happiness in Him who is everywhere, who is all-pervading, your own Self, this is real happiness" (Lannoy 1996, 147). Indian religion not only helps people see sources of well-being, but helps people turn to these sources when they face hardships in the external world.

In a Bengali language essay, India's first psychoanalyst Girindrasekhar Bose (1886–1953) notes how Indian religion pushes people to see happiness as in the mind:

> [In the West] human beings usually try to attain happiness by extending their control over the external world. All the material sciences help [people] in this endeavor. The Hindu *sastras* advise that there is no permanent happiness in external objects; genuine happiness comes from restraint over mind. The serene person is happy under all circumstances. (Nandy 1995, 129).

Sociologist D.P. Mukerji ([1953] 1958, 238) quotes Gandhi as emphasizing control of material wants:

> We notice that the mind is a restless bird; the more it gets the more it wants, and still more unbridled they become. Our ancestors, therefore, set a limit to our indulgences. They saw happiness was largely a neutral condition.... We had no system of life-corroding competition.

Indian religious traditions, then, provide a well of resources that people can draw on to find an approach to address the world's inevitable hardships and disappointments.

Perhaps as important is that contrariety and contradictions are fundamental to religious thinking—and they were important in Western religion thinking, too, at least before the Enlightenment (Koslofsky 2011, 62–68). Thus, Daya Krishna (1989, 113) concludes that "religious discourse ... is replete with contradictions. There seems something in the religious experience which necessitates its articulation in statements which appear contradictory to the rational intellect." Krishna (1989, 115) argues that religious experience "tends to formulate itself ... into contradictory statements simultaneously asserted as true. The language in which religious experience tends to express itself is not the language of mathematics or even of the empirical sciences but of parable and paradox which still claims to convey truth." Radhakamal Mukerjee ([1936] 1960, 178) similarly points out that "mysticism always seems to involve a contradiction" of a deep personal relationship with a God who is both the self and separate from the self, who is immanent, yet "beyond existence." Mukerjee ([1936] 1960, 178) concludes the actual experience of the "mystic ... is supralogical and by its nature 'polar' and thus reconciles the logical extremes." This book shows that life satisfaction comes only from contradictory experiences. Since religious discourse "is replete with contradictions," in places where religion is pervasive people may more easily recognize feelings of enduring life satisfaction come from contradictory experiences

The subordination of reason in religion to love, experience, and non-rational ways of thinking may also support practices that lead to well-being. Drawing perhaps on Indian sensibility, Benoy Kumar Sarkar (1941, 24) criticizes Western assumptions that the person is "rational, reasonable or logical animal." Rather, Sarkar says the "unreasonable, illogical and irrational features of human personality" coexist at the same time. D.P. Mukerji ([1955] 2013) argues that Sufi and bhakti traditions lay great stress on love. As a result of emphasizing love and experience, Mukerji (1955 [2013], 221) argues, "rationality has not had much chance in our social system." Radhakamal Mukerjee (1950, 2005, 434–35) argues that while Western psychology sees the mind as having a basement (subconscious) and a ground floor (conscious), Hindu psychology includes a "purely spiritual second floor, having no roof, but communicating directly with the open sky." This second floor allows Hindus to be open to nonordinary experiences and psychic phenomenon. Some sociologists may recognize Pitirim Sorokin's (e.g., 1954; 2002, 83) idea that sociology had neglected humans' "supraconsciousness, a 'genius,' 'creative *élan*,' or 'divine inspiration' that lies above the level of any conscious and rational thought." And Sorokin influenced Indian sociologists like Sarkar and Indian philosophers like Krishna. But perhaps Indian thinkers were attracted to Sorokin *because* his thought was consistent with Indian thought's lack of surety that reason is the only path. Hence Sarkar (1941, 493) concludes that "Sorokin's prayer for the future" sounds like the prayer of "old Hindu social philosophers for the advent of *Yugavatara* (God-incarnate-in-man) and in virtually the same terms." In other words, Sarkar sees commonality with Sorokin whom Sarkar seems to regard as a Hindu philosopher.

Seeing reason as only one path to truth facilitates the contradictory paths that lead to well-being. The recognition of reason's limitations also facilitates "noncognitive awareness as the highest reality" (Dehejia 2008, 82), an awareness that facilitates pleasures more than thinking. An awareness of reason's limitations also facilitates what Dehejia (2008, 82) calls "epistemic rest": "When all the senses are stilled when the mind is at rest, when the intellect wavers not, then say the wise, is reached the highest state." For Dehejia (2008, 83), epistemic rest "comes at the culmination of joyful activity, it is the pleasurable stillness that succeeds the excitement of orgasm, it is the silence that follows speech and yet contains within it all sounds, it is the glow of restful knowledge that seeks knowledge no more." Niranjan Kamboj enters the "zero zone" when he rings the bells above his head on entering temple. So do I when I ring the bells above my head when I surmount Pinnacle Hill—my local Kedarnath—every morning. Religion's subordination of reason facilitates transcending language and entering silence—and is reflected in religious traditions of mantra and silent meditation (Muller Ortega 1989, 15). The *Maitiri Upanishad* says:

> By closing the ears with the thumbs, they hear the sound of the space within the heart. Of it there is this sevenfold comparison: like rivers, a bell, a brazen vessel, a wheel, the croaking of frogs, rain, as one speaks in a sheltered place. Passing beyond this variously characterized sound, [devotees] disappear in the supreme, non-sound, the unmanifested Brahman. (Muller-Ortega 1989, 71)

With such religious traditions, people like Niranjan Kamboj can more easily enter the zero zone in temple.

For Niranjan Kamboj, India's many religious festivals provide "mental relief" by offering opportunities in which he can share joys and sorrows with others. In a wedding process, he says, "there is happiness in every step we take. We experience well-being [khushhali]." Tenth-century Kashmiri Shaivite philosopher Abhinavagupta recognizes how religious rituals facilitate well-being by bringing people together:

> Consciousness, which is composed of all things, enters into a state of contraction due to the differences generated by separate bodies, but it returns to a state of oneness, to a state of expansion, when all of its components

are able to reflect back on each other.... For this reason when a group of people gather together during the performance of a dance or of song, etc., there will be true enjoyment.... All of the bodies of all those present are in reality as if they were our own body. (Muller-Ortega 1989, 61–62)

Merging, mixing, and connecting in felicitous positive interactions is central to well-being. Given the number and centrality of Indian festivals and understanding of such festivals in philosophers like Abhinavagupta, it's no surprise that Niranjan Kamboj, an oil and gas executive with a commerce degree, understands the mental peace he gets from participating in festivals.

Radhakamal Mukerjee's ([1936] 1960) analysis of religion highlights that it is religion itself—rather than distinctively Indian religion—that provides joy by turning attention away from the little self, by providing meanings, by embracing community, and by recognizing contradictions. Radhakamal Mukerjee wrote more than 50 books of sociology and published in mainstream sociological journals in the USA and UK, but also translated the *Astavakragita* and the *Srimad Bhagavata* from Sanskrit into English. Radhakamal Mukerjee's ([1936] 1960, 221–22) analysis of mysticism (which can be described as both joyous and analytic) draws on his "unpublished diary" of his mystical experiences:

I saw ... the vast sea under the lovely moonlight.... I heard the humming of the bee full of the sensuousness of spring or the soft languorous note of the flute wafted from a distance reminiscent of things that no longer belonged to me. Then the morning Star arose, shining in dark, blue, unfathomable space, and it lured me into the infinite. What strange kinds of space are hidden in the recesses of the brain! What a rude shock to our ideas of time! And what wonder when a streak of light sounds like a song and a shining figure turns into the sensation of a sweet unforgettable smell! At times for days and months I lived among beings apparelled in a celestial light. There was a luminous procession of gods and angels, dazzling glades, lakes and forests.

Both Radhakamal Mukerjee and D.P. Mukerji enjoyed sociological work, but also literature, poetry, art, and mystical experiences, confirming the importance of participating in diverse aspects of life as a source of well-being.

As a sociologist, Radhakamal Mukerjee analyzed how religious sensibilities encourage well-being. First, thinking of the "religious object" as "akin" to the self provides positive "feelings of awe, wonder, holiness, and unity" (Mukerjee 1949, 90). Second, with such "joy, serenity, and poise," people form intimate connections with others (Mukerjee 1949, 90). Religion encourages such connections by encouraging the perception that "God shines through" in all fellow humans (Mukerjee [1936] 1960, 8). "Religion," Mukerjee (1949, 91) argues, "gives to the world the social idea of an infinite charity, compassion or love that bind together all in one simultaneous and eternal relationship with God." "Religious rites and observances" regularly bind people in "fellowship, love and service" (Mukerjee 1949, 92), in relationships of "equality and fraternity," not "domination and subordination" (Mukerjee 1949, 90). Third, religious meanings—especially the insight that there are realities that transcend the self and the world (Mukerjee [1936] 1960, 3)—sustain the person's "imagination, love and social sympathy" in the face of "manifold crises and defeats" (Mukerjee 1949, 92). Religion, Mukerjee ([1936] 1960, xiii) says, provides "training in the art of contemplation" which "safeguard[s] against strains and tensions in inner life" (Mukerjee [1936] 1960, 183). Inevitable "disharmonies and tensions" are transformed to "poise" through "strenuous contemplation" that sees a reality that transcends self and the world (Mukerjee [1936] 1960, 3).

Social Structure: *Living* the Uncertainty

My study of the effects of globalization emphasized the relative importance of structural realities over cultural understandings: Globalization changed India more because of new opportunities to participate in the global economy than because of global media that entered India (Derné 2008). In this chapter, I have emphasized how Indian cultural traditions influence Indians' understandings of well-being.

While Indian religion emphasizes an approach that finds well-being in the self, rather than circumstances, Lata Mani (2009, 50) is right to argue Indian conditions push in this direction, too: "Life in India," she says, is fundamentally shaped by the principle of uncertainty." Thinking, perhaps of power cuts, disruptions of water supply, and air pollution, Mani reasons that in India "nothing in the material environment can be taken for granted, be it water, air, or electricity. For most," she says, "unpredictability and impermanence are *not* theoretical concepts; rather they shape daily experience. In such circumstances, one either develops a sense of humour or else is irremediably miserable."

Thus, Indian realities (alongside Indian religious traditions) push people to find well-being outside of external circumstances. The very contingencies and uncertainties of material life push one to find well-being in the mind, in humor and in small pleasures when accomplishments in the material world are difficult to pursue. *Both* Indian life and Indian thought, then, help Indians find well-being outside of transient material circumstances.

References

Bellamy, Carla. 2011. *The Powerful Ephemeral: Everyday Healing in an Ambiguously Islamic Place*. Berkeley, CA: University of California Press.

Bennett, Peter. 1990. "In Nanda Baba's House: The Devotional Experience in Pushti Marg Temples." In *The Divine Passions: The Social Construction of Emotion in India*, edited by Owen Lynch, 182–211. Berkeley, CA: University of California Press; Delhi: Oxford University Press.

Bokhare, Narendra. 2006. "Small Shaiva Bronzes of Maharashtra," In *Gods Beyond Temples,* edited by Harsha V. Dehejia, 35–41. Delhi: Motilal Banarasidass.

Chaudhuri, Nirad C. 1979. *Hinduism: A Religion to Live By*. New Delhi: B.I. Publications.

Ciotti, Manuela. 2012. "Resurrecting *Seva* (Social Service): Dalit and Low-Caste Women Party Activists as Producers and Consumers of Popular Culture and Practice in Urban North India." *Journal of Asian Studies*, 71(1): 149–70.

Dehejia, Harsha V. 2008. *Parvatidarpana: An Exposition of Kasmir Saivism through the Images of Siva and Parvati*. Delhi: Motilal Banarsidass.

Derné, Steve. 1995. *Culture in Action: Family Life, Emotion, and Male Dominance in Banaras, India*. Albany, NY: SUNY Press.

———. 2008. *Globalization on the Ground: Media and the Transformation of Culture, Class, and Gender in India*. New Delhi: SAGE Publications.

———. 2013, November, 16. "Shiva Lives in Rochester: A Jogging Professor of Sociology Experiences the Power of Shiva atop Pinnacle Hill in New York." *Economic and Political Weekly*, xlviii(45–46): 84–85.

Diener, Ed. and Eunkook M. Suh, eds. 2000. *Culture and Subjective Well-Being*. Cambridge, MA: MIT Press.

Diener, Ed., E. M. Suh, H. Smith, and L. Shao. 1995. "National Differences in Reported Subjective Well-Being: Why Do They Occur?" *Social Indicators Research Special Issue: Global Report on Student Well-Being*, 34: 7–32.

Easwaran, Eknath. 2006. *The Constant Companion*. Mumbai: Jaico.

Eliade, Mircea. (1958) 1969. *Yoga: Immortality and Freedom*, 2nd ed. Translated by Willard R. Trask. Princeton, NJ: Princeton University Press.

————. 1981. *Autobiography Volume I: 1907–1937, Journey East, Journey West*. Translated by Mac Linscott Ricketts. Chicago, IL: University of Chicago Press.

Gupt, Bharat. 2004. "The Genesis of the *Nayika* in the *Natyashastra*." In *A Celebration of Love: The Romantic Heroine in the Indian Arts*, edited by Harsha V. Dehejia, 17–22. New Delhi: Roli.

James, William.1902. *The Varieties of Religious Experience: A Study in Human Nature*. New York, NY: Penguin.

Kakar, Sudhir. 1981. *The Inner World: A Psycho-analytic Study of Childhood and Society in India*, 2nd ed. New Delhi: Oxford University Press.

Kent, Eliza F. and Tazim R. Kassam, eds. 2013. *Lines in Water: Religious Boundaries in South Asia*. Syracuse, NY: Syracuse University Press.

Kinsley, David R. 1982. *Hinduism: A Cultural Perspective*. Englewood Cliffs, NJ: Prentice Hall.

Koslofsky, Craig. 2011. *Evening's Empire: A History of the Night in Early Modern Europe*. Cambridge: Cambridge University Press.

Krishna, Daya. 1989. *The Art of the Conceptual*. New Delhi: Indian Council of Philosophical Research.

Lannoy, Richard. 1996. *Anandamayi: Her Life and Wisdom*. Shaftesbury: Element.

————. 2002. *Benares: A World Within a World*. Varanasi: India.

Larsen, Randy J. and Michael Eid. 2008. "Ed Diener and the Science of Subjective Well-Being." In *The Science of Subjective Well-Being*, edited by Michael Eid and Randy J. Larsen, 1–13. New York, NY: Guilford.

Luhrmann, T.M. 2012. *When God Talks Back: Understanding the American Evangelical Relationship with God*. New York, NY: Vintage.

Lynch, Owen. 1990. "The Mastram: Emotion and Person among Mathura's Chaubes." In *Divine Passions: The Social Construction of Emotion in India*, edited by Owen Lynch, 91–115. Berkeley, CA/New Delhi: University of California Press/Oxford University Press.

Madan, T.N. 1989. "Review of Fruitful Journeys: The Ways of Rajasthani Pilgrims by Ann Grodzins Gold." *Contributions to Indian Sociology*, 23(1): 230–31. Also cited in Prem Saran 2008. *Yoga, Bhoga and Ardhanariswara: Individuality, Wellbeing and Gender in Tantra*. New Delhi: Routledge.

————. 1997. "Tradition and Modernity in the Sociology of D.P. Mukerji." In *Social and Cultural Diversities: D.P.Mukerji in Memorium*, edited by Abha Avasthi, 167–92. Jaipur: Rawat.

Mani, Lata. 2009. *SacredSecular: Contemplative Cultural Critique*. New Delhi: Routledge.

Mathews, Gordon and Carolina Izquierdo. 2009. "Anthropology, Happiness, and Well-Being." In *Pursuits of Happiness: Well-Being in Anthropological Perspective*, edited by Gordon Mathews and Carolina Izquierdo, 1–19. New York, NY: Berghahn.

McDaniel, June. 1989. *The Madness of the Saints: Ecstatic Religion in Bengal*. Chicago, IL: University of Chicago Press.

Muller-Ortega, Paul Eduardo. 1989. *The Triadic Heart of Siva: Kaula Tantricism of Abhinavagupta in the Non-Dual Saivism of Kashmir*. Albany, NY: SUNY Press.

Mukerjee, Radhakamal. (1936) 1960. *The Theory and Art of Mysticism*, 2nd ed. Bombay: Asia Publishing House.

———. 1949. *The Social Function of Art*. Mumbai: Hind Kitabs.

———. (1950) 2005. *The Dynamics of Morals: A Sociopsychological Theory of Ethics*. New Delhi: Radha Publications.

———. 1951. *The Indian Scheme of Life*. Mumbai: Hind Kitab.

———. 1957. *The Horizon of Marriage*. Mumbai: Asia Publishing House.

———. (1960) 2005. *The Philosophy of Social Science*. New Delhi: Radha.

Mukerji, Dhurjati Prasad. (1942) 1948. *Modern Indian Culture: A Sociological Study*, 2nd ed. Mumbai: Hind Kitabs.

———. (1958) 2002. "Mahatma Gandhi's View on Machines and Technology." In *Diversities: Essays in Economics, Sociology and Other Social Problems*, edited by D.P. Mukerji,234–59. New Delhi: Manak. First published in 1953.

———. (1955) 2013. "Indian Tradition and Social Change" In *Sociology at the University of Lucknow: The First Half Century (1921–1975)*, edited by T.N. Madan, 212–24. New Delhi: Oxford University Press. Also cited in D.P. Mukerji, (1958) 2002. *Diversities: Essays in Economics, Sociology and Other Social Problems*. New Delhi: Manak, 261–75.

Nandy, Ashis. 1995. *The Savage Freud and Other Essays on Possible and Retrievable Selves*. Princeton, NJ: Princeton University Press.

Naravane, Vishwanath S. 1978. *Modern Indian Thought*. New Delhi: Orient Longman.

Oberoi, Harjot. 1994. *The Construction of Religious Boundaries: Culture, Identity and Diversity in the Sikh Tradition*. Chicago, IL: University of Chicago Press.

O'Flaherty, Wendy Doniger. 1973. *Siva: The Erotic Ascetic*. Oxford: Oxford University Press.

Pant, Pushpesh. 2006. "The Divinity of Food." In *Gods Beyond Temples*, edited by Harsha V. Dehejia, 209–14. Delhi: Motilal Banarasidass.

Paranjape, Makarand. 2006. "Ten Meditations on the Guru." In *Gods Beyond Temples*, edited by Harsha V. Dehejia, 215–22. Delhi: Motilal Banarasidass.

Raine, Kathleen. 1990. *India Seen Afar*. New York, NY: George Braziller.

Rao, Raja. (1960) 1986. *The Serpent and the Rope*. Woodstock, NY: Overlook Press.

Roland, Alan. 1988. *In Search of Self in India and Japan: Toward a Cross-Cultural Psychology*. Princeton, NJ: Princeton University Press.

Saran, Prem. 2008. *Yoga, Bhoga and Ardhanariswara: Individuality, Wellbeing and Gender in Tantra*. New Delhi: Routledge.

Sarkar, Benoy Kumar. 1941. *Villages and Towns and Social Patterns*. Kolkata: Chuckerverty Chatterjee.

Shweder, Richard A. 1991. *Thinking Through Cultures: Expeditions in Cultural Psychology*. Cambridge, MA: Harvard University Press.

Spink, Walter. 2004. "The Quest for Krishna" In *A Celebration of Love: The Romantic Heroine in the Indian Arts*, edited by Harsha V. Dehejia, 30–37. New Delhi: Roli.

Sorokin, Pitirim A. (1954) 2002. *The Ways and Power of Love: Types, Factors, and Techniques of Moral Transformation*. Philadelphia, PA: Templeton Foundation Press.

Suh, Eunkook M. and Jayoung Koo. 2008. "Comparing Subjective Well-Being across Cultures and Nations: The 'What' and 'Why' Questions." In *The Science of Subjective Well-Being*, edited by Michael Eid and Randy J. Larsen, 413–27. New York, NY: Guilford.

Taneja, Anand Vivek. 2013. "Nature History, and the Sacred in the Medieval Ruins of Delhi." PhD. Dissertation, Columbia University, New York.

Trawick, Margaret. 1990. *Notes on Love in a Tamil Family*. Berkeley, CA: University of California Press.

Trivedi, Ramendra Sundar. 1921. *Yajna-Katha* [Bengali; *The Doctrine of Yajna*]. Calcutta. (As quoted and translated by Sarkar 1941.)

Varma, Pavan K. 1993. *Krishna: The Playful Divine*. New Delhi: Penguin.

———. 2001. *The Book of Krishna*. New Delhi: Penguin.

PART III

Lessons

8

WHAT HAVE WE LEARNED
ABOUT WELL-BEING?

In the old days, the yatra (pilgrimage) to Hemkund Sahab used to take a whole week. During that time, the person on pilgrimage finds mental peace. He remains focused only on the yatra, *forgetting worldly things for the whole of one week. But when he boards the returning bus, he again gets involved in the same old routine. The mental peace one gets from pilgrimage is not lasting. It is neverlasting and has never lasted. In our religion, there is term for the person who has ostracized himself from society and lives on his own terms and conditions. That person is called a brahm-gyaani, a pure saint who leans in the direction of God. Only the brahm-gyaani could have a permanent and lasting peace of mind.* Otherwise, for the ordinary person, 36 times in a day he gets mental peace and loses it 36 times as well. It happens that way with me; I can't say about the others.

—Suraj Singh, 58-year-old Sikh male real-estate seller

In life happiness keeps coming and going. Sukh [comfort, happiness, pleasure] and dukh [sadness, sorrow, grief] are two sides of the same coin.

—Yakin Kaur, 43-year-old Sikh housewife

Do I contradict myself?
Very well then I contradict myself,
(I am large. I contain multitudes.)

—Walt Whitman

The only people for me are the mad ones...desirous of everything at the same time.

—Jack Kerouac

A rmaan Singh, the 65-year-old who contemplated suicide when his son died, talks of health, wealth, and connections to others—what he calls "fame" or shoharat—as necessary to well-being. For Armaan, individual achievements, such as his sporting triumph celebrated at an assembly, are a source of well-being, too. After floundering when his son died, Armaan eventually found a mental approach to facing the trauma, learning from a guru who helped him understand that really the body is nothing. Echoing the Gita, but not quoting it, this unobservant Sikh says one must keep on working without any expectations of the fruits; that one can't change one's circumstances, but can change how one thinks about one's circumstances. By seeing happiness as inner, recognizing one can't change one's circumstances, and recognizing that ultimately the body is nothing, Armaan transcends the despair he felt at his son's death. Armaan has pleasures that allow him to continue living with joie de vivre. He watches cricket and cinema with friends, enjoys morning walks and delicious food, gets thrill from his motor-cycle and pretends to flirt with the girls who call him Uncle. By keeping a positive outlook, Armaan enjoys felicitous interactions with everyone around him: "If you're good, everybody is good; if you're happy, everybody is happy." Armaan cultivates interactions that generate a chain of well-being that spreads from himself to others and back to himself, transforming an inner approach into an external situation of well-being.

Although cultivating *some* sort of pleasure is necessary for well-being, Armaan's *particular* pleasures—food, motorcycle-riding, cricket-watching, and ghumna—are perhaps no better than other pleasures—bathing, singing, and going to temple. The diversity of pleasures this book describes shows what is important is the ability to find pleasures that separate from daily life. Armaan's approach to handling difficulties—seeing happiness as inner—is not the only approach that will bolster well-being. One might instead focus on controlling one's ambitions or seeing the beauty of each day. What is important is having *an* approach to handling inevitable troubles in life.

Armaan's approaches and actions are contradictory—and this is fundamental to well-being, too. After telling me the body is nothing, Armaan immediately headed out for a cup of tea and he also says that health, wealth, and sex are essential to well-being, too. Although Armaan enjoys pleasures, he also has a productive worklife that involves stocking goods for sale. This study shows that well-being comes from living inconsistently, from engaging in different, contradictory aspects of life. One gets well-being from throwing oneself into all things whole heartedly. When alone, embrace solitude; when with others, embrace togetherness. The distinctive wisdom of Hinduism is the recognition that it's all good if everything is embraced wholeheartedly. Hinduism makes imperative *both* renunciation of the world *and* embracing affairs of the world, including bodily pleasures such as sex and exercise. This study demonstrates that a diversity of *contradictory* things produce well-being—sex and renunciation, work and play, purpose and purposelessness, and body and mind. Engaging in activities and pursuits that *contradict one another* is also necessary for well-being.

The wisdom of the Gita and of Armaan Singh rightly recognizes that, ultimately, *external situation* has little to do with well-being. Instead, well-being comes from how people think about their situation. Well-being, then, does *not* rest in particular circumstances or situations. While people need *some modicum* of health and income, connections to others and opportunities to strive individually, what constitutes this modicum is shaped by outlook. Very limited income and health, and limited connections and opportunities are not inconsistent with well-being—the important thing is how people *see* their income, health, connections, and opportunities. Both Prakash Tyagi and Ishwar Kumar have poor health and are neglected by their family, but for Ishwar this is a source of venom and sourness, while Prakash maintains well-being by focusing on how he can still walk, if slowly, and how every day offers a new elegance. As the Gita rightly recognizes, well-being is primarily inner. As Prakash Tyagi puts it, "if circumstances do not smile on you, smile yourself on circumstances."

A feeling of well-being doesn't rest in particular conditions, but in particular interactions, interactions over which each person has some control. Armaan is right to see that he maintains well-being by happily interacting with others. Garhwali singer Sunil Sharma says when his wife criticizes him for his lack of seriousness about earning, he just looks down in shame, nodding his head and listening. But mostly Sunil cultivates interactions about his musical talent that induce prideful feelings of well-being. He pushes me for praise about his accomplishments. After playing me one of his cassettes, he asks, "Aren't I a great singer?" Sunil says that while most children are more attached to their mothers, "spiritually [E] I love [*prem*] my father too much." Sunil plays over in his talk and in his mind how his father, whom he describes as a "gentle fellow who never earned much," is so "emotional that he weeps [with joy] when he sees me singing on television." Sunil experiences a lack of well-being when interactions with his wife force him to "look down" when he thinks of how it's her earnings that provide his five-person family with a small two-room flat. But he experiences well-being in thinking of how his father might view his musical talent. Sunil cultivates inter-actions that generate praise for his creative work and focuses on interactions with those, such as his father, who assure him of the importance of his music.

As I describe in Chapter 6, women, laborers, and the elderly often face trying circumstances, but the ill-being from them is often tempered by well-being in other areas. Fulmala Rajput, a 31-year-old, feels sorrow (dukh) when her family members scold her with sharp words and compel her to do housework. But reading is a pleasure for Fulmala and she describes obtaining a job and giving birth to a son as the source of khushhali in her life. Janki Kumar, a 25-year-old, is so distressed by the alcohol-fueled fighting in her family that she wants to convince her husband to leave the family. Yet Janki experi-ences khushhali in doing housework and in thinking of how the man she married is a good husband and father. Although pressed down by their jobs, Vashisht Kumar gets a little pleasure from listening to the radio, Yashoda Kumar thinks hopefully of her children's future and Raghu Kumar enjoys talking and laughing at the worksite. These people's well-being is mixed, waxing, and waning (see Singh 2015) as interactions and situations sometimes push them to think about and engage in areas of life that provide vitality, while pushing them at other times into discouraging aspects of their lives.

Recognizing that well-being is situational, coming and going in tran-sient interactions calls into question the very concept of well-being as an *enduring* sense of life satisfaction. Armaan Singh comes across as a mauj and masti individual with joie de vivre. Nonetheless, he was close to committing suicide in the despair of his son's death. Sunil Sharma experiences well-being when he thinks of his musical talent, but has an absence of well-being when he thinks about his earnings. Vashisht Kumar experiences ill-being when thinking of his children's failure to support him, but well-being when he listens to the radio. Fulmala Rajput experiences ill-being when she thinks of being scolded by family members, but well-being when she thinks of her job and her son. Janki Kumar experiences ill-being when her drunk in-laws create scenes, but well-being when she thinks of her loving husband who cares well for the children. The people I interviewed recognized the mixed, transient nature of well-being, suggesting that well-being may be a social-scientific construct produced by the interview situation. The interview interaction itself produces people's well-being as people enjoy being the center of attention and telling their life story. Well-being—a feeling of enduring life satisfaction—may not actually endure. People enjoy feelings of enduring life satisfaction, but usually don't have an enduring feeling of life satisfaction!

Well-being, then, is more like a flow, rather than some "enduring state." Most fundamentally, well-being is actually in interactions. Sunil Sharma's father supports his creative work; so when Sunil interacts with his father—*or imagines such interactions*—he feels well-being. But when his wife criticizes his earning capacity—*or he imagines her criticisms*—he looks down (a sign of shame), feeling a lack of well-being. As Armaan shifts his focus from his son's death to enjoying a cup of tea, his experience of life satisfaction shifts. The rapid movement in focus from one arena of life to another in our own interior interactions shifts our well-being quickly.

Arlie Hochschild (1983) revolutionized understanding of emotions by highlighting emotions in interaction. This book similarly suggests that well-being is not primarily a persistent inner state, but exists in interaction. This shifts attention from the external factors shaping well-being to how well-being arises in meanings and interactions. Radhakamal Mukerjee ([1965] 2005, viii–ix) argued that sociology could bring about a "revolution" in the social sciences by shifting from studying "properties of objects" to studying "relations of objects" within the "whole sociological situation." Sociology's distinctive contribution to understanding well being is to see well-being *in* interactions rather than within the individual psyche.

Multiple Foundations of Well-being

Part I of this book showed that well-being rests on multiple foundations, each of which is important: income, health, individual pursuits, connections with others, pleasures that provide breaks from daily life, and meanings to get through difficulties. Maitreyi Chatterjee, a 65-year-old, says her life aim is: "[To] pray to God to keep me healthy so that I can spend more time with my friends and relatives." "I also enjoy kitty parties," she says, using an English phrase associated with meetings of women to eat, chat, and play cards. She also says she "experiences happiness by [her] knitting and stitching" and in providing food to the beggar who comes to her house every day. In these few sentences, Maitreyi describes her well-being as arising from connections to other people (helping others, meeting her friends), pleasures (food and cards at a kitty party), meanings (praying, helping others), and individual achievements (her knitting and stitching). Gira Kumar, a 22-year-old beautician who passed Class 9, begins describing well-being by emphasizing the money she earns as a beautician. She proudly notes that she used to work for a parlor but now earns more money on her own. The happiest moment in her life was completing her beautician course so that she could stand on her own two feet. Gira also enjoys the pleasures of ghumna-phirna, wearing good clothes, and chatting with her friends. For Gira, too, individual pursuit (earning a degree), pleasure (nice clothes and walking), and connections to others (chatting with friends) are fundamental to well-being. Gajendra Rajput, the 69-year-old retired forestry official, gets well-being from his ability stay focused on doing a good job to help others, the pleasures of yogic exercise, and a life philosophy that focuses on service to others. Abbas Khan, a 24-year-old with a masters degree in computer science, gets well-being from his achievements ("when I won the intercollegiate footrace there was much happiness") and connections to others ("well-being comes from living in the family; if I'm with my family I'm happy"). For Abbas, poetry provides both pleasure and meaning: "Through [my hobby of] *shayri* poetry I get the experience of life through Urdu." Harish Mishra, a 40-year-old, similarly gets well-being from meanings—his belief in God, which provides "tremendous inspiration"—pleasures ("In my opinion, well-being means to have a sound sleep every night and have abundant food in the house"), and connections to others ("When I depart this world there should be at least five people, apart from my family members, who are shouldering me [in my coffin] and who will say 'he is a nice man'"). Harish dismisses his successful business—he owns a clothiers shop—as something he only does to earn his bread, but he still mentions the well-being from individual striving when he shares with me the "emotional poetry" he writes.

Over the years, the meanings that guide people, the pleasures they enjoy, the connections that move them, and the pursuits that satisfy them change. But the sense of enduring life satisfaction persists even if particular pleasures, meanings, connections, and pursuits change over time. Connections to friends may shift to connections to family; meanings may shift from religion to poetry; and pleasures may shift from filmgoing to religious ritual. Continuing to find satisfaction in these areas of life is what is important for well-being.

Contradictory Foundations of Well-being

These foundations address contradictory aspects of life—pleasures are often bodily, meanings are of the mind. People get happiness and joy at striving to their potential, but they also need meaningless pleasures that escape the day-to-day activities, such as sleeping, bathing, and drinking tea. Achievements (and pleasures) can be solo, but people need to connect to others, too.

In a range of ways, utopians saw work—at least at a job!—as detracting from well-being. Marx argued that wage labor prevented us from pursuing "free conscious activity." Herbert Marcuse and Norman Brown were skeptical that we could pursue our deepest desires when we were caught up in the workaday world. Max Weber argued that our culture was so organized for "a vocational worka-day life" that there was room for neither neighborly love ([1915] 1946, 357) nor for the search for ultimate meanings of life ([1919] 1946, 152). But as Victor Turner knew, humans need back and forth between effort and pleasure, work and play, connections to others and individual achievement. The source of well-being is contradictory because people need that back and forth. Too much striving to reach goals doesn't provide well-being, just as singing *all the time* would not be a source of well-being. Being a mystic merging into others isn't well-being—people need a sense of self, too.

There are *contradictory* foundations of well-being, all of which contribute to well-being. Sukhraj Singh, the 33-year-old newspaper hawker, describes well-being as coming from his love (pyaar) for his wife and being blessed with a daughter, but also from "plants and trees" and from his "inner voice." Despite his obvious focus on his love for family, Sukhraj describes getting well-being from going to the gurudwara because he gets the feeling he has "no relations, no family and just am in the service of God, chanting 'Wahe guru, wahe guru' all the way." Akaldeep Kaur, a soon-to-be-married 27-year-old who has just completed her degree in computer applications, describes well-being as "meet[ing] new people and talk[ing] to them." But when Meenu asks her to describe a situation of well-being, she refers to meeting "old friends and go[ing] for ghumna-phirna." For Akaldeep, both meeting new people and enjoying old friends provides well-being. Nitin Kumar, a 36-year-old driver, who passed Class 10, finds well-being in materialism *and* spirituality. He characterizes well-being as the mental peace (maansik shanti) he gets from going to temple, but describes his happiest moment as the day he got married and says he would get the most happiness (khushi) from "owning a great vehicle."

Because the interview situation is usually a one-time affair, contradictory aspects of well-being don't always come through as interviews often capture where the person is at the moment. Because the interview is cognitive, people are perhaps more likely to be consistent. But the contradictory foundations of well-being were particularly evident in the people whom I knew well and in my own reflections. One day after I ate a delicious *makki roti* (corn chapati), Armaan Singh said that was a bodily happiness (*sharirik khushi*), but that real (*asli*) happiness comes from the mind. But knowing Armaan, I know he takes great delight in the body, too. In speech, he sometimes takes the side of renunciation, but his life shows the importance of both—indeed both taken to their extreme. He is a mauj and masti individual who loves living to the extreme, *but at the same time* says that the body is *nothing*—not that it's unimportant; it is *nothing*. I get pleasure from love-making and bodily pleasures such as bathing and great food. But in India, I enjoy a bit of renunciation—no sit-down toilet, no hot showers. While I know those things are available in India, a little renunciation feels good in life. Himalaya trips with no electricity and climbing "peaks"—small,

13,000 foot ones!—is ascetic, too. And no sex or love-making, either! (But I used to enjoy eroticism by going to a film or two and I can still watch Shilpa Shirodkar and Mithun Chakraborty dance on YouTube!) Like Shiva, I'm the erotic ascetic.

People get pleasure from both being a special person and from connections to others. Indeed, people sometimes feel special because of their ability to help others: Rajendra Rana, the 21-year-old news reporter, takes pride in his individual accomplishments as a journalist *because* (he says) his accomplishments help other people understand AIDS or polio, or the need to go to medical doctors rather than relying on superstitions. Pradeep Kumar, the 50-year-old laborer, takes pride in his individual success in building a home *because* his mother chooses to live with him rather than his other siblings. Sunil Sharma probably gets the most well-being from his creativity, but he also obviously has deep love for his wife and children.

Well-being is *not only* in the mind—how one sees things—*but also* in external circumstances. Lochan Mishra, a 68-year-old, says that well-being comes from a mental approach—keeping expectations in check: "Khushhali means that you don't expect much so that you will always be satisfied and you will never regret. But if you expect something and are disappointed, then you can't have khushhali." Yet he describes feeling the most well-being when he managed to build a family home after his father lost his possessions and land at partition:

> When the country was partitioned, my father's land was left in Pakistan.... My father died in 1986, without a home. But in 1989, I built my house and all my brothers and sisters came here when the house was completed. That was the happiest moment of my life because we were starving for the home. That was the first home out of the four brothers. Everybody was so happy.

Although Lochan says well-being involves having no expectations, when the starvation for a home was quenched, he felt great well-being—he found well-being in external circumstances. Or recall Raj Pattial, the flashy 19-year-old Punjabi business student who says that the key thing is to have a mental approach—to not give attention to tensions—but also that he got great well-being when he eats good food and feels the air-cooled breeze of an apple orchard he found in the hills. So, both a mental approach and external circumstances are essential for well-being.

In *The Elementary Forms of the Religious Life*, Durkheim ([1912] 1915, 25) argues that acceptance of the principle of noncontradiction depends on social conditions. Durkheim notes that in many religious myths, beings have "contradictory attributes" being "at the same time one and many, material and spiritual." Psychologist Richard Nisbett (2003, 174–84) confirms Durkheim's insight, showing through clever empirical studies that Americans often prefer to justify preferences with a simple rule in order to avoid contradiction, while Chinese, Japanese, and Koreans have a dialectical reasoning style that embraces contradictions to find the truth. Indians have traditions that celebrate contradiction, perhaps making it easier for Indians to act in the contradictory ways that provide well-being compared to people like Americans who embrace the principle of noncontradiction. In its attention to cleanliness and eating pure food, Hinduism connects body with spirit. Hinduism celebrates renunciation, yet much of Vaishnavism emphasizes the erotic and, in Tantra, spiritual growth is linked to sexuality. The Gita proposes contradictory paths: being a warrior and being a vegetarian, pursuing truth and pursuing action. Indians celebrate Shiva's asceticism *and* his eroticism. Some Sufism similarly sees sexual play as the path to spiritual cultivation (Kugle 2007, 194). Islamic traditions in South Asia include theology and philosophy, but also focus on fasting and prayer strings to fight physical and emotional ailments, yogic postures to improve digestion, and the therapeutic use of plants (Khan 2012, 15). When Naveeda Khan (2012, 15) found books addressing these topics among her grandfather's possessions, she admits she was puzzled by the "coupling of the cerebral with the gratuitously bodily." Durkheim saw a split between body and soul as fundamental to religion, but in Indian traditions there is no such divide. So, the *Yoga Sutra* connects the most cerebral—consciousness or mind—with physiology: control of mind is accomplished by control of breath (Alter 2004, 20). Tantrism realizes the highest spirituality through realization of a divine body (Alter 2004, 20; Eliade [1958] 1969, 227; Muller-Ortega 1989, 101–02).

Of course, this style of thinking is not completely alien to the West, just subordinate in the contemporary era. The mystic Jacob Boehme proclaimed "nothing can be revealed...except through contrariety" (Koslofsky 2011, 63). Craig Koslofsky (2011, 62) argues that prior to modernity Western thinking emphasized "polarity, duality, antithesis, and [especially] contrariety" as the best way to understand "all natural, intellectual, and social phenomena." Western thought includes many from Boehme to Jung who find wholeness in the union of opposites (Obeyesekere 2012, 259). Koslofsky trances how over time contrariety as a way of thought was subordinated in the West, but it hasn't disappeared. In the rock musical *Hair*, mind and body pleasures are combined: "My body is walking in space/My soul is in orbit with God face to face.... My mind is as clear as country air/I feel my flesh, all colors mesh." Yes it is all good: "Red black/blue brown/yellow crimson/green orange/purple pink/violet white." Or on a run, the body exercises, the mind is invigorated. The mystic Evelyn Underhill encouraged her correspondents to allow "the tobacco smoke of the parlor and the incense of the chapel to mingle and mix," to "learn how to enjoy both the passions of spiritual life and the pleasures of a good cup of coffee" (as paraphrased by Kripal 2001, 47).

A lot of the social-science research on well-being, perhaps influenced by Western assumptions about the principle of noncontradiction, misses how fundamental contrariety is to well-being, but ethnographic research theorizing from actual individuals' experiences *does* recognize contradictory facets of experience as producing well-being. Thus, Gordon Mathews's (1996, 18) intensive interviews with Americans and Japanese showed that Japanese use contradictory conceptions—self-realization *and* feeling of unity with a group—to understand what makes life worth living. Mathews (1996, 22) reports that the majority of the Japanese he interviewed seemed to think of their *ikigai*—that which makes life worth living—"neither as *ittaikan* [sense of commitment to a group] nor as *jiko jitsugen* [self realization] but as ambiguously balanced between the two." Legal scholar and public intellectual Patricia Williams (1991, 10) argues that the fact "that life is complicated" is of "great analytic importance." Avery Gordon ([1997] 2008, 3), a sociologist brave enough to study experiences of ghosts, argues that this fact is not a "banal expression of the obvious" but, rather "a profound theoretical statement—perhaps the most important statement of our time." The statement is important because so much social science is reductionist, missing the complexity of things—a complexity that is necessary for well-being. As I'll argue in Chapter 9, sociology needs a new epistemology that recognizes this diversity, but perhaps it's more important to realize that embracing this complexity allows us to live fuller lives. Thus,

Indian sociologist D.P. Mukerji (1894–1961) argues that complexity is a virtue because it is the "outcome of an intenser form of life" (1924, 232). Daya Krishna (1989, 139) is right to conclude that there is a human "need" to look "at oneself in countless embodiments." Living what Rilke called all the lines in the body provides well-being (Brown 1959, 108).

Contextual Basis of Well-Being

One reason for the contradictory foundations of well-being is that well-being ultimately depends on context. What provides well-being at work might not provide well-being at home. What provides well-being with one's spouse might not provide well-being with one's friends (or lover!). What provides well-being as a child in a family might not provide well-being as a parent in a family. What provides well-being at school might not provide well-being at a dance club. When Armaan Singh is thinking about his son's death, the idea that the body is nothing provides well-being. But when Armaan is riding his motorcycle fast or eating at his favorite dhaaba the idea that the body is nothing does *not* lead to well-being. When Sukhraj Singh is living life day-to-day in Dehradun, he focuses on his wife and children as providing well-being, but when he is at the gurudwara he gets well-being from the "feeling" that he has no relationships or family. Women often say they get well-being from different sources after marriage than they did before marriage. Sushma Sharma said her job gave her happiness before marriage, but afterwards she got happiness from her children. Sunil Sharma gets well-being from his creative life, but his creative life does not provide well-being in the context of earning a living.

The Mixed Experience of Well-being

The well-being Sunil experiences from his musical creativity conflicts with the simultaneous ill-being from failing to earn enough to satisfy himself or his wife. Sunil's well-being is *mixed*. His well-being shifts as his attention shifts from one arena of life (his musicality) to another (his support of his family), from the way he imagines he is seen by his father (who praises his music) to how he is seen by his wife (who criticizes his lack of seriousness). He experiences *both* well-being and lack of well-being in the course of each day. His experience of well-being as fleeting and mixed is not uncommon. Subjective well-being is defined as a sense of enduring of life satisfaction, but this study suggests that "sense" doesn't usually endure. Well-being is instead mixed and shifting.

Raj Pattial, the 19-year-old business student with joie de vivre, gave me a sense that he had a lot of well-being: He had pleasures such as enjoying exploration of a lonely place in the mountains and said food was the best part of life. He had an approach to life: it is important, he said, to not give attention to tensions and to avoid chasing money. Raj showed connections to others, describing the taste in doing another person's work as the best taste. Raj seemed happy and I said he seemed like a "well-being person," but he replied,

> [I would] never say that because according to me that is nothing about the nature of well-being. When you are in a bad mood, your good mood is going to come back and when you're in a good mood, one day your bad mood will come back.

Yakin Kaur, the 43-year-old housewife, concluded that "in life happiness keeps coming and going. Sukh [comfort, happiness, and pleasure] and dukh [sadness] are two sides of the same coin." A 68-year-old widow said that "sukh and dukh in life just go together [*saath saath*]." A 70-year-old Hindu laborer with no schooling beyond Class 4 offers a profound understanding of well-being:

> In life, we get khushi [happiness]. In life, sometimes it's down, sometimes it's up [*uthna*]; sometimes it's low [niche], sometimes it's high [*uper*]. In all lives, it's like this—sometimes up, sometimes down, sometimes sukh, sometimes dukh. It is all the game of the Almighty. When there is too much [zyaada] khushi, we shouldn't start jumping up and down and when things are down [niche] we shouldn't cry, either.

I often saw the experience of such ups and downs in people's day-to-day lives. One morning 48-year-old Gurkeerat Singh told me that he was feeling good today "for no reason." Later that day, his feeling was gone and I asked him why, and again he said there was no reason.

Raj Pattial, just 19, put it well in answering my question about whether he was a person with consistent well-being: "That is not in the nature of well-being."

In the quotation that opens this chapter, Suraj Singh describes how the peace he finds on a pilgrimage evaporates quickly after boarding the returning bus and getting involved again in his daily routine. The 70-year-old widow Tavleen Kaur similarly describes getting "mental peace" after doing the darshan and bathing at the tenth guru's sacred birth spot. But when I ask her if that mental peace is lasting, she laughs: "This peace of mind is not for always. If we always had it, what else shall we want? When we return back from the yatra we again get caught up in the day-to-day routine of the world and that peace fades away." Suraj Singh, the 58-year-old real-estate magnate, is right to say that only a saint can maintain mental peace all the time: "For the ordinary person, 36 times a day he gets mental peace and loses it 36 times as well." Suraj is cautious enough to say that he only knows that, "it happens that way with me; I can't say about the others." Yet his generalization from his own experience is a fine piece of indigenous sociology and philosophy!

Niranjan Kamboj, a 48-year-old, is one of many who experience happiness and sadness simultaneously. Niranjan seems to be genuinely content: he cultivates felicitous interactions and regularly enters the "zero zone" when hearing temple bells. But Niranjan says, "Although there is no such moment when I didn't get happiness [khushi], there are still some moments when all of a sudden [achanak] we get much [zyaada] sadness [dukhi]" Niranjan lived through a horrible experience when his brother was kidnapped and murdered. Thousands of people, he said, searched for his brother in the hope that he was alive, but he was dead, and Niranjan was the first to see the dead body—which he calls the "biggest, saddest [dukhi] moment of my life." Although he describes himself as having "no moment" where he doesn't get happiness (khushi), thoughts of his brother return. So, if he eats food of his brother's liking (pasand), tears roll down his face. A week before our interview, he said he was searching through some old files for some papers related to his gas business and he came upon his brother's high school admission and photo card and he found himself feeling sad again. "Although I am a happy person," he says, "this is all in my heart [dil] still." Niranjan has never experienced a moment in which he's not been happy, yet the sadness of his brother's murder is always in his heart, too.

It was surprisingly common for people to describe the *same situation* as a situation of greatest well-being *and* the greatest lack of well-being. In our 10th interview we were incredulous when a 21-year-old coaching student said his greatest khushhali was when "a big bus accident happened." "How did you feel well-being?" we asked. "Twenty people died and nine survived that accident. At that moment, I felt khushhali since I survived." When we asked him about a time of an absence of khushhali he replied, "Also that accident. Seeing those twenty people dead gave me the biggest lack of well-being, while I also felt most happy that I had survived." A 22-year-old Muslim female student got her greatest well-being when she was admitted into a college program, but this was also the greatest anguish because she had to leave her one-month-old daughter in the village while she pursued her degree. Arvind Rana, a 30-year-old, felt the most ill-being when he had to leave his family to earn money while his wife was pregnant, but, in turn, experienced the "greatest happiness" when he heard by phone of his son's birth. Jaspal Sidhu, the 22-year-old clean-shaven Sikh coaching student, describes his greatest well-being as being called to interview for the defense forces. "I felt a lot of happiness [khushi] but when I faced the board I failed to qualify. So my happy [*khushiwala*] time was also my sad time [*dukhwala*]." Jaspal himself emphasizes experiencing happiness and sadness simultaneously, even if it might seem that the incidents are separate: "At the time I got the most well-being [khushhali] I simultaneously got a lack of well-being in the same place." Perhaps the common phrasing of sukh-dukh makes people more likely to recognize how sukh *and* dukh are generated by the same circumstance.

Often, intense feelings of well-being can lead to intense feelings of an absence of well-being. Armaan Singh says wealth (dhan) is important to well-being and concludes his philosophizing by saying that "to make the most of your money, you should have a successor [*varis*]. Everyone wants a son." But, then he starts crying thinking of his son's death—the "worst moment of my life." This hurt, he says, "is not a subject of 1–2 days, which ceases. It's a lifelong process which gives dukh as long as a person lives." Thinking about the heights of well-being—having a son—prepared Armaan for the depths of a lack of well-being. Fareed Khan, the 58-year-old fruit seller who tries to stay emotionally level, described his greatest happiness when his first son was born. But he quickly cautioned that "one shouldn't be so happy" and started crying, saying

> Whenever there is extreme happiness in someone's life, a sudden gam [unhappiness, sorrow, woe] also arrives the next moment, spoiling your happiness. Our son is having his first *id* after marriage and, unfortunately, my daughter-in-law has gone to her parental house, leaving us inlaws behind in this sorry state. The wife has gone; the wife has gone.

Just as Fareed Khan's and Armaan Singh's intense happiness led to an intense experience of sadness, intense sadness makes happiness greater. Thus, 51-year-old Upjeet Kaur's happiness at her son's birth was so intense because in her seven childless years of marriage her in-laws "used to say bad words to me and wanted my husband to arrange another marriage to get children." When asked about experiencing an absence of khushhali, the 36-year-old mother Pyara Kaur started by describing woe, but her thoughts quickly shifted:

> When my brother died four years ago, I was very dukhi because I wondered how my bhabhi [brother's wife] would fulfill all her responsibilities to five children. I brought one of his daughters with me to share their responsibility and am now happy she is in class X in a public school.

Niranjan Kamboj, whose brother was murdered, describes sadness as necessary for happiness:

> If you love sukh, you should love dukh, too. If dukh doesn't stick to you, you won't experience sukh. You won't realize the value of sukh until you have dukh.

Whenever one of Niranjan's friends' brothers marry, "I experience the sukh and the dukh at the same time." Niranjan's experience of sukh that a friend's brother has married is enhanced by the dukh he feels because his own brother was killed before he could ever marry. Niranjan wasn't trained as a philosopher, but what insights he has!

When asked to talk about a situation of well-being, respondents often think first of a lack of well-being. When I ask Sukhraj Singh about a situation of well-being, he immediately refers to the "very bad phase" he went through when he lacked even food to eat after his father's death. He had to ask for donations to conduct his father's funeral. But he quickly turns his thoughts:

> After my marriage, when I was blessed with a daughter I got so much happiness. After the second daughter, it added great happiness. It is by the virtue of the fortune of those two daughter that I am having happiness and well-being in my home.

Significantly, Sukhraj prefaces his discussion of his period of greatest well-being by talking about the bad phase. Experiencing and reflecting on the depths of despair make happiness more satisfying. Mohit Mishra, a 65-year-old, similarly introduces his discussion of a situation of great well-being by mentioning a time in which he lacked well-being:

> I was deprived of any happiness in my childhood in the absence of any guardian. I had to make my own choices. I am a self-made man who earned for himself and [arranged my own marriage]. I have educated my five children and both of my sons are now government servants. What else do I need? All my kids were grade-A in their studies. No one needed tuitions [paid private class] to get through school. After the family grew and my children got married, [in-laws] are coming and going and attending to those guests is part of my happiness. My children respect me and care for me and this gives me well-being.

Mohit, whose father died when he was young, was raised by an aunt and uncle, whom he describes as a constant "hurdle," who offered him no encouragement in his studies, but instead wanted him to do farm labor. Mohit is proud of his inclination to study and says the encouragement of teachers provided him with well-being. What I want to emphasize here is that for Mohit, the well-being that he got caring for his children is associated with thinking about the *absence* of well-being that he felt in not being similarly nurtured by his own guardian when he was young.

Feelings of well-being are not only mixed, then, they can even be contradictory. It's not just participating in *diverse* aspects of life that leads to well-being, but participating in pleasant *and* unpleasant aspects of life that helps a person feel well. While in the USA there is a negative relationship between positive and negative emotions, in Japan the correlations between good feelings and negative were mostly positive (Kitayama and Markus 2000, 138–39). That is, in the USA, people who feel positive emotions don't feel negative ones as much, while in Japan people who are more emotional feel more emotions in general, positive *and* negative. Similarly, for people such as Niranjan, Fareed and Armaan, a strong feeling of dukh is combined with strong feelings of sukh. This is a dialectical approach, different from tempered well-being—it's having both strong, positive well-being and strong, negative well-being *simultaneously*. Sunil Sharma feels intense passion about his creative pursuits, intense love for his father, intense love for his wife and children, *and* intense unhappiness about his ability to earn enough to make himself and his wife happy. When Fareed Khan and Armaan Singh think of their joy at having sons, they also feel intense sorrow at the disappointment in what has happened with their children. Niranjan Kamboj has intense enjoyment of food or a wedding that is accompanied by intense unhappiness that his dead brother can never marry or enjoy such food again. What's exhilarating and wonderful can also be wrenching, depressing and unbearable *at the same time*.

Indian religious traditions don't attempt compromise between eroticism and asceticism, but even urge pushing both to extremes. Given Indian religious traditions' recognition of such complexities, it's no surprise that an Indian sociologists like Benoy Kumar Sarkar emphasized the need for back and forth between hardship and glory; in my terms between well-being and ill-being. Sarkar (1941, 498) argued humans could never create conditions free from evils because "spirituality" can not "flourish without some doses of evil to be counteracted and overpowered by creative intelligence and will." For Sarkar (1940, 26), vitality comes from turmoil: "There is to be no peace while there is progress and there can be no progress while there is peace" (cited by Bandyopadhyay 1984, 18). "The mental, spiritual or social condition," Sarkar (1941, 521) writes, "is one of discord and unrest. No stage of the psyche can be envisaged as one of harmony, concord or equilibrium. It is a condition of unending disequilibrium, disharmony and discord that accompanies onward march." It's more than that well-being is always mixed; rather, feeling low is necessary to feel high; intensity of depths prepares ground for intensity of heights. Unless you're a mystic, you can't experience the glory of oneness all the time. The fact of the complexity of well-being was recognized by Indian sociology 70 years ago, even though today's well-being scholars continue to try to explain an individual's "level" of well-being, which they assume to be stable.

The fleeting, mixed, and contradictory nature of well-being suggests that there really isn't an *enduring* sense of life satisfaction. Rather than looking for the sources of well-being in *the individual's* objective situation, we should look to how well-being works in people's interactions. How does Sunil cultivate interactions that remind him of the value of his creative pursuits? How does Sunil shift his interaction with his self to feel more pride at his father's praise and less shame at his wife's criticisms? Kitayama and Markus (2000, 115) are right to argue that scholars looking for the sources of well-being in "seemingly individual attributes like optimism, extroversion, efficacy, mastery or self esteem" are using the assumptions of a "North American cultural complex." While I think Kitayama and Markus believe such attributes are an important source of well-being in American "social worlds" but not in East Asian ones where well-being is "very much a collaborative project," I believe the insights from India (and East Asia) are in fact true in the USA and other non-Asian places, too. Experiences of dukh are necessary to experience sukh. Well-being is a collaborative project that depends on the nature of one's connections and relations to others and, ultimately, this study suggests well-being is found not in the individual but in situational interactions.

The focus on the situation rather than the individual has long been recognized in Indian sociology (Bose 2014; Singh 1983). D.P. Mukerji argued, for instance, that a focus on the abstract individual, borrowed from the West, could not capture the multiple relationships through which the person attains unity and universality (Bose 2014, 192).[1] Mukerji argued the sociological focus on individualism offered a poor understanding of *Indian* society; this book suggests that a focus on situations, interactions, and relationships may provide a better understanding of well-being than a focus on individual characteristics, not just in India but everywhere.

---

[1] Bose is citing Mukerji's 1933 Bengali book, *Chintayasai*. (I do not read Bengali!)

Well-being: An Interactionist Approach

The social-scientific understanding of emotions was revolution-ized by an interactionist perspective that saw emotions not as arising within the individual but through interactions and meanings (Hochschild 1983; Lutz 1988; Lynch 1990). It was useful to see emotions as shaped by cultural paradigms. So, in the USA, the idea of love as certain, lasting, overcoming obstacles, and directed at a special person shaped the Americans' experiences of love (Swidler 2001). The Indian idea that love should be directed toward many in a joint family and that exclusive, intense love between husband and wife potentially threatened relationships with the husband's parents and brothers shaped Indians' experiences of love (Derné 1995). It was useful to see emotions not as natural biological responses within the organism, but as shaped by meanings and social interactions. A mixed-up feeling one has after being abandoned by a friend becomes more clear and focused after talking with other people about the feeling. It was useful to recognize that emotions are not just biologi-cal but are shaped by emotion norms. If the norm is to feel joy at one's wedding, people work to feel that joy. These approaches also recognized that people spoke of emotions not only to express feelings but to communicate a message to other people. To talk about one's justifiable anger might not reference inner feelings but might argue for the rightness of one's own conduct and to point out the transgres-sions of another's conduct (Lutz 1988; Lynch 1990). To talk of love might be to assure the loved one of one's constancy.

This book has been building toward a conclusion that an interac-tionist perspective that focuses on how well-being exists in interac-tions between people, and between a person and his or her self, could similarly revolutionize the study of well-being. Rather than searching for individual circumstances (such as health, income, and social con-nections) that generate well-being, we should study how interactions, situations, and meanings generate well-being. Perhaps it's not social connections that lead to well-being, but how we think about our social connections. Perhaps well-being is not found within the individual, but within the interactions the individual cultivates. Perhaps cultural paradigms shape the experience of well-being. Perhaps norms about well-being—one should feel well-being because of a long marriage, a good salary, or helping others—lead people to work on their feelings of well-being. Perhaps talk about well-being is used to justify the rightness of one's conduct.

Rather than arising through circumstances, well-being may come about primarily through the *meanings* people use to understand their situations. As recognized by both the Gita and many of the people I interviewed, well-being rests in the mind. It's not one's circumstances that lead to well-being, but how one thinks about one's circumstances. As so many Indians I interviewed reasoned, it's often impossible to change one's circumstances. But because a person can change their thinking about those circumstances, each person can attain inner well-being. Both Prakash Tyagi, a 79-year-old, and Ishwar Kumar, an 80-year-old, have poor health and their families neglect them, but Prakash's outlook provides well-being, while Ishwar remains discontented. Ishwar, who walks with a cane but seems more hale and hearty than Prakash, complains about medical problems, saying his inability to move outside Dehradun "has added to my sufferings." Prakash, whose health is in grave decline, focuses on still being able to walk to the park, if slowly. Ishwar is "fed up" with his family and "curses" modern India in which there is no respect for those without a bank balance. Prakash is neglected by his family, but approaches life with zeal and focuses on forming new relationships. Ishwar grumpily focuses on the (unlikely) prospect of changing his situation by moving out of his nephew's house. Prakash has a felicitous approach to facing troubles: he deemphasizes tensions and attachments, focuses on the transience of things, and sees each morning as its own beauty. The similarity of Prakash's and Ishwar's circumstances and the difference in their subjective well-being shows that an individual's well-being depends on their ability to develop a meaningful approach to handle difficulties and challenges.[2] As Prakash Tyagi puts it, khushhali "depends on attitude and temperament—on what we think and believe."

---

[2] Vaillant (2002, 219–22) draws a similar comparison between two 75-year-old American men. One focuses on having to give up work he loved while the other focuses on "every day" as offering "a new experience." Vaillant concludes that the first man's unhappiness stems from focusing on the glass as half empty, rather than half full. The first man sculls regularly and was completing a carpentry project with his children, yet remained grumpy about having to retire. "If only he could have focused on the glass half full, on his carpentry, on the next generation, and on the light on the water as he rowed, he might have found his life very interesting indeed."

Interactions also shift people's focus to areas of life that induce differing feelings of well-being. If a news reporter calls to interview Sunil Sharma about Garhwali songs, he will feel well. But if one of his wife's friends buys a car or he has to make a payment for his children's schooling, he will focus on his earning capacity and feel an absence of well-being. Emmons and McCullough (2003) reported an experiment in which they asked people to list one of three conditions—hassles, things they were thankful for, or mundane activities—for three weeks. As might be expected the group that was asked to think about hassles experienced less well-being than the group that was asked to think about what they were thankful for (Larsen and Prizmic 2008, 278). This simple experiment demonstrates how even internal interactions with oneself can push an individual to think about things that either contribute to or detract from feelings of well-being.

More fundamentally, well-being actually resides in interactions themselves. Girish Aggarwal, the married 48-year-old living with his wife, 17-year-old daughter, and 20-year-old son, says that being "part of the sukh and dukh [joys and sorrows] of others gives me happiness." Echoing Girish, Sudhir Kumar, 18, says that "sharing sukh-dukh [happiness and sadness] with my friends makes me feel very good [bahut achcha laga]." When Sudhir's mother died the year before I interviewed him, he remained alone and sad for months. But "mixing with friends and talking to them" "provided support in that time" so that now he feels happy and fresh. By contrast, the absence of good interactions leads to an absence of well-being. Ishwar Kumar, the 80-year-old living with his nephew, is caught in a circle of woe because "there is no one to listen to," and "no one with whom one can share one's woes and sorrows." Unloved and neglected by his nephew's family Ishwar finds it hard to form felicitous interactions that build well-being—even as he himself realizes good interactions even with rough-tempered people is the path to khushhali.

That some of the interactions that provide well-being are interactions with the self echoes the symbolic interactionist insight of Charles Horton Cooley and George Herbert Mead that an image of self emerges by taking the viewpoint of imagined others toward the self. So, reflection about one's life and situation from the viewpoint of others is what ultimately produces a feeling of life satisfaction. Using interviews conducted with Americans by herself and my other undergraduate students, Rachel Greenberg (2010) argued that well-being comes from people's own reflexivity—from their reflections on their circumstances. Working through how one thinks about the ups and downs of life produces meanings that give people a sense of feeling well.

Well-being arises, then, through cultivating positive interactions. Armaan Singh, enjoys talking and interacting and seeks out these interactions. He often turns on the television in his shop and watches cricket with friends and acquaintances. "My motto," he says, "is to give enjoyment. If you're good, everybody is good. If you're happy, everybody is happy." Niranjan Kamboj similarly recognizes that if he is able to "experience happiness others will experience happiness, too" while if he has a problem and is

> alone or lonely, the stress keeps on increasing due to not sharing with others. My smiling face will look sullen [latkana, literally hanging] and I will keep on thinking. By sharing and cracking jokes, the stress level is automatically reduced and we forget our dukh.

Sharing sorrows dissipates sorrow. Cultivating one's own masti makes others happy, increasing one's own well-being. Armaan and Niranjan each point to the positive chains of well-being where the well-being of one supports the well-being of another.

With teatime in India, people of modest means can introduce felicitous interactions of hospitality by sharing tea. I have even had people who live on the street offer me tea in a tea stall with money earned from begging. Everyone wants to engage in a felicitous interaction in which their value is affirmed. That is the source of well-being.

It's no surprise, then, that interviews reveal that people have well-being *because the interview situation itself produces it*. When Narendra Sethi and I conduct interviews, the person is the center of two persons' attention. I almost always can honestly tell the interviewee how much I learned from what he or she said. If the interviewee becomes upset because they're discussing something that is disturbing, Narendra Sethi and I support the person and try to help them through their difficulties. In talking with Narendra and myself, a person is outside their usual day-to-day situation—often taking a break from work. As my wife Lisa Jadwin said to me one day, it's powerful for people to be able to tell their own stories. In short, the interview is a felicitous interaction that itself produces well-being. That's also why we found that people interviewed by Meenu were more likely to say that they got well-being from helping others. By talking of what they sensed would make Meenu respect them, people pursued well-being sensed felicitous interactions.

Durkheim understood the contagion of good (and bad) emotions. When people collect together, Durkheim ([1912] 1915, 215) argued, every emotion

> expressed finds a place without resistance in all the minds, which are very open to outside impressions; each re-echoes the others and is re-echoed by the others. The initial impulse thus proceeds, growing as it goes, as an avalanche grows in its advance.

So, for Durkheim, the despair of mourners spreads from person to person and the excitement of a corroboree intensifies passions of collective effervescence. Thomas Scheff (1990) described the shame-rage spiral that occurs when bad interactions build on each other. When a criticism or slight (real or imagined) produces a feeling of shame or embarrassment, that shame can, in turn, produce shame and embarrassment in the person who initiated the chain reaction with a criticism or slight. Randall Collins (2005) understood how positive interactions build emotional energy. Interactions in which people reaffirm each other and express good feelings mutually build confidence, enthusiasm, and positive energy, creating a positive chain of emotional energy. This book suggests that well-being, too, arises not from internal states or characteristics but from interactions (even with the self) that build positive feelings, creating a sense of enduring satisfaction with life.

Well-being, then, operates in chains and connections. One's own lack of well-being can depress the well-being of another person. But, more important, the happiness, joking, and masti (joie-de-vivre) that someone feels can transform the sullenness of someone else facing tensions. This happiness, joking and masti that transforms doesn't reside within the person, but *within the interaction*. Putnam (2000) is right to argue that well-being resides in connections to others through a statistical analysis looking at things such as commuting, tv-watching, and membership in volunteer associations. In this book, I argue that it may also be productive to think of well-being, not as residing in the individual, but as arising in interactions with others.

Overcoming the Blues through Interactions

Felicitous interactions with others appear to be a key method of managing the blues. "Mixing with friends and talking with them" pulled Sudhir Kumar out of the despair he felt when his mother died. Niranjan Kamboj says that the "social atmosphere in which we are always interacting" helped him remain happy even after his brother was kidnapped and murdered. Jayant Aurora, a 77-year-old, is sometimes disappointed at the lack of support of his sons—although this came through only subtly—but his interactions with his long time friend keep him refreshed: "We meet every morning and have a lot of fun, throwing abuses at each other."

I myself notice how I overcome the blues through interactions. I found myself blue in India one fall. I felt bad for a friend who took time off for an out-of-town excursion that was not as pleasing as he had hoped. My department had—without telling me—assigned me to chair a departmental committee, while I was on leave, and there was a messy situation to deal with on my return. My back had been sore and I had a persistent cough. After going to Tapkeshvar—a Shiva temple—at which I meditated on my wife's beauty and asked for Shiva's help, I ran out of hot water I wanted to use to clean my feet after walking barefoot on the temple grounds. I thought I'd send some mail, but there was no one in the booth, there was no glue to paste the stamps on, and when I got glue, it got on everything. But I felt better by cultivating good interactions. I took time to print some photos and gave them to my barber and two friends. This was not just the pleasure of giving, but the pleasure of good relationships as all three were happy with the photos. My barber looked completely delighted with the photos and one friend asked if I could email them to him, too, so he could make one photo his main Facebook photo. I had sweet relations with all three and took the friend who put the photo on Facebook out for lunch. I felt better doing something for other people.

Of course, most people cultivate felicitous interactions in the course of each day. Going to the temple and doing puja connects to others. When a beggar who receives a donation points to God for thanks, can the giver help but feel connected not just to the beggar but to that God that represents society? Doesn't one have pleasant interactions with one's spouse (bringing a cup of tea) as one begins one's day?

In India, I smile at beggars, tea-stall workers, and the workers at the dhaaba as I begin each morning. On my morning walk, I exchange pleasantries with the ancient old ones enjoying the morning sun. Later, I enjoy positive back and forth with fruit-sellers or someone who operates a small store. As Lakshman Negi, the retired 61-year-old, says, sweet words are the important thing. Or as 73-year-old Gopal Chopra says, "[Khushhali] comes from having the human qualities—believe in truth, don't harm others, speak politely to others, and help others." Gopal knows that good interactions with others are the source of well-being. When one has the blues, one cultivates the interactions that produce well-being.

Focusing on Interactions and Meanings to Understand Variation

Focusing on interactions and meanings may be a fruitful way to understand some of the variations observed in people's subjective well-being.

Some of the lower levels of well-being found among the disadvantaged can be explained from this perspective. Laborers are more often pushed into interactions that discredit or shame them. Laborers more often confront nonreciprocal interactions in which they are ordered about. To the extent that the poor have less well-being, then, it may not be due to external circumstances but nonfelicitous interactions.

Similarly, because so many people in the middle years of life are caught in the circle of raising a family, their interactions tend to focus on this circle and, so, people in these years find well-being from supporting a family by earning a living or keeping house, rather than from spirituality or self-development.

A focus on meanings suggests that *discourses shape the nature of well-being*. So, if Americans' discourses connect money to well-being, Americans more easily recognize the deficit they feel when they lack money. Since Indian discourses emphasize the richness of social relations as a source of well-being and helping others as a source of well-being, Indians feel a deficit in well-being when social relationships are not rich and easily experience well-being through helping others. Indian religious discourses, emphasizing that well-being comes not from circumstances but how one thinks about these circumstances, make Indians more likely to recognize the role of finding an approach to life in obtaining well-being. People's differential exposure to discourses may also shape what gives people well-being. I interviewed a couple of *pujaris*, both of whom found well-being more from religion than others did probably because they are moving in religious circles of thought and interaction.

This Study's Contributions to Scholarly Understandings of Well-being

Correlational studies show health, income, religion, and connection to others are associated with higher well-being. The open-ended *Everyday Well-being Study* (Markus et al. 2004) on which my study is modeled showed Americans recognized these factors as a source of well-being. This study shows that Indians recognize health, income, religion, and connections to others as a source of well-being, confirming these studies' conclusions. The study may be useful in showing *why* certain conditions are associated with well-being. Thus, it's long been known that religion correlates with well-being—religious people report greater life satisfaction than nonreligious people (e.g., Kim-Prieto and Diener 2009; Liu, Harold, and Wei 2012; Myers 2008). This study shows that enjoyable ritual activities, connections to others, and meaningful ways to handle the inevitable difficulties and disappointments of life are reasons why religion is associated with well-being. For Gurkeerat, religious rituals are a pleasurable break from work; for Armaan Singh, a guru helped him see things differently after the trauma of his sons' death; for Tavleen Kaur, the gurudwara provides a glimpse of community. Such findings only confirm the suggestions of well-being researchers, such as David Myers (2008, 326–27) who details how religion provides "social support" (connecting people together), helps people "cope with loss" (by providing meaning), and provides "durable self-esteem" (through ways of seeing one's place in the world). Income is associated with well-being. This study suggests that a fundamental reason for this is that income allows people to contribute to others and engage in felicitous interactions with family members and people at work.

Still, this study gives more importance, perhaps, to meanings and pleasures than has been the case in previous studies. I think, too, this study suggests that *contradictory* experiences are necessary to experience well-being.

This study's focus on interactions as shaping well-being helps overcome some conundrums in the study of well-being. It's often noted, for instance, that demographic factors such as health, income, and age account for little of the variance in subjective well-being (Diener [1984] 1989, 12, 33). One reason may be that it is not a person's external circumstances that produce well-being, but how people think about those circumstances. It is often seen as surprising that people describe their lives as characterized by well-being (Biswas-Diener and Diener [2001] 2009; Bok 2010, 25; Kesebir and Diener [2008] 2009). One reason may of course be that the interaction of the interview situation or even simply thinking positively about well-being produces well-being. It's often seen as surprising that *reports* of health correlate more strongly with well-being than people's actual health (Bok 2010, 21). This is of course because it's not empirical health that is associated with well-being, but people's interpretation of their health. So, if people see themselves as healthy, that is more important than their empirical health. Vaillant (2002, 13), who found that "objective good physical health was less important to successful aging than subjective good health," reasoned that "it is all right to be ill as long as you do not feel sick." Similarly, the relatively low correlation between income and well-being can be explained by the importance of how people interpret their income. This book argues that how people attribute meaning to their income and health is more important than the amount of their actual income and health. An infirm person (like Ishwar Kumar) who focuses on his or her limitations has less well-being than the infirm person (like Prakash Tyagi) who focuses on what he or she can still do.

The primary contribution of this study is to show that well-being is shifting and arises in interactions. This suggests that in addition to studying the effects of individual traits and external circumstances, we should be studying actual interactions. The "unit of analysis" of well-being is probably the interaction, rather than the person. This is the implications of recent research suggesting that positive interactions with others are a primary source of well-being (Fredrickson 2013; Larsen and Prizmic 2008, 274–75; Seligman 2011). Number, quality, and frequency of relationships, all correlate with subjective well-being (Diener and Seligman 2002; Larsen and Prizmic 2008, 274). Larsen and Prizmic (2008, 275) are right to conclude that socializing with other people regulates negative feeling by providing the opportunity to reappraise and reframe situations. Such socializing can induce positive emotions, changing how a person feels. Larsen and Prizmic (2008, 278–79) also show that showing gratitude is a prime source of well-being. Or, as psychologist Martin Seligman (2011, 20) puts it: "Other people are the best antidote to the downs of life and the single most reliable up."

Barbara Fredrickson (2013, 24–25), a psychologist of emotion and well-being, is right to emphasize "positivity resonance"—what she calls love—as crucial: "One person's sincere, heartfelt smile can trigger a powerful and reverberating state between two people, one characterized by the trio of love's features: a now-shared positive emotion, a synchrony of action and biochemistry, and a feeling of mutual care." The back-and-forth "ripples" of positivity resonance affect each person, "establish[ing] and strengthen[ing] healthy communities and cultures" (Fredrickson 2013, 86). And it's no surprise, perhaps, that Fredrickson finds that love-and-kindness meditation (with its Indian roots) is one of the best ways to cultivate moments of positivity resonance that increase well-being. Indian philosopher Daya Krishna (1989, 195) emphasizes that there "exists the world of colours and sounds and tastes and smell" as well as a "world of imagination where these are transmuted into a realm where beauty reigns supreme." But "above all these," he says "is the world of interpersonal communication where flesh strains for flesh, mind for mind, and soul for soul. Krishna argues "art, religion and contemplative enjoyment of nature" give people's lives significance and that

> interpersonal communication can crown [the person's] experience of "significance" by an intense give-and-take where each feeds on the other and increases a thousandfold. In short, heaven and hell are not far from [each person] and it depends, to a very great extent, on [each person] whether [the person] would make of his [or her] life and that of others a heaven or hell.

References

Alter, Joseph S. 2004. *Yoga in Modern India: The Body between Science and Philosophy.* Princeton, NJ: Princeton University Press.

Biswas-Diener, Robert and Ed Diener (2001) 2009. "Making the Best of a Bad Situation: Satisfaction in the Slums of Calcutta." In *Culture and Well-Being: The Collected Works of Ed Diener*, edited by Ed Diener. New York, NY: Springer.

Bok, Derek. 2010. *The Politics of Happiness: What Government Can Learn from the New Research on Well-Being.* Princeton, NJ: Princeton University Press.

Bose, Pradip Kumar. 2014. "Abstract Individual, Concrete Person: Overcoming Individualism in the Sociology of D.P. Mukerji." *Sociological Bulletin,* 63(2, May–August): 185–205.

Brown, Norman O. 1959. *Life against Death: The Psychoanalytic Meaning of History.* Middleton, CT: Wesleyan University Press.

Collins, Randall. 2005. *Interaction Ritual Chains.* Princeton, NJ: Princeton University Press.

Derné, Steve. 1995. *Culture in Action: Family Life, Emotion, and Male Dominance in Banaras, India.* Albany, NY: SUNY Press.

Diener, Ed. (1984) 2009. "Subjective Well-Being." In *The Science of Well-Being: The Collected Works of Ed Diener*, edited by Ed Diener, 11–58. New York, NY: Springer.

Diener, Ed. and Martin E. P. Seligman. 2002. "Very Happy People." *Psychological Science,* 13(1): 81–84.

Durkheim, Emile. (1912) 1915. *The Elementary Forms of the Religious Life.* Translated by Joseph Ward Swain. New York, NY: Free Press.

Eliade, Mircea. (1958) 1969. *Yoga: Immortality and Freedom,* 2nd ed. Translaed by Willard R. Trask. Princeton, NJ: Princeton University Press.

Emmons, R.A. and M.E. McCullough. 2003. "Counting Blessings versus Burdens: An Experimental Investigation of Gratitude and Subjective Well-Being in Daily Life." *Journal of Personality and Social Psychology,* 84(2): 377–89.

Fredrickson, Barbara L. 2013. *Love 2.0.* New York, NY: Plume.

Gordon, Avery (1997) 2008. *Ghostly Matters: Haunting and the Sociological Imagination.* Minneapolis, MN: University of Minnesota Press.

Greenberg, Rachel. 2010. "Walk Down Memory Lane: Reflexivity as a Component of Well-Being." Geneseo Undergraduate Research Conference. Geneseo, New York, USA.

Hochschild, Arlie. 1983. *The Managed Heart: Commercialization of Human Feeling.* Berkeley, CA: University of California Press.

Kesebir, Pelin and Ed Diener. (2008) 2009. "In Pursuit of Happiness: Empirical Answers to Philosophical Questions." In *The Science of Well-Being: The Collected Works of Ed Diener*, edited by Ed Diener. New York, NY: Springer.

Khan, Naveeda. 2012. *Muslim Belonging: Aspiration and Skepticism in Pakistan.* Durham, NC: Duke University Press.

Kim-Prieto, Chu and Ed Diener. 2009. "Religion as a Source of Variation in the Experience of Positive and Negative Emotions." *Journal of Positive Psychology,* 4(6): 447–60.

Kitayama, Shinobu and Hazel Rose Markus. 2000. "The Pursuit of Happiness and the Realization of Sympathy: Cultural Patterns of Self, Social Relations and Well-Being." In *Culture and Subjective Well-Being,* edited by Ed Diener and Eunkook M. Suh, 113–62. Cambridge, MA: MIT Press.

Koslofsky, Craig. 2011. *Evening's Empire: A History of the Night in Early Modern Europe.* Cambridge: Cambridge University Press.

Kripal, Jeffrey J. 2001. *Roads of Excess, Palaces of Wisdom: Eroticism & Reflexivity in the Study of Mysticism.* Chicago, IL: University of Chicago Press.

Krishna, Daya. 1989. *The Art of the Conceptual.* New Delhi: Indian Council of Philosophical Research.

Kugle, Scott. 2007. *Sufis and Saints' Bodies: Mysticism, Corporeality & Sacred Power in Islam.* Chapel Hill, NC: University of North Carolina Press.

Larsen, Randy J. and Zvjezdana Prizmic. 2008. "Regulation of Emotional Well-Being: Overcoming the Hedonic Treadmill." In *The Science of Subjective Well-Being,* edited by Michael Eid and Randy J. Larsen. New York, NY: Guilford.

Liu, Eric Y., Harold G. Koenig, and Dedong Wei. 2012. "Discovering a Blissful Island: Religious Involvement and Happiness in Taiwan." *Sociology of Religion,* 73(1): 46–68.

Lutz, Catherine A. 1988. *Unnatural Emotions: Everyday Sentiment on a Micronesian Atoll & Their Challenges to Western Theory.* Chicago, IL: University of Chicago Press.

Lynch, Owen. 1990. "The Social Construction of Emotion in India." In *Divine Passions: The Social Construction of Emotion in India,* 3–36. Berkeley: University of California Press; New Delhi: Oxford University Press.

Markus, Hazel Rose, Carol D. Ryff, Katherine B. Curhan, and Karen A. Palmersheim. 2004. "In Their Own Words: Well-Being at Midlife among High School-Educated and College-Educated Adults." In *How Healthy Are We? A National Study of Well-Being at Midlife,* edited by Orville Gilbert Brim, Carol D. Ryff, and Ronald C. Kessler, 273–319. Chicago, IL: University of Chicago Press.

Mathews, Gordon. 1996. *What Makes Life Worth Living? How Japanese and Americans Make Sense of Their Worlds.* Berkeley, CA: University of California Press.

Muller-Ortega, Paul Eduardo. 1989. *The Triadic Heart of Siva: Kaula Tantricism of Abhinavagupta in the Non-Dual Saivism of Kashmir.* Albany, NY: SUNY Press.

Mukerjee, Radhakamal. (1965) 2005. "Preface to the Second Edition." In *The Social Structure of Values,* viii–x. New Delhi: Radha Publications.

Mukerji, Dhurjati Prasad. 1924. *Personality and the Social Sciences*. Kolkata: The Book Company.

Myers, David G. 2008. "Religion and Human Flourishing." In *The Science of Subjective Well-Being*, edited by Michael Eid and Randy J. Larsen, 323–41. New York, NY: Guilford.

Nisbett, Richard E. 2003. *The Geography of Thought: How Asians and Westerners Think Differently ... and Why?* New York, NY: Free Press.

Obeyesekere, Gananath. 2012. *The Awakened Ones: Phenomenology of Visionary Experience*. New York, NY: Columbia University Press.

Putnam, Robert D. 2000. *Bowling Alone: The Collapse and Revival of American Community*. New York, NY: Simon and Schuster.

Sarkar, Benoy Kumar. 1940. "Creative Disequilibrium in Freedom, Democracy and Socialism." *Calcutta Review* (January).

———. 1941. *Villages and Towns and Social Patterns*. Kolkata: Chuckerverty Chatterjee.

Scheff, Thomas. 1990. *Microsociology*. Chicago, IL: University of Chicago Press.

Seligman, Martin E.P. 2011. *Flourish*. New York, NY: Free Press.

Singh, Bhrigupati. 2015. *Poverty and the Quest for Life: Spiritual and Material Striving in Rural India*. Chicago, IL: University of Chicago Press.

Singh, Yogendra. 1983. *Image of Man: Ideology and Theory in Indian Sociology*. Delhi: Chanakya.

Swidler, Ann. 2001. *Talk of Love: How Americans Use their Culture*. Chicago, IL: University of Chicago Press.

Vaillant, George E. 2002. *Aging Well: Surprising Guideposts to a Happier Life from the Landmark Harvard Study of Adult Development*. Boston, MA: Little Brown.

Weber, Max. (1915) 1946. "Religious Rejections of the World and Their Directions." In *From Max Weber*, edited by H.H. Gerth and C. Wright Mills, 323–62. New York, NY: Oxford University Press.

———. (1919) 1946. "Science as Vocation." In *From Max Weber,* edited by H.H. Gerth and C. Wright Mills, 129–58. New York, NY: Oxford University Press.

Williams, Patricia J. 1991. *The Alchemy of Race and Rights: Diary of a Law Professor*. Cambridge, MA: Harvard University Press.

9

TOWARD A BETTER SOCIOLOGY

I am not a sociologist as sociologists would like me to be.

—Dhurjati Prasad Mukerji, Presidential Address to the First Indian
Sociological Conference, Dehradun, 1955 (1955 [2013], 213)

*Truth is not fashioned by the human mind; truth is revealed to the mind.
Hence the importance in Indian tradition of the practice of learning the
truth by listening to one who speaks it. This is known as* sravana, *"hearing."
But hearing the truth is not enough. The student must internalize it,
mull it over, imbibe it. There must therefore be a process of reflecting
or "meditating" on it* (manana) *and there must also be a process of
"contemplating" the insights thus gained so that the student is better able
to apply that truth in his or her own life.*

—William K. Mahony (1997, 233)

Sociology should return to studying the good life, something deep
within sociological traditions, but neglected in recent decades.
Rather than trying to reduce complex reality, sociology should
embrace nonreductionist epistemologies to better recognize contradictions and contrarieties in the social world. Embracing continuity between observer and observed creates a fuller understanding
than that provided by distanced objectivity. Following the Indian
tradition Mahoney describes in the epigraph, sociological understanding improves if we listen to the people we interview, contemplate their insights, and apply their truths to our own life. Such
sociological introspection can be combined with interviews to help

the researcher better understand and learn from what interviewees say. Haridas Chaudhuri (1965, 29–30) points out that in contrast to "modern western psychology's" "empirical study of the psyche," the "integral psychology" pioneered by Indian psychologists learns through "active participation in the creative growth and self-fulfillment of the psyche." While Chaudhuri admits that learning through activity is "trans-empirical" in the narrow social-science sense, such knowledge is not "trans-experiential." By acting on the wisdom of the people we interview, we gain knowledge from experience rather than from "external perception"—knowledge that is "empirical in the broader sense of the term."

An approach that studies the good life, combines introspection, fieldwork, and interviews, and relies on a nonobjectifying, nonreductionist, experiential epistemology is consistent with the sensibility of a distinctively *Indian* sociology and philosophy. While postmodern thinkers have emphasized nonreductionist, nonobjectifying experiential epistemology, Indian sociologists Benoy Kumar Sarkar (1884–1949), Radhakamal Mukerjee (1889–1968), and D.P. Mukerji (1894–1961) embraced this epistemology in the first half of the twentieth century. This chapter argues that a nonreductionist, nonobjectifying methodology and epistemology are not only good for research, but good for the researcher, too. Embracing these methods benefits sociology and sociologists, contributing to the good life and confirming this study's insights about well-being.

This chapter nonetheless recognizes that there are intractable ethical dilemmas in studying others. My inherent optimism is reflected in the chapter's argument that sociology can be spiritual practice with heart, but studying others always involves the perils of objectification and misapprehension.

This chapter is perhaps heretical to American sociology, but recently a few others are following the same lines. Consistent with the thought of Indian sociology, but unaware of that thought, Christian Smith (2010) recently theorized that we must recognize the plurality of human personality, rather than reducing the human to first principles. Consistent with Indian sociology and the argument of this book, Smith (2010, 220) argues against "variables sociology" that focuses on the individual as the unit of analysis, urging a move to making social relationships the primary unit of analysis. Unbeknownst to Smith, Radhakamal Mukerjee made a similar argument half a century ago.

Considering the Good Society

I ultimately question the concept of well-being as an *enduring* sense of life satisfaction. But returning to a study of how to live a good life would make for a better sociology.

Anthropologist Joel Robbins (2013) recently argued anthropology needs to move "beyond the suffering slot" to look at the good life. Martin Seligman (2011, 103–05) similarly indicted psychology for focusing on "the psychology of victims and negative emotions and alienation and pathology and tragedy" and urged a turn toward examining a psychology of why people flourish. Sociology has turned so much to studying suffering that there is little room to study how to live well. When Radhakamal Mukerjee (1997, 174) visited the University of Chicago sociology department in 1937, he was "surprised" with its "preoccupation with social pathological problems" rather than "normal community structure and processes." Ruut Veenhoven (2008, 44), one of the few sociologists studying subjective well-being today, correctly reports that well-being "is no great issue in sociology; the subject is not mentioned in sociological textbooks and rarely discussed in sociological journals."

As I started writing this book, I was excited about sharing my findings with other sociologists. But looking through the scores of calls for papers for the American Sociological Association conference in 2012, there was nothing on the good life. Ultimately, I submitted a paper to a theoretical tradition—symbolic interactionism—and the field of emotions. But there was really no place, among sociologists, to study well-being. This was particularly ironic because the theme of the meeting was "Real Utopias: Emancipatory Projects, Institutional Designs, Possible Futures." Surely learning how to live a good life is the true emancipatory project! The paper I submitted was initially rejected (although the session organizer later found a place for it on the panel when another paper dropped out [Derné 2012a]), showing, I think, the lack of space to discuss the good life. When I attended those ASA meetings, session after session focused on suffering and disadvantage. When the ASA organizer rejected my paper, I submitted another paper to an adjacent meeting—the Society for the Study of Symbolic Interaction (Derné 2012b). This more ethnographic, qualitative group was more congenial to me than the more anonymous ASA and the methodological traditions were more in keeping with the direction of this book. But I was still placed on a panel with two other papers, both of which related to the suffering of persistent illness and physical troubles. I tell this tale of conferences to highlight just how peripheral well-being is to studies in sociology.

Studying suffering may even lead to the suffering of scholars, which surely limits what they can know. Religion scholar William P. Harman (2006, 27) described a goddess shrine in India that attracts "the ill and the infirm, many of whom suffer obvious pain and discomfort." Worshipers "leave quickly," staying just long enough to "discharge obligations contracted by vows." Harman found that he, too, avoided "tarrying" at the shrine. It isn't easy, he says, to spend much time "among the constant throngs of thousands of afflicted and suffering people who go there to live and await the healing of the goddess." Harman couldn't return to do research more than five consecutive days at a time without developing "a low-grade depression." Constant contact with "open wounds, running sores, and misshapen limbs" is just plain depressing! To understand the people we study, we have to identify with them and see ourselves as fundamentally like them. To see ourselves as like them is to feel their pain! If the suffering is so great that the researcher can't bridge the difference with the sufferer, the study of the sufferer is unlikely to reveal much truth.

The classical sociological traditions were all concerned with moral questions about how to live a good life. Karl Marx argued that "free conscious activity" is humans' species being and that capitalism prevented humans from freely and consciously producing, reducing them to being little more than animals. He suggested that only when the general production was socialized could humans—and he actually meant men!—have the freedom to use the time remaining for creative productive pursuits. This book's conclusions suggest that Marx is right that providing time for creativity is an important part of living the good life, but that Marx was too narrow in focusing on creative productive pursuits—there are many other pleasures that are important to well-being. Marx was notably incorrect in dismissing the pleasures of "eating and procreation" as animal functions. We're human, but we're also animal and these bodily pleasures are an important part of the good life. Marx mocks the worker who thinks he's free when he "dresses up" in the home, but this study has found that grooming, too, is part of the good life. Marx had a good understanding of how long work hours prevented people from being free, but his view of the freedoms that people would pursue to find a good life was far too narrow. Marx, moreover, missed the role of work—even constrained work—as a source of well-being.

Max Weber argued that the ability to attribute meanings to things was what made us human and criticized modern society for turning humans into "order addicts" who used an instrumental rationality to attain things without thinking about substantive reasons for attaining these things. So, people want to earn more and more money without thinking about the meaning of that money. Or I want to publish a paper in the *American Sociological Review* without much thought about what that paper says. This book suggests that Weber was right that *meanings* are a key source of well-being. People want to understand their contributions to others and want to have some way of understanding life's ups and downs.

For Emile Durkheim, the primary ill of modern times was the loss of social connections that occurred as people began striving as individuals, rather than being embraced in close social groups. This book suggests that Durkheim was right that social connections are a fundamental aspect of well-being (but that we also must emphasize how individual striving *also* is key to well-being).

With but a few notable exceptions (e.g., Bellah et al. 1985), sociology has turned its back on the project of understanding the path to well-being. I have followed with interest the Successful Societies project led by Peter Hall and Michele Lamont (2009), but the work done so far focuses on external measures—such as health—and social problems—such as AIDS—and how social institutions can help improve those measures, without focusing much on internal signs of well-being.

Operating outside the hegemony of American sociology, *Indian* sociology has given more attention to studying the ultimate questions about living a good life. Noting that the specialization of the different social sciences have narrowed their scope, Benoy Kumar Sarkar (1912, 8, 11) complains that using specialized methodologies to answer narrow questions has "withdrawn the attention of scholars from the study of the hopes and aspirations of [humans], the progress and decay of civilizations and the ultimate gains and losses of humanity" (cited by Dandyopadhyay 1984, 29). D.P. Mukerji (1955 [2013], 223) argues that Indian sociological traditions should draw on

Indian religious traditions. "All our *shastras* are sociological," he said. Looking at *paataal*—the depths—he said, should allow sociology to "*ultimately* show the way out of the social system." In Chapter 7, I describe how Radhakamal Mukerjee (1949 [2005], 90) recognized how religion fulfills "the all-important social function of creating and maintaining the conditions of enduring and satisfying human relationships." Mukerjee ([1936] 1960, 1) complains that most studies of religion concentrated on its "abnormal aspects." He says that the "psychoanalytic school" is wrong to focus "dissociation, repression and sublimation" in mystics' lives because "there is a large mass of religious experience" characterized "by full participation of thought, emotion and will that establishes a balance and integration of the ego" (Mukerjee [1936] 1960, 2).

Radhakamal Mukerjee (1949 [2005], 96–97, 104) urged sociology to focus on identifying positive values of "commonality." Action in crowds, he said, is instinctual and nonmoral, action in interest groups is rational-emotional and amoral, and action in society is emotional-rational, and moral. But in commonality, action could be "transmoral," using norms of "love, equality and solidarity." Mukerjee ([1965] 2005, ix) despaired that the "scientific, technological and industrial revolutions" in "Western civilization" had led to an emphasis on values as "relativistic" and had turned humans away from addressing "universal claims" stemming from the "transcendent dimensions" of the self. He urged replacing the "prevalent empirical ... theory of mind or self" with "a multi-dimensional theory that can do justice to the self's deep and expansive cosmic affinities and transactions" connected to "intrinsic and ultimate values and norms." In 1965, Mukerjee ([1965] 2005, vii) wrote hopefully that "discover[ing] values" and "clarify[ing], harmoni[zing] and adjust[ing] values" were "essential features of the new outlook in sociology." Mukerjee reasoned that sociology could identify values that would provide such felicitous connections. T.N. Madan (2013, 13) is perhaps right to conclude that this focus pushed Mukerjee "away from sociology (as the subject is generally understood and practiced) towards a mystical view of human sociality." "In Commonality," Mukerjee (1949 [2005], 98) wrote, "the distinction between altruism and egoism [and] between social consciousness and self-consciousness vanishes" as the person "loves and serves" a neighbor because the neighbor is actually part of the self. "One who does not love [one's] neighbor" fails to understand "the potentialities of [one's] own nature.... The love, the compassion, the sympathy that the neighbor arouses are no more [the neighbor's] than the self's." Mukerjee (1949 [2005], 99) argued that "instrumental values such as wealth, property, standard of living, social status and the interest of the class are competitive in character" and divide people. Mukerjee (1949 [2005], 99) urged moving to "intrinsic values including health, appreciation of beauty, development of understanding and the great moral virtues" all of which are "unifying, defined as these are in terms of individual need and worth and social well-being." He urged identifying values that would unify and provide well-being.

Before the recent hegemony of quantitative methods and narrow questions in American sociology, Pitirim Sorokin (1889–1968) urged the sort of focus on searching for a better society that I describe in the works of Indian sociologists. Although he founded the sociology department at Harvard and served as president of the American Sociological Association, Sorokin has been neglected in recent years. I didn't learn of his work in graduate school, but rather I came to know his work because it influenced some of the Indian sociologists (like Sarkar and Mukerjee) and philosophers (like Krishna) whom I cite here. I think Indians were perhaps attracted to Sorokin because his message was consistent with the concerns of Indian traditions. And I think Sorokin's goals, methodologies, and epistemology may also have been influenced by his Russian background. (It's notable to me, too, that he seemed to find academic politics more distressing than being jailed by the czars and, later, the Bolsheviks!) Sorokin identified different methodologies for knowing associated with the multiple aspects of human character. Because we are bodies, we know empirically; because we are minds, we know through reason; but because of our souls or supersensory capacities we learn transcendent truths through intuition and revelation (Johnson 1998, 14; Sorokin 1943, 105; see also Meyer 2008). Witnessing the tragedies of the mid-twentieth century (World War II, Stalinism, and Nazism), Sorokin (1950, v) argued that while there were times when humankind "urgently need[ed] an upsurge of scientific discoveries and technological innovation," and there were other times when the "paramount need" was for a release of "aesthetic or religious or philosophical creativity," "an exuberant blossoming of ethical creativity seems to be the most desperate need of humanity today." Noting the scientific advancements that had been made, Sorokin (1950, v) argued human-kind would survive "if there are no great scientific or philosophical or artistic or technological achievements during the next hundred years," but he doubted the survival of humanity unless the "egotism of individuals and groups" is "transcended by a creative love ... as a dynamic force effectively transfiguring individuals, ennobling social institutions, inspiring culture, and making the whole world a warm, friendly, and beautiful cosmos." Just as Marx (1845–46 [1978], 193) argued that people needed to be transformed to gain the benefits of a communist society, Sorokin argues that to live well people need to be transformed to gain "harmony," "freedom," and "happiness." By the time his influence had waned, Sorokin lamented that love and altruism had been largely ignored by sociologists, who instead focused on negative social acts such as crime, violence, and discrimination while stigmatizing "the study of prosocial behavior and love as nonscientific exercises in sociological preaching" (Johnson 1998, 20).

Sociology should return to studying what makes people well and considering how society can be structured to encourage feelings of well-being by encouraging connections between people. Feminists have long argued (e.g., MacKinnon 1989, 101–02) that sociological knowledge disempowers if it doesn't help people act in ways that can improve their lives. So, sociology must address not only how societies can be structured to encourage feelings of well-being, but how people can live in ways that encourage well-being. I suggest the implications of this study for living well and structuring a society to encourage living well in the next chapter.

Non-reductionist Theorizing

This book suggests that sociological theory could be transformed by focusing on the relationship, rather than the individual. Radhakamal Mukerjee ([1960] 2005, 78) argues that the "entire group of humanistic studies" suffers "gravely" from focusing on the "abstract, detached individual," instead of seeing persons as "social." As I note in Chapter 7, D.P. Mukerji (1955 [2013], 217) found that Parsons's action system did not apply for the simple reason that action for the Indian is "not individualistic" but rooted in group life.

But D.P. Mukerji (1924, 241) also saw *both* the "group" *and* "the uniqueness of the individual" as unreal. What is needed, Radhakamal Mukerjee argued, is a focus on *relations* as the key sociological unit of analysis. So, Mukerjee ([1965] 2005, viii–ix) argued for a "Copernican revolution in the field of sociology" that would shift "the stress from the method of Aristotle to that of Galileo with reference to social phenomena: the former dealing with the *properties* of objects, the later dealing with the *relations* of objects to the whole sociological situation" (Mukerjee's emphasis). This book argues that understanding relationships and interactions, rather than individual circumstances, is what we need to understand well-being.

Sociological theory should not, I argue, reduce human beings to any fundamental first principle, but should focus on the plurality of human personality. The people whom I interviewed often recognized *contradictory* bases of well-being, a focus consistent with Indian religious traditions as in the Gita's description of different paths to well-being, and Shiva's manifestations as both erotic and ascetic. Nisbett (2003, 174–5) demonstrates that while Westerners rely on the principle of non-contradiction and, so, often try to reconcile opposites, Asian traditions emphasize transcending contradictions or finding truth in both sides of a paradox or anomaly. This Indian sensibility was taken up by D.P. Mukerji[1] and Radhakamal Mukerjee,[2] but my focus here will be on Benoy Kumar Sarkar. Coming from a Hindu tradition and drawing on Sanskrit texts' approaches to sociology, economics, and politics, Sarkar also referenced German, French, American, and Bengali sociology, the *American Sociological Review*, the *Mahabharata,* and Robert Browning! Sarkar translated Marx into Bengali and spent much of his mature career translating *The Sukraniti*, a Sanskrit text providing knowledge of secular society. With this diverse and still *Indian* background, Sarkar (1941, 25) opposed Marx, Durkheim, and other theorists who emphasized one aspect of social existence over another. Recognizing how classical

---

[1] Mukerji (1924, 28) argues we must recognize a "multipersonality within the same individual mind."

[2] Mukerjee (1960b, 11–13) argues people operate in spheres of politics, economics, and religion. So political scholars are wrong to see people as focusing only on power, just as economic scholars are wrong to see people as only focused on wealth. Thus, we must recognize humans' "multi-dimensionality."

Sanskrit texts identified four "fundamental instincts"—kama (sex), kamchana (wealth), kirit (reputation) and karma (work, action, or creation), Sarkar (1941, 25, 79–80) criticizes sociological interpretations for tending to emphasize one arena (be it sex or economy or politics) over the diverse aspects of life. Sarkar (1941, 25) urges that sociologists should "stress" "the pluralistic make-up of the mind or personality," and recognize that human behavior always reflects the working of some combination of the four instincts he identifies in Hindu thinking: sex, acquisition, power, and creativity (Sarkar 1941, 79–80). Sarkar (1941, 25) holds that humans' reasonableness, compassion, rationality, and secular nature exist alongside irrationality, selfishness, superstition, and religiosity; just as rivalry, jealousy, envy, malice, enmity, hatred, and repulsion exist alongside friendliness and sympathy (Saha 2013). I think of how Delhi sociologists responded to my 2011 talk by emphasizing how I needed to move beyond interviews because often what people say at first turns out to be only part of the story and that people are not likely to admit to an interviewer the pleasures they get from harming other people. Sarkar (1912, 11; 1937, 24) argues that the fundamental aspect of humans cannot be found in religion, economics, ethics, or the state alone (quoted by Bandyopadhyay 1984, 26). None represents the whole person (Sarkar 1937, 24). Sometimes, "human life manifests itself ... in art and literature, at other times in political conflicts and religious movements" (Sarkar 1912, 11 cited in Bandyopadhyay 1984, 26). Thus, "not 'truth,' but truths constitute the objective verdict of philosophy" (Sarkar 1905, 1 cited by Bandyopadhyay 1984, 20).

Today postmodernists argue against "absolute, universal, general or abstract" truths in favor of truths that are "individual, personal and concrete." But that idea was apparent in *premodern* Indian thinking—the quotes in the first sentence of this paragraph are not from a postmodern theorist, but an Indian political scientist's summary of Sarkar's ideas (Bandyopadhyay 1984, 20)! Both postmodern and premodern thinking recognized the complexity and contrariety of life, while modernity and enlightenment tried to reduce to universal principles. Avery Gordon (1997 [2008], 3) argues that the fact that "life is complicated is of great analytic importance." Sociology should recognize the complexity that appears in interviews and fieldwork and avoid simplifying complex realities. D.P. Mukerji (1924, 23) describes life's complexity as a "virtue" because it is "the outcome of an intenser form of life." And, so, embracing complexity helps in living a rich life.

Before postmodernism, Sorokin (who influenced Sarkar, D.P. Mukerji, and Radhakamal Mukerjee) recognized the contradictory human drives for peace and war, love and hatred, and independence and domination (Johnson 1988, 8). Sorokin theorized that humans are three-dimensional, possessing a body, mind, and soul, each with its own epistemology or way of knowing (Johnson 1998, 14). Barry Johnson (1998, 14) summarizes Sorokin's theory saying,

> The body experiences reality through the senses and knows the world empirically. The mind sees knowledge through reason and understands the world rationally. The soul, or supersensory capacity, develops from intuition, grace, and revelation. Through this third dimension, humans grasp the sublime or transcendent truths of their existence.

Thus, Sorokin (1943, 105–06) contends that "sociocultural reality" is a "complex manifold" with an "empirical aspect to be … studied through sensory perception," "a logico-rational aspect of sociocultural phenomena" "to be apprehended through the discursive logic of human reason," and a "supersensory, superrational and metalogical aspect" that could be apprehended through intuition, revelation, and mystic experiences (see also Krishna 1989, 140–43). Indian philosophy highlights noncognitive ways of knowing that might access the supersensory aspect of life. Dehejia (2008, 82) quotes the *Katha Upanishad* as describing how high states are accessed through noncognitive awareness "when all the senses are stilled" and "when the mind is at rest." Sociologists should explore ways of knowing all aspects of life, rather than reducing social dynamics to a single dimension.

Non-Objectifying Epistemology and Methodology

Feminist theorists Dorothy Smith (1989, 1990) and Catharine MacKinnon (1989) critique an epistemology of objectivity as contributing to a way of thinking that leads to objectification of other people, leading especially to men's objectification of women. For Smith, objectivity—stepping outside of situations of which we are part—is associated with abstract, extralocal "relations of ruling."

The ability to see others abstractly, from a distance, and outside of local, real situations facilitates distancing oneself from others' feelings and experience. Linking objectivity to the objectification of women, MacKinnon (1989, 124) argues that "objectivity is the methodological stance of which objectification is the social process. Sexual objectification is the primary process of the subjection of women." Since women have been "objectified as sexual beings, while stigmatized as ruled by subjective passions," women's interest, MacKinnon (1989, 120–21) maintains, is in "overthrowing" the distinction between knowing subject and known object.

More recently, Lata Mani (2009) has pointed out that secular Marxists who criticize "Hindu fundamentalists" neglect emancipatory streams of religious traditions. Mani (2009, 84) points out that ultimately it is the "sense of separation" (whether the Left's separation from religion or "Hindu fundamentalists'" separation from Muslims) that ultimately "underwrites" "cruelty, prejudice and suffering." Mani (2009, 9) argues that "spiritual truth" makes us aware that the "qualities we are so tempted to decry in others may also be present in us" and also that our own positive qualities are present in those we may criticize. Both secular activism (the Marxist left) and spiritual philosophy (decried as Hindu fundamentalists) "spring from a common source, the desire to end suffering and bring harmony to human existence. Both posit a positive essence to humans—'humanity,' 'loving spaciousness'—and each seeks to address this core by means of its own specific rationality. Secular activism focuses primarily on changing unjust social arrangements.... Spiritual philosophy explains what prevents fellow feeling from being manifest in us" (Mani 2009, 150). Recognizing the harm of separation, Mani sees unity with others, suggesting the same nonobjectifying approach I urge here.

Dorothy Smith (1989, 43) shows how sociology is implicated in objectifying others by its distanced method and epistemology. By distancing readers and researchers, sociology situates sociologists and readers of sociology in ways that "subdue local positions, perspectives and experiences." While there are many counter-tendencies within sociology (e.g., Stacey 1990), too often sociology still takes a distanced stance toward those we study. Sociology routinely, I think, raises that "sense of separation" that Mani points to as the source of suffering. Feminist sociologist Kristin Luker (2012, 627) describes how the "ten minutes at the end of the interview remind [her] of the morning after a one-night stand. The abrupt end of so much intimacy, especially when it is one-sided, creates gnawing social discomfort." She quotes another researcher, Karen Lacy, who describes herself as a "nimble interviewer" but who nevertheless doesn't want to "reciprocate" (by answering interviewees' questions; Luker 2012, 627). These sociologists sense their unease—and even examine it—but seem to keep putting interviewees in the same one-sided situation. MacKinnon links objectivity with objectification, and feminist researchers recognize that their own interview process feels like a one-night stand in which the intimacy is one-sided, the researcher using the object of research.

I have always participated in this process of objectification—studying others for my purposes, a process that now disheartens me. I was pursuing interviews to get "data." The "friends" I talked with in interviews usually saw very little of me after that. Like many researchers, I've become uneasy with this process and now emphasize dialoguing with, learning from, and being transformed by the people I interview. Rather than seeing the people I interviewed as unlike me, I see them as not fundamentally different from me. While the relationship with those I interview is still unequal—I am asking the questions and setting the agenda—it is no longer *completely uni*-directional. Even from my first interviews in the 1980s, I would give the people I interviewed a chance to ask me questions, but now I try to have much more back-and-forth about sources of well-being. I didn't keep in contact with anyone I interviewed in the 1980s for very long, but now I often stay in contact with some people—certainly a small minority—for years. In the preface, I suggest that perhaps Dr Christensen (2012) seems to see himself as a different species from the pickup artists whom he studies. Frankly, I am now objectifying Tony Christensen, creating a picture of his talk for my own purposes. But as I thought more about Luker's description of the interview process as a "one-night-stand" in which the interviewer wrangles the interviewee into bed, I began to see the sociological researcher as a "pickup artist." My career as a sociologist includes that process—finding people to interview and wrangling them into doing the interview. As this study reached its end, I found myself searching for people to interview who fit certain categories: How can we recruit lower-middle-class housewives? Or less educated Muslim women? Or laborers? This process has disturbed me more and more as the years go by.

I've quoted Luker's frank admission that she sees the last ten minutes at the end of the interview as the end of a one-night stand, but she also approvingly quotes Howard Becker's "insistence that we not distance or pathologize those we study" (Luker 2012, 627). In his 1955 presidential address at the first Indian sociological conference, D.P. Mukerji (1955 [2013], 216) spoke of how Indian scholars are too often "taken in by that mysterious phrase"—"scientific detachment." Mukerji held that the advantages of "insight that comes from participation" are far greater than the advantages "of being in the swing and being internationally recognized as scholars in accordance with a supposedly common standard of 'scientific' technique." As later feminist theorists recognize, we better know society by being part of it rather than standing separate from it. Thus, MacKinnon (1989, 98) argues women are "able to have access to society and its structure because they live in it and have been formed by it, not in spite of those facts." We can understand situations by "moving and being moved, changing and being changed" (MacKinnon 1989, 91). Citing Gloria Anzaldua's focus on "open-hearted listening," Luker (2012, 627) recognizes the value of sociologists writing fieldwork notes not only about "what we observed, but what we *felt*." And it's worth noting—given my subject position—that Mukerji (1955 [2013], 216) recognizes that "foreign scholars" can also participate in this process when in India!

Indian religious traditions—I'm especially focusing on Kashmiri Shaivism—offer a particularly valuable approach to nonobjectifying epistemology. These traditions that see nondifferentiation between self and other facilitate nonobjectification of those we study. Thus, Abhinavagupta (tenth century) says that "within itself," "the reality of Siva" "embraces all principles, which are in effect identical with it" (Muller-Ortega 1989, 86–87). Sanskritist Paul Eduardo Muller-Ortega (1989, 29) concludes that because of Shiva's "unboudedness, any attempt to pin him down theologically results in his manifesting himself as the opposite quality as well." Thus Muller-Ortega (1989, 85–86) concludes Abhinavagupta's writings are flexible because they seem to result from "an attitude that holds that while distinctions are real and true on their own level, they are also continuously being undercut by absolute reality," the larger truth which is the "multifarious nature of Siva."

Harsha Dehejia (2008)[3] has explored how Kashmiri Shaivism creates an epistemology that overcomes the distinction between subject and object. Gazing at Parvati, Shiva creates the initial duality between subject and object—Shiva experiences joy looking at Parvati as different from him (Dehejia 2008, 45). But the goal of Kashmiri Shaivism is to resolve this duality into oneness. In Abhinavagupta, *Spanda*—the throbbing vibration like the in-and-out breath—"bridges the cognising subject with the cognitive object," ensuring Shiva and Parvati are never adrift, and the two unite in marriage (Dehejia 2008, 46). Not only are Shiva and Parvati united, but Parvati acts as a mirror for Shiva, ensuring that what Shiva sees in Parvati is ultimately part of the self. "The mirror of Parvati ensures" that the "cognition of Siva turns back upon itself, becomes *reflexive*, assuming that this objective cognition leads ultimately to *self* awareness, for Siva in his second and subsequent cognitions sees none other than himself in the mirror" (Dehejia 2008, 60; my emphases). The mirror ensures that there is a "continuity of the pulsation between the subject and the object. Throughout the epistemic dialogue between Shiva and Parvati the biune unity of the subject and the object is affirmed for it is a unity born of affirmation and not negation" (Dehejia 2008, 60). While Shiva is attracted to Parvati because of difference (her curves!), he ultimately sees Parvati as nondifferent from Shiva.

Thus, Kashmiri Shaivite epistemology suggests that objects of knowledge ultimately reveal the self. The people we interview are like us, not different from us. They help us learn not just about them, but about who we also are. Parvati creates vibration

> between Siva's awareness of the world around and self-awareness. That self-awareness that has been brought about by the mirror is a *pratimilana* or a coming together of ... expansion ... and ... introversion in which all traces of *difference have vanished*. For this state of *pratimilana* is nothing other than ... the undifferentiated and joyous state of consciousness, a state of consciousness that is fully awakened and *enlarged*, in which the subject-object duality ceases forever, where there is a shattering of the initial illusion of duality. (Dehejia 2008, 65; my emphases)

---

[3] Dehejia, a practicing physician with a doctorate in Ancient Indian culture, embodies the multiplicity of selves this chapter also focuses on.

Thus, the *Vijnanabhairava* holds that "knower and known are one and the same" and Dyczkowski (1987, 101) concludes "there is a movement [spanda] of awareness from one to the other as Siva becomes Sakti[4] and Sakti becomes Siva. They are reflected within one another like two mirrors facing each other." Thus, Dehejia (2008, 73) concludes, "objectivity no longer remains a hindrance but a doorway to self-discovery ... a stepping stone to *shuddha-vidya* [pure knowledge which blends the objective with the subjective, Parvati and Siva]." Dehejia (2008, 73) points out that the *Siva Sutras* hold that the yogi is able to "convert the world drama into a pleasing revelation of the true inner self." Or in the *Spandakarika*: "When the yogi desirous of seeing, stands fixed, covering all objects with the light of his [or her] consciousness [the yogi] experiences the entire objective world" within the yogi's own self (Dehejia 2008, 67).

The knowledge that comes from seeing the self in objects reflects the approach of Shiva's joyous affirmation of Parvati, rather than distancing objectification. The knowledge that comes, moreover, depends on Shiva's emotions of delight and wonder at the transformation of "an initial dualistic cognition into unitary cognition" (Dehejia 2008, 70). While Luker describes the encounter between interviewer and interviewee as similar to a one-sided, one-night stand, Dehejia (2008, 47) links "epistemology with romance, for the joy and excitement of a cognising subject in the process of acquiring knowledge is best reflected by the amorous relationship of Siva and Parvati." So, the *Vijnanabhairava* prescribes "that the mind should initially be joyous before it can undertake realisation, that this joyousness is the prerequisite for a higher epistemic step" (Dehejia 2008, 68). The joy of the unity of Shiva and Parvati is an "essential step in the growth of knowledge and the subsequent expansion of consciousness" (Dehejia 2008, 68). If one dismisses the pickup artists one studies, is depressed by the sick people seeking healing, or hates the "Hindu fundamentalists'" hate, one misses the joyous attitude of oneness that advances understanding. Shiva is "wonderstruck and amazed" when his initial cognition of Parvati as different is "transformed through the mirror into a cognition of none other than

---

[4] In this context, *shakti*, the goddess or feminine energy, can be seen as referencing Parvati. Of course, all the goddesses are ultimately one, ultimately part of Shakti. In Shaivism, the goddesses are ultimately part of Shiva, too!

himself" (Dehejia 2008, 69). The resulting emotion (*rasa, bhava*) of wonder (*adbhuta*), exults his mind, shattering "Siva's egoistic, limited self-absorption," giving birth to a "larger self awareness" that includes Parvati (Dehejia 2008, 65, 69). For Kashmiri Shaivites "the excitement and thrill" at wonder is a "necessary prelude in the process of knowledge" (Dehejia 2008, 72).

Considering my own emotions and the emotions of those I interviewed, this book suggests that *emotional knowledge* contributes to our understanding. In his exploration of mystic ways of knowing, Andrew Greeley (1974, 16, 18), sociologist (and defrocked Catholic priest and writer of racy romances), pointed to "truths unplumbed by the discursive intellect" that follow instead from the "joy" at seeing "all things are well." Dehejia (2008, 7) describes the *Agamas* as "joyous rather than reasoned," "effervescent rather than subdued," "life affirming, rather than life denying." As anthropologist Monique Skidmore (2003) notes, this kind of "emotional knowledge" is "usually disregarded or unacknowledged by the ethnographer in the presentation of fieldwork data." But perhaps the *barttaman-panthis* of Bengal (often referred to as "Bauls") are right to suggest that emotion and passion are a better path to knowledge than dry renunciation and passionlessness (Openshaw 1998, 7). This book argues that using our own emotions and the emotions of those we interview can provide an *emotional intelligence*, which advances sociological understanding and an understanding of how to live well.

For some time some anthropologists (and a smaller number of sociologists) have focused on experiencing what the people we study experience. So, while Tony Christensen resists becoming a pickup artist, Robert Desjarlais (1992) insists he can only understand shamans' experience by going into trance, by becoming, as it were, a shaman. Desjarlais (1992, 19) says that "by participating in the everyday life of a society distinct from one's own the ethnographer slowly learns (often tacitly but always partially) patterns of behavior previously unfamiliar to his or her body." Thus, the knowledge becomes "embodied" to be examined. Consistent with Kashmiri Shaivism (e.g., Muller-Ortega 1989, 84, 282), knowledge only comes through experience. Thus, in Kashmiri Shaivite epistemology, knowledge "is not passive but active" (Dehejia 2008, 69). "Knowledge turns into action and action leads to knowledge" (Dyczkowski 1987, 80). Desjarlais (1992, 35) says such embodiment depends on the researcher's "empathy"—an empathy that "rides on the faith that the grounds of experience between two people are similar, such that we can 'know' what another is feeling based on what we ourselves would feel in that situation." While ethnographers have constantly reminded themselves—and been reminded by their colleagues—not to "go native" (Goulet 1994, 16–17) and not to try to "live other people's lives" (Geertz 1986, 373), ethnographers have recently argued that we can learn from paying attention to our own lives, including our inner lives (Goulet 1994, 16–17). Thus, Jean-Guy Goulet (1994, 19) argues that "the ethnographer's *experiences* of interaction in another lifeworld ought to be viewed for what they are, namely viable tools for research" (my emphasis). Goulet (1994, 19), like Desjarlais, suggests we can learn not just from our observation of others but from ourselves engaging in others' lifeworlds. So, David Haberman (1994, xv) found that to understand Indian pilgrims in Braj, his "own body" was a "most valuable tool for research." He learned about suffering from his own bleeding feet. His bodily experiences taught him pilgrimage is not "refined intellectualism, but concrete bodily experience of the material." Monique Skidmore (2003, 5) investigates her own experiences of fear in living with the military dictatorship in Burma to understand not just Burmese people's fear but the experience of fear more generally. Examining our own experiences is a source of insight. Seeing our experiences as similar to those we study militates against distancing objectivity.

We learn not just from experiencing what others experience but from back and forth with others about their experiences and our own. Gananath Obeyesekere (1990, 226) recounts that even from the beginning "even the most objectivist" of fieldworkers "must be able to relate to our informants as normal human beings." Obeyesekere (1990, 226) continues:

> As I close my notebook or shut off my tape recorder, I am once again thrown into normal human interaction, from which I learn a great deal about the other culture. I begin to understand the other culture, not on the basis of accumulated data ... but when I can relate to my informants dialogically, such that their actions make reasonable sense to me, as mine do to them.

Goulet and Young (1994, 329–30) describe the benefits for ourselves and those we study when we "take our informants seriously." Participating with an open mind in their lives opens us up to "aspects of human experience which were blocked by the basic assumptions and taboos of our own cultures." As we introduce our own "interpretive schemes" in our interactions with our "hosts," we open them to new experiences and understandings as well. Goulet and Young's focus is on how we should take seriously how our informants report extraordinary experiences associated with, for instance, shamanism, but the concept of taking our informants seriously has much broader applicability. Seeking to learn from what the people I interviewed say about well-being also facilitates my nonobjectification of the people I study. As Dehejia (2008, 60) argues, the mirror of another "ensures that the object is upheld and given an epistemic bonafides and not dismissed as illusion or unimportant." Rather than learning about why they approach well-being the way they do, I can learn about how to approach well-being.

Milton Erickson held that action is more likely to lead to insight than insight to action. By participating in the approach to well-being of those we study—that is, by trying to act on what they say gives them well-being—we learn not just about their approach to well-being, but the value of that approach to well-being, too.

Early in the twentieth century, D.P. Mukerji developed a nonobjectifying approach to sociology consistent with postmodernism, with the Shaivite sensibility of Indian religious traditions, and with the insights of anthropologists such as Obeyesekere. Mukerji (1924, i–ii) was just 30 years old when he recounted that it came to him "rather late that objectivism was only the other side of subjectivism—that both were unreal as springing from a disturbed and unbalanced psychical state." Mukerji (1924, 240) held that neither the objective nor the subjective point of view was sufficient by itself for a complete visualization of truth, which came only through a dialectic relation of subject and object:

> The true position is that the subject is always to be understood in relation to the object.... The subject knows, feels.... The object is an object by being known, felt and willed, too.... The objects display a unity only when they are related to the subject.... *The only way out of this difficulty is to recognise the relation between subject and object.* (Mukerji 1924, 26–27; my emphasis)

Mukerji held, the truth lay beyond both the possible "delusion, illusion and hallucination" of subjectivity and the "sensation and materialism" of objectivity. Mukerji (1924, 25) found the "continuum behind the subject and the object" in "personality" (which he associated with the Sanskrit concept of *purush*), encompassing *both* subject and object. Mukerji (1924, 26) holds that by recognizing the "relation between subject and object" we can come to see that "the subject and object are now included in the self" that is "more than subject." For Mukerji (1924, 46) personality includes *both* subject and object, while "individuality drifts from" subject to object and back. "Personality is joy, individuality is pain or pleasure. Personality is freedom in thought and action, individuality is enmeshed in the tentacles of determinism" (Mukerji 1924, 46). By seeing the objects of our study in relationship to ourselves "a new spiritual life of Self is lived," "bridg[ing] the gulf between the Subject and the Object" (Mukerji 1924, 33).

Mukerji (1924, i) finds *joy* in this nonobjectifying approach. He describes developing this approach "for myself," because it helped find a "position beyond a petty self consciousness and flurried quest of physical comforts," a position beyond a "totally subjective and a totally objective point of view." The "personality" beyond subject and object is a "measure of joy" (Mukerji 1924, 33). Mukerji describes the scholar who recounts "a dozen arguments for and against a system of protective tariff in India" as feeling no joy because of a reliance on "spurious impartiality." But Mukerji (1924, 33) describes how Gokhale "so personalised India that his arguments for protection" "transmuted a debate into a work of Art. There was joy in his expression, for his arguments helped him to realise himself, his self being identified at that moment with the good of his country. Similarly, a scientific historian marshaling an array of facts cannot produce a book half so enjoyable as that of a nationalist historian however unscientifically partial [the historian] may be." It is *joyful* to connect with the people we study. Apparently quoting Sufi poetry,[5] Mukerji (1924, 35) again identifies the unity between the subject and

---

[5] Mukerji does not clearly identify the source of this quotation. He explains "the large number of quotations in the book" by saying he wanted to "show the extent of my indebtedness" (Mukerji 1924, vi). Mukerji (1924, 346) resisted the convention that "demanded an immediate indication of the sources," saying he had "an earnest desire to avoid pedantry," and so "wove" the quotations "into the texture of the argument" "postpon[ing]" references "until the very end of the book." I was unable to identify clearly the source of the quote.

the object: "I am He whom I love and He whom I love is I, we are two spirits dwelling in one body. If thou Seest Me, thou Seest Him and if thou seest Him thou seest us both." Mukerji (1924, 35) quotes the poet of the Isha Upanishad:

Thou who moves alone, who dost regulate the creation, who art the spirt of the Lord of all creatures, collect Thy rays, draw together Thy light, let me behold in thee the most blessed of all forms, the Person who is there, He I am.

"Science and logic," Mukerji (1924, 35) says, would "laugh at" such sentiment "for they deal with facts which are not related to Personality and as such do not evoke the 'rasas' [emotions]." So, for Mukerji sociology connects him to other people evoking such emotions of joy: "Personality creates beauty and joy by establishing relations not recognized by science" (Mukerji 1924, 35).

Mukerji (1924, 33) recognizes that joy comes not just from understanding, but from doing, from engaging in lessons learned: "A gardener in [the] garden is ... more delightful ... than the botanist in [the] laboratory; [the gardener] will sing, but the other will not" (Mukerji 1924, 33).

Thus, Mukerji argues sociology can be spiritual if sociology recognizes unity with others and connects with others in action:

So the restless *spirits* among the social scientists are trying to discover interrelations.... Much *heart* searching is going on among them today to attain some form of unity in diversity. I do not mean that the barriers have been demolished, or that the unity has been established. But this dissatisfaction is *divine*. (1955, [2013], 214; my emphases)

For Mukerji (1955 [2013], 213) "sociology has a floor and a ceiling, like any other science, but its specialty consists in its floor being the ground floor of all types of social disciplines, and in its ceiling remaining open to the sky." Thus, Mukerji (1955 [2013, 224] hopes that "the cause of spirit" is not a "lost cause," that "the method of insight" is not a "decadent, futile method," and that "interpretation" is not without use "in human knowledge." Mukerji urges sociology to contribute to the weakening of barriers, establishing more unity—unity that will lead to better understanding and making the world better.

Meyer (2008, 218) similarly holds that "knowledge that endures" is a life force connected to all other life forces." Knowledge is spiritual if it connects us, rather than separates us from others. What we need today, Meyer (2008, 221) argues, is knowledge that heals, brings us together, and challenges, surprises, encourages, and expands our awareness. Spiritual meanings are "whole, contemplative, intuitive, metaphoric, joyful, liberating. Within research," she says, spiritual knowledge provides "answers you will remember in your dreams" (Meyer 2008, 229).

A nonobjectifying epistemology that connects to others, then, is part of a unitive project that is itself a source of well-being. D.P. Mukerji (1924, 28–29) argues that we must not oversimplify human motives, but should recognize "multipersonality within the same individual mind." Mukerji argues that recognizing "multipersonality" not only helps us better understand humans and society, but also helps us see a "Fundamental Unity," that reflects "Universal Spiritual Being ... that ultimately unifies the different selves of different individuals."

Catharine MacKinnon's (1989, 130) feminist analysis of women's subordination emphasizes that women's "second class" status is related to "being a thing for sexual use," which in turn is related to an objectifying way of knowing:

> The eroticism that corresponds to the male side of the epistemology ... its sexual ontology, is "the use of things to experience self."[6] Women are the things and men are the self. (1989, 123).... Woman through male eyes is sex object, that by which man knows himself at once as man and as subject (1989, 122).... Indeed, objectivity is the methodological stance of which objectification is the social process. Sexual objectification is the primary process of the subjection of women (1989, 124).

Too often social scientists like myself have used an objectivist epistemology to understand those we study. A more spiritual approach is to recognize unity with those we study.

In his later years, Radhakamal Mukerjee ([1965] 2005, viii) wrote hopefully that sociology was overcoming "the dualism between facts and values, individual and society, egoism and altruism, community and cosmos, self-actualization and self-transcendence that has

---

[6] MacKinnon references Andrea Dworkin's (1981, 124) phrasing here.

thwarted sociological analysis" in the past. Mukerjee moved beyond the distinction of subject and object:

> Finally there is neither witness nor witnessed, but there simply Is. The Is remains eternal.... It is the unity of the seer and the seen.... The Is is one indivisible impersonal consciousness. ([1936] 1960, 230)

Radhakamal Mukerjee sees the benefit of overcoming these distinctions for the sociologist as well as the for sociological analysis. In religion, a human finds "perfection of human relations lie[s] not in domination and subordination, but in equality and fraternity, not in *the use of fellow-humans for [the person's] own end or interest*, but in reciprocal love and tenderness" (Mukerjee 1949 [2005], 90; my emphasis). So, rather than using the objects of our study for our own purposes, sociologists should interact lovingly with those we study. Drawing on his own diary of his mystical experiences, Mukerjee ([1936] 1960, 221–23) sees mysticism as providing an understanding that totality of all beings is experienced in the "I" of the mystic ([1936] 1960, 4–5), involving both "self-realisation" and "self transcendence" ([1936] 1960, 225). "Emotion and reason" "fuse" in the mystic's understanding ([1936] 1960, 223). Mukerjee ([1936] 1960, 4, 25, 158) uses words such as "joy," "wonder," "mystery," "awe", "veneration," and "ultimate concern" to describe the feelings the mystic's knowledge produces and applies these mystical insights to a method and epistemology appropriate for sociology: "An ecstatic contemplation of the relation of self to another self reveals the infinite and the universal in the finite and the particular other person" (Mukerjee 1949 [2005], 90). Like D.P. Mukerji, Radhakamal Mukerjee is suggesting a nonobjectifying, nonreductionist epistemology can make sociology a spiritual discipline. By seeing the people we study (be they pickup artists, people suffering serious illness, Hindu fundamentalists, or the men and women Narendra, Meenu, and I interviewed) as nondifferent from us, we experience joyful connections to all, and better understand others' perspective by relating to it fully and trying to live the insights of those we interview.

T.N. Madan (1994, 194) describes being asked if he expected anthropologists to like those we study. "The point," he replied, "is not one of like or dislike, but of mutual respect, or at least of taking the other seriously as a human being. In the absence of such an attitude, one wonders" how anthropologists can capture others' "visions of the good life, their innermost spirit." Madan (1994, 159) counsels against "dividing humankind into "ourselves" and "others," urging that we must strive "to see ourselves in others and others in ourselves—to bring about what ... Hans-Georg Gadamer calls the 'merger of horizons.'"

Christian Smith (2010, 406) argues that the "promotion of the realization of the personhood of other persons is always included in the natural telos of every person pursuing realization of his or her personhood." "The underlying model of the good of personhood is therefore one of gift giving and exchange—as opposed to ... competition, conflict or domination.... Self-fullness is thus achieved in part by selflessness" (Smith 2010, 407). If sociologists' "self-serving" calculations turn the people we study "from a person into a means that is useful for our own benefit," we do not contribute to others' personhood (Smith 2010, 408). Smith doesn't know the works of D.P. Mukerji or base his understanding of the person on the Sanskrit concept of purush. But his conviction that sociology can develop its insights by promoting the personhood of those we study and that by doing so we contribute to the well-being of the sociologist gives me optimism that Mukerji may be right that the cause of spirit is not a lost cause.

Transforming Sociological Method: Sociological Introspection

Recent theorizing from feminism to postmodernism (e.g., MacKinnon 1989; Seidman 1991; Smith 1990) has argued there is no objective view of situations, that the scholar is always seeing the world from a particular standpoint. This should not lead to despair, however, but should encourage scholars to *add* consideration of their own experiences to the text, as anthropologists have been doing fairly regularly for decades. This book argues that reflecting on one's own experiences— what Carolyn Ellis (1991) calls sociological introspection—should be an essential part of every sociological study.[7] This impulse to sociological introspection is supported by Kashmiri Shaivite epistemologies

---

[7] Lata Mani (2009, 25) makes a similar case for sociological contemplation.

that see the linkages between ourselves (the subject) and those we study (the object). In his cross-cultural study of mysticism Radhakamal Mukerjee's (1936, xix) argues "introspection establish[es] an inward continuity of self and the universe as a whole." Such introspection "generates reverence for all [humans] as seats of the ultimate values, and for all human and social experiences as channels of their experience." Mukerjee is not referring to sociological introspection, but the mystic's meditation; the result is the same: Introspection connects us to the experiences of others beyond the self. Introspection facilitates nonobjectification.

Thinking about how I would answer the questions that my assistants and myself put to our respondents keeps me honest. Was the question really something I could expect them to answer? What experiences would I be less likely to open up about in my answer?

Trying out my respondents' wisdoms helped me evaluate the insights of the people I interviewed. Would I find well-being from what my respondents said gave them well-being? Would I find a lack of well-being from what my respondents said harmed their well-being? Thinking about these questions and my experiences of life in India gave me a sense of the universality and comparability of our experiences, but also helped me critically consider the fullness of the answers that people gave to the questions that I put to them.

One day my wife (Lisa Jadwin) commented that any conclusion from interviews that don't allow the interviewee to ask questions are probably flawed. When I was interviewing Raj Pattial, I asked him what he got from going on pilgrimage and he turned it around to ask *me* what I got from fasting. I stumbled around and said that fasting changed my consciousness. Raj added that fasting shows "you have a purpose. You are not fasting for your normal life, but for some other purpose—a purpose beyond the normal self." Such back-and-forth is so important for understanding that it should not be unusual.

Exploring my own well-being in India helped give greater confidence in what I was learning from interviews and faces. Thus, this book includes my own reflections on well-being that were prompted by the people whom I interviewed and got to know. The pleasures—great food, a good haircut, moviegoing—and problems—the time it takes to mail a letter!—gave me some insight into well-being and its disruptions. I kept a file—"me and well-being"—as I was going along and that turned out to be part of the "fieldwork" of this book.

Ara Francis (2012) recently described a chasm between sociological knowledge and her lived experience. Years of her sociological work focused on critiquing over-involved parenting. But when she herself became a parent, she found herself doing many of the same things that she had previously critiqued. Francis concluded that her distanced sociological practice had produced this dissonance. The disjunction suggested that she had perhaps not fully engaged with her interviewees' way of seeing the world. Francis described other sociologists who contribute to racial segregation they oppose in their own housing practices. These sorts of disjunctions highlight how important it is to apply our findings to our own life to better understand our findings' validity—and to see how fully we've truly understood the statements of those we interview.

A sound feminist maxim is that the personal is political. Feminism holds, of course, that women's position is unjust, imposed, and *needs to be changed*. As MacKinnon (1989, 101–02) puts it, to understand the world in a feminist sense is to understand that it can be otherwise. That is, we must be able to apply our knowledge to our own lives. If we learn of social troubles *but can't do anything about them*, the knowledge is disempowering. But it's not just the political that's personal—the academic is personal (and political) as well. We better understand what we study by living what we study. We can only understand well-being sociologically by considering how our findings apply to our own lives. Applying one's sociological insights to oneself confirms the veracity of these insights and suggests the value (for living!) of them as well.

Multiple Methods

Through sociological introspection, I learned not to *overvalue* what people told me in interviews. Interviews led to a bias towards the cognitive and the meaningful, making people unlikely to talk about the purposeless, the bodily, and the sheerly pleasurable. It's surprising that I saw as many contradictions as I did in interviews as interviews had a tendency to bias people toward increasing consistency.

Important discourses—especially about helping others—affected what people said—perhaps more than what they actually felt. Hearing the chorus of women referencing helping others—*"dusro ka madad,"*

I heard over and over as a response to what gives well-being—made me see that a discursive power (while surely influencing how people experienced well-being) perhaps more powerfully affects what they say than what they actually feel. Interviews have a tendency, then, to reveal *publicly acceptable discourses*. People's general statements about well-being often follow respectable discourses (even as their answers to a question about "particular situations" of well-being very often depart from those discourses).

More important, publicly-acceptable discourses of helping others and sweet relationships militated against people relating antisocial pleasures in interviews. As a professor at the University of Delhi told me, people are not likely to mention harassing others as a source of their well-being. Although I have seen people enjoying harassing others, no one mentioned this in interviews. As part of a subsidiary study, we asked people over 30 what they thought about changes in women's status over the last 20 years. None of the men we interviewed mentioned decreased eve-teasing (which men used to enjoy) as one of the losses associated with a change in women's status. (Public eve teasing in cinema halls and streets has diminished in Dehradun in the 20 years I've been studying there [Derné, Sethi, and Sharma 2013].) I happened to know that a man whom I interviewed sought out and enjoyed extramarital relationships—often through deception. But he didn't mention sexual relationships (even with his wife) as a source of well-being in his interview. People didn't talk about scheming for extramarital sex or the pleasures of harassment in interviews! (But the pickup artists studied by Tony Christensen might mention the pleasures of scheming for extramarital sex in their interviews because they are part of a seduction community. On the other hand, if I "picked them up" to interview them about well-being, that context might have led them away from mentioning the pleasures of scheming pick-ups.)

After my return from India, I opened a seminar on well-being by asking students to consider what gave them well-being. One of the students noted that the responses of the 15 American students had all referenced external things—being with animals, enjoying a room that was colored blue, or drag-racing on dodgy streets. She noted that none of them had talked about well-being stemming from any internal feelings. Another student said that this was because we were talking in the first day of class with strangers whom we didn't know well.

She suggested that well-being might be associated with internal feelings, but people might not be comfortable talking about it ("yet," she added!). This discussion with a group of talented American college students made me realize the interview situation might produce a bias toward the cognitive and the external. It is through reflecting on how we ourselves—who are ultimately *like* the people we study—would respond to questions in this situation and what we might obscure that helps us evaluate what those we interview tell us.

Thus, interviews *always* must be supplemented with fieldwork and active consideration of people's faces. The faces of women toiling at making chapatis contrasts with statements that cooking was a hobby that gave them well-being. The faces of people in an autorickshaw, laughing at children falling off the back of another vehicle was not something that came up in interviews. The obvious pleasures of a husband when he received tea his wife had made did not come in interviews. People enjoyed drinking tea at stalls, exercising, and dancing at parties, but these were not things that came up in interviews. Lakshman Negi enjoyed alcohol very much, commenting with a gleam in his eye that he always slipped a bottle in his pocket, but didn't mention it when the recorder was going, instead talking about maintaining a peaceful countenance to create felicitous interactions with others. I have quoted Lakshman's discussion of chains of well-being, but the interview did not tell much about Lakshman's pleasures—his gardening came up, but not his love of alcohol. Indeed, pleasures came up rarely in interviews. Thus, interviews tell part of the story of well-being, but not the whole story. It's not that what interviews tell is untrue, but that it's partial. We need to look at the faces to find out especially about pleasures of the body and about taken-for-granted pleasures and un-pleasures.

The gap between interview statements and reality was most apparent in those I knew well. So, Armaan Singh said that the body is nothing, but loves to ride motorcycles, flirt with schoolgirls, see sexy movies, and eat delicious alu paranthas. But Armaan mentions none of these pleasures in a formal interview. A sober Hindu believes in living virtuously, but has a flirtatious relationship with a neighbor. A business executive says helping others is his main source of well-being, but is happy about the privileges (free parking, free housing) of his position. Harjit Singh said that all he does is read the Guru Granth Sahab, but when we arrived at his house he was reading an

English-language newspaper. I interviewed Gyan Prakash because of his obvious pride and well-being at his athletic accomplishments, but he didn't mention these in the interview at all. I interviewed Hemant Kapoor because he told me about the well-being he got bathing in a stream, but he didn't raise this issue with a recorder rolling. I interviewed Sunil Sharma because he seemed to find well-being from his clever design and construction of household furniture, but this did not come up in a formal interview. A man of about 30 said in an interview the basis of khushhali was khushhali in the family, but I knew his main pursuit was forming extramarital relationships.

It's no surprise that Prakash Tyagi, Armaan Singh, and Sunil Sharma appear so often in this book as these were people whom I got to know well and so learned a great deal about because I knew them outside interviews. They, thus, are the best illustrations of the complexity of well-being and the processes that people use to overcome the absence of well-being. (And all of these people are men. The fact that I didn't get to know any women I interviewed outside the interview situation limits what I can say about women—especially regarding their pleasures.)

Still Objectifying: Intractable Ethical Quandaries

In 1992, Umesh Pandey wrote a letter to the *Anthropology Newsletter* describing the benefits—but especially the harms—he felt he and his family had received by assisting Susan Wadley (1994, xxvi) and others in their anthropological research. "Day by day," Pandey (1992) recounts, "we talked to these new anthropologists in friendship" not knowing "the information would go into books and disclose our privacy." While Pandey enjoyed learning English and helping the researcher learn village Hindi, he seems to regret telling the researcher stories "to get things and money out of you," since what was written will "hurt the feelings of village people if they could read"—and will certainly "hurt" future generations who will undoubtedly be able to read. Pandey describes his connection with the researchers as starting with "excitement and love" but turning to "hate, anger, fear, and suspicion, and finally to hope." Pandey especially has difficulty understanding how the researchers "disappear all of a sudden" and while there is "excitement" when the researchers return there is confusion when they say again at the end of their stay that they do not know when they'll return. Not knowing how many researchers have earned PhDs through him and his villagers or how many papers have been written about them, Pandey (1992) recounts that "our" "love" for the Americans has "destroyed our peace of mind," while "greed" for the researchers' money has "destroyed our dignity." The one-sidedness, it seems to me, is what Pandey (1992) describes as leaving a "question mark on our hearts." "We," he says, want friendship, life-long relationships and to think of "you" as part of a family, while the researcher wants "information." "You anthropologists come and go like a dream. It is difficult to know what to like or hate. Still, we love you." Anthropologists, he says "have made a path into our private worlds." Pandey asks whether the anthropologist "will make for us— the people you study—a path into your private circle." Wadley (1994, xxvii) herself concludes that "ultimately we must ask whether it is possible to do truly ethical research. Or do our friendships mask our exploitation and betrayal of our 'friends'?"

We're used to thinking that the main ethical threat of our research is people being harmed should other people learn the identities of the people we study. We go to great lengths to maintain anonymity of the people we interview so that the people we interview are protected from being harmed by others who could learn what it is they told us—but the process is difficult. Wadley (1994, xxvii) realizes that despite the use of pseudonyms her "friends in Karimpur will often recognize themselves and probably their neighbors." The fact that I learned the most from people I knew best—making them more recognizable to those who knew me in Dehradun—creates dilemmas. It doesn't take much to see who I was hanging out with. Like Wadley (1994, xxvii), I've also tried to be sensitive about revealing anything that might hurt people should their identity become known. But it is difficult to predict what people will find objectionable. In the introduction, I describe how I once spoke about my research with a government administrator, who wanted to be interviewed. I had no recorder, but I took notes as she talked. I found what she said admirable, but wanted to confirm what she said, so I sent her an email transcript of the interview. She replied by saying that she did not like at all what I had written down. I erased the interview and, in fact, have managed to forget what she told me. What I want to highlight here is that I found what she said much to be admired, but when confronted with my notes about what she said, she did not want what she said revealed. Maybe seeing it in print was different. Maybe being objectified always feels like harm. My experience with the government administrator was one of the most disheartening experiences I've had. At that point, I wound down the interviews and started writing. There were a number of other Forster-like experiences where there were confusions and miscommunications associated with hospitality. I found myself treating even my friends like objects of study. It is said that no author is to be trusted—and the same might be true of the social scientist as well. When I read Peggy Trawick's *Notes on Love in a Tamil Family* I was enthralled. But as I did this research, I wondered how that family—all the photos of them, so personal, affairs hinted at—felt about what Peggy had written. Like Wadley (1994, xxvii), I've tried to spare my "friends" "any pain from writing of this book." Like Wadley, I know "I have probably not fully succeeded."

When our respondents are also our friends, they may be harmed in ways quite different from the threat of having their identities revealed. As Pandey's (1992) letter to the *Anthropology Newsletter* revealed, objects of research are also harmed by being befriended by ethnographers, like me, who may not reciprocate friendship. It's now possible for me to stay in touch with those I interviewed via email—and I have. This happens with just a small minority of the people whom I interviewed. But I'm not able to act in friendship with people who were very important to me by attending weddings or other rituals. More and more there are gaps in the emails, and my correspondents lament that I have forgotten them. Kristin Luker's analogy of the one-night stand may be right for the interviewees whom we never see again. But for those we see over the years, a researcher's increasing distance can be probably more distressing. "Steve was once my friend!" I can choose to travel to India to see my "friends," but few of my "friends" in India have the resources to travel to see me. So, it's not so easy to avoid objectifying other people in sociological research.

My discussions of presentations at sociological conferences have also made me uneasy. I wrote them up on my portable Eee PC at the conference—much like writing up field notes. I'm perhaps particularly uneasy because the people I'm writing about move in the circles that will read this book. While their statements were made in a public setting, the statements are not definitive, but preliminary. It's because

I'll meet Dr Christensen and Dr Francis again at conferences that I'm uneasy about reporting what they said at conferences and how this illuminates North American sociology. But still this unease, alongside the strong objections of the administrator whom I interviewed in India, highlights the dilemma of speaking for the people whom we interview and interpreting their feelings. Despite my embrace of a nonobjectifying epistemology and a recognition that the people I interview are fundamentally similar to myself, I still control what stories are told and not told.

I'm concerned about my tale objectifying Dr Christensen. I hope readers realize I identify with him. While I'm inferring that he objectifies pickup artists as a separate species, I *know* that I have been involved in the process of objectifying the people I study. I am ashamed to admit that in the 1980s and 1990s, I thought of the people I interviewed mostly in terms of what I did with their stories in my books than how their stories related to my self-understanding. Sometimes I would sing a joking verse that denigrated the foibles of those I interviewed, while celebrating the books I wrote. The "joking" nature suggests that I was not quite serious in objectifying, but it nonetheless suggests I knew what was going on in the interview process. I have told the tale in more explicit terms in conference settings but have been asked not to do so in this book. I would not want to offend people by telling them of my offensiveness. Jeffrey Kripal (2001, 25) recounts being "deeply moved … by the stories … that fellow historians of religions have shared … over meals and telephone conversations and in hotel hallways and convention rooms across the country."[8] Kripal reflects on "how it is that these experiences, which seem to be so meaningful, energizing and creative, are so seldom allowed a clear voice in public, published scholarship." Kripal doesn't blame his colleagues for not "revealing their own secrets" since the "political dynamics" of the academy make revealing such secrets seem equated with "fuzzy thinking" or "rampant subjectivity." I'm convinced—as Kripal is, too, I think—that attending

---

[8] Turner (1994) similarly reports anecdotes about extraordinary experiences are brought up in "informal conversation, at parties, in students' kitchens, and in other non-structured contexts," but aren't seen by writers or publishers as "suitable for inclusion in a serious anthropological publication." I, too, have heard scholars like Gloria Raheja and McKim Marriott tell personal stories at conferences that illustrate the points of their publications at least as effectively as the objective stories that appear in their publications.

to the personal world of scholars helps us understand their work and its limitations. There still are secrets—I can't provide details of my joking (but still relevant) reference to the objectification of the men I interviewed in earlier studies between 1986 and 2001. (And I have also been asked to limit personal references to my continuing Shiva devotion that appear in the Afterword.) Just know that I have been involved in the process of objectifying those I've interviewed. While I hypothesize that Dr Christensen took a distancing stance toward the pickup artists, I am objectifying him in the process and I admit to taking the approach I attribute to him in my previous studies. I see myself as fundamentally like Dr Christensen. As Lata Mani (2009, 9) rightly recognizes, contemplation usually makes us aware that the characteristics we "are so tempted to decry in others may also be present in us."

I learn from Dr Christensen's online CV that he delivered a conference paper asking "Am I the Only Bathrobe Clad Ethnographer?", which examines "How Studying Everyday Life Online Challenges Our Conception of Ethnographic Research" (Christensen 2006). Perhaps, I thought, Dr Christensen turned to researching online communities because of some of the ethical challenges of objectifying the friends who take part in interviews. In the preface, I describe how Dr Dolloff, another presenter at the Qualitatives conference, discomforted with imposing research on an arctic community that is so often the "object" of research, continues to go back and forth over the years, renegotiating her place in the community. I wondered if Dr Christensen had been able to stay in touch with members of the seduction community over the years and whether many "pickup artists" might have found sweet, lasting relationships, just as he himself has done—a relationship that he originally feared was threatened by his research on a "seduction community" of pickup artists, the kind of relationship that contributes to well-being.

References

Bandyopadhyay, Bholanath. 1984. *The Political Ideas of Benoy Kumar Sarkar*. Kolkata: Bagchi.

Bellah, Robert N., Richard Madsen, William M. Sullivan, Ann Swidler, and Steven M. Tipton. 1985. *Habits of the Heart: Individualism and Commitment in American Life*. New York, NY: Harper and Row.

Chaudhuri, Haridas. 1965. *Integral Yoga: The Concept of Harmonious and Creative Living*. Wheaton, IL: Theosophical Publishing House.

Christensen, Tony. 2006. "Am I the Only Bathrobe Clad Ethnographer? How Studying Everyday Life Online Challenges our Conception of Ethnographic Research." Symbolic Interaction and Ethnographic Research Conference. Niagara Falls, Ontario.

———. 2012. "Friends Don't Let Friends Do Ethnography: Reflecting on Ethnography's Tolls on Personal Relationships." 29th Annual Qualitative Analysis Conference, St. John's, Newfoundland.

Dehejia, Harsha V. 2008. *Parvatidarpana: An Exposition of Kasmir Saivism through the Images of Siva and Parvati*. Delhi: Motilal Banarsidass.

Derné, Steve. 2012a. "Well-Being: An Interactionist Approach—Notes from India." American Sociological Association Annual Meetings, Denver, August.

———. 2012b. "Bodily Pleasures and Well-Being: Notes from India." Annual meetings of the Society for the Study of Symbolic Interaction, Denver, August.

Derné, Steve, Narendra Sethi, and Meenu Sharma. 2013. "Structural Changes Rather than the Influence of Media: 20 Years of Economic Liberalization in India." In *Consumer Culture, Modernity and Identity*, edited by Nita Mathur, 143–65. New Delhi: SAGE Publications.

Desjarlais, Robert R. 1992. *Body and Emotion: The Aesthetics of Illness and Healing in the Nepal Himalaya*. Philadelphia, PA: University of Pennsylvania Press.

Dworkin, Andrea. 1981. *Pornography: Men Possessing Women*. New York: Perigee.

Dyczkowski, Mark S.G. 1987. *The Doctrine of Vibration: An Analysis of the Doctrines and Practices of Kashmir Shaivism*. Albany, NY: SUNY Press.

Ellis, Carolyn. 1991. "Sociological Introspection and Emotional Experience." *Symbolic Interaction*, 14(1): 23–50.

Francis, Ara. 2012. "Mom Can't Walk the Talk: The Chasm between Sociological Knowledge and Lived Experience." Annual Meetings of the Society for the Study of Symbolic Interaction, Denver, August.

Geertz, Clifford. 1986. "Making Experiences, Authoring Selves." In *The Anthropology of Experience*, edited by V.W. Turner and E.M. Bruner, 373–80. Urbana, IL: University of Illinois Press.

Gordon, Avery (1997) 2008. *Ghostly Matters: Haunting and the Sociological Imagination*. Minneapolis, MN: University of Minnesota Press.

Goulet, Jean-Guy. 1994. "Dreams and Visions in Other Lifeworlds." In *Being Changed: The Anthropology of Extraordinary Experience*, edited by Jean-Guy Goulet and David Young, 16–38. Peterborough: Broadview.

Goulet, Jean-Guy and David Young. 1994. "Theoretical and Methodological Issues." In *Being Changed: The Anthropology of Extraordinary Experience*, edited by Jean-Guy Goulet and David Young, 298–335. Peterborough: Broadview.

Greeley, Andrew M. 1974. *Ecstasy: A Way of Knowing*. Englewood Cliffs, NJ: Prentice Hall.

Haberman, David L. 1994. *Journey through the Twelve Forests: An Encounter with Krishna*. Oxford: Oxford University Press.

Hall, Peter A. and Michele Lamont. 2009. *Successful Societies: How Institutions and Culture Affect Health*. Cambridge: Cambridge University Press.

Harman, William P. 2006. "Negotiating Relationships with the Goddess." In *Dealing with Deities: The Ritual Vow in South Asia*, edited by Selva J. Raj and William P. Harman, 25–41. Albany, NY: SUNY Press.

Johnson, Barry V. 1998. "Introduction." In *On the Practice of Sociology*, edited by Pitirim A. Sorokin, 1–55. Chicago, IL: University of Chicago Press.

Kripal, Jeffrey J. 2001. *Roads of Excess, Palaces of Wisdom: Eroticism and Reflexivity in the Study of Mysticism*. Chicago, IL: University of Chicago Press.

Krishna, Daya. 1989. *The Art of the Conceptual*. New Delhi: Indian Council of Philosophical Research.

Luker, Kristin. 2012. "Review of *Sociologists Backstage: Answers to 10 Questions about What They Do* by Sarah Fenstermaker and Nikki Jones." *Contemporary Sociology*, 41(5): 626–27.

MacKinnon, Catharine A. 1989. *Toward a Feminist Theory of the State*. Cambridge, MA: Harvard University Press.

Madan, T.N. 1994. *Pathways: Approaches to the Study of Society in India*. New Delhi: Oxford University Press.

———. 2013. "Introduction; Sociology at a Particular Place in a Particular Time." In *Sociology at the University of Lucknow: The First Half Century (1921–1975)*, edited by T.N. Madan, 1–66. New Delhi: Oxford University Press.

Mahony, William K. 1997. "The Guru-Disciple Relationship: The Context for Transformation." In *Meditation Revolution: A History and Theology of the Siddha Yoga Lineage*, edited by Douglas Renfrew Brooks, Swami Durgananda, Paul E. Muller-Ortega, William K. Mahony, Constantina Rhodes Bailly, and S.P. Sabharathnam, 223–76. South Fallsburg, NY: Agama.

Mani, Lata. 2009. *Sacred Secular: Contemplative Cultural Critique*. New Delhi: Routledge.

Marx, Karl. (1845–46) 1978. *The German Ideology*. In *The Marx-Engels Reader*, 2nd ed., edited by Robert Tucker, 146–200. New York, NY: Norton.

Meyer, Manulani Aluli. 2008. "Indigenous and Authentic: Hawaiian Epistemology and the Triangulation of Meaning." In *Handbook of Critical and Indigenous Methodologies*, edited by Norman Denzin, Yvonna S. Lincoln, and Linda Tuhiwai Smith, 217–32. Newbury Park, CA: SAGE Publications.

Mukerjee, Radhakamal. (1936) 1960. *The Theory and Art of Mysticism*, 2nd ed. Bombay: Asia Publishing House.

——— (1949) 2005. *The Social Structure of Values*. New Delhi: Radha Publications.

Mukerjee, Radhakamal. (1960) 2005. *The Philosophy of Social Science*. New Delhi: Radha.

———. (1965) 2005. "Preface to the Second Edition." In *The Social Structure of Values*, viii–x. New Delhi: Radha Publications.

———. 1997. *India: The Dawn of a New Era (An Autobiography)*. New Delhi: Radha.

Mukerji, Dhurjati Prasad. 1924. *Personality and the Social Sciences*. Kolkata: The Book Company.

———. (1955) 2013. "Indian Tradition and Social Change." In *Sociology at the University of Lucknow: The First Half Century (1921–1975)*, edited by T.N. Madan, 212–24. New Delhi: Oxford University Press. Also cited in D.P. Mukerji, (1958) 2002. *Diversities: Essays in Economics, Sociology and Other Social Problems*. New Delhi: Manak, 261–75.

Muller-Ortega, Paul Eduardo. 1989. *The Triadic Heart of Siva: Kaula Tantricism of Abhinavagupta in the Non-Dual Saivism of Kashmir*. Albany, NY: SUNY Press.

Nisbett, Richard E. 2003. *The Geography of Thought: How Asians and Westerners Think Differently ... and Why?* New York, NY: Free Press.

Obeyesekere, Gananath. 1990. *The Work of Culture: Symbolic Transformation in Psychoanalysis and Anthropology*. Chicago, IL: University of Chicago Press.

Openshaw, Jeanne. 1998. "'Killing' the Guru: Anti-Hierarchical Tendencies of 'Bauls' of Bengal." *Contributions to Indian Sociology*, 32(1): 1–19.

Robbins, Joel. 2013. "Beyond the Suffering Subject: Toward an Anthropology of the Good." *Journal of the Royal Anthropological Institute*, 19(3): 447–62.

Pandey, Umesh. 1992. "Would You Like to Listen or Not?" *Anthropology Newsletter*, (May): 3.

Saha, Suhrita. 2013. "Benoy Kumar Sarkar (1887–1949): A Tryst with Destiny." *Sociological Bulletin*, 62(1): 4–22.

Sarkar, Benoy Kumar. 1912. *Science of History and the Hope of Mankind*. London.

———. 1937. *Positive Background of Hindu Sociology Book I*, 2nd ed. Allahabad.

———. 1941. *Villages and Towns and Social Patterns*. Kolkata: Chuckerverty Chatterjee.

Seidman, Steven. 1991. "The End of Sociological Theory: The Postmodern Hope." *Sociological Theory*, 9(2): 131–46.

Seligman, Martin E.P. 2011. *Flourish*. New York, NY: Free Press.

Skidmore, Monique. 2003. "Darker than Midnight: Fear, Vulnerability, and Terror Making in Urban Burma (Myanmar)." *American Ethnologist*, 30(1): 5–21.

Smith, Christian. 2010. *What Is a Person?* Chicago, IL: University of Chicago Press.

Smith, Dorothy. 1989. "Sociological Theory: Methods of Writing Patriarchy." In *Feminism and Sociological Theory*, edited by Ruth A. Wallace, 34–64. Newbury Park, CA: SAGE Publications.

Smith, Dorothy. 1990. *The Conceptual Practices of Power: A Feminist Sociology of Knowledge*. Boston, MA: Northeastern University Press.

Sorokin, Pitirim A. 1943. *Sociocultural Causality, Space, Time*. Durham: Duke University Press. Cited in Barry V. Johnson, ed. 1978. *On the Practice of Sociology*. Chicago: University of Chicago Press, 104–114.

———. 1950. *Altruistic Love: A Study of American 'Good Neighbors' and Christian Saints*. Boston, MA: Beacon Press.

Stacey, Judith. 1990. *Brave New Families: Stories of Domestic Upheaval in Late Twentieth Century America*. Berkeley, CA: University of California Press.

Turner, Edith. 1994. "A Visible Spirit Form in Zambia." In *Being Changed: The Anthropology of Extraordinary Experience*, edited by Jean-Guy Goulet and David Young, 71–95. Peterborough: Broadview.

Veenhoven, Ruut. 2008. "Sociological Theories of Subjective Well-Being." In *The Science of Subjective Well-Being*, edited by Michael Eid and Randy J. Larsen, 44–61. New York, NY: Guilford.

Wadley, Susan S. 1994. *Struggling with Destiny in Karimpur, 1925–1984*. Berkeley, CA: University of California Press.

10

LIVING THE GOOD LIFE

What have we learned about living a good life? How can we as individual persons and as members of society find well-being and contribute to the well-being of others?

Find an Approach to Hardships

Finding meanings in life, especially finding an approach to dealing with hardships and the necessities of life is fundamental. My friend Bert Sandell wrote to me around Thanksgiving 2011 to suggest levels of happiness. A lower level would involve things such as the well-being of enjoying food or the lack of well-being of spilling your tea. A middle level would involve finding a job and a higher level finding a marriage. The last, he said is higher because it's more enduring. But *nothing* that gives us well-being truly endures except an *approach* to life. We'll always spill tea or not enjoy our food. Unfortunately, most of us will also lose a job or be dissatisfied with parts of it. We won't all lose a spouse, but logic dictates that half of married people will lose a spouse who predeceases them. There's an old story in Buddhism where a woman who lost her son went to the Buddha and asked her how to overcome her grief. He told her to find a person who has not suffered loss and bring a mustard seed from that house. Of course, she went from house to house only to hear story after story of grief. She learned, but never found that mustard seed. We all experience hardships and losses in life. Those who say well-being is ultimately inner are right in that what really provides well-being is an approach to deal with these hardships and losses.

The approaches we develop may prove inadequate as we face different trials and losses. So, Armaan Singh considered suicide after his son's death because the approaches that he had developed were inadequate to deal with such a hard blow. He got through his crisis with the understanding that ultimately "the body is nothing"—even if he wasn't consistently guided by this approach and continued to enjoy good food and riding his motorcycle fast. The approaches we find may not always endure, but our *willingness to find an approach to handle hardships* does endure.

Ultimately finding an approach to living with the ups and downs of life can endure and anchor well-being.

Pursue Pleasures

An approach is mental—but we also need pleasures of the body. The out-of-the-ordinary pleasures are important, but we especially need pleasures that can regularly release us from the purposeful pursuits of our day-to-day lives. Go for a run; do qi gong meditation; sing with your friends; take a walk in nature; go camping; do the hula.

All of the things I've just listed separate from the day-to-day world. Although some people may see running as contributing to a larger goal of fitness or health, all of these things—including running—are a good in themselves. That is, they can be done for reasons *other than* some larger purpose. While this might not be obvious for those who don't know qi gong meditation, all of these things involve the body, too. With the exception of going camping, all can be done as a part of the day.

Social-science researchers are scurrying around to figure out what pleasures are best. Some have highlighted dancing (such as hula), singing, and camping, which is why I highlight them above. But this book shows that the key thing is to find pleasures that are good in themselves, that use the body and that refresh for a return to day-to-day realities.

Not all pleasures can endure. Certainly 100-year-olds surf, but not all 100-year-olds can! But for most people pleasure *can* endure. Bert and his friends have been doing a summer backpacking trip for 30 years! And it's an old saw, but it's true: We don't stop running because we get old; we get old because we stop running. Plenty of people do hula or singing for their whole lives. But the thing that can endure and that provides well-being is a commitment to find pleasure in life.

And get a good sleep (Naiman 2006).

Find pleasures that combine many goods. *Bahri alang* combines intoxication, bathing, meeting with friends, and going outdoors.

Engage in Important, Meaningful Work That Connects to Others

Although pleasures and approaches partly provide well-being by providing relief from unpleasant necessities, work itself is an important part of well-being. As I learned from the pensioner whom I met on the train in 2011, finding a *technique* at which one is good and through which one can support oneself and others is vital to well-being. Work provides money. It gives us a sense of contribution.

My friend Bert sent me this quote from Shawn Achor: "Happiness is the joy we feel striving after our potential." Bert is right: Striving to accomplish something important as best we can gives us well-being from being special. If we can turn that *technique* into something that makes a living, it connects to others, too.

Make work as enjoyable as possible. Use it to cultivate sweet relationships. Use it to develop the self. If it's a mind job, try to work in some bodily activity. If my students are listless, we can always play Can Jam—a game competing to throw a frisbee in a can—or do the hula! If it's a bodily job, find ways to engage the mind.

Connect

Plenty of social-science research shows that social connections are fundamental to well-being. So, cultivate social connections.

Especially important is to cultivate positive interactions that create chains of well-being. Spread love. Be generous with praise—especially when it's deserved. Recognize contributions of others. Fredrickson (2013, 38) is right to counsel people to "recognize positivity resonance" and "seek it out." Cultivate micromoments of positivity resonance, getting benefits and giving benefits, a back and forth (Fredrickson 2013, 86).

Manulani Aluli Meyer (2001, 139–40) was told by the Hawaiians she interviewed of the dangers of cursing at people. She describes a Hawaiian who always

> told you put plenty love into it. Don't grumble, if you're doing it with love, your [meal] will come out delicious but if you grumble, then everything will sour, you know? Okay, you give an assignment to a family. Maybe that family you'd say "you cook the long rice and chicken." Come that night it starts to bubble, then you would know they grumbled, they didn't put their heart and soul in making this, so you can find out who grumbled, I mean, by the taste.

It may be a metaphor. Or maybe not. But the idea is sound. Cultivate positive interactions. Put love in, you'll get love out.

Or as Lakshman Negi told me, highlighting what I came to see as positive chains of interaction: "Saying sweet words is the important thing—much more important than money. You can't take back whatever words come out of your tongue. My internal self should not be giving abuse. We shouldn't utter anything untoward which hurts someone because that spreads unhappiness." Or as a 73-year-old Hindu man told me, "We should live with love [prem] with each other. We should live equally with love [prem] with everyone. Remaining with love [prem] is the source of khushhali. There is nothing else needed other than living with love [prem]." Love is all you really need.

There's a qi gong exercise (taught to me by qi gong master Lisa O'Shea) that encourages sending positive feelings to those you dislike. If you can feel connected to even those you dislike, it's a way of connecting to the unity of the world.

There will be times when you feel disconnected. Scheff analyzes these disconnections as feelings of shame. So, find techniques for managing shame. Can you feel more connected by doing things for others? By going for a run? By throwing yourself into work? Does a sense of humor help?

Don't do things that harm others—such as smoking, bad driving or littering—as these harm your relationship with others, harming your well-being. Don't objectify other people!

Be Moderate

Don't go overboard with any one thing. As Raj Pattial said, religion is good, but excessive religion—becoming a baba—is not. Yash Singh does meditation every day, but doesn't do fire-pit sacrifices.

Don't go overboard with any one pleasure. Yash finds a little alcohol after work relaxes the mind but drinking at work would be a sign alcohol has taken over one's life. You may think you want to be on safari all the time, but you can't be "on safari to stay."

Don't go overboard with work. Gurkeerat Singh recognizes that "work is worship" and uses work to get through troubles. But he also exercises and meditates daily, enjoys a break at teatime, and looks forward to ritual celebrations.

As I was writing this book, I saw a comment on YouTube about the lyric from Simon and Garfunkel's "Only Living Boy in New York," that goes, "half of the time you're gone and you don't know where." The comment said that Paul Simon might be half right: "Actually, all of the time you're gone and you don't know where." But, then, you've become a mystic. One day while doing qi gong meditation and sending healing energy to the smokers whom I typically hate, the tears rolled down my cheeks. I asked Lisa O'Shea, my qi gong practitioner and teacher, what would happen if I felt that way all the time and she replied that, then, I would be a mystic. And I suppose some people can be a mystic, but most people get well-being by being in the world and its ups and downs some of the time even if some of them finding joy in mystic experience some of the time.

I've urged a focus on connection to others; I've urged generosity with praise. But this should not go so far as to praise people who have not performed well. An "A" to all the students means nothing and doesn't reward the performing students.

Be moderate even in moderation! Taking things to extremes gives well-being, too. Climb the Himalayas. Experience extreme emotions. Run a marathon.

Don't Try to Be Consistent

One of the fundamental themes of this book is that it's all good. So, be both erotic and ascetic. Enjoy the mind and the body. Find well-being through work. And through pleasure. It truly is all good. Be moderate and immoderate.

While the last section urged moderation, take everything to extremes and, then, move on. Like Shiva, be the most intense erotic. And, then, be the most intense ascetic. Explore full connection to others. And, then, explore the fullness of the self.

The sociologist (and mystic!) Radhakamal Mukerjee (1960, 5–6) says,

> The psychology of healthy, mature and wholesome persons rather than of stunted, immature and desperate ones shows that basically the higher and the lower needs, egoism and altruism, instinct and conscience, intrinsic and instrumental ends, sensate and ideational modes are *not in conflict* but in agreement. The mature person *abolishes these and many other polarities.* (my emphasis)

You Don't Need It All

Focus on what you do have. One day in November 2011, I didn't sleep well, but I still had a nice run, a great alu parantha for breakfast and did some good writing. I didn't have it all, but I still had well-being. Prakash Tyagi lacks health and his family connections are frayed, but he still is able to see each new day as a new elegance.

I usually find I can just forget troubles when engaged in something that's good. But this is partly an interaction. Don't focus on troubles.

Cultivate Nonwork Time

Part of being moderate is to limit work's demands. Free time is central for pleasures. Free time is central to the purposelessness and emptying the mind.

When I first arrived at SUNY-Geneseo, at one of the first departmental meetings I made some crack that surely we'd all like more time and less money. People around the table looked at me like I was insane. (Geneseo has this work-ethic thing. Like whenever I go to sit outside and enjoy the day—other faculty would look at me like I was crazy, making cracks like I was just "out standing in a field.")

This study shows that laborers' lack of time is a key part of their lack of well-being.

Cultivate nonwork time. Take time to cook and enjoy food (rather than saving time by eating Soylent). No matter the pressures of work, take time for a run.

Cultivate Health

My respondents are right that without health, it's hard to have well-being. Although an approach can overcome ill health, it is difficult to do when health issues assert themselves.

Partly, this is the luck of the draw. My mother-in-law lived a good lifestyle but still died of colon cancer.

But there are things you can do: Avoid doing things (such as smoking and too much alcohol) that harm the body.

While exercise is a good in itself, it also builds health that allows you to do things such as kayak the Molokai north shore, climb small peaks in the Himalaya, or ride horses fast across the Sahara.

Don't do things that harm your body.

Constructing a Good Society

As I started writing this section in 2014, I remembered (in an instant) that in college (living in "revolutionary Berkeley" just as Reagan was being elected president) I tired of people who, as they say in *Hair*, "only care about the bleeding crowd. How about a needing friend." I proposed a politics of love in those early 1980s, recollecting an old saw that if we want to be a better society, we have to be a better people. Circumstances can be improved to help people live a good life, but ultimately I think living the good life will bring well-being. The Indian sensibility that holds that we can't change our circumstances but we can change how we think about them has a great deal of value. Radhakamal Mukerjee (1951, ii) was right to conclude that "the basic Indian postulate is that no good society is possible without good [people],[1] and that for the good society it is more important to form good understandings, affections and morals than to frame good laws and rights." During the cold war, Mukerjee (1960, 6–7) reflected that both "Democracy and Totalitarianism" seek "higher sociality" that comes ultimately not from institutions, social arrangements, and rights but from people's "conscience, love, and sharing." Mukerjee (1951, ii) does not see people as "instinct-bound" or "institution-ridden," but as capable of pursuing their own freedom. He sees this deep within Indian traditions. Quoting the *Mahabharata*'s counsel that the "highest virtue" is doing good for others and "the greatest wrong is to oppress others," Mukerjee (1951, v–vi) says that "India has depended far less than any other social culture on laws, techniques and constraints for group harmony and the prevention of domination ... of man over man." India "has aspired," instead to produce "good" people, "who through a real sharing of life [and] an effective mutuality of experience produce the good and just society."

While I think well-being comes from individuals developing approaches to troubles and finding pleasures in life, society could be better structured to help people on this path. As Clive Hamilton (2003) shows in his important book *Growth Fetish*, the primary efforts of governments today tend to focus on economics. Governments want to encourage job growth. They want to train members of society for productive jobs. But they don't try to help us experience well-being. Aren't there ways society could be structured and things governments could do to make well-being more likely?

Perhaps schooling, which appropriately trains people for jobs, could devote more attention to *non-economic* means to a good life. Could students study philosophical approaches to hardship? Could co-curricular activities focus more on developing pleasures? D.P. Mukerji (1924, v) argued the "dynamic individual" should be

---

[1] He referred to "good men," rather than good people. While he may have just been using the time's noninclusive language, he may have had in mind males. Nonetheless, I think his point applies to all people.

developing "toward the Absolute." Mukerji (1924, 240) saw the "development of Personality" as the "object of society and the Social Sciences." For Mukerji, personality is that element of the person that cannot be explained in behavioral terms by social, cultural, and biological influences (Nagendra 1997, 152). Mukerji (1924, 240) complains that until now education has been an "auxiliary science" "aimed at an evolution of the ideal sought by Economics or Politics" through "vocational or civic instruction." Mukerji urges that, instead, education should aim at producing people fit for a "higher," more fulfilling social life.

Economic changes might focus on *moderating* work demands. This book suggests that people need both work and play—purpose and pleasure. In Volume III of *Capital*, Marx ([1894] 1978) held that the "realm of freedom actually begins only where labour which is determined by necessity and mundane consideration ceases." Beyond the realm of necessity "begins that development of human energy which is an end in itself, the true realm of freedom, which, however can blossom forth only with the realm of necessity as its basis." Thus, Marx concludes, "the shortening of the working day" is the "basic prerequisite" of such human freedom. While less optimistic that our "natures" would allow us to attain well-being, Keynes (1932, 366–67), too, saw decrease of working hours—which he saw as an inevitable result of new technologies—as a great opportunity to live fuller lives. Yet for many people, job demands eat up more and more of their time, leaving less space for the development of other facets of life that can be combined with purposiveness to produce well-being. D.P. Mukerji (1932, 29–30, cited by Madan 1997, 172) argues that it is "in leisure alone" that a person can "conquer the tyranny of time, by investing it with a meaning, a direction, a memory, and a purpose." Mukerji especially places significance on having moments outside of social contact so that one has space to reflect: "What is of vital significance is that our time-adjustments should be made in such a way that we should be free from the necessity of remaining in social contact for every moment of our life." "This is why," Mukerji says, "the Hindu philosopher wisely insists on the daily hour of contemplation." With modern civilization's "growing" "bustle," he says, this need only increases. I find myself becoming edgy if my time is taken up with social contacts and I have no time for reflection. Mukerji is right that a good society is one where people are able to find time outside of social demands.

D.P. Mukerji ([1958] 2002, 237) analyzes how Gandhi's opposition to colonialism was "not merely on the limited ground of political and economic subjection but on the much wider issue of the conflict of civilizational values." Gandhi (quoted by Mukerji [1958] 2002, 241) described himself as "socialist enough to say" that factories

ought only to be working under the most attractive and ideal conditions, not for profit, but for the benefit of humanity, *love taking on the place of greed as the motive*.... The mad rush for wealth must cease and the laborer must be assured not only of a living wage but a daily task that is not a mere drudgery. (my emphasis)

So efforts by employers to limit work hours and by governments to incentivize limiting of work hours would do more for well-being than constantly trying to increase GNP and productivity. Mukerji's ([1958] 2002, 253) analysis of Gandhi suggests a reorientation of values to balance profit with love is important to make that a reality.

Much like D.P. Mukerji, Radhakamal Mukerjee emphasized that moderating demands of segments of life (like work) is key to well-being. Since "the psychology of healthy, mature and wholesome persons" shows the combination of "polarities and contradictions," Mukerjee (1960, 5–6) concludes that "the psychology of healthy and mature rather than of sick culture" would establish "a balance, collaboration and synergy of antinomic values and ways of living." Mukerjee ([1949] 2005, 183) complains that with the dominance of "science and technology" humans' "thoughts, feelings and attitudes" have become "assimilated to a general standardised pattern." With the prominence of work, "instrumental values such as wealth, property, standard of living, [and] social status" take priority over "intrinsic values" such as "health, appreciation of beauty, development of understanding and the great moral virtues" (Mukerjee [1949] 2005, 99). For Mukerjee ([1949] 2005, 185), the demands of the "daily toil of life" leave little room for "normal emotions and intellectual faculties."

Like D.P. Mukerji, Radhakamal Mukerjee ([1949] 2005, 95) recognizes the value of "meditation in isolation." Such meditation allows the individual to "experience a most intense 'self consciousness'" in which resides "the sense of the whole and the eternal that elicits cooperative and infinite love." Without such time separate from social demands, the individual is more likely to be shackled with "eager desires, trivial thoughts and little deeds."

Like D.P. Mukerji, Radhakamal Mukerjee sees contemporary society as making so many demands that the individual is "merge[d]" with various secondary groups, promoting a "dead and deadening uniformity" in the interests, values, and lives of people. Radhakamal Mukerjee, like D.P. Mukerji, then, suggests that moderation of demands in any one sphere will allow people to be more multidimensional, promoting the good life.

Resonating with Durkheim, Radhakamal Mukerjee ([1965] 2005, x) argued sociology could play a role in evaluating and reshaping values to provide people with "new moral and spiritual equipment." For Mukerjee, an important role of sociology was to identify the values that promote "human growth, wholeness and transcendence beyond the biological and social dimensions." So, Mukerjee gives sociology an important role in fostering the good life. Only with "universal values, ideals and symbols understood, interpreted and fostered by sociology" can the "coming world society" flourish.

While finding an approach to troubles and finding pleasures are the most enduring elements of a good life, society can certainly help people avoid troubles by insuring that people are paid enough to live and have access to adequate health care. My respondents recognize that income and health are essential parts of the good life. The world is rich enough to be sure that everyone has these things.

People flourish when they find productive activity that they do well and makes them feel special. Governments should continue helping people do that—alongside doing more to help them develop pleasures and approaches to life. But whatever technique people find to support themselves, governments can work to be sure compensation and health care is adequate for life.

References

Fredrickson, Barbara L. 2013. *Love 2.0*. New York, NY: Plume.
Hamilton, Clive. 2003. *Growth Fetish*. London: Pluto.
Keynes, John Maynard. 1932. *Essays in Persuasion*. New York, NY: Harcourt Brace Jovanovich.

Madan, T.N. 1997. "Tradition and Modernity in the Sociology of D.P. Mukerji." In *Social and Cultural Diversities: D P Mukerji in Memorium*, edited by Abha Avasthi, 167–92. Jaipur: Rawat.

Marx, Karl. (1894) 1978. *Capital, Volume Three*. In *The Marx-Engels Reader*, 2nd ed., edited by Robert Tucker, 439–42. New York, NY: Norton.

Meyer, Manulani Aluli. 2001. "Our Own Liberation: Reflections on Hawaiian Epistemology." *Contemporary Pacific*, 13(1 Spring): 124–48.

Mukerjee, Radhakamal. (1949) 2005. *The Social Structure of Values*. New Delhi: Radha Publications.

———. 1951. *The Indian Scheme of Life*. Mumbai: Hind Kitab.

———. (1960) 2005. *The Philosophy of Social Science*. New Delhi: Radha.

———. (1965) 2005. "Preface to the Second Edition." In *The Social Structure of Values*, viii–x. New Delhi: Radha Publications.

Mukerji, Dhurjati Prasad. 1924. *Personality and the Social Sciences*. Kolkata: The Book Company.

———. (1932) 2004. *Basic Concepts in Sociology*. Kolkata: Rupa.

———. (1958) 2002. "Mahatma Gandhi's View on Machines and Technology." In *Diversities: Essays in Economics, Sociology and Other Social Problems*, edited by D.P. Mukerji, 234–59. New Delhi: Manak. First published in 1953.

Naiman, Rubin R. 2006. *Healing Night: The Science and Spirit of Sleeping, Dreaming, and Awakening*. Minneapolis, MN: Syren.

Nagendra, S.P. 1997. "D.P. Mukerji as a Sociologist." In *Social and Cultural Diversities: D P Mukerji in Memorium*, edited by Abha Avasthi, 147–66. Jaipur: Rawat.

Acknowledgments

[Paying] debts to ancestors, debts to the universe, and debts to the teacher ... provide a person with the satisfaction needed to attain real peace.... The real debt owed to the teacher is that of passing on teaching to others. Every student in turn has to become a teacher and pass on the teaching, preferably by adding his or her own experience to it.... Real satisfaction comes by fulfilling desires related to the well-being of others ... which is part of paying our debt to the universe.

—Peter Marchand (2006, 66), student of Tantric Harish Joshi

Part of my well-being from writing this book comes from the idea that this book might contribute to sociology and to living the good life. This book will also contribute to well-being if I'm able to celebrate what I've learned from my teachers, students, assistants, and friends. Thinking about what one is grateful for increases well-being. These concluding acknowledgments, then, give thanks and highlight the themes of this book.

Sweet friendships in India taught me as much, perhaps, as interviews. Harkirat Singh Jassal's family embraced me. I shared their festive times and ate great food at their house. I learned from their wisdom. One day (which by chance was Thanksgiving in the USA) I commented on how the *makki parantha* I was eating was the food of heaven. "Heaven is right here," Harkirat said to me. "The wife is here. The children are here. The best food and drink are here. Good work is here everyday in the shop. Not in America. Not in Orissa. Not in Punjab. Here."

I also shared many meals with Sudhir Kumar Rana, friend and extraordinary travel agent (who also helped me with many practicalities, including computer repair). Sudhir included me in his pilgrimages, visits to local temples, and family celebrations, and also offered a lot of wisdom. (While I'm on the subject of travel agents, thanks as usual to Vinstring travels—and thanks to Philip Lutgendorf, friend from my Banaras days, for suggesting I work with them!)

Journalist Narendra Sethi worked as my research assistant in 1991, 2001, 2007, and 2011. In 1991, I was just over 30, studying filmgoers, and I met Narendra at the dusty *Dainik Jagaran* newspaper office above Dehradun's Kanak theater. By 2001, he arrived on motorcycle and was moving up in the world. In 2007, he had a car and was working for a cable news outlet. He used to bring gladiolas to my room. I was impressed with how easily he recruited interview subjects and his sensitivity that made interviews so successful.

One of my lucky days was when educator Meenu Sharma became my research assistant in 2011. Working for me was her third shift (her first was working at a college and her second was cooking and doing housework). But she did more than I ever could have imagined. She was incredible at going to laboring areas and Muslim areas to find women from these groups. She was remarkable in finding lower-middle-class housewives to interview. She helped me with my Hindi and made translation a breeze. And she welcomed me into her household, where I tasted some great foods that I had never had before! I watched cricket with her husband and was introduced to her children.

Narendra and Meenu helped me rework my interview schedule. They helped me recruit respondents and assure that we protected human subjects from any harm. They did an extraordinary job translating interviews into English. This book couldn't have been written without them, but the friendship shared is what is most important to me.

Of course, the greatest thanks is owed to the more than 200 people who talked to me about well-being. I surely got more from this than they did at least in material terms, but I hope—and think—that our interactions were a positive chain of well-being for me and my "respondents." I got a sense that people enjoyed talking about well-being and telling me their life stories. I felt I benefitted from the wisdom of everyone I interviewed and, even more, from connecting with my respondents. I feel blessed to have met people such as Prakash Tyagi, Sunil Sharma, Armaan Singh, and many others.

I have always been grateful—perhaps not expressed enough—by the warm welcome I have received at the University of Delhi, which has always been my academic home in India. My relations there have been fleeting, but memorable for me. I was green in 1986 when

I turned up at André Béteille's office at the Institute of Economic Growth. My recollections of meeting with Dr Béteille are vivid and I appreciated his help; I learned even more from his books over the years. It must have been in 1991 that Veena Das was my advisor at the University of Delhi—it was the summer of economic liberalization and I remember her large desk that still had those symbols of pre-liberalization status—plenty of paper weights under a fan. Radhika Chopra welcomed me warmly in 2001 and 2011. By the time I got to the University of Delhi in 2011, I had friends there in Sanjay Srivastava and Satendra Kumar, both of whom I had met in conferences in the West. Sanjay and Satendra are some of the finest sociologists working today, Satendra exploring caste relations and Sanjay exploring an increasingly postmodern India. But it was their welcome that I especially appreciated—it was Satendra with whom I shared lunch at the famous D-School canteen. Janaki Abraham arranged a valuable talk on campus and we shared tea afterwards. I am grateful for the help, the pleasures, and the sweet connections.

SUNY-Geneseo, my home institution, granted me a sabbatical to conduct the 2007 research, a leave of absence to conduct the 2011 research, and a 2014 sabbatical to finish this book. Joyce Peter, sociology department secretary, kept my Geneseo work going and grant administrators Betsy Colon and Traci Phillips facilitated the research going smoothly. Helen Thomas was an extraordinarily helpful grant writer that is probably the main reason I received a grant. President Christopher Dahl has built a great public liberal-arts institution and always supported engaged faculty research as an essential part of student achievement. It gives me pleasure to thank Joyce, Betsy, Traci, Helen, and Chris because they've been great friends as well.

Geneseo undergraduate student Aru Ray helped me prepare the interview schedule before I left for India in 2007. We also read Rahul Sankrityayan's *Gummukarshastra* together and this was a great help in improving my Hindi for the study.

The US Department of Education funded this work with a Fulbright-Hays Faculty Research Abroad grant. I'm pleased to thank S. Bharati and Harsh Singh in India for their help.

In the years between the two interview stints, I learned a great deal—as always—from my undergraduate students at SUNY–Geneseo. I taught three senior seminars in which about 60 students each did about two interviews like those I did in India. It was from my students that I learned that well-being might really be mixed. One of the senior seminar groups asked people whether they'd ever experienced well-being and lack of well-being simultaneously. They gave as their example a respondent that got well-being from receiving soccer ball on a birthday but being unable to run out and play with it because it was raining! Student Karen Sperber (2010) wrote a paper about the mixed nature of well-being and presented it at a professional conference. Related to my focus on well-being as arising in interactions, another student Rachel Greenberg (2010) wrote a paper on the role of reflexivity in well-being and Patrick Maney (2010) insisted that bodily pleasures were a source of well-being neglected by interviews, themes I have taken up in this book.

Not only did these students' work help me understand well-being, but working with them on their projects and presentations was a highlight of my teaching career. I feel proud that these students conducted good research and wrote good papers. And I felt great well-being when one of these students told me the well-being senior seminar was her favorite class.

My friend Gordon Mathews, Chinese University of Hong Kong anthropologist, was the person who helped me turn to the study of well-being. I've long admired his book on what makes life worth living in Japan and the USA (Mathews 1996) and modeled my interview question about life's purpose on the questions he asked in that study. I don't really remember how we met, but I remember a long walk at an American Anthropological Association meeting in San Francisco to get a burrito in the mission district. We ended up in a bookstore looking at a travel guide on Hong Kong to see the description of Chungking mansions—center of low-end globalization, which he was studying (Mathews 2011). Gordon even visited Rochester, New York—he had gotten his degree down the road in Ithaca—and we had a meal at a Thai restaurant. Gordon and I got together again to present research on well-being at a psychological anthropology conference in Pacific Grove, California one March. I talked about what it was like interviewing people about well-being, reading from the transcript of Raj Pattial's interview, getting a laugh (a source of well-being) when I quoted Raj as saying one "must not give attention to tensions." A fond recollection of the panel is Gordon jamming on the piano before the session. Thanks, Gordon, for putting me on to the study of well-being.

I've enjoyed my discussions of well-being with friends such as Bert Sandell, Brian McGuire, Mark Berry, Ginny Sandell, Joel Gilman, Tom Carlson, and Arlene Messer; their insights have appeared in this book. Bert, Brian, Mark, and Tom discussed well-being with me during our annual backpack trips as I was planning and doing this research. My friend Bert appears in this book and gives me well-being—he laughs at my jokes, he helped me start running, and he invited me on an annual summer backpacking trek that is one of my favorite events of the year.

My wife Lisa Jadwin is a great scholar and a wonderful partner and companion. While I was in India and she was in the USA, we could talk twice a day by phone on skype this time, keeping me close to her and the kitties, even while I was far away and she was encountering family difficulties. We could even watch the San Francisco Giants together on mlb.tv while talking on skype halfway around the world. Her insights also guide this book—I always learn the most from Lisa. It gives me pleasure to thank her for being the best.

This book should also pay homage to my longest standing supporters from Berkeley. Gerry Berreman helped me with contacts when I first got to India and put me in touch with people for whom I wrote my first chapters. He knew the importance of connections and I always loved seeing him over the years. I'm sorry I didn't get this book finished before Gerry died in December 2013.

Ann Swidler was the star of my last book (Derné 2008), in which I confirmed her argument that cultural consistencies come not from socialization but from confronting similar structural realities. Arlie Hochschild had given me a few chapters of her *Talk of Love* (Swidler 2001) in manuscript when I headed off to India for the first time in 1986. It deeply affected my earliest work, too. It was great to see her again at the conference in Pacific Grove after many years.

I worked with Claude Fischer as an assistant on his study of the telephone's history in the USA (Fischer 1994), first studied methods with him, and took a class on academic writing with him, too, all of which made me the sociologist I became. He has supported me in many ways, but what I want to emphasize here is that he introduced me to the great cycle of explanation—the back and forth between evidence and explanations that had an effect on my research and teaching over the years. And I saw him after many years at the conference in Pacific Grove, too. Claude and Ann may live in the San Francisco

Bay area, but you still can't beat walking in Pacific Grove in March! Although we see each other rarely (including once when we ran into each other going to Ellis island in 1992), I feel a connection to Claude and Ann and am thankful for all they've done for me. What were they doing at an anthropology conference in Pacific Grove?—maybe our circles aren't that different!

Arlie Hochschild was my dissertation advisor and wrote hundreds (literally!) of letters of references. Just as she took an interactionist perspective to emotions in *The Managed Heart* (Hochschild 1983), I take an interactionist perspective to well-being here—and it was Arlie who pushed me to think about the chains of well-being. So, her influence on this book's biggest conclusion is quite direct! But really this book follows her method more than anything else. Many years ago, in a graduate seminar, I parroted something that was said in a book we were reading and she asked me whether I really believed it. I thought, and just said, "no." So, from the beginning she taught me that sociological introspection should be applied to anything we read. But it's taken a long time for my academic work to reflect that!

For a long time Arlie has been encouraging me to look at the contradictions and complexities in people more than I have. But I think in the past, I've been smoothing over differences, resolving inconsistencies. But with this book, I tried to *foreground* rather than *resolve* the contradictions. And it's because of this that I've realized it's all good—that well-being draws not just on diverse elements— but contradictory ones. With Arlie, too, our connection is more than an academic one—I'm always thankful to be in touch with her and share a bit of our lives.

I find well-being in this book's culmination connecting me to both my students and my teachers. I think of Maslow's description of being in a graduation and seeing the scholars—Socrates, Plato, and the bunch—who had been there before him. It gives me well-being to connect with three generations of scholars—my teachers (Arlie, Ann, Claude, Gerry), my generation of scholars (Gordon, Satendra, and Sanjay), and my students (Karen, Rachel, Patrick). These connections across academic generations give me a feeling of a positive chain of well-being.

With these acknowledgments, I'm getting well-being by giving thanks, connecting to others and finding meaning, and also by being a bit playful with this manuscript.

References

Derné, Steve. 2008. *Globalization on the Ground: Media and the Transformation of Culture, Class, and Gender in India.* New Delhi: SAGE Publications.

Fischer, Claude S. 1994. *America Calling: A Social History of the Telephone.* Berkeley, CA: University of California Press.

Greenberg, Rachel. 2010. "Walk Down Memory Lane: Reflexivity as a Component of Well-Being." Geneseo Undergraduate Research Conference. Geneseo, New York.

Hochschild, Arlie. 1983. *The Managed Heart: Commercialization of Human Feeling.* Berkeley, CA: University of California Press.

Maney, Patrick. 2010. "Well-Being and the Sensory Construction of Happiness." Geneseo Undergraduate Research Conference. Geneseo, New York.

Marchand, Peter. 2006. *The Yoga of the Nine Emotions: The Tantric Practice of Rasa Sadhana.* Rochester, VT: Destiny.

Mathews, Gordon. 1996. *What Makes Life Worth Living? How Japanese and Americans Make Sense of Their Worlds.* Berkeley, CA: University of California Press.

———. 2011. *The Ghetto at the Center of the World: Chungking Mansions, Hong Kong.* Chicago, IL: University of Chicago Press.

Sperber, Karen. 2010. "An Interesting Mix: The Possibility That Well-Being and a Lack of Well-Being Can Be Experienced Simultaneously." Geneseo Undergraduate Research Conference. Geneseo, New York.

Swidler, Ann. 2001. *Talk of Love: How Americans Use their Culture.* Chicago, IL: University of Chicago Press.

Postscript: Living Shaivite

This book argues that we learn only by recognizing similarities with those we study, an imperative that goes against the common anthropological insistence that we not go native.

Frederique Apffel-Marglin is one who has told the tale of the pull of India. She worked in Orissa from 1975 to 1993, but turned to studying an NGO in Peru because by the late 1980s she found that whenever she went to Orissa to do fieldwork she "simply wanted to be there, participate in rituals and make offerings; I could hardly bring myself to do fieldwork" (Apffel-Marglin 2008, 2–4). She eventually realized that her "years in India, particularly in Orissa, the people, the landscape, the other-than-humans I interacted with in those places ... acted powerfully upon me, they changed me and the course of my life." The "people, landscape and deities" she found herself among in India taught her not just about "themselves but as significantly about [her]self and about ways of being with them and with the world in general that were totally unsuspected by the person [she] then was." Apffel-Marglin found herself transformed from "a secular modern person eager to professionalize herself in the field of anthropology into a person feeling responsible not only to the human persons she encountered but to the 'holiness of the holy' in the other-than-humans and the world" she encountered in India.

I, similarly, came to Nepal as a 22-year-old secular modern. But, over the years, I drifted into becoming Shaivite as I went to temples and did pilgrimages with friends. In the fall of 2012—30 years after I first arrived in Nepal—I discovered a sacred spot atop Pinnacle Hill in Rochester NY, USA. Every day I would run to Rochester's highest point. I noticed fires burning and tridents scratched in the ground and realized quite suddenly that the triple communication towers atop the hill represented a huge trident.

On my daily run the day before Thanksgiving 2012, I installed a bell on a tree at the approach to Pinnacle Hill in honor of Shiva. The next morning, exactly a year after I had eaten delicious makki parantha in the home of my best friends in India, as I headed toward Pinnacle Hill's crest, I came upon a deer atop the hill. I slowed as I approached the top and was greeted by prayer flags. Sometime between Wednesday late afternoon and Thanksgiving morning, prayer flags appeared alongside my bell at the approach to the summit. "Happy Thanksgiving, the devotees have arrived," I shouted as I returned home.

Winter arrived in Rochester, but I kept running. Some days, I carry a bell with me on my run, hearing the ringing as I run. As I ring the bell atop Pinnacle Hill, I experience, I think, something like the zero zone described by Niranjan Kamboj. The morning after Mahashivaratri in 2014, at sunrise, in subfreezing temperatures, I saw a vertical ice rainbow-column shining down through the trident made of communication towers.

Everywhere people make the sacred out of the ordinary (e.g., Eck 1998). I have sat on the banks of the Ganga in Rishikesh and watched someone build a Shiva lingam in the sand. Others will subsequently worship that sand lingam with color and flowers. Still others will pour Ganga water on Shiva, destroying the lingam and rebuilding it. When the Berkeley city council put up traffic barriers to improve traffic flow, local Hindus worshiped those poles as Shiva lingams, too. Some pilgrims go to the four dhams in the Himalaya, others to the four dhams of the compass—Puri in the East, Dwarka in the West, Rameswaram in the South, and Badrinath in the Himalayas. Each morning I complete a char dham yatra culminating in a visit to Shiva on Pinnacle Hill.

Seeing the people I interviewed as being like me, I embraced some of their practices. Their wisdoms taught me about living the good life, how to find the sacred in the ordinary, and how to simultaneously enjoy the material and the spiritual, connections and individual pursuits, pleasures and meanings. My visualization of readers also learning from the wisdoms of the people I interviewed contributes to a chain of well-being that connects us all.

References

Apffel-Marglin, Frédérique. 2008. "Introduction: Are Goddesses Real?" In *Rhythms of Life: Enacting the World with the Goddesses of Orissa*, 1–30. New Delhi: Oxford University Press.

Eck, Diana L. 1998. "The Imagined Landscape: Patterns in the Construction of Hindu Sacred Geography." *Contributions to Indian Sociology*, 32(2): 165–188.

Glossary

Bhagwan: God

bhajan: Hindu devotional song.

bhang: intoxicating hashish mixture of ground cannabis buds and leaves mixed with milk, clarified butter, and spices.

bahri alang: a secular ritual involving activities like moving through crowded city lanes to a quiet lonely place, grinding and consuming bhang, "doing latrine", bathing, washing clothes, exercising, massaging the body with oils, combing hair, putting on clean clothing, and eating paan.

char dham yatra: pilgrimage to four holy spots in the Himalaya—Yamunotri, source of the Yamuna; Gangotri, source of the Ganga (or Ganges); Kedarnath, a mountain abode of Shiva; and Badrinath, a mountain abode of Vishnu. With motorized transport, it can now be done in weeks, although there are still steep walks up to Kedarnath and Yamunotri that need to be undertaken.

chaat: savory fried snack.

dhaaba: inexpensive eatery.

daal: lentils, a simple food.

dargah: Islamic shrine built over grave of religious figure or saint.

darshan: taking the auspicious sight of a holy person or deity.

dukh: sadness, sorrow, unhappiness, suffering, grief, distress.

dukh-sukh: sadness and joy, pleasure and suffering. Hausner (2007, 102) says dukh-sukh refers "to a complete range of human emotions. Dukh-Sukh is a term that refers not only to the pain or pleasure arising from a particular experience, but more accurately to the nature of suffering and delight in the universe."

ghats: stone steps leading to the banks of a sacred river, pond, or lake.

ghumna or *ghumna-phirna*: wandering, strolling, moving around, roaming.

gurudwara: Sikh place of worship.

hijra: eunuch.

khush: happy, joyful.

khushhali: well-being, state of happiness, state of flourishing; prosperity.

khushi: joy, delight, happiness.

kirtan: religious chant in both Sikhism and Hindu devotional traditions.

langar: Sikh ritual serving of food to the wider community, usually at a gurudwara.

mast: to be intoxicated with life or passion, to have *joie de vivre*, wanton, lustful, happy, radiant with joy, lively and carefree.

masti: intoxication, joi de vivre, carefreeness, passion, joyous radiance.

mauj: whim, caprice, delight.

paan: mixture that includes betel leaf and areca nut; chewed to produce mild intoxication.

prasad: food offered to a deity and returned, consecrated; consumed by devotees after the offering

puja: prayer, worship, including offerings to a deity.

pujapath: worship, meditation.

pujari: Hindu temple priest.

roti: bread

sadhu: religious ascetic or holy person, usually, a renunciant who has abandoned family, possessions, and worldly life.

samsara: the world as perpetual flow of events; the cycle of birth and death.

seva: selfless service to others, often associated with religious devotion.

shanti: peace, serenity, calmness, tranquility.

sharaab: alcohol

shauk: hobby, fondness, or fancy for something.

sukh: happiness, pleasure, comfort, contentment, joy.

sukh-dukh: pleasures and sorrows. See *dukh-sukh*.

sukh-shanti: happiness and pleasure, contentment and peace.

uddeshya: purpose, object, motive.

yatra: pilgrimage to a holy place; also, journey.

Index

About the Author

Steve Derné is Professor of Sociology at the State University of New York at Geneseo. He has received fellowships from the Fulbright program (1986–1987, 2012), the Rockefeller Foundation (2002), the National Endowment for the Humanities (1997, 2005), and the American Institute of Indian Studies (1991). In five research stints over 30 years, he has conducted 31 months of fieldwork in India. His previous books explore family life and emotion in India (*Culture in Action*, 1995), filmgoing in India (*Movies, Masculinity, and Modernity*, 2000), and cultural, economic, and family changes since India's economic liberalization (*Globalization on the Ground*, SAGE, 2008). The interviews on well-being engaged him and the people he interviewed more than any of his previous studies in India.

Derné enjoys India's people, food, music, religions, ambiance, and ways of life. He once lived in Banaras for 15 months, has been visiting the Himalayas for more than 30 years, and has completed a bus pilgrimage to Yamunotri, Gangotri, Kedarnath, and Badrinath. He has been to four *jyotirlingas* and discovered a fifth in North America! Insights and practices from life in India shape his daily life in the USA: He starts his morning with Indian tea, worships Lord Shiva atop a local hill, lives in walking distance of a samosa shop, and listens to *ragas* on his way to teach at university. He has kayaked off Burma in the Bay of Bengal, in Baja, California, and around the islets off the Hawaiian islands. One of his pleasures is riding horses fast in places like the Sahara, Patagonia, and the Genesee valley. He has ridden horses with his wife in Rajasthan and in Assam. He enjoys running every day, whether through crowded lanes in Indian cities or amidst the vibrant spring, steamy summer, colorful fall, or snowy winters of upstate New York. He lives in Rochester, New York, with his wife Lisa Jadwin and three cats.